THE HIDDEN FACE

ST THÉRÈSE OF LISIEUX

A photograph taken in June 1897, three months before her death

THE HIDDEN FACE

A Study of

St Thérèse of Lisieux

by

IDA FRIEDERIKE GÖRRES

IGNATIUS PRESS   SAN FRANCISCO

Originally published as *Das Senfkorn von Lisieux*
8th revised edition of *Das verborgene Antlitz:*
Eine Studie über Therese von Lisieux
Herder Verlag, Freiburg im Breisgau
© 1959 by Ida Friederike Görres
Published with ecclesiastical approval

English edition translated by Richard and Clara Winston
Pantheon, New York

Cover art: Carmelite Kneeling and Reading a Book
© Hulton-Deutsch Collection/ CORBIS

Cover design by Riz Boncan Marsella

Published by Ignatius Press, San Francisco, 2003
ISBN 978–0–89870–927–8
Library of Congress catalogue number 2002113184
Printed in the United States of America ∞

*Dedicated to
Esther von Kirchbach
in friendship*

CONTENTS

I

THE STORY AND THE PROBLEM

I. THE ASCENT

THE CULT of St Thérèse of Lisieux has a history unequalled in recent centuries. This young nun, who was born in 1873 and entered a convent at fifteen, died at twenty-four of galloping consumption. Never, in this short span of life, did she do anything that struck her contemporaries as extraordinary, anything that even attracted attention. The general estimate of her among the nuns of the convent community, with whom she had lived in close association for nine years, is expressed in a well-known anecdote: from the window of her sickroom Thérèse, during the last months of her suffering, heard one nun say to another: "Sister Thérèse will die soon; what will our Mother Prioress be able to write in her obituary notice? She entered our convent, lived and died—there really is no more to say." [1]

Yet it was this very obituary notice—one of an unusual sort, as it turned out—which after only a few months begot an incredible storm of spontaneous veneration. It began on a timid note, like a plucked string, and swelled to a thousand-voiced chorus extending over whole countries and continents—long before the authorities approved of these demonstrations. As early as 1909—had she lived, Thérèse would then have been thirty-six years old—veneration of her was so widespread, and so many urgent petitions had been submitted to Rome pleading for a decisive pronouncement, that steps towards her solemn beatification were initiated. This was a breach of the express convention of canon law that no such procedure should be undertaken less than fifty years after the death of a believer. "We must hurry to raise the little saint to the altars," said Cardinal Vico, Prefect of the Sacred Congregation of Rites, which is in charge of such matters, "otherwise we shall be anticipated by the voice of the people." It was popular demand on the part of Catholic Christendom

---

[1] The obituary notice is a circular letter sent out by the superior of a convent to sister houses of the Order, in which a brief sketch of a deceased member's life is given, and prayers are asked for her soul's peace.

which was fulfilled, in the years 1923 and 1925, by Pope Pius XI's beatification and canonization of "little Thérèse".

The two roots of this strange religious movement, which is without its counterpart in recent Church history, are a book and a mass experiencing of miraculous aid, the so-called "shower of roses".

The book was the above-mentioned obituary notice. Deviating from the custom of the Carmel, the Prioress allowed the deceased nun to speak for herself. She published two notebooks that Sister Thérèse had written during her last two years for her elder sisters, nuns in the same convent. These contained childhood memories, girlhood experiences, a letter, and finally, at her Superior's request, some practical lessons on convent life.[2]

Sent out to the convents of the Order under the title of *The Story of a Soul*, it was a fairly large volume as compared with the modest proportions of the usual obituary notices. Its effect outran the wildest expectations. Within a very short time, the existing copies had been lent out by the various convents, at first to relatives, priests and "devout souls"; all over the world readers began demanding new editions. The book's public swelled like an avalanche; between 1898 and 1932 the autobiography was in constant demand, and 700,675 copies were circulated, while the abridged popular edition ran to almost two-and-a-half million copies in the original language alone. Up to Thérèse's canonisation the book had been translated into thirty-five languages.[3]

The book contained the young nun's proclamation: "After my death I will let fall a shower of roses." The phrase derived from the life of one of the saints, read aloud at table in the convent, in which a sick man sees roses fall upon his bed as a sign that his prayers have been heard.

Was it this uncommonly bold promise, or was it the total impression of the autobiography, that aroused such confidence? In any case, thousands of hands stretched out to receive the promised "shower of roses". It fell and has not ceased to fall.

In the year 1909, twelve years after her death, an average of fifty letters daily were pouring in, gratefully and jubilantly relating prayers that had been heard. These were faithfully collected, and the most striking events, conversions and cures were published in volumes under the title of *Pluie de Roses*. By 1925 the collection contained three thousand closely printed pages. One has a curious sensation leafing through these badly printed volumes, cheap in their format, virtual museum-pieces of tasteless book-

---

[2] In addition there was a sizable appendix consisting of correspondence, poems and conversations.

[3] Figures from the survey of the veneration of St Thérèse contained in the *Annales de Ste Thérèse de Lisieux*, Nov. 1932, p. 327. These figures have since enormously increased.

making. On the frontispiece of the last issue, 1923–25, the saint is shown in sentimental pose, eyes raised to Heaven, surrounded by cherubs in the devotional style of 1900. Underneath are the simple words: "I shall come back to the earth to teach others to love Love." Then, in 608 pages, follow 427 accounts: two-thirds of them concerning miraculous cures, the rest narrating conversions, succour in the midst of dangers, accidents, and so forth. The stories of cures generally have appended to them affidavits by the doctors and nurses in charge of the patients, and by other eyewitnesses. We read of cancer of various organs, blindness, tuberculosis in its last stages, gastric ulcers, meningitis, and many other severe illnesses, of cures of very small children in whom imagination and suggestibility could play no part. We find reports of conversions of unbelieving and apostate Catholics who had lived for twenty, forty and sixty years on a hostile footing with the Church; reports of spiritual illumination, of peace descending upon tormented, struggling persons, of Christians of other denominations coming to the Church. A special section is devoted to the "shower of roses" in missionary countries. Here are reported cures, conversions, rescues from imprisonment, plagues, and floods in Peking and Tientsin, in tiny towns in the Chinese provinces, among Mohammedan Arabs in Tunis, in India and Madagascar, in South Africa and the Equatorial regions, Dahomey, Nyasaland, in the Canadian Lakes region, Manchuria and the Solomon Islands, Alaska and Siam—from all places where missionaries and their parishes, and even pagans, trustfully called upon the "little saint".

Since 1926 the journal *Les Annales de Ste Thérèse de Lisieux* has continued the chronicle of the shower of roses and the account of the veneration of Thérèse throughout the world. These constitute remarkable documents in the history and psychology of religion. The testimony is overwhelming. In the face of the stories and affidavits, one would have to assume a worldwide conspiracy of persistent and shameless liars if one wished to challenge wholesale the credibility of these plain, grateful accounts. It may be that some experiences were only felt to be "miracles" by the persons concerned; but the quantity of sheer inexplicable events far outweighs such dubious cases.

Equally astonishing is the fervour with which new Christians everywhere received this message. We hear of mission churches in the Sahara and the Manchu steppes, of orphans in Madagascar who went without their rice to send a contribution for the building of the basilica in Lisieux; of Japanese lepers and Ceylonese pariahs who made similar sacrifices; of Japanese, Annamite and Chinese parishes, and seminars of native priests in the Belgian Congo and Basutoland, who placed themselves under Thérèse's protection. Three years after the initiation of her cult, a

Canadian city sent out seven thousand pilgrims to celebrate the anniversary of her canonization. On the Fiji Islands her image stopped a tidal wave and drove Chinese bandits away from a mission station they were attacking. And the cult had spread beyond the limits of the Roman Catholic Church. In the Anglican church of Our Lady of Walsingham a relic (a piece of Thérèse's blanket) is publicly exhibited. In 1928 a group of Protestant natives on Malabar made a pilgrimage to her shrine in the Catholic church. A Maronite archpriest from Lebanon reported on an Office and a journal in Arabic which he had to write for his Theresian congregation. The Chaldean Patriarchal Seminary in Mosul sent a photograph of five new priests gathered around the portrait of their patron saint. Even a Shiite Moslem, a man from the strictest sect of image-hating Islam, having been cured by Thérèse, kept her picture in his house and told the Syrian Archbishop of Zahlé that "neither Mohammed nor the prophets outweigh this lovely saint".[4]

These incidents, selected at random, are mere chips from the vast block of material accumulated in the seventeen annual volumes of the magazine, and this, in turn, represents only a sprinkling of the enormous number of letters received by the Central Office in Lisieux.

Lisieux has become one of the frequently visited places of pilgrimage in the world. Above the bones of the young saint has risen a tremendous cathedral, which was consecrated in 1937 by Cardinal Pacelli, who later became Pope Pius XII. The literature devoted to the dissemination and strengthening (alas, not always deepening) of Thérèse's cult is still increasing.

And not only the masses—the Popes, too, have been enthusiastic supporters and promoters of her cult, above and beyond the canonization. When she first appeared, St Pius X is said to have called her the "greatest saint of modern times" (according to Abbé Combes)—a mysterious pronouncement which we shall have to discuss later. Pius XI called her the star of his pontificate and commended to her the countries which gave him the greatest concern, Russia and Mexico. In 1927 the "Little Flower" was placed beside Francis Xavier as the patroness of all missions and missionaries of the Church. Pope Pius XII appointed her (if we may use such a phrase) the second patroness of France, "*à l'égal de Sainte Jeanne d'Arc*".

---

[4] In 1932 a Carmelite father reported from Chicago on the truly American dimensions of the Theresian movement in his native land. He introduced himself as head of a "Society of the Little Flower", which in the first eighteen months after its foundation had gained two hundred thousand members (mostly men). He described the "National Shrine of the Little Flower" in Chicago, and the incessant mass influx to the impressive ceremonies in this church, which were promoted by high-pressure advertising: "People stand in the streets for hours until their turn comes to enter the shrine."

In 1946 a "jubilee for the fiftieth anniversary of her precious death" was initiated in Lisieux. Almost all French dioceses held a solemn exhibition of her relics. In 1947 an equally solemn "conclusion of the Theresian year" was held.

The appendix to Abbé Combes's collected edition of her letters contains a table seven pages long: "*Dates de la Glorification de Ste Thérèse de l'Enfant Jesus*", which according to a footnote represents only a brief extract from a whole volume, "*Sainte Thérèse . . . glorifiée par la Sainte Église. Actes officiels et Discours Pontificaux.*" The worker-priests, too, have placed their heroic project under her protection, and the seminary of the Mission de France in Lisieux was opened under her wing. Eleven hundred altars have been erected in her name.

Who, early in the twentieth century, would have imagined that such a torrent of worldwide veneration for a saint was possible within the Church? For the cult of saints seemed plainly in process of being relegated to Catholic "paganism", that is to say, to a realm which is the subject of mild ridicule—the realm of convents, villages, children's devotions, of the unenlightened and reactionary believers. The cultivated Catholic felt obliged to explain away this cult, with forbearance or embarrassment, as a tolerated survival and curiosity, like the tribal customs of an Indian reservation.

And now this movement, emerging in the years of the most crushing kind of middle-class materialism, burst forth out of the religious decadence, indolence and hollowness of the pre-war period. Moreover, during the chaos of the war and the post-war eras, it yielded no ground and grew.

2. THE QUESTION

Christian believers had received Thérèse as they have, for centuries, hailed their saints: questioning her no more than one would question the rising of a new star in the sky; responding to her with astonishment, faith, delight. A saint is an exemplar and a helper in need; the repute of his virtues and experience of his aid are his passports. More is not asked for.

The cult of Little Thérèse has from the first been a mass movement. It does not emanate from a group of sharply defined spiritual character, from a specific movement, such as gathered around the figure of St Francis or St Ignatius. It is directed simply towards "the devout" of the age, and they have enthusiastically responded.

The astonishing "career" of this saint has been a surprise to her admirers, but no problem. Rather, it is the most powerful confirmation of all their views on piety and the virtues. Thérèse seems to them the most glorious, the most successful embodiment of their ingrained ideals. She is precisely what they expect a saint to be. She provides overwhelming justification for the traditional elements within the Church, for the kind of devoutness that has always been held good, and for its ways and methods. She is the child of an ideal Catholic family, the product of an ideal Catholic education, the model of a nun. To the masses of those who venerate her she is "flesh of our flesh and bone of our bone"; she is with utmost intensity "one of us".

Precisely here is the point at which our uneasiness begins.

For more than two generations (and even longer, counting initial stages) there has been going on within the Church a struggle for the renewal of Catholic Christianity. It has been waged with a tremendous amount of quiet fervour and has remained inside the Church, only gradually working its way outwards. That it exists is testimony to the vitality of the Church in times both of outward complacency and of extreme affliction. This struggle is not aimed, as it was during the period of the Cluny Reform or the Counter-Reformation, at the elimination of crassly scandalous abuses; it is concerned with overcoming a host of factors which may be regarded, in their totality, as a sclerotic condition of old age, characteristic of an era approaching its end. It would be erroneous to imagine that the Church has to defend her sacred heritage only against assaults from without. Weeds grow luxuriantly in her own acre. There are special dangers to the Christian religion which flourish only in the soil of faith. And these are not only due to the "bad Christians" on whom we would so gladly heap the blame when the name of God is blasphemed among the pagans, and seekers of good will are unable to find the door of the Church. There are peculiar malformations springing up out of an originally sound base; there are spiritual ulcerations on the healthy body which are especially nourished by religious zeal and aspirations. There are a thousand influences of the *Zeitgeist*, on both the positive and the negative sides, which give rise, in the substance of the Church, to strange and questionable alloys. There are periods of decadence and zones of decay within the Church also.

And it is part of the nature of the Church, of her humanity and her catholicity, that all these things should exist side by side and simultaneously with all the qualities of divinity, greatness, goodness and vitality with which she has ever been identified. Where the negative manifestations mount—almost always when a historical epoch is coming to an end, for the faithful, too, are children of their times and must participate in the general doom—there arise tensions, crises, experiments and questionings, a groping for new ways and goals within the ancient truth. The twentieth century is undoubtedly such an era of transition. The struggle for rebirth—for the Church is the phoenix—is already a historical phenomenon in our time. Its course is at once full of mistakes and blessed triumphs, full of humiliations and of promise. It will continue to go on for the remainder of the twentieth century.

Various as are the groups and factions, the circles and currents within the Church, and bitter as their mutual feuds occasionally become, they all seem to be united in one general view: rejection of the forms of Christianity of the late nineteenth century. They see that time as an era of bourgeois Christianity, as a period of rigidity, calcification, weakening, undermining, falsification and distortion of the true Church. They see the era as one of masks and ugly overlayers. The cure must be sought, they think, in a resolute breakthrough of these conventions, back to the sources, forward to a purer form of Christian life cleansed of slag and trash.

Naturally, anyone adhering to this view regarded the phenomenon of the Theresian cult with a certain distrust, if not with outright repugnance. Was it not, in all its forms of expression, the hardest crystallization of everything such progressives were fighting and seeking to eliminate? Did not the fantastic trumpery, the endless *kitsch* surrounding the figure of Thérèse, betray the sources from which her cult sprang, the persons she appealed to, the kind of people who identified themselves with her?

But a spirit of trashy popularity also tends to hang over some of the places of pilgrimage dedicated to the Blessed Virgin. Perhaps, then, we ought not to allow ourselves to be influenced by such external trappings. Yet, even when we conquer all our prejudices and turn to the texts Thérèse has left to us, do we not usually feel the same insurmountable uneasiness?

For let us be honest with ourselves: Who among us has ever read *The Story of a Soul* for the first time without being disappointed? Who among us has really liked the book spontaneously, without the aid of an uneasy conscience which leads us modestly to ascribe our discontent with this famous work to our own inferiority?

We believe we speak for many others when we confess that at first, repeated readings of *The Story of a Soul* did not bring us the hoped-for enlightenment. For at first the book displays not a trace of greatness. *At first*, we say! How small everything is, how painfully little. It is as though we must stoop to enter into a world where everything is made to a birdlike measure, where everything is sweet, pale and fragile, like the lace in which the saint's mother dealt.

What a shut-in, faintly perfumed air seems to rise from it. The air of middle-class parlours full of miniatures and knick-knacks, full of idealized family portraits in gilt frames hanging against flowered wallpaper. It is an air that smells of memories like the morocco leather backs of old volumes of poetry. The little figures, hand-painted and touched with gilt, standing everywhere about, lovingly dusted and regarded every day, may be precious to members of the family because so many mutual recollections are linked with them. But to the stranger they are unimportant and banal. The events narrated in the story are also like simple-hearted *bric-à-brac*: childhood games and childhood tears, sorrows in school and joys in the holidays. In between are little sacred scenes: First Communion and Confirmation, first awakening of vocation for the convent. Then follow the struggles for the realization of this heart's desire—struggles which seem to the writer the grandest of experiences, involving a call upon the bishop, a trip to Rome, a visit to the Holy Father. All this is painted in detail, a veritable china-closet piece behind the fine bright glass of memory. This first and longest section of the book is full of candid effusions to the child's "little mother", full of pet names and outcries, of exclamation marks, dashes and allusive rows of dots. One can literally feel the typically feminine underscoring of all the important words.

The next chapters, too, seem like filigree work and loving miniature painting. They tell of the sorrows and joys of life in the convent. The tone changes, however; in place of the girlish chatter there are now simple little didactic pieces on convent life, on the novices, on charity—the kind of writing the Prioress wished. The third section is the real heart and soul of the book; here strong fire glows through all the lace frills and painted glass. But it is greatly to be feared that most readers will not get as far as this.

You, the reader, who have been expectantly looking for some sign of greatness, read on more and more wearily from page to page. How sweet all this is, how well meant, how finely observed, how pleasantly narrated—but how "little", here too. This story confines the heart instead of expanding it. What a narrow horizon and what a poverty of content. There is much talk of sorrows and crosses: the little novice is scolded; Papa cannot come to her Clothing; her Profession is postponed by half a year. There is talk of sacrifices and mortifications, and then come the examples: how Sister Thérèse patiently bore another nun's rattling her rosary; how Sister Thérèse in the laundry gently endured, for the love of God, her careless workmates splashing her with dirty water; how she practised perfect poverty by not objecting when a pretty water jug was removed from her cell and replaced by a chipped one, or by saying nothing when a fellow nun borrowed a brush or crayon from her paintbox and failed to return it. Or there is a grave description, spread over several pages, of how for a time as a postulant—and voluntarily—she led a half-paralysed old lay sister from the choir to the refectory, and for ten whole minutes— she expressly mentions the length of time—she endured the poor old thing's pedantic and anxious grumbling.

What lay person, the reader muses unhappily, what average "Christian in the world" as such pious souls would call him, who never in his life thought of perfection and who has only tried to live as best he could before God and his conscience, would ever have the courage to pick out such trivialities of his daily life as "sacrifices" and "acts of virtue"? What average Christian would presume to remember them, let alone write them down? The reader thinks of mothers of many children, of hard-worked servants, of innumerable persons engaged in difficult, monotonous work in oppressive domestic surroundings, of women fettered to a domestic cross day and night. Do they not endure every day a hundred times the trials so solemnly described here? And do they not take these silently and patiently for granted, bowed under the yoke of their lives and consenting to it, possibly cheerful and grateful about it? Do they look in the mirror every hour of the day to note down their "sacrifices"—even though in gratitude for the grace of God? Where would it end, the reader thinks, if everyone kept such careful account of each drop of sweat and each pinprick?

Does not such self-observation, such weighing everything in the most delicate of balances, constitute a serious weakening of the genuine Christian concept of sacrifice? Is it not a falsification and distortion? What can be the effect of such ideas on an unbeliever who bravely fights his way through the difficulties of his existence; would they make him see the strength and dignity of the Christian view of man? Would he not turn aside, with a contemptuous shrug, from something that can seem to him only an extreme form of self-satisfied philistinism and rather seek for models of courage and magnanimity among the austere pagans? And can even a Christian thirsting for honest instruction find here that stimulus to perfection for which his soul hungers?

Disappointed, the reader lays the original aside and leafs through one of the ordinary biographies, hoping to find in the testimonies of others things that the saint, in her humility, may have concealed. And once again he feels as if he were being forced to look through the wrong end of a telescope. It is as if the biographer in the sweat of his brow were trying to elevate such trivialities into heroic deeds. Alas, if only he were conscious of the effort. But how luxuriantly and innocently and with what conviction the easy praises flow: "She was given a worn-out habit *of rough wool*! She *never complained* when she was given only light sandals to wear." But, for Heaven's sake, that is what she entered the Carmel for! What did you expect, my dear sir? Fur-lined boots? (In fact, she had them.) And were any of the other nuns dressed differently?

Further: "In the middle of winter she did the washing in cold water, although this made her hands cracked and sore." Well, after all, washing has to be done in winter, too (although there is no real call to do it in cold water), and every washerwoman and housewife has cracked hands. Moreover, such work in the convent was taken by turns, and we know that Sister Thérèse was frequently employed in other domestic duties.

Moreover, the average Christian in the world cannot feel especially shocked when he hears that Thérèse as a fifteen-year-old postulant "right after her entry into the convent took upon herself the most modest and often strenuous duties *such as sweeping the stairs*", and that she "*never shirked any work*".

The story of the nun who rattled her rosary appears in these biographies as an "amazing sacrifice that goes beyond the ordinary measure of self-denial". Thérèse silently accepts a reproach by her gentle, good-hearted Novice Mistress on account of a vase that someone else had broken. "With what admirable magnanimity", the biographer exclaims, "she seized the first opportunity, even though it came hard to her, to mortify herself in humility!"

What a view of the world lies behind such judgments!

Is it any wonder that a great many readers are repelled by this insipid food after a few chapters, that they do not stick it out to the end, fearing to hear the same paeans to mediocrity in the account of our saint's suffering and death? The disillusioned reader henceforth abides by the impression that the much-praised sanctity of the "little way" consists in fashioning an extraordinarily high opinion of oneself on the basis of insignificant achievements and that natural fulfilment of human obligations which every other ethic passes over silently out of good taste, if not out of humility or modesty. The reader knows many persons who have only a pitying smile for all the acts the world considers great and important: "Imposing, yes, but such steps do not follow the way—those poor unfortunates gain no merit from all their efforts." While these same persons are firmly convinced that their smallest "sacrifices", of which they diligently keep lists, are the "truly great things" before God, and secretly determine the course of the world. He would gladly leave them their complacency—for after all, it must be a highly satisfying feeling to be so convinced of the preciousness of one's own person—were not profounder matters at stake.

There is no help for it—in spite of all the talk of pure supernatural grace, Thérèse of Lisieux seems to be no more than the pinnacle of the bourgeois ideal, the embodiment of a single virtue: the perfect goodness of a ductile child who appears more than life-size only against the middle-class and puritanical horizon of a certain type of mentality. She cannot bear comparison with any other saint. To be sure, all the saints have done little things, but none of them exclusively little things.

And then the Catholic reader is brought up short, alarmed by his own judgment.

For what does it mean if this person has been canonized, that is to say, presented to the entire Church as a standard and a model to follow? Has the canonization not rendered absolute a form of Christian piety which seems to him the most trivial, dubious, possibly dangerous form of piety in the entire history of the Church?

When I began work on this book at the beginning of the Second World War, not a single encouraging or interested voice was raised among my friends and acquaintances. I was met only with expressions of surprise, of criticism, or with attempts at dissuasion. "Really, can't you choose a more important figure, one more significant for our times? Thomas More, John Henry Newman or St Hildegard? Is it not enough that boarding-school girls, seminarians and novices are dinned with this sweet and harmless but, alas, so insignificant subject? Has not all that is necessary, and far more, already been said about this holy little nun? What can she teach us, Christians who live in the world in this chaotic moment of history—she, this 'little white flower transplanted from one closed garden to another'? Did she not think of herself in these very terms? What good to us laymen who are struggling so hard to be 'mature Christians' is a piety whose guiding figure is a small child: to be more precise, a baby? A baby that must ride in the lift because the stairs are too steep for it, that 'does not want to grow so that it will never have to stand on its own feet'." Is this the kind of childlikeness of which the Gospel speaks? Can it serve as a model to us upon whom there has been imposed, in a world falling apart at its seams, the responsibility for the Kingdom of God?

Even sympathetic ecclesiastical writers at first saw in Thérèse's personality nothing but a rather remarkable example of traditional bourgeois and conventual piety. The instructive book *Die Heiligkeit der Kirche im 19. Jahrhundert*[5] by the Jesuit Konstantin Kämpf devotes to Blessed Sister Thérèse in 1929 (that is, after her beatification) only a very modest place among fifty-four saintly nuns. "The magic of youth and innocence...fervent love of the Cross...": this devout author with a profound acquaintance of hagiological literature seems to have noticed nothing more striking about Thérèse. Alongside the studies of forty-four foundresses of modern Orders and seven women set apart by stigmata or visions, the section on Thérèse seems thin and unimpressive.

The great Bremond, that incomparable student of the history of piety, especially in his native France, wrote in the second volume of his tremendous book:[6] "Who can explain to us the posthumous history of the saints? Today a mighty stream of worshipful reverence surges up to the grave of a young Carmelite nun, who passed away only yesterday, who all her life was known to no one, and whose canonization may now well be

[5] Published by Benziger.
[6] *Literary History of Religious Thought in France.*

expected. Will the Catholics of the twenty-first century still know the name of Sister Thérèse of the Child Jesus?"

Yet how has the course of events surpassed the boldest dreams of Thérèse's venerators! Of the fifty-four holy figures of whom Kämpf treated perhaps a dozen are known to contemporary believers—aside from the small communities in which they are revered as founders; the others have, so to speak, sunk into oblivion in Heaven. Thérèse has outshone them all.

And to what saint's grave in Christendom do such hordes of worshippers come?

But what does all this mean?

Among all the opinions, doubts and emotional reactions, two facts remained, firm as rocks and indisputable: the canonization and the shower of roses. Of what significance were these if Thérèse really represented only the perfection of narrow, tame, charming, thoroughly respectable goodness, seeming larger than life only against the background of the lower middle-class Catholic ghetto of her time? Of what significance was it that the *Church* canonized such a person, presenting her to the entire world as a standard and an exemplar—and did so at such a moment in history as ours? It certainly seemed as if the Church were elevating into an absolute, a form of Christian devotion which had been increasingly regarded by many of us as the most dubious and fleeting kind of piety in the history of the Church. We had thought this sort of thing was dying out. To put the matter more sharply: did not such a figure as Thérèse, and the host of her venerators and proclaimers, embody the very type of bourgeois Christianity which we were resisting, which in our youth we had fought to overcome, in our maturity striven to transform, because we believed that history demanded new responses from the Church in each succeeding epoch? Why, then, cling to a response already so painfully old-fashioned?

Then came a more difficult, more bewildering question: What is the meaning of the *divine* testimony on which the canonization is based, the "shower of roses"—that unique, fabulous manifestation of otherworldly, celestial power in the sphere of our lives? What was it testimony of, and for whom?

This last question impelled me to study Thérèse of Lisieux, to overcome many intellectual and psychic resistances. A small, unforgettable incident shaped my decision.

During a meeting at Burg Rothenfels, then the centre of the Catholic Youth Movement in Germany, a student showed me a small picture, like a passport photograph. "This is the true appearance of Little Thérèse", he said. "Dom Willibrord Verkade, the monk-painter of Beuron, discovered and published it. The Carmel at Lisieux, and a French bishop as well, protested vehemently against its publication."

A small group of young people gathered around him; the picture passed from hand to hand. In stunned silence we gazed at the familiar and yet so alien features, and someone said: "Almost like the face of a female Christ." From that August morning on I was determined to pursue the riddle of her look and her smile—so different from the honeyed insipidity of the usual representations of her. Who was Thérèse of the Child Jesus in reality?

The present book has sprung from this question. I call it, deliberately, only a study. Its aim is nothing more than to consider and present Thérèse's life and character, insofar as they are known from the available sources, as conscientiously and objectively as possible, and finally to offer an interpretation.

A similar experience has probably been the lot of many Catholics who, having been deeply disappointed with bourgeois Christianity, or having gradually grown away from it, nevertheless feel compelled to meet the challenge of this saint. The second generation of biographers of Thérèse, all differing widely in origins, language and approach, are in agreement on one thesis: that the existing portraits and interpretations of Thérèse cannot have represented her true self. Rather, each of us, proceeding independently and ignorant of the others' work, has found in her, to our surprise, a confirmation of our own boldest dreams of renewed Christianity. The task then was to communicate this discovery.

But Thérèse had now become a figure of interest, having attracted the curiosity of the intellectuals. That development had to run its course. Involuntarily, we find ourselves repeating Georges Bernanos's exasperated sigh: "These literati are all alike.... As soon as they want to lay hands on sanctity, they smear themselves from top to bottom with sublimity [*ils se barbouillent du sublime*]—they smear the sublime around everywhere. *But sanctity is not sublime.*"

Once the rosy, saccharine glaze of sentimental bad taste and moralism had been pierced, every effort was made to show Thérèse in as strong as possible contrast to that sort of "distortion". Thérèse was now presented as a psychological problem, a misunderstood woman of great importance, a repressed artistic nature, and so on. An effort was made to introduce some drama into the, alas, so gentle and monotonous outlines of her character and life, to throw in a few wild, discordant notes that would convey an element of adventurousness, and thus suit the changed tastes of the contemporary public. This trend is still growing.

So there arose the image of a modern Thérèse, a philosophical, conscious reformer, even a revolutionary; a tormented, defiant fighter; and finally a Titanic figure beset by daemonic impulses. And as a further outcropping there developed the sensational legend that theologians, examining her posthumous works, had trembled at the possibly explosive effects of these writings and had deliberately formed a conspiracy to keep this "atom bomb" from blowing their tottering, senile structure to smithereens. According to this tale, they had decided to remove the fuse from Thérèse's time bomb and had gone to enormous trouble to rewrite all of her writings, to "purge" them line by line, expunging all that was new and unique and "adjusting" everything to the banal level of nineteenth-century bourgeois Christianity. For fifty years, the story went, this conspiracy succeeded in offering to the Catholic public a saccharine devotional figure as the true Thérèse of Lisieux. Now, however, the veil of falsifications was being ripped away from this brilliant revolutionary, and her long-withheld testament was being restored to Christendom.

Among the tradition-bound devout, too, her image had already assumed virtually superhuman proportions. She is seen as a female Father of the Church, a towering mystic creatively defining in words her discoveries in the abyss of Divinity; a feminine Pascal in her childhood, later a conqueror of the Augustinian spirit. Her book has been placed beside the Gospels themselves, her personality (that tragic Christ Child doll) beside that of the Mother of God.[7]

Probably one of the most remarkable characteristics of our saint is her ability to attract the most contradictory, the most mutually hostile types, into the ever-growing circle of her silent and loud (often very loud) venerators. Radical avant-gardists, novelists, journalists, Catholically inclined conservatives, nuns and seminarians, simple servant-girls and prominent ladies of Catholic organizations dispute with one another for the privilege of having this little nun—of all persons—serve as their figurehead, of proclaiming her the forerunner and herald of their ideals, and of identifying themselves with her as their archetype.

3. THE SOURCES

Our concluding chapter attempts to analyse the intellectual background of this curious dispute. For the present, however, there comes to the fore the question of the genuineness of the existing documents concerning Thérèse. This is a problem of first importance, for even with the exercise of considerable imagination the existing sources, on which all previous biographies have been based, do not contain any suggestion of this new Thérèse and certainly offer no proof of the "revolutionary" saint. This school of thought consistently postulated an unknown Thérèse who would

---

[7] Ida Görres was writing this book in 1957 and it was published in 1959. On 19 October 1997, Pope John Paul II declared St. Thérèse to be a Doctor of the Church.—ED.

be revealed when her complete and authentic posthumous papers at last became accessible to the public.

Now the time has come. In 1948 a volume was issued containing the critical edition of her whole correspondence, from the four-year-old's first dictated note to the dying nun's last lines, scribbled hastily in pencil upon the back of a devotional picture. The editor of this work is Abbé André Combes, long a devoted student of Theresiana, who enjoys the highest reputation.

In 1956 appeared a four-volume critical edition, *Manuscrits Autobiographiques*, edited for the Carmel by the Carmelite Father François de Sainte-Marie. It includes a photostat copy of the manuscripts which form the major part of *The Story of a Soul*. Even the outward format is imitated: two notebooks of different sizes, and two small folders of loose sheets, reproduced with the greatest faithfulness. We feel as if we had the original manuscripts in our hands. The saint's handwriting is often difficult to decipher; the manuscript is full of deletions, corrections, erasures, is scrawled hastily with poor pens on ordinary lined paper. The handwriting of the last page is extremely unsteady.

The other three volumes contain commentaries on the text, tables, comparative lists of variant readings, lists of all books and quotations mentioned, statements by handwriting experts on the various characters, even an index of all the words used by Thérèse; as in a concordance of the Bible. Few works of world literature have been accorded the honour of such an elaborate edition produced with such painstaking scholarship.

There is no doubt that the manuscripts have had a strange history. Thérèse Martin never "wrote a book". The work here and elsewhere referred to and quoted as *The Story of a Soul* has reference to that memorial volume which her convent published immediately after her death.[8] That volume, however, was a collection. The basis of it was the two notebooks containing her recollections of her parental home and her brief years in the convent. Added to these, as an eleventh chapter, was a long letter to her eldest sister, Marie, who lived in the same convent. In this letter she detailed the spiritual experiences which she called "her way". Later there also appeared as a separate little volume the *Novissima Verba*, a collection of conversations noted down at Thérèse's sickbed.

---

[8] In this present book we have retained the numbers given by the author in her references to *The Story of a Soul*. There have been different editions of this book and their arrangement has differed. Therefore the chapter numbering Ida Görres uses will not match some available modern translations. Despite the differences in enumeration we refer the reader to the definitive edition *Story of a Soul: The Autobiography of St. Thérèse of Lisieux*, a new translation from the Original Manuscripts by John Clarke, O.C.D. (Washington, D.C.: ICS Publications, 1972, 1976).—ED.

Not a page of these posthumous writings was intended for the public when it was written. The first notebook was not even meant for the entire convent, only for Thérèse's relatives in it. Basically, all three parts can be regarded as letters; indeed, they are replete with personal salutations and exclamations. They are pure dialogue, first with the "mother" of her childhood, Pauline [Sister Agnes], then with her eldest sister and godmother, Marie [Sister Marie of the Sacred Heart], finally with the mother of the convent community, Prioress Marie de Gonzague. Not until Thérèse was confined to her sickbed did the thought occur that these notes also "might do good" to other human beings. More and more strongly there arose in the dying girl a sense of mission, a feeling that she had not had her religious insights and experiences for herself alone and the few relatives of her own blood who were dearest to her, but for many.

> For others the noble good rests within me,
> I can and will no longer hide the treasure.
> Why did I seek the way so yearningly
> If I am not to show it to my brothers?

These lines from Goethe express Thérèse's feeling with surpassing clarity. After her death she wished her sisters to pass on her spiritual bequest. Thérèse herself was concerned with that alone. Not so her sisters. From the very start they were at least as much interested in drawing the world's attention to the person of their sister, whom they unshakably believed to be a saint. The memorial volume they published was intended to serve both ends.

After Thérèse's death the Prioress was quickly won over to the plan. The two notebooks, which supplemented one another, were merged into a continuous autobiography, the letter to Sister Marie inserted as an eleventh chapter, and a description of Thérèse's illness and death added to form a twelfth chapter. A selection from her letters and devout poems, notes on conversations and a section called "Counsels and Recollections"[9] rounded off the whole. The Prioress insisted—"for the sake of uniformity", say some; "out of morbid vanity and jealousy", say others—on having the numerous personal addresses in the first three pieces altered, so that it appeared as if all were addressed solely to her. This change deeply embittered Thérèse's sisters and left behind a heritage of incurable resentment; even in the latest commentaries indignation over this arrogation can still be felt. On the other hand, this stylization undoubtedly

---

[9] Written by the third of Thérèse's sisters in the convent, Céline (Sister Geneviève).

made the book as a whole readable; since nobody even knew Thérèse's name, the patchwork succession of notes to various persons would otherwise have seemed thoroughly chaotic. Moreover, this much-discussed imposition of unity was relinquished as early as 1914, and in all subsequent editions the original arrangement was restored.

There remained, however, the page-by-page editorial work, to my mind far more important, which Mother Agnes—later Prioress for life of the Lisieux Carmel—carried out on the entire text.

She had a perfect right to do so. Thérèse herself was well aware that her casually written notes constituted only an inadequate, fragmentary expression of what she felt to be her message. She solemnly enjoined her dearly beloved sister, her *petite mère*, to put some kind of order into her literary bequest. "My little Mother, you must once more go over everything I have written. If it seems well to you to cut something out, or to add something that I have said to you or... be it so as if I myself had done it. Remember this later and have ... les. For you know every little wrinkle of my soul, you alone!" [10]

Thus Mother Agnes had received a com... power of attorney", which the other members of the family in the ... incidentally, also took upon themselves.

The original texts were, moreover, an inadequate instrument to serve the second purpose of this group—the annunciation of Thérèse's glory. They were childish, unpolished, rough drafts, full of intimate allusions and hints, to a considerable extent comprehensible only to the addressees. They had to be edited for the public. And this, it seems to us, is the point of the much-discussed and much-lamented manipulations of the texts which have resulted in grave reproaches against the Carmel of Lisieux, and even in charges of falsification and distortion. To our view, these charges are unjust and unfounded. Few editors have ever received from an author such unlimited authority as did Mother Agnes from Thérèse. Yet we cannot doubt that, with the best intentions, her sole purpose was to present to the world not a picture of her youngest sister, but *her own* picture of Thérèse.

That is the aim of all the editorial work. We find three types of changes in the original: cuts, stylistic corrections and insertions. The first are very extensive and are for the most part objectively justified on grounds of discretion—we must remember that in the year of Thérèse's death all the persons mentioned were still living and were well known to one another in the narrow circle in which the nun had moved. Other passages were cut because they were really inessential—too intimate or commonplace

[10] *Novissima Verba.*

family events; scenes out of childhood such as, for example, a detailed account of a fall into a pail as a baby.

The stylistic corrections are extremely numerous, but do not affect the content. The insertions seem to me the one considerable and questionable element. Curiously enough, the critical edition has hitherto made no reference to them and drawn up no lists of them, whereas some seven thousand stylistic changes have been carefully counted.

The deletions and insertions, however, have virtually nothing to do with Thérèse's message and doctrine; they serve, it seems to us, solely to stylize her portrait along the lines of the conventional ideal saint of the period—and of the sisters themselves.

At this point we must make one thing clear: in so doing, the sisters were not distorting. Not a single essential trait has been falsified or suppressed; nothing alien to Thérèse has been superimposed upon her. The reshaping of *The Story of a Soul* serves precisely the same purpose and is of precisely the same nature as the millions of little portraits which were intended to familiarize the public with the face of the new saint. For naturally there was bound to be public curiosity about the physical appearance of the young nun, and pictures were made ready beforehand. The printed collection contained no genuine photographs, although many of these existed. Rather, as it was discreetly put, what was published was "a very conscientious synthesis, chosen with the greatest care, of the best expressive elements contained in various photographs". In other words, the picture was a careful composite of several which were, in the sisters' judgment, the most beautiful, and these were probably retouched to accord with Céline's paintings. This third of the deceased nun's sisters had had the benefit of painting lessons in the eighties. Now she tirelessly turned out, on the basis of old photographs, and probably from imagination also, sketches for devotional pictures: Thérèse as a tousel-haired three-year-old; Thérèse in curls and veil, making her First Communion; Thérèse as a young girl with long hair, her head leaning on Papa's shoulder; Thérèse as a nun, with a crucifix wrapped in roses, or writing in her cell; Thérèse on her deathbed, in a radiant glow; and even a transfigured Thérèse floating on heavenly clouds. These pictures formed the mass conception of the new intercessor in Heaven. They enjoyed enormous popularity among simple souls—and caused aesthetic shudders among the less simple. Probably they were instrumental in erecting the stoutest wall between more intellectual Catholics and a deeper knowledge of the saint.

The pictures correspond exactly with the literal description of Thérèse's person that accompanied older editions of the book: "She was tall of figure. She had blonde hair, grey-green eyes, a small mouth, fine and regular features. Her countenance, of the colour of the lily, was harmoniously carved, well-proportioned, always sweetly serene, as if stamped with heavenly peace. Her carriage was full of dignity, at once simple and graceful."

Comparison with actual photographs is sufficient to show the difference and provides us with our finest clue for judging the editing of the original texts.

In both content and language Thérèse's original manuscripts produce a dual impression. Her handwriting is usually hasty and careless, the passages scribbled down in snatches of time. Quotations, however, Scriptural passages, sacred names, and important words (love, grace) are interspersed in solemn, ornamental script. Similarly, the artless conversational tone, tender and spontaneous, full of pet names and exclamations, alternates with long stretches of school-essay style. In school Thérèse had been a shining light in "composition". All her life, like many young girls and like her epoch in general, she loved a lyrical, pompous sort of "poesy", especially in descriptions of nature and pious reflections. The language is replete with lilies and dewdrops, flowers and birds, the flush of dawn and the twinkle of stars, doves and palms—precisely as we find these elements in the devotional pictures and convent paintings of the time. The entire sensibility of the period stretching from Rococo to Late Romanticism has been preserved in this language. Her letters are exactly the same.

We may put it this way: Mother Agnes recast her sister's scribble into "calligraphy" and her personal notes into "school theme". Possibly she did so out of regard for what she thought to be the taste of the public; possibly in order to clothe her sister's extreme youth and *naïveté* with somewhat more dignity and solemnity. The content remained the same. Thus, the seven thousand corrections are, ultimately, without significance. Who is really troubled if the original says, "I loved snow", and *The Story of a Soul* "choicely" puts it: "Have I ever told you, Mother, how fond I am of snow?" The difference is that between the fresh impulsiveness of a child's drawing and an "embellishment" to suit grown-up standards, imposed by a governess with ruler and eraser. For Mother Agnes, her sister whom she revered as a saint nevertheless always remained the youngest, the baby of the family whom she had once primped and dressed for visits. Now she polished the sister's notebooks with the zeal of a schoolmistress, in order to make sure that they would be presented respectably to the world. It must be remarked, of course, that her sister's writings made their way in the world in spite of, not because of, this embellishment.

The facsimile manuscripts afford no sensational revelations, no fundamental transformations in our picture of the saint. In this respect, the mountain of critical research has brought forth a mouse. Neither in the letters nor in the original text of *The Story of a Soul* have I been able to find so much as a single sentence which in any way altered my view of the saint. Anyone who understood how to read the texts, as they have been printed hitherto, within the framework of the historical period, and who worked through the extensive documents on the beatification and canonization, will already have found enough sidelights and material to supplement the portrait shaped by the sisters. The new publications, aside from a very few corrections on factual details, such as the trip to Rome, have provided me only with innumerable confirmations of the conception of Thérèse which underlies this book. I had been able to advance that view only as a personal hypothesis, however; now the new publications offer scholarly support to it. Because of limitations of space, I have been able to include only a small part of the new corroborative material in the present book.

This book, then, cannot be more than an attempt at a translation from the language of yesterday, which has already become inexpressibly alien to us; an essay to clarify, for a few persons, at least, the enigma and the sealed glory within the countenance of this saint. She has been hidden from our sight by so many veils: the cheaply gilded veil of insipid bad taste; the opaque, rigid folds of an outmoded ideal of sainthood; the deceptive curtain of stylization; and, finally, the radiant gauze of her own resolute silence, which no human effort can ever entirely lift away.

2

THE NEST

I. ORIGIN AND HERITAGE

To MANY PERSONS their own childhood, at least in their conscious minds, means very little: a beginning only in the sense of a point in time at which life started; a groping sketch without lasting validity, vague and half-erased, outmoded by "real" life, neither prelude nor rehearsal for one's actual being, but only a fragment of vegetative or, at most, animal existence.

But along with these there are persons, though they probably do not appear often, for whom childhood means something different: a beginning fraught with meaning, full of promise and anticipation, containing the future; an overture which sounds the dominant theme; a dress rehearsal for life, which can be as perfect as a work of art and may even surpass the later, the "real" performance. It is a sketch, but not a groping inadequate schoolboy's sketch scarcely indicating the intention; rather, the sketch of a master's hand, using the sparest of means, barely suggesting the outlines, and yet perfectly, transparently, setting forth with incomparable economy and sureness the finished work of art.

That is the case with the childhood of Thérèse Martin. Her first four years were her life, filled with her essential being as a plump, round fruit with its own juice, unique and complete, early and gloriously perfected. From the very first she appears like a complete human bud—not like Pallas provided with helmet and shield from the start, but in the most delicate stage of blossoming. Through no fault of her own, an early shock causes her to lapse from this radiant beginning, and she spends the time which is ordinarily for a child the second strong, significant period of enrichment and growth in a statelike exile; "beside herself", in "the saddest stage of my life", she phrased it in retrospect. The third period, when she regained her self, lasted until her death.

Thérèse on her deathbed, in spite of the long road of purification over which she had passed, was much more like the four-year-old Thérèse than the struggling, spiritually aspiring girl of her confirmation period. Her "way of childhood" actually proceeds, in a strangely literal sense, from one childhood to a new form of purest childhood. In the light of this we may already begin to see that the concept of the child had, for Thérèse, a peculiar overtone and a special weight; it derived from her own experience of childhood as, so to speak, the state of original perfection—not with any petty inclination on her part to sentimentalize great things.

It is curious to observe the unerring certainty with which Thérèse felt this very early stage of her life, from the ages of two to five, to be her true, valid self, to be the perfected embodiment of her "idea", if we may phrase it this way. Up to the time of her early, always anticipated and gently longed-for death, childhood represented the true measure of her self, her starting point in an essential rather than merely temporal sense. Her life was a return to this early perfection, which had been received as pure grace. Consequently, we cannot speak of her in terms of "development". All her life she added nothing to her dowry. Her growing-up was only an unfolding, a refinement of what she had brought with her into the world, what already existed within herself; it was not the absorption of influences from without. Whatever affected her afterwards, as the result of elementary and boarding school, and later the Carmel, always remained alien to her, and in some sense—in spite of all her humble receptiveness of the heart and will—secretly invalid for her. The outside world caused her unspeakable pain, but it did not penetrate into her; it added nothing to her nature and took nothing away. With a highly singular mixture of extreme gentleness and tenacity, her being defended its intact wholeness and self-containedness. To this is due much of the simplicity of her character, but also its impenetrable narrowness.

Childhood is all heritage, all dowry. It is important for us to know the forces which shaped this childhood, which produced the substance of this life, and impressed their ineradicable seal upon it.

Those forces are very few: her father, mother, sisters, and perhaps the Norman countryside. These—and we must not forget the times. "For", Goethe writes in his preface to *Dichtung und Wahrheit*, "this seems to be the chief task of biography: to represent the man within the relationships of his age, and to show to what extent the currents of the Whole oppose him, to what extent they favour him; how he forms out of this conflict a view of the world and men; and how, if he is an artist, poet, writer, he reflects it back again. However, this is demanding something scarcely attainable [by the autobiographer]: that an individual should know both himself and his century. Himself, to the extent that he has remained the same under all circumstances; the century in that it carries along with it both the willing and the unwilling, determines and shapes them, so that one can say: If such and such a person had been born only ten years earlier or later, he would have become, in his own development and in his effect upon the outside world, a totally different person."

During the process of canonization, the question was put to Céline, the shrewdest and most articulate of the sisters: What aspect of the Christian life in her parental household had made the deepest impression? She replied: "The chief virtues I saw practised at home were the observance of the holiness of Sunday, and contempt for the world."[1] This reply was by no means a spontaneous inspiration; it was almost certainly the product of long and penetrating consideration and discussion. It does indeed define the elements that were actually of highest importance within the family. At the same time it reflects, in as sharp a focus as the view-finder of a camera, certain essential features of the nineteenth century.

The great experience of nineteenth-century Catholics was the "secularization" of the Western world, and, consequently, the expulsion of the Church from its position of eminence. Of course this process had begun long before, and had been foreshadowed and in part accomplished over many generations. But those who experience great historical changes at first hardly notice them, only feel that they are being dragged along willy-nilly; some time must always elapse before such changes pierce to the deeper levels of consciousness and engender new attitudes, new modes of behaviour.

Even though the Church had retained, of her once uncontested dominion, far more prestige and special privilege than we today can imagine, an enormous displacement had nevertheless taken place. Certainly there had always been rebellion and resistance, but hitherto the Church had always embodied the very principle of order and justice, her primacy so unchallenged that anyone who rose up against her was by definition a rebel, an opponent of sanctity itself—though his contemporaries might feel this to be crime or glory. Now the position had changed fundamentally. Primacy was enjoyed now by the world; the world alone was taken for granted, sufficient unto itself; the world was the protagonist and the Church only the antagonist, to be viewed and treated as troublemaker or ally, as tool or rival. In any case, in the consciousness of the peoples she had irrevocably lost her first place and would have to struggle henceforth, to exert herself to the utmost, to maintain second, if not third or even a still lower place. The Church had moved into a defensive position; she had not abdicated, she had been deposed; she was on the way to becoming the private affair of individuals or groups.

---

[1] 2 S., 63. For abbreviations used in the footnotes, see list of abbreviations on p. 421, below.

Catholics were aware of this development with varying degrees of clarity; at times they were burningly conscious of it; at times it was only a dull grief. Not only the mind, but far more intensively their whole sense of life and self was incessantly steeped in the problem. For their attitudes, shaped and nourished by past experiences and conceptions of a very different sort, were adjusted to the new situation only gradually and with great difficulty. Out of their surprise and perplexity two crucial responses formed in the hearts of the devout, responses which have continually influenced the character of Catholic life. The one was a fervent, unconditional affirmation of love and loyalty to the Church, in which all the pathos of the piety of the period was expressed; the other was a never-ending, equally passionate and exclusive negation of the victorious, usurping power of "modernity" in all spheres of life.

Perhaps never before and never since has there been so painfully vigilant, so sensitive, so unconditional and uncritical a devotion, such blind loyalty, to the Church, and not only to her, but to everything connected with her. This devotion was the kind of passionate, fervent emotion, afire with repressed indignation, which is offered to an abandoned wife, an abused mother, a dethroned queen. The devout laid stress, eagerly and assiduously, upon everything that distinguished them from the others, everything unmistakably pertaining to their particular faith. They were more popish than the Pope and more Catholic than the Church. They wanted constantly to display their adherence to Rome by banners, glaring colours, prominent badges. Here was the nucleus of that emotional and aggressive type of zeal which nowadays so strongly offends our tastes: the coloured caps of Catholic student associations, which the young people sport as they stroll about their universities, as if they were in a public procession; the wide blue sashes of the Children of Mary; the medallions worn with evening dress; the ostentatious observation of the fasts; the delight in mass demonstrations, resolutions, processions, which no longer have a religious, but rather a political character. In their eyes, all such acts are confessions of faith and an apostolate. There is a strange and touching blend of contradictions: sincere pride to the point of arrogance and challenge, and inner uncertainty which continual loud assertion is supposed to smother; a claim for the validity of the Church's message in all things, and a kind of passive, though fanatical defensiveness. Their fanaticism was at once chivalric and plebeian, diplomatic and tactless, intimate and indiscreet, wholly spiritual in intent, yet with a childlike and childish obstinacy insisting upon the most petty superficialities. We might almost say: the very secularization of life which they were condemning and rejecting penetrated, in the methods which were used to combat it, through all back doors into the heart of the Church. The devotion of the devout was deflected from its sole real significance, was focused upon men instead of God, kept one eye at least cocked for the impression it was making upon the "world". In their devotion the devout were constantly endeavouring to make apologias or give instruction, to edify or to convert. And this all-dominant tendency found its way into the most personal depths, right down to the gestures made during prayer and the attitudes people assumed while receiving the Blessed Sacrament.

In this struggle against secularization lies at least one very important root of that idolization of obedience, and that blind submission to every utterance of the ecclesiastical authorities, which aroused the scorn of contemporaries and brought forth ashamed and angry criticism from later generations. Perhaps the commandments and the canons have never been so punctually and zealously honoured, been so followed to the letter, with such tenacity, to such excess and with such intransigence. Not that their content was understood with any greater penetration and affirmed out of this deeper understanding, but simply because they were commands. Perhaps never before has the Law been so *loved*. To it was offered obedience for the sake of obeying, *art pour l'art*; obeying, the individual could be conscious of himself as a loyal child of the Church. Newman, who must have had a great deal of experience with this attitude in his circles, recognized clearly the grave danger which could arise from this originally noble impulse. He once spoke of the "lust for servility" in which certain ecclesiastical circles revelled and attempted to outdo one another.

Out of this attitude, too, there no doubt arose that tactic—practised in the Church with astonishing unanimity and consistency—of hushing up all past and present weaknesses and errors of the Church. There was an unspoken but unbroken conspiracy steadfastly to approve, embellish, excuse and praise every expression of ecclesiastical life, whether Roman policy or monastic pedagogy, whether the intellectual content of a sermon, editorial or Catholic novel, or the aesthetic values of devotional pictures, church buildings or hymns to the Pope, whether a Catholic historical hypothesis, a philanthropic institution or the private life of personalities who stood high in the estimation of the Church. All such matters were immune from criticism, were unassailable, sacrosanct. Anyone who ventured a criticism of the excellence of all such things was under suspicion of disloyalty, secret freethinking and unreliability.

There is a great deal of decency and honour, an astonishing sense of solidarity and responsibility, underlying this sort of fidelity. To gather with closed eyes around the beloved, threatened banner is noble. And yet how much narrowness and intolerance, how much injustice and falsehood, how much servile renunciation of responsibility, how much mental laziness and cowardice—to the point of abdication of common sense—assembled in the course of time behind the broad shield which those faithful warriors held out to protect their endangered heritage!

With equal resolution, with equal refusal to make concessions, everything that belonged to the world, everything that in any way reeked of the "modern spirit", was shunned, rejected and condemned unexamined, unquestioningly, with no reference to objective factors, solely on principle and for the sake of protest.

For the devout of this type the world was divided plainly into a chessboard of black and white squares; there were no shades between, no questionable boundaries, no development, no special cases. The designations "Catholic" or "modern" decided all questions. French *esprit* created for the pious Catholics of that era the pointed, perhaps malicious, perhaps melancholic name *émigrés de l'intérieur*, a phrase revived in the twentieth century as a political concept: exiles who have remained at home and who nevertheless have emigrated from the prevailing order, who are fugitives from the whole life of the nation, leftovers of a vanished era, quietly longing for a return to or restlessly bent upon reconquest of the past.

Repeatedly reformers, gathering around the leading intellects of the time, sought to re-establish the severed link with contemporary life and society. But these efforts were restricted to the cultivated few; they did not extend to the people. The *émigrés* remained outsiders, wanted to remain so. The epithet possibly derives from the conceit of the victorious new elements, but possibly, too, from the painful, tragic defiance of those who affirmed the gulf and kept it wider than necessary, feeling at once noble pride and unconfessed impotence, the dignity of renunciation, and a resentment that slowly poisoned their spirits.

We believe we are not far wrong in assuming that the situation of the French Catholics, product of the times that it was, exercised a far-reaching influence upon the whole development of piety from the middle of the last [nineteenth] century up to the eve of the First World War. This influence extended far beyond the borders of France. The strong tendency to expansion in the French teaching Orders, and later the governmental attacks upon the monasteries and convents, led many members of the Orders to take refuge in neighbouring, more tolerant countries. For generations the daughters of the leading social classes in almost all European countries were reared by French nuns who steeped their charges in Catholicism of this particular character and atmosphere: a cultural process whose significance should not be underestimated. For in their methods of education, pedagogically highly effective and conscious of purpose, the *émigré* attitude was soon completely separated from its historical premisses; the reasons for it were swiftly forgotten, and it was referred back to purely religious premisses. It developed into an independent ascetic system and laid claim to being the sole valid expression of elevated Christian piety.

An age-old heresy, often refuted, often condemned, but repeatedly reviving with uncanny tenacity inside Christianity because its deepest roots lie within human nature itself, returned at this time unrecognized and over byways. It entered not through the open conflicts of theological schools, but by the overlooked gateway of a defeatism both traditional and tainted with secularism. It emerged from the world-weariness and the fear of life inherent in an epoch tinged with doom. In earlier forms it had been called Puritanism and Jansenism; now, under the guise of strictest orthodoxy, it seized power in almost the entire Catholic world.

That "contempt for the world" which Céline cited as one of the qualities in her parents' home, and in which the devout of those days luxuriated, undoubtedly possessed fairly often a high ethical earnestness. This was expressed in inner freedom from the enormous rapacity and pleasure-seeking of the age, in a lofty personal dignity and purity which marks the distance between the world of *The Story of a Soul* and the world of Zola's novels. Nevertheless, the religious basis of that ethical earnestness—where it was not simple inherited faith—was not strictly valid. Secular hopelessness engendered in the emotional life of believers a conviction of the hopelessness of secularism; the taste of sour grapes was, alas, too eagerly pronounced to be the tartness of the Cross. An anxious hostility towards body and mind became established. That hostility was not rooted in Catholic doctrine, but in the attitudes towards life of those who did not adjust well to secular society. It led, furthermore, to indifference and, in fact, to principled refusal to share in the responsibility for this modern world. The relationship between the world and the devout became solely a strategic one; the Church was more and more felt to be a front, and devoutness a kind of patriotism. Life behind this front lost meaning insofar as it was not directly in the service of the fighting forces. Only expressly religious activities were held to be of value and worthy of a Christian. Hence the monastic life was necessarily esteemed the true, supreme model of Christian life; and hence the value of marriage was thrown into question.

The forces necessarily released by the withdrawal of believers from participation in secular life could not remain idle. Since they no longer found any field of activity in a world stripped of religious references, they were applied exclusively within the Church herself. There developed a strange byplay alongside secular developments: a tremendous eagerness for the establishment and building of purely religious organizations, a world in itself. This movement has frequently been dubbed "the revival of the

Catholic Church in the late nineteenth century". But the contemporary believer, looking back upon the phenomenon, finds himself wondering whether the astonishing outpouring of devout diligence, the tremendous accomplishments in charity and education, the clubs and "cultural endeavours", may not also appear in a rather curious light—if we consider as a parallel phenomenon the increasing, inexorable dechristianization of the entire white race in all realms of life. The Christian's duty to the world, it would seem, cannot be supplanted by any amount of pious activity outside the world. The contemporary believer must also ask himself whether the unprecedented number of foundations of Orders, or rather congregations, during that era was really a healthy outgrowth of the idea of monasticism. Was it not mostly an unsound excrescence of that superstition so prevalent among the laity: that the world offered no room for a pure, godly Christian life? In his crippled religious condition the layman no longer possessed any standard of his own, and comparison with the standards of religious life in the monastic Orders led to dual consequences. The permanently felt gulf between the unattainable ideal and personal reality might result in inferiority feelings. The average Catholic therefore would leave piety to the pious, that is, to specialists who had the time and desire to occupy themselves with the multitudinous obscurities of the "higher spiritual life"—a special world arranged only for initiates. He, the ordinary mortal, would meanwhile limit himself strictly to "meeting his religious obligations", to being a so-called "practising" Catholic. An alternate development was for religious life even in the world to be placed entirely under imitations and surrogate forms of the monastic rule. In line with this was the widespread attempt to observe monastic obedience in the relationship with one's confessor, and the taking of private vows of celibacy. Clericalism among the laity found fruitful soil; more was offered voluntarily than the priesthood would ever have obtained by demand. At the same time, however, this artificial subsidiary society of the "unadulterated Catholics" was infiltrated by purely secular standards which betrayed the superficiality or the self-deception of its "flight from the world". For in this society numbers, conventions, success, social rank and titles were more important than ever before. Class snobbery of the crassest sort was justified on a religious basis, with a clear conscience; social problems were disregarded with innocent ignorance. Even during the First World War a lady of above-average devoutness, belonging to these circles, could boast that she never shook hands with either Protestants or members of the middle class.

Thérèse's environment was still free from such excesses, but the basic elements of that *"émigré* attitude"—preference for emphatically visible forms of religious life, the cult of the Law and the Commandments, the pro-scription of all "worldliness", overestimation of monastic forms of conduct—emerged clearly in the life of the family.

Thérèse Martin was of French provincial origins. Her family tree, as far as it is known, goes back to a stock of long-settled Norman peasants, possibly also to the artisan class of small towns. These were people such as Charles Péguy, Thérèse's contemporary, knew and loved, people like his mother, the maker of cane chairs in Orléans, and his neighbours in the poorer quarter of the town. Péguy has described them and sung their virtues with keen sorrow for things irrevocably lost: a poverty-stricken, hard-working, sturdy, rude, contented and irrepressible folk, endowed with boundless strength for enjoying and enduring life; a medieval folk, far more closely related to the people of guilds and brotherhoods out of the days of Joan of Arc than to the class-conscious proletariat among whom Péguy's lot was cast in later life.

Thérèse's parents did not belong to this world and wanted no part of it. The Napoleonic Age had interposed a stratum of military life and soldier's blood between them and their more settled forefathers. Both their fathers had fought in Bonaparte's army. Zélie Guérin's father later continued to serve in the gendarmerie. The children turned to trade—perhaps it would be more accurate to say, to the modest independent business enterprises to which the class of richer artisans was everywhere tending. Both were veritable models of the respectable rising bourgeoisie who were beginning a tremendous economic and social upsurge in the second half of the nineteenth century. Soon the Martins enjoyed a degree of prosperity which permitted them a comfortable style of life, journeys to spas during the summer holidays, and extended pleasure trips, a small country house, and for the children the typical education of young ladies: boarding school and private lessons. As has been mentioned, Céline was given painting lessons; Thérèse remarks that as a young girl she never had to do any household work. The girls were never allowed to go to school unaccompanied by the maid, even in pairs or groups. The family had become bourgeois, outwardly and inwardly.

The memory of Monsieur and Madame Martin has suffered a fate sim-ilar to that of the canonized daughter: a loving stylization, based on the accepted patterns of holiness, has smoothed out and retouched the uniquely personal elements; the two have been presented to posterity as *the* holy parents of their holy child. All human weaknesses and flaws have been effaced. Nevertheless, the wealth of material permits us to form a fairly clear picture of them.

Both, in their youth, had sought the religious life; both had been barred from it by purely external obstacles. Louis Martin wished to enter the

Augustinian Monastery of the Great St Bernard. His application was turned down because of insufficient educational background, and he had not the character which enables many whose vocation comes to them late in life to resume and carry through the struggle with school books. He returned home, and for fifteen years after this disappointment he lived as a single man and in such retirement that his friends whispered of a secret vow of celibacy. His final decision to marry Zélie Guérin evidently was due more to her and to his mother's urging than to any impulse of his own. Gentle and shy, he was guided more by others' decisions than his own.

Zélie Guérin had knocked on the door of the Sisters of Charity of St Vincent de Paul; possessed of a strong, active temperament, she wished to serve the sick. Since the Mother Superior rejected her, without giving any specific reason, she soon appointed another goal for herself. Sober, tenacious and enterprising, she did not passively mourn the loss of her heart's desire, but resolved to devote many children to the service of God. This intention alone led her to marriage and undisguisedly dominated the many years of her married life. Nine times she was privileged to hope, and her persistent desire was fulfilled in her five daughters, although only after her death. She lived to see the desire for the convent awaken only in her favourite daughter, Pauline, the second oldest, and she carefully nourished this inclination. Moreover, Madame Zélie never abandoned her wish to fulfil herself the dream of her youth some day, in her old age, when all her children had taken the veil. Like many strong and vital women, she seems to have taken it for granted that she would survive her husband.

"I have just been reading the life of St Jeanne de Chantal", she wrote to Pauline in the winter of 1875, when Thérèse was two years old. (St Jeanne-Françoise de Chantal, herself a widow and the mother of several children, had founded the Order of the Visitation.) "And I am utterly beside myself with admiration. It interests me all the more since I have always thought highly of the Order of the Visitation" (which is one of the few that accepts widows). "But now I love it still more. How happy all those who are called to it seem to me!" A few weeks later: "I am thinking only of the cloister and solitude. I really do not understand that, given my inclinations, it was not my vocation to remain unmarried or to enter a convent. I should like to grow very old, in order to withdraw into solitude once all my children are taken care of." Another time, when her mind was occupied with the great figure of Madame Acarie, one of the first French Carmelites in the seventeenth century, she said: "How happy she was, being privileged to give her three daughters to God."

"I always wished to have many children in order to rear them all for Heaven"—that was this strong woman's consolation when she four times lost a child, two small daughters and two sons. More and more ardently she longed for a son who would be a priest, a "missionary", a saint, who would more than make up for her own desire to devote herself to an Order, which had been denied by God's inscrutable counsel. It must have been an ultimate disappointment for her—though she fought through to resigned acceptance—when her late-born child Thérèse, the ninth and last, who marked the end of her childbearing years, apparently banished this hope for good—in the outcome, to fulfil it gloriously beyond all measure.

In all matters Zélie Martin remained the stronger partner, the leader within the marriage. "Our mother had an unusually energetic character and a tremendous capacity for self-denial, which always made her forgetful of herself. She laboured with great courage in order to be able to give us a careful education." Her daughters describe her, but not their father, in this fashion.

In the eighteen fifties, within the strict conventionality of French provincial life, it was extraordinary indeed for a girl still in her parents' household to set up independently in business—and, moreover, with the practical purpose of improving her own dowry and therefore her chances for marriage. Her determination to take up lace manufacture must have lain entirely outside her experience, and the advice of her relations, for all her life Zélie considered her impulse to do so a direct inspiration from the Blessed Virgin. She sought out lacemakers, trained them herself, sketched patterns for them, supplied drawings, took the orders, dealt with customers and suppliers, and so built up a home-crafts industry which quickly proved highly profitable. Her father was a sergeant of the gendarmerie, had served for forty years in the military under the Empire and the Restoration; her mother, of whom we know little, must have shared the instability of a soldier's life until she settled down in Alençon. Thus Zélie's decision, and the consistent good fortune which attended her in it, shows independence and initiative, commercial efficiency and a certain gift for handling people.

The relationship with the honest watchmaker Louis, who was no longer so very young, was not initiated by him. The official biographers agree that Zélie, chancing to encounter him on a bridge, received a divine inspiration telling her that this was her destined husband. Thus she recognized, with remarkable insight, her affinity to this taciturn and dreamy solitary. It was not too difficult for her to establish contact between her family and his. She must then deliberately have directed matters towards the desired conclusion. Ten months after their marriage Zélie once again proved the stronger partner when she converted her husband from his ideal—probably one he had held for a long time—of a "Josephite marriage", in other words a marriage in name only, to her own concept of a family blessed by many children.

Her superiority in practical realms was so great that in spite of her large household and the rapidly growing flock of children, she kept her lace business. Later, Louis Martin sold his own business to a nephew and entered the one his wife had established. He took over the travelling, part of the purchasing, and the bookkeeping. All the rest Madame Zélie continued to run herself, in spite of nine confinements, a variety of illnesses among the children, and all the duties and cares of a housewife in those years when the domestic economy was still a sizable enterprise. In sum, here was a woman of extraordinary energy and capability. Zélie combined the life of a model wife and mother and a successful business woman with the inclinations of a nun, and she merged all this into a remarkably impressive harmony. Her letters leaven the impression of an efficiency and strength of will that might well appear somewhat alarming; we see in them a cheerful, tender heart, a lively, gracious nature, wit, a gift for observation, and a happy mother wholly devoted to her children in spite of all other concerns. Her portrait, which Céline painted from photographs, has undoubtedly been stylized and made to accord with prevailing ideals of beauty, like so many of the pictures of her famous daughter. Nevertheless, we can discern a curious similarity to the features of the youngest daughter during the last years of Thérèse's life. Beneath the dark hair is a clear, wide face in repose. Her forehead, unusually high for a woman, is somewhat concealed by her coiffure. Her large, dark eyes are slightly too close together; with the almost horizontal eyebrows, the strong, straight nose, the firm chin and straight, tightly closed mouth, they lend an air of sternness, and almost of hardness, to the face. But it is not the hardness which stems from lack of feeling, rather from mastery over a passionate heart. Such must have been the appearance of the woman who, solicitous as she always was for the welfare of her husband and children, concealed from them for sixteen years her own severe illness. As a girl Zélie had bruised her breast; the injured spot gradually developed a tumour which in the end became malignant; she died of it at the age of forty-six. Disinclined always to have others fuss over her, ever optimistic and at the same time ascetically severe towards herself, she maintained silence until it was too late. (From a letter published for the first time in 1942, in the *Annales de Sainte Thérèse*, it appears that Madame Zélie began to be concerned about this disease in 1864 and questioned her brother Isidore about it.)

We find Thérèse displaying the same inexorable harshness towards herself. How strongly the daughter's attitude reminds us of Céline's comment on her mother: "When our little sisters died, people said: There is no need to try to console Madame Martin; she does not suffer at all from the loss of her children!" "And yet", Pauline adds, "her letters showed that her heart was broken."

Alongside this strong, tender, but undeniably domineering woman Louis Martin seems to have been made of much softer stuff. He was a dreamer and brooder, an idealist and romantic. These traits can be seen still in the picture of him as an old man, which his indefatigable daughter Céline probably adapted from a photograph. It shows the head of a pleasant-looking patriarch, with a steep, bare forehead, large eyes which must have been blue-grey like those of his youngest daughter (who is shown leaning against his shoulder), sharply arching eyebrows, and a tidy white beard framing a small, fine mouth.

He loved nature with a deep sentimental enthusiasm. From him Thérèse inherited her passion for flowers and meadows, for her native landscape, for clouds, thunderstorms, the sea and the stars. There was, too, something rather un-French about his wanderlust, which in youth and age tempted him again and again to abandon the sedentary comforts of bourgeois life. Even when he dreamed of the cloister, he was not drawn to a famous house nearby, noted for scholarship and pastoral care, but to the cloud-wrapped solitudes of the Great St Bernard where intrepid monks lived on the edge of glaciers to watch over pilgrims and travellers, and with the aid of their almost legendary dogs fought against all the demons of the alpine night to rescue those lost in the snow. How this dream of his combined escape from the world with adventure! Some of this unforgotten youthful romanticism still survived amid the peaceful idyll of retirement in Lisieux. Unlike his sober-minded wife, who deferred her dream of the convent until her daughters were taken care of, Louis Martin engaged in a rather wistful game: he arranged a little den for himself high up in the attic, a true monastic cell for praying, reading and meditation. Even his daughters were allowed to enter it only if they wished spiritual converse and self-examination. As in a monastery, he divided the day into worship, garden work and relaxation. His Jesuit friend Father Pichon reports that even as a widower and the father of nine children he gave the impression of a monk who had been driven by contrary winds out into the world.

Along with this impulse towards withdrawal, his old, inextinguishable delight in travel came to the fore. He made pilgrimages to Chartres and Lourdes, went to Germany and Austria, travelled twice to Rome and even to Constantinople, and planned but did not live to carry out a pilgrimage to the Holy Land.

He certainly loved his craft also, the deliberate, reverent absorption in detail and precision. He loved the precious things with which he dealt as a jeweller. To his daughters he gave touching and naïve pet names: Marie was his "diamond", Pauline his "noble pearl", Céline "the bold one", and the "guardian angel". But Thérèse was his "little queen", to whom all treasures belonged. "Little queen" meant far more than "princess"; it testified to the unconditional dominion this child wielded over his heart. "It can't be helped, she is the queen", he would always reply to Zélie in the early years, when she warned him not to spoil the child. He loved to recite poems holding Thérèse on his lap, and to sing her to sleep. His excessive sensitivity, his tendency to have moods and weep easily, has been noted.[2] Thérèse may well have inherited from him this affliction of her childhood, which she later overcame when her character once more reverted to that of her mother.

"Papa" was the centre of the quiet house, "Les Buissonnets", in Lisieux, to which he retired after the loss of his wife. The daughters, all of them disinclined towards marriage even before the desire for the convent awoke in them, had no other ideal in life than to lavish care and attention upon him. While he still lived they were already venerating him as a saint. "A saint's child prays" is the title of a long, emotional poem in which Thérèse paid tribute to all the joys and cares of their years together, and invoked her late father with trustful reverence, as if he were one of her heavenly patrons. Marie, who during her father's lifetime sometimes shook her head at his lofty and austere views, and who hid the lives of the Desert Fathers from him to keep him from going too far in imitation of them, later wrote: "How right our father was when he said to us: 'My children, fear nothing for me; I am a friend of God.'"

Nevertheless, almost every word of *The Story of a Soul* which deals with the father, almost every reference to him in the published letters and in statements of the older daughters during the canonization trial, indicates how strongly there had developed in the family a tacit agreement to treat Papa as a peculiarly fragile treasure. A veritable conspiracy of tenderness spread protective wings over his life. The comment on Zélie already cited, "She laboured with great courage in order to be able to give us a careful education", indicates that the mother felt this responsibility rested upon her own shoulders, though according to the view of the times it was certainly the father's concern. Again and again we feel the implicit tremulous anxiety: Papa must be spared, Papa must not be troubled. Because it pleased him, Thérèse was allowed to wear her hair down— only for that reason, Céline stresses. Such "vanities" violated the stern principles of the mother and the sisters in charge of Thérèse's upbring-

[2] P. Ubald, 16.

ing, and they tried to make up for it by telling the child again and again that she was not at all pretty.[3] Thérèse concealed all the tribulations of her school years so that Papa would not know of them; her so-called conversion of Christmas 1886, of which we shall have more to say, was the outcome of overcoming a childish disappointment lest Papa's joy in the holiday should be spoiled. As each successive sister entered the convent, the only real difficulty was the question of who would now continue to care for their father. Thérèse's heart-rending grief at her own early decision to enter the Carmel was, again, concern for the suffering she had to impose upon his submissive heart. For all that she admired him so deeply and responded to his "little queen" with the pet name "my king", for all that she took his opinions on everything as the ultimate in wisdom, she also viewed him from earliest childhood as somehow menaced, as exposed to the buffeting of the world. She was only seven when she had the curious experience of her waking dream or second sight, her "prophetic vision", as she and her sisters called it, which was probably connected with unconscious anxiety in her love for her father—whether the root of this anxiety or the fruit of it, none can say. One bright afternoon when Monsieur Martin was away, Thérèse was standing by a window in high spirits. Suddenly she saw a man come out from behind the wash house and walk slowly across the garden. In dress, in height, in walk, he was exactly like her father, but he was strangely stooped and aged, and his head was concealed by a heavy veil.

The child's horror-stricken cries alarmed her sisters. They searched the garden, but there was no sign of the uncanny figure. From that time on Thérèse always felt an unknown dire fate hanging over her father, and this feeling probably made for the intensity of her emotional struggle when the time came to part from him. A year after her entrance into the convent, the vision was fulfilled and explained: her father suffered several strokes which produced at first severe psychic disturbances, hallucinations and attempts to flee his home, then led to partial paralysis of the brain, and later to general paralysis of the body. Still fully conscious of his tragic and humiliating state, Monsieur Martin had to be transferred to an institution. After three years, when complete immobility rendered his care easier, he was moved back home, where he was tended by Céline and Léonie. He died five years later, his mind completely shattered. In the early stages of his long suffering the poor man used to cover his face with a towel, as if out of an impulse of shame; this action often recalled to the sisters Thérèse's premonitory vision.

[3] 2 S., 88.

The two elder sisters had a deeper influence upon the formation of Thérèse's character than either of the parents. We shall speak in greater detail of this later on. For the present we can anticipate to say that Pauline and Marie successively guided their little sister's education, and that their combined influence was far greater than that of the convent school and of their relatives in Lisieux, Uncle and Aunt Guérin, for all Thérèse's closeness to these.

Two of her sisters were still living in 1944: Pauline, as Mother Agnes of Jesus, whom Pope Pius XI appointed Prioress of the Carmel of Lisieux for her lifetime, and Céline, as Mother Genevieve of the Holy Face, in the same convent. Thus, much about these two sisters is still hidden under the veils of the Order. We know only that Pauline resembled her mother in all things, that she was dark-haired and dark-complexioned, lively and ardent in temperament,[4] and sensible beyond her years. Her mother wrote to her at fifteen as to an adult confidante: "You are a true friend to me; you give me courage to endure life with patience. I thank you for giving so much joy to all of us." [5] Intelligent and firm, intellectually gifted and imbued with a clear, purposeful piety, physically so small and delicate that the name *petite mère* appears half teasing, half tender,[6] Pauline almost represented for Thérèse her lost mother. As long as the younger sister lived, she held this maternal role and represented the strongest guiding and shaping element in Thérèse's growth.

Marie died at the age of eighty, in January 1940, as Sister Marie of the Sacred Heart, in Lisieux. Her biography, related in loving detail in her obituary, presents a distinct picture of her kind, forceful and simple nature. Earthy and straightforward, natural and a little angular, with refreshing love of liberty and a pleasant portion of obstinacy, she was of the stuff out of which—in the next generation—eccentric, professionally active spinsters were made. In another country she might have plunged into the awakening Suffragette movements and distinguished herself for her energy in the cause. In the Convent of the Visitation, where she spent a few years as a pupil, she was a highly gifted though difficult child, won many prizes and distinctions for achievement, had many friends, and was passionately attached to her aunt, Sister Dosithea, who was one of the teachers. Nevertheless, homesickness almost broke her bold little heart; at last a bout of typhoid fever forced her to return home. She was convinced ever afterwards that she had fallen sick because of her suffering at

---

[4] "*Des ardentes fillettes brunes et pleines de vie*", the biographer of Sister Françoise-Léonie says of the two eldest.

[5] Laveille, 49, unpublished letter of 5 December 1875.

[6] Dolan, 11.

being separated from her dear ones, a suffering she had concealed. In boarding school she steadfastly refused to recite the "prayer for priests and religious" which her beloved aunt pressed upon her in the hope of awakening a desire for the convent in the schoolgirl. But upon her return home she was equally stubborn in refusing to dress fashionably, "as though I wished to offer myself for sale". And she wept with defiance and indignation when her mother, who did not dare to hope that this daughter of hers would have a vocation, once cautiously began to speak with her about the holy state of matrimony (presumably in tones implying that it was a last spar to cling to in a shipwreck).

Later Marie wanted to dedicate her life to her father, and it may have been a greater and more painful surprise to her than to him when her sister Pauline's confessor, the famous Father Pichon, S.J., discovered in her also a call to the Carmel; we may put it, when her sister and Father Pichon joined forces to persuade her to take this step, since she had not yet decided upon any definite path in life. The formula "It is the will of God" worked its magic, and Marie submitted to her destiny. Under other circumstances she might well have submitted, like so many of her contemporaries, to the will of parents in entering upon an arranged marriage. She went into the Carmel without enthusiasm, but willingly enough, with a pure readiness for obedience and devotion. And she lived for nearly sixty years grateful and contented with her chosen vocation—as she might equally well have done as a wife and mother. It would seem that Thérèse, during her years in the convent, must have learned much about "little souls" from observing this sister who was without especial "gift" for religion—about the simple and average souls whose sole greatness consists in their unconditional loyalty.

"Our parents were considered extraordinarily devout", said Marie at the canonization trial. "Daily, they attended the earliest Mass at half-past five, which they called the Mass of the poor." They communicated four or five times a week—amazingly often in those days of Jansenistic practices in matters of the sacraments. Their sole diversions consisted of pious converse and edifying reading, the daughters reported. After the mother's death Monsieur Martin moved away from Alençon. One of his principal motives was to remove his growing daughters from their old circle of acquaintanceship in the town; although these persons were of course good churchgoers, they seemed to him too worldly-minded. The traditional charities of the wealthy bourgeois household were practised as a matter of course. On certain fixed days the needy came for their support; the children were early accustomed to giving alms. On the day of a child's First Communion it was the custom of the countryside for a well-to-do family to provide some poor child with her communion dress and invite her to table; the Martins gladly followed this custom. The divergent temperaments of the two parents emerge somewhat humorously in their practice of Christian charity. Louis Martin once sweetly conducted home a drunk who had been lying in the gutter; at the railway station he took up a collection in his own hat to obtain the fare for a poor epileptic. Madame Zélie fought out a bitter struggle in court against two malignant women from whom she had snatched away a foster child they were in the habit of mistreating. The parents' respect for priests was so great, Céline relates, "that I have never seen the like of it. I remember as a child considering priests *something like gods,* so accustomed was I to seeing them placed altogether beyond ordinary mortals." [7]

No wonder, then, that the children were all raised unequivocally to view the convent as their destiny. The father, too, "sought no worldly disposition for his daughters," a friend of the family said, "but wished they would all dedicate themselves to God." When the last of the daughters confided to him that she, too, would enter the Carmel after his death, the old man said joyfully, "Come, let us go together to the tabernacle of the Lord to thank Him for the graces He has showered upon our family, and to the honour He has shown to me in choosing His brides from among my daughters. Yes, God does me great honour in asking for all my daughters. Had I anything better, I would gladly offer it to Him." [8] His house was long considered "a kind of little convent". [9] Another friend of the family calls Monsieur Martin a venerable patriarch living entirely in the supernatural realm, a Christian of the first days, "not in the least tainted by the modern spirit". [10]

Anxiously, the parents watched for every sign of virtue in the children. That Marie upon her return from boarding school attended Mass every day did not content her mother; Madame Zélie thought her daughter did not look devout enough, and this was a great wrong. After the death of five-year-old Hélène her mother recollected a petty lie of the dead child and underwent great fears for her punishment in purgatory, until she was consoled by prayer. "Our parents always seemed like saints to me", Pauline testified. "We were filled with reverence and admiration for them.... They had no use for the things that glitter.... Our mother despised all worldliness and would tolerate nothing luxurious in the house." "She would not have us wear choice clothes", Céline declared. "In regard to vanity she let nothing pass." No wonder that Thérèse, raised in this atmosphere,

[7] 2 S., 63.
[8] Laveille, 216.
[9] 2 S., 76, 525.
[10] 2 S., 56.

suffered severe pangs of conscience at the age of twelve because she took a childlike delight in the gift of some blue silk hair ribbons. Only in the description of the bridal dress that Thérèse wore for her Clothing is there tender mention of the shimmering splendour of swan's down, white velvet, and those famous laces, the *points d'Alençon*, which had made their mother's fortune; for this occasion alone could Thérèse adorn herself, when all the finery celebrated the perfect sacrifice of earthly beauty. When, many years later, Céline was about to attend a ball at the home of friends, the sisterly trio in the convent were so agitated that Thérèse called her sister to the visiting room especially to warn her against such a reckless act and shed rivers of tears at the perils she might encounter. Many years later, at the time of the canonization trial, the sisters recollected this incident as proof of Thérèse's "heroic chastity".

To be sure, there was a certain irony in the fact that both parents derived their considerable income exclusively from the vanity of their fellow men, the father as a jeweller and the mother as producer of handembroidered lace, which at the time cost up to five hundred francs a yard and was used only for the most luxuriant toilettes. Here was exemplified the sharp separation between occupation and the private religious world which was so typical of the Catholics of the period.

Sundays were kept with puritanical strictness. The parents would never have permitted a journey on this day, "not even a useful one", says Marie. In Alençon it was customary for certain shops, those of the jewellers and watchmakers, for example, to stay open on Sundays when the country folk of the vicinity came into town to stroll and window-shop. Even in strict churchly circles the right to do business on Sunday must have become established by custom, for Marie emphasizes that her father's pastor gave him permission to act fully in accord with his own judgment in this matter. But their shop remained closed, and Louis Martin also steadfastly rejected the suggestion that he at least leave open a side door for the customers, "to avoid giving offence". This observance cost him considerable loss of profits in the course of time—as all the daughters and biographers go out of their way to stress and repeat with admiration.

With equal zeal the parents kept all prescribed fasts. "Our mother was frail and delicate by nature; nevertheless she fasted and did penances just like Father." Both, as a matter of principle, did not avail themselves of the dispensations and alleviations which had become common at this time. "Such things are nothing for good Christians." Even when severely ill and having just finished a strenuous journey, Madame Martin refused to eat supper on an ember day.

Does it surprise us that out of such a puritanical atmosphere should grow that message of inner freedom, pure love and simplehearted candour

before God which is Thérèse's bequest to Christianity? Let us not forget
that the spiritual property of an individual, as well as a nation, is never
limited to what he consciously possesses. In the French in particular there
still dwells, deep in the blood and by now become nameless, an inesti-
mable Christian heritage: drops of that great tide of mysticism which swept
through devout France in the seventeenth century, which was later parched
by the withering breath of Jansenism, frozen by the icy winds of freethinking and finally swallowed by the earthquake of the Revolution, but
which continued to trickle in hidden rivulets out of deep springs in many
Christian families. In the final analysis the Martins derived from this heritage; it contributed more than their fidelity to the law and their contempt for the world; and it came to light in them, in all their children,
and most radiantly in their youngest daughter.

2. CHILDHOOD

Thérèse Martin was a happy child. The experiences of the dawn of life
create the premisses for all later experience, or at least the key by which
we interpret that later experience. A "happy" childhood is therefore inexpressibly more than a mere "childhood paradise" in the sentimental
usage of that phrase; more than an idyll before "real life"; more than a
kind of nature preserve fenced off from raw reality, sheltering something
that cannot exist under other circumstances. A happy childhood means—or
ought to mean—that one's first experience of the world is a "true"
experience—not yet comprehensive, of course, yet comprehending the
prime reality, so that it becomes an experience of an essential order which
thenceforward will serve as a basis of comparison, in whose light all future falsification, all disorder, will be recognized as wrong and invalid.

A happy childhood means above all a loved child. Because Thérèse was
a happy child, her beginnings could contain perfection. Because she was
a loved child, she received from the beginning the knowledge that others
must struggle towards so consciously, with such difficulty, by painfully
strenuous detours: the simple truth that to so many of us seems the most
incredible and amazing lesson of religion: *that we can be loved without having deserved it*: that grace comes first. "Love resides, not in our showing
any love for God, but in His showing love for us first." [11] The core of the
Christian revelation is prefigured, secretly and compellingly, in this experience which precedes all anticipation, all expectation, all questioning;
the knowledge that childhood is bliss. It is bliss simply to be someone's

[11] 1 Jn 4:10.

child, child of a father, of a mother, living, moving and having its being in a love which is unmerited, unmeritable, anticipatory, unconditional and immutable.

On this basic mystery and reality Thérèse's childhood was built. This was the source of her subsequent doctrine of the "way of spiritual childhood". And it was as if her family were called upon to incorporate this particular reality in living pictures.

Thérèse was one of those few happy mortals for whom Father was really the simple model, reflection and symbol of God the Father. The love which surrounded her from the first day of her life was more than tenderness, more than care, more than joy in the continuance and renewal of the life of the parents in their children. Looking back upon her parents, Thérèse had no need to forgive them for anything, apologize for them, be "understanding" about them.

We might expect that the rather narrow piety of the parents would manifest itself in the home as pressure and gloom, as sharpness or even harshness: this particular sort of shadow is, alas, often cast by that kind of light. But in the Martin family piety was a dense, protective hedge with all the thorns turned outward towards the world, shielding the nest from all disturbing, foreign, indifferent and inquisitive elements. Inwardly, it folded the young in a wrapping of pure love, bright as blossoms, warming as the down around a young brood. Only in the fate of Léonie did its limitations become apparent.

The monastic, almost puritanical severity of the two parents towards themselves was apparent to the children only in the sweet fruits which grew from this pitiless pruning and bending of human nature: in the "tremendous self-conquest" of the mother, whose toil and illness never cast a shadow of despotism, unrest or tension upon the sunny comfort of the household; in her inexhaustible patience and leisure, so that she always had time to squander on games and serious conversations, on long letters, gladsome observation, tenderness and gaiety. They tasted these fruits in the gentle justice of the father, who "never spoke a single uncharitable word",[12] in the deep concentration of his face in church, which told them more about the reality of prayer than all catechisms.[13]

Clear and alive as in a speeded-up motion picture which shows the opening of a bud, we see a human heart blossoming unhindered in the steady sunlight of a great and rich parental love. There is nothing special in all the long letters which Zélie sent to Pauline in the distant convent boarding school at Mans, nothing more remarkable than the story of the

[12] S.S., vii.
[13] S.S., iv.

growth of a small human being. Perhaps the astonishment and delight of the parents was more deeply felt this time because their happiness still throbbed with their barely surmounted anxiety over this last child. For Thérèse had been given to them against all hope, and then given twice over; the newborn infant had come very close to succumbing because of the mother's disability. Zélie had been unable to nurse, and the child's life was preserved only by the painful sacrifice of separation, a year in the care of the good peasant nurse Rosalie, in the forests of the Bocage—the same nurse who had cared for their dead brother.

The mother's joyous, humorous letters summon up a vivid picture of the baby Thérèse. That picture is supplemented for us by Thérèse's own recollections in *The Story of a Soul*, and by her sisters' memories. We see the Benjamin of the family, the "little queen", the imp, the urchin, the little monkey, the little darling—quick and lively, bright and tender, enterprising and independent, droll and obstinate, full of joy in life, full of ideas and jokes, excessive in affection and sorrow, imbued with the most touchy sense of honour. "She really seems to be very clever", Madame Martin wrote to Pauline[14] before Thérèse was a full year old. "I also think her nature is good; she is always smiling." A year later: "My little Thérèse is gentle and sweet as an angel. She has a delightful character; one can see that already. She has such a dear smile." [15] "She has a blonde little head and a golden heart, and is very tender and candid." [16] "She is cleverer than any of you was as a baby." [17] "The dear little one is our sunshine. She is going to be wonderfully good; the germ of goodness can already be seen." [18]

She was an exceedingly thoughtful child, Marie said in the trial; precociously intelligent from the age of two on.[19] Pauline recalls that she was "especially intelligent and loving, very sympathetic and attentive, especially towards Father"; Céline describes her as a very lively child, full of élan and high spirits, exceptionally communicative.[20]

At the same time, no one was blind to the faults which were just as clearly in evidence in this precociously conscious, highly emotional child. "Céline seems to be quite naturally good, for as for the other little monkey, I don't know what is to become of her, she is such a little madcap",

[14] Laveille, 37.

[15] *Sur la vraie physiognomie morale de Ste Thérèse*, special edition published by the Carmel of Lisieux, 1937, p. 2.

[16] Laveille, 65, letter to Pauline of 14 May 1876.

[17] Laveille, 47, unpublished letter to Pauline of 22 March 1877.

[18] Laveille, 56, unpublished letter to Pauline of 4 March 1877.

[19] I S., ii, 30.

[20] Ibid.

Madame Zéline wrote to Pauline when the two youngest girls were six and three years old. "She is intelligent enough, but not nearly so docile as her sister. When she says 'no' nothing can make her change, and she can be terribly obstinate. You could keep her down in the cellar all day without getting a 'yes' out of her; she would rather sleep there." Thus Thérèse quotes her in the first chapter of *The Story of a Soul*, and she adds that she had a fault that her mother did not mention in her letters: pride. One day her mother promised her a penny if she would kiss the floor, "to see just how far my pride would take me.... A penny was a fortune to me in those days... but my pride was up in arms, and drawing myself up to my full height I replied: 'No, Mother! I'd rather go without the penny.'" Another time the four-year-old was being made ready to go to some friends in the country. She tried to seem indifferent as to how she was being dressed, but secretly she was sorry when Marie gave her a long-sleeved dress. "I should look so much prettier if I had my arms bare."

These last three stories (and the one about the famous basket of doll's things) have latterly been cited as proofs for the fashionable contention that Thérèse was a "problem" child with perilous inclinations. But we must not pick these elements out of context—as did Thérèse herself. The letter with the celebrated passage about putting her in the cellar in fact continued: "But you know, my Pauline, all these matters do not lie very deep, and we think our 'Benjamin' very sweet, even with her tiny baby faults."[21] And again: "She is so extraordinarily candid. It is charming to see her running after me to confess: 'Mother, I pushed Céline once and smacked her once, but I won't do it again.' It is that way with everything she has done."[22] "Not for all the gold in the world would the little one lie.... She is unusually frank. As soon as she has done the least thing wrong, everyone has to know about it. Yesterday she tore a little corner off the wallpaper and got into a pitiful state. She wanted to tell her father about it as soon as possible. By the time he came home four hours later, everyone else had forgotten all about it; but she ran to Marie saying, 'Quick! Tell Father that I tore the paper.' She stood like a criminal awaiting sentence, but she had got the idea into her little head that he would forgive her more easily if she accused herself."[23] This respect for judgment was lodged deep in her—for the love that surrounded her was neither blind nor weak. She was the recognized, uncontested favourite. Her father submitted with untiring love to her smallest whims in regard to

[21] *Sur la vraie physiognomie morale de Ste Thérèse.*
[22] Laveille, 65, letter to Pauline of 14 May 1876.
[23] *S.S.*, i.

play.[24] She could interrupt her mother at any work.[25] Her sisters wanted nothing so much of letters from home than to hear precisely what little Thérèse had said, done, disarranged; at home they competed to take care of her. Nevertheless, no one overlooked her faults. Thérèse learned very quickly that she did not "fall into disfavour" for little, everyday, unavoidable misdeeds and accidents such as tearing clothes, dirtying hands and dress, breaking a fine vase, knocking her head on the table leg. But the slightest attempt to be naughty, affected, demanding or moody was frowned upon. The two cases of reproaches which she mentions in *The Story of a Soul*[26] are important only because they demonstrate the remarkable alertness, firmness and sensitivity of her upbringing.

One day she was playing on the swing when her father passed and called to her, "Come and give me a kiss, my little queen." "*Dérange-toi, Papa!*" Thérèse replied pertly—an untranslatable compound of "Come for it yourself" and "If you want it, you'll have to go to the trouble of getting it", with perhaps even, "Don't be so lazy." Her father went by, with a grave expression, but without a word, while Marie said: "You naughty little thing, how can you be so rude to your father?" "I got off the swing at once; I had really learned my lesson, and the whole house echoed with my cries of contrition." Another time her mother wanted to kiss her in the morning, but Thérèse pretended to be asleep; then, when her ruse was seen through, she hid herself under the sheet and said with the air of a spoiled child: "I don't want anyone to see me." This time no one laughed; the mother left, with some stern words of reprimand.

These are nothing but trivialities, everyday occurrences such as are common in any united family. But from the very beginning they operated to form an extraordinarily tender, impressionable, lively conscience guided and impelled solely by love. "Being good" in little Thérèse's world meant only one thing: doing the will of her father and giving her mother joy. Naughtiness was but one thing: making her parents sad. Contrition and forgiveness wiped out all faults entirely, instantly, without reservation. That was her basic ethical experience, and it remained with her all her life. From the very start, all formalism in fulfilment of the law was excluded.

In a book on family life in the present day, a mother[27] writes that the child must learn from the mother's comforting how God comforts us; this was the way Thérèse and her sisters learned it. "It is not only because

---

[24] S.S., i; Laveille, 62.

[25] Laveille, 62.

[26] Ch. i; Laveille, 65–66.

[27] Esther von Kirchbach, *Von Sonntag und Alltag*. Ein Buch der christlichen. Gemeinde, 1939.

I have been preserved from mortal sin that I fly to Jesus with such confidence and love; even if I had all the crimes possible on my conscience, I am sure I should lose none of my confidence. Heartbroken with repentance, I would simply throw myself into my Saviour's arms, for I know how much He loves the prodigal son. I have heard what He said to Mary Magdalene, to the woman taken in adultery, and the Samaritan woman. No one can make me frightened any more, because I know what to believe about His mercy and His love; I know that in the twinkling of an eye all those thousands of sins would be consumed as a drop of water cast into a blazing fire;"[28] for "I have plumbed the depth of more than one mother's heart".

When Sister Thérèse lay upon her last, long sickbed, Pauline—now Mother Agnes—said to her, reflecting on the past: "I am convinced that Mama often exaggerated and somewhat embellished your little childhood faults, in order to have something amusing to write in her letters to me—for all I ever wanted to hear was about you babies, and she sometimes had to rack her brains to find something to tell." "I think you are right," Thérèse said, "and it is true that it was never necessary to scold me harshly in the least, even before I was three years old. A single word spoken lovingly and gently was enough for me, and would have sufficed for my whole life to make me see and repent what I had done wrong." Marie, who during the early years had a share in the upbringing of Thérèse, gives the same testimony: "When she was still very small it was never necessary to scold her when she had done something wrong. It was enough to say to her: that is not right, or: that offends God, and she would not try it again."[29]

Was Thérèse, then, a model child?

She was not, if we mean by the phrase a child that *has* no difficulties because it is too docile, too timorous, too unimaginative, too dull, too feeble or too placid to feel or practise resistance to the wills of others. She was, if we mean that Thérèse *made* no difficulties. That was strikingly the case. Thérèse was an extraordinarily good child as a baby, as a schoolgirl, as a young girl, as a novice—all her life. This goodness was characteristic of her whole nature, was the one "special" quality about her. And we may say that such goodness always came both extremely hard and extremely easy to her.

Hard because, as we have already seen, she was uncommonly intelligent and emotional.

"God graced me with intelligence at a very early age, and He so engraved the events of my childhood on my memory that it seems they

[28] *S.S.*, x.
[29] I *S.*, 30.

happened only yesterday", she herself says, writing about the period from her third to her fifth year. "Without showing it, I took in everything that was going on around me, and all that was said, and *I think I passed the same sort of judgment on things as I do now.*"[30]

Even at that early age she was consciously sensitive to the beauty of landscape, of flowers, of an evening mood. "I love to think of... those Sunday walks, when Mother came with us. I can still feel the deep and poetic impression which the wheat fields made on me when I saw them all studded with poppies and cornflowers and daisies. Even then I loved far distances, wide spaces and the trees. The whole of nature, in fact, enchanted me, and raised my soul towards Heaven."

Her passionate heart awoke early: "God has surrounded me with love all my life; the first things I can remember are tender smiles and caresses, and while surrounding me with all this love He gave me a warm and sensitive heart to respond to it. No one can imagine how I loved Father and Mother; I showed my affection for them in thousands of ways, for I was very demonstrative."

Enterprising and fearless though she was, she liked to cling to her mother's apron; the briefest separation caused her grief. She worshipped her big sisters, who were so frequently away from her on mysterious journeys. Barely able to talk, she would regularly answer when her mother asked what she was thinking about: "Pauline." "I used to dream of you from morning till night."

Her attachment to Céline was passionately intense and tender. The two children, three years apart in age, were inseparable "just like the little white chickens"—their dearest possessions. Thérèse would leave her full plate of dessert and clamber down from her high chair if Céline had finished first. Every time the elder girl was taken off by the grown sisters for lessons, Thérèse was "bathed in tears"—anew every day; parting for only a few hours wrenched her heart. In order to enjoy the presence of this dearest sister, she would sit still as a mouse for two or three hours in Marie's room, blotting herself out utterly, until the long lesson was over. If she thought she had caused her parents sorrow, the whole house rang with her sobs; in her long nightgown she would climb out of her bed and run barefoot through the rooms until she had asked and obtained forgiveness. She could not bear to feel guilty.

Children possessed of such force of emotion and self-assertion are, as a rule, not easy to rear. But alongside these "expansive" forces, as Thérèse herself calls them—her demonstrative outpourings and insistent commu-

[30] S.S., i.

nicativeness, her possessiveness—there was manifest from the beginning a happy tendency towards restraint, reticence, renunciation, recollection in all senses. When she was still too small to reach the door latch, she was found by Marie lying peacefully on the threshold of her room; she had been there for hours because she did not want to call for aid. She never objected to or resisted a command. "She cried a little, I suppose, but never tried to change my mind", Pauline declared. Never, all the sisters unanimously testify, did she make use of her privileges as the "Benjamin" of the family to force fulfilment of a whim or desire of hers by begging, pouting or tears. "I think my disposition was the same then as it is now", Thérèse writes in her candid manner. "I had acquired considerable self-control already, for I never complained when any of my things were taken away from me, and if ever I was unjustly accused I would keep silent rather than excuse myself." The sisters repeat, confirm and emphasize this trait of hers.

Marie, upon her return from the boarding school of the Visitation, brought an old conventual custom with her: a kind of rosary with movable beads on which "acts of virtue" could be counted by shifting the beads. The classical practice, recommended by St Ignatius, among others, called for a totalling up of faults. When, one wonders, did this aid to self-admonition become a complacent bookkeeping of virtues? It is possible to hold different opinions on this late form of "particular examination". The pharisee does very well with it: I have not only fasted twice this week, but have overcome myself eight times in the forenoon and nine times in the afternoon. Nevertheless, there are still simple souls who can utilize unharmed, and even genuinely profit by, such methods. Marie and her mother, at any rate, saw no danger in presenting six-year-old Céline with such a chaplet and teaching her how to use it. And Thérèse, who had to imitate Céline in everything, was also given one. Very soon she outdid her bigger sister. "Even Thérèse wants to start making sacrifices now", Madame Zélie, to whom this sort of piety was commonplace, wrote to Pauline. "But the most charming thing of all is to see Thérèse slip her hand into her pocket time and time again, and move a bead along as she makes some sacrifice." These self-conquests, Marie explains, consisted in giving in to her sister in games and on all possible occasions. "She really had to do violence to herself, for her character was already firmly pronounced." Whereas Céline, we will remember, was at this time gentle and yielding. Certainly pride also played a part in this remarkable rivalry in asceticism; therein lies the danger of such methods. Thérèse remarks herself that this impulse partly underlay her "growth in virtue": "I had a love for virtue, but I was proud too, so I only had to be told once: 'You mustn't do that,' and I never wanted to do it again."

This contest in virtue, and its effects, are part of the inventory of "signs of early saintliness" which is regularly invoked whenever the childhood of the saint is discussed. We must be somewhat more cautious in our estimate of these "signs".

Thérèse at the age of two spoke her first words of prayer "with charming reverence".[31] She could not fall asleep without having said her prayers.[32] She was bent on having the adults take her along to Vespers, which she called "my Mass". She would cry when she was taken for a walk instead or had to stay home; in one such case she escaped from her nurse and ran alone to church in the pouring rain.[33] She was fond of praying before the May altar, which her sisters had adorned "up to the ceiling with branches of a wild plum and fresh greenery along all the walls (for 'Mama is very hard to satisfy, much harder than God's Mother!')."[34] She chattered away delightfully of the angels and God and asked all sorts of questions about them.

But all these "signs of early saintliness" are no more than natural. Every devout mother or aunt, every nun who works in a children's home, could tell hundreds of such stories. Why should the imitative nature of a bright, imaginative child not venture into this sphere, all the more so since religion so emphatically constituted the core of the family's life? Thérèse herself gratefully acknowledged this: "With only good example about me, it was only natural that I should tend to follow it."

Her early asceticism, too, is susceptible to a simple, offhand explanation. Speaking of her great self-control, Thérèse adds: "There was no real virtue in this on my part for it came naturally."[35]

We may unreservedly take that statement literally. The capacity for overcoming oneself is in fact "natural" to many children; they may even display distinct pleasure in such conduct. Even without a counting-up of virtues, such a tendency can mount to a kind of mania for establishing records—which springs not only out of ambition to win the praise of others, but out of a profound delight in experiencing mastery over oneself—this first manifestation of the realm of the spirit. It is a kind of pride, not haughtiness nor vanity, but rather a peculiar, still unconscious and unselfconscious but very distinct sense of human dignity in oneself—the same pride which makes a small child remarkably "sensitive" to real or apparent humiliations, to a mocking tone or a remark which it cannot yet

[31] Laveille, 42.
[32] Laveille, 46.
[33] Laveille, 42.
[34] Laveille, 64.
[35] S.S., i.

"understand". It is this pride which Thérèse characterized by *amour-propre*, that scarcely translatable French expression which means literally "self-love", but differs in emphasis from our "self-love" or "vanity". *Amour-propre* suggests rather a high opinion of oneself, a desire to measure oneself by an exacting standard; it is a "noble", high-hearted pride. This sort of pride seems to have been particularly characteristic of Thérèse as a child.

"She had an extraordinary strength of will", Céline declared in summing up. This trite expression immediately suggests a further question. For "will in itself" does not exist; we must always ask what power stands behind the will, impelling it, strengthening it, making of it a force imbued with mind and spirit, rather than a mere instinct. More than pride, more than *amour-propre*, lies behind little Thérèse's self-control. Namely: conscience. That is the key to the secret of her unfailing, astonishing "goodness".

Her uniqueness lay in her pure and powerful conscientiousness. Perhaps it is fairly common for children to display a pronouncedly "moral" character, just as there are some who have a surprisingly pedantic, driving impulse towards orderliness and cleanliness; and some who have a distinct feeling for propriety in every sense. But such behaviour nevertheless seems essentially connected with a sense of pleasantness and unpleasantness, or in the second case with what is permitted and what prohibited; there is often a certain rigidity and anxiety about it, especially when the child's upbringing has been strict. Only later, when ideas of good and evil are "read into" the child's conduct, does it turn its attention towards these ideas. Most children have to develop from "behaviour" to "principles". In the case of little Thérèse, we will remember, fear of punishment played no part. In her, the development of conscience began at a point that is usually the goal of such development: with obedience that was free because it sprang from love. Her "will to love goodness" developed, inevitably, by experience with the goodness which she came to know through obedience; at the same time her acquired behaviour was her own because her heart was impelled by love, because she eagerly grasped and affirmed the desires of those she loved. And she comprehended these commandments of love as supremely important, the crucial elements in her life. This the child demonstrated, long before she could understand such words as value, importance, nobility, by painful, self-conquering obedience. The will of her parents took absolute precedence in her life; she *always* obeyed it, and that meant for the "little monkey", the imp, the little princess, the small, impulsive, passionate, spoiled little thing, nothing less than that she obeyed it at all costs. Nothing else was possible for her.

It is clear from this that the most innocent and best-natured of children must pay a price if they are to remain unconditionally faithful to conscience, to recognized good. None can say when, for young Thérèse, the will of her parents began to be a translucent medium for the will of God, in whose place they stood; when she began consciously to obey God in obeying her parents; when the "Little Lord Jesus" became a real person rather than a word willingly but uncomprehendingly repeated. This seems, however, to have happened very early. Let us recall Marie's testimony: "When she was still very small, it was necessary only to say to her... 'That offends God....'" Of course we cannot know whether the tone and look of the adults did not make the decisive impression upon the child. Céline declares more expressly: "Thérèse was by nature proud and obstinate, but only so long as there was no question of offending Jesus; for from this time on she went to great pains to please Him in all things and never to offend Him." [36] Speaking of her fifth or sixth year, Thérèse tells of always asking her "little mother" Pauline, after she had been tucked into bed: "Have I been good today? Do you think God is pleased with me?... I always got the answer, 'Yes.' I would have cried all night otherwise."

And there is the overwhelming statement that Thérèse made, in all simplicity, upon her deathbed: "Since the age of three I have refused God nothing." [37]

This goodness was partly, as she herself said, her "nature", not any especial virtue of hers. It was a simple harmony with the inner and outer laws of her environment and with the love which prompted her to be in accord with her beloved parents and sisters. It was the product of a healthy, happy and strong disposition. She was as "natural" as a string responding with a round tone to the masterly touch of a musician's hand, as natural as a clever animal which has been perfectly trained. The fact that her nature was such, and that at the same time she was able to awaken and to flourish in a compatible environment in which real goodness was implanted into this willing, eager love—this was pure grace.

This grace was not received by unconscious forces, as in sleep, and was not taken into herself as a precious seed in order to sprout later on. Rather, in feeding the roots of her being it also overflowed into the consciousness of this little soul, so that Thérèse "knew" what she was doing. And that was again pure grace, unfathomable and mysterious.

And that this grace, which by the law of our fallen and redeemed nature we must help to purchase and hold at the price of sacrifice, for all that it comes unmerited—that this grace so irresistibly attracted the child's heart, that she took it into herself and held it with all the force of her

---

[36] I S., 54.
[37] C.S., 266.

small soul, always, however, sustained by a gracious force that incomparably surpassed her own: this was again grace unalloyed.

This, then, was one other fundamental lesson of those precious years, a lesson Thérèse was never to forget: goodness is a gift, is grace, freely conferred apart from all deserving, by God's mercy and unfathomable choice, and yet a gift whose giving she must help to perfect at every moment with devoted receptivity, with receptive devotion. "Jesus called to Himself whom He Himself wished." These Scriptural words stand, solemnly and deliberately, at the beginning of *The Story of a Soul*, and by way of introduction Thérèse tells the simple story of the "little white flower": "If a little flower could talk, it seems to me it would say what God has done for it quite simply and without concealment. It would not try to be humble by saying it was unattractive and without scent, that the sun had destroyed its freshness or the wind its stem, when all the time it knew it was quite the opposite. This flower, in telling her story, is happy to make known all the gifts that Jesus has given her. She knows quite well that He could not have been attracted by anything she had of her own. Purely out of mercy, He gave these gifts."

In the childhood of this girl, as in her whole life, one after another of the basic concepts of Christianity stands forth with the precise purity of a snowflake under the microscope. Here, first and foremost, is the concept of holiness.

Holiness is not, in the Christian sense of the word, surpassing ethical achievement, ascetic record-breaking, possession of rare and strange forces drawn from mysterious marginal realms of the psychic life, like clairvoyance or healing powers. It is not genius expressing itself in religious vision. Holiness is hallowedness, is a state of being seized and marked by God who alone is holy. That human soul is holy who responds to the hallowing divinity, "Yes", who responds with all his forces and at any cost, in free and loving obedience. "What God asks of you is that you should sanctify yourselves".[38] That the seed and the seal of all holiness, sanctifying grace, is received in baptism; that the human being permits himself, in freedom, to be moulded by it in imitation of his Lord, though also in pain; that he recognizes the will of God and submits to it, is filled and sustained by it as is the skin by flesh and bone—these are the realities, these are indispensable.

Such grace can take possession of an adult, but of a young person and of a child as well. A good many persons object to taking a "saintly child" seriously, for we have had deeply impressed upon us the principle that

---

[38] 1 Thess 4:3.

saintliness, holiness, must necessarily, essentially, be the result of "achievement", won by blood and sweat. We resist the idea of a childlike halo, so plainly "given" for nothing; we resist this idea with our reason, see it as a cheapening, prettifying devaluation and emptying of the concept of saintliness. We feel it to be an insult towards those who toil and struggle and nevertheless are denied saintliness. That is to say, in a secret corner of our minds we resent it as discrimination against ourselves.

"You and Marie will have no difficulties with her upbringing", Madame Martin wrote to Pauline in the spring of 1877, when she felt the approach of death. "Her disposition is so good. She is a chosen spirit." In voicing this, which must console her for the anguish of parting, she meant more than "choice" in the sense of precious. This devout mother already glimpsed something she would see only after she had crossed the threshold: that God had laid his hand upon Thérèse.

3. "PETITE REINE"

Five months later, on 28 August 1877, Madame Zélie Martin died of cancer. By medical standards her disease was hopeless; in June she had gone to Lourdes to seek, with firm confidence, a miraculous cure. But when no divine sign was forthcoming, she submitted calmly and devoutly to the inevitable: "The Mother of God has not healed me because my time is up, and because God wills me to repose elsewhere than on this earth." [39]

Thérèse was barely four and a half years old. Hitherto she had heard nothing but innocuous fine words about death as the gateway to Heaven and to the Child Jesus. Thus, in moments of passionate affection, when caresses would not suffice her ("when her love gets the better of her", her mother wrote), she would follow the logic of childhood and laughingly, blithely cry out her wish that her parents were dead. [40] But by now she knew precisely what was happening and what death meant as the lot of humanity; she knew it as children know, in dark, unanswerable insight beyond words, as she knelt in the sickroom during Extreme Unction, and when her father took her in a few hours later to give her dead mother a last kiss. "I do not think I cried very much, and I told no one of all that was going on inside me. Without saying anything, I just watched and listened, and saw a lot that they wanted to keep from me. On one occasion I was all alone near the coffin, which was left standing on its end in the corridor. I stood there, deep in thought, for ages. It was the first

---

[39] Laveille, 78, unpublished letter of 16 August 1877.
[40] Laveille, 47.

time I had seen one, but I knew what it meant well enough. As I was so little I could not see all of it without raising my head. How big and gloomy it seemed!"

The mother's death destroyed this sunny, happy family life at the core. What followed was still dear and sweet, peaceful and sheltered, but also perceptibly muted, fragmentary. It was a surrogate.

Soon afterwards Monsieur Martin left the town where he had spent his youth and the years of his marriage and moved to Lisieux. His wife had given up the lace business in the last months of her illness. He bought a pretty, spacious country house, Les Buissonnets, situated in a large garden on the slope of a hill overlooking the town. Suddenly aged after the death of his wife, he led henceforth the quiet life of a well-to-do retired businessman, aloof from the world and the times. His grown daughters, who so resembled their mother, kept house and brought up the younger ones. Lisieux had been chosen in order to make it possible for Aunt Guérin, whose home it was, to take the place of a mother for the half-orphaned children. But this soon proved to be unnecessary. In those days girls married at sixteen and seventeen and promptly took charge of a large, elaborate household and a family of children that annually increased. Hence, Pauline and Marie were felt to be no longer "young girls" in our present sense of the phrase, but mature young women. With gentle firmness they gave shape to the new home in their own way. Pauline had long since set her heart upon the Carmel; Marie still did not yet know what life would demand of her.

Monsieur Martin established an almost monastic schedule, a touching combination of heavenly and earthly inclinations, of remote dreams of his younger days and the duties and hobbies of a good paterfamilias: attendance at church every morning and "visiting" in the afternoons; hours of contemplative reading and prayer in the belvedere, his fine room on the roof, where he had a view far out over the countryside; work in the garden and long walks; and the sport of the meditative soul, angling. A large part of his time was devoted to his beloved youngest daughter, his "little queen". He was her most faithful and sympathetic playmate, her beloved, idolized "king". Céline was three years older than Thérèse; at that age the distance was very great. But her father delighted in everything she liked to do. Thérèse was never very interested in playing with dolls,[41] although she did not lack toys, as the reverential display of her toys at Les Buissonnets shows to this day. We are probably not far wrong in assuming that a profound, tacit inhibition restrained her from playing

---

[41] *S.S.*, ii.

"mother" so directly and unequivocally. Nor did she ever speak of her mother and of the many lively memories she had of her. She preferred "romping around Father in the garden", playing with flowers, which she loved beyond all else, building altars in a niche in the garden wall, and busily brewing colourful *tisanes*, concoctions of seeds and bark and berries of all sorts, which she served to her father in her doll's cups. He would taste her teas earnestly, with the expression of a connoisseur, would inspect, praise and suggest improvements for the garden altars. He taught her the names of plants, took her on long walks through the broad Norman meadowlands, and let her carry home enormous bouquets of flowers. She could sit in the grass by the water and watch his earthworms while he fished, and even try the high art of angling with her own little rod at times—though she was not very keen on this. When a thunderstorm surprised them, he carried her home in his arms, in spite of the burden of fishing tackle, to guard her feet from the wet grass. On dark winter nights, when he brought her home from her uncle's, they would gaze together at the star-studded sky and delight in deciphering a "T" in Orion's belt, Thérèse's own initial sparkling on the vault of Heaven. Holding her father's hand, Thérèse went to church on Sundays, and people whispered, deeply moved, when the tall, white-haired man, "this venerable patriarch", walked down the nave "hand in hand with his little daughter".

"If ever St Teresa was mentioned, Father used to bend down towards me and whisper: 'Listen, my little queen, he is talking about your patron saint.' Then I would really listen but I am afraid I kept my eyes on Father far more than on the preacher because I could read such a lot in his noble face." Sometimes her father also spoke to her about the world and life, and Thérèse felt as if she were grown up. Then, overwhelmed, she would hope that Father would conceal his wisdom, for: "If you talked that way to the great men in the government they would make you King for certain; then France would be happier than ever before. The trouble is you would be miserable because Kings always are, and also you would not be my very own King, so I am glad they do not know you." (In this remark we can easily detect the firmly royalist principles of the Martin family—and that Thérèse's imagination had been filled with stories about the "martyr king", Louis XVI, and the unfortunate little Dauphin in prison.)

"At that time I had so little courage that the very thought of losing Father would have terrified me", she confesses. One day he had climbed to the top of a ladder in the garden and called out to her: "Move out of the way, my little queen; if I fall down, I shall squash you." Whereupon she went up closer, thinking: "If he falls down I will not have the grief of seeing him die; I shall die too."

Evenings, while her sisters played a game of draughts and then read aloud something edifying or entertaining, she sat on her father's lap, rocked like a baby, and finally sung to sleep by one of his beautiful lullabies. And when they said their night prayers, she had only "to look at him to know how saints must pray". Later, when she was already a Carmelite, this recollection of familial happiness in childhood merged with her conception of heavenly bliss. "Céline, dearest sister," she wrote twelve years later in that naïve and stiff composition style in which she nevertheless contrived to express genuine feeling, "soon the shadows will be scattered, soon the rude winter frosts will be followed by rays of the eternal sun... soon we will be in our homeland. Soon the joys of our childhood, *our Sunday evenings*, our deepest outpourings of the heart, will be given back to us—for ever!"[42]

The big sisters divided up maternal duties; Céline had taken Marie, Thérèse Pauline, for *petite mère*. After their mother's funeral, when the five girls were looking sadly at one another, the nurse had exclaimed in sympathy: "Poor darlings, you haven't got a mother any more!" Céline "threw herself at once into Marie's arms, saying: 'You shall be my mother now, then.' As I always used to do the same as Céline, I might have followed her example in this, only I thought Pauline might be rather hurt, and feel she had been left out, if she did not have a little daughter, too. So I looked lovingly at her and buried my head in her breast, saying in my turn: 'Pauline's going to be *my* mother!'"[43] Léonie, who was at the time fourteen, stood about, rather at loose ends. That was to be her fate all her life.

Pauline continued Thérèse's education in the spirit of their deceased mother. What Thérèse received was the solid, old-fashioned education which was at her time the common heritage of good families of all stations and languages in the West. Social class and national emphases made for certain differences, but the spirit was everywhere essentially the same. It is the type of education which has been under furious attack for half a century, which has been blamed for all disasters for the past three generations. Yet no adequate substitute for it has so far been found. For it is one of those precious things which in unskilled hands lose all their radiance. Its practical strength, as well as its intellectual weakness, lies in the unthinking, unquestioning assumption that the child is unfinished, ignorant and unreliable, the grown-up unquestionably wise, knowing, finished, and a perfect model. The educator proceeds, on the confident assumption of his complete superiority in all realms, to raise the pupil

[42] 26 April 1891.
[43] *S.S.*, ii.

with kindliness and sternness, in his own image. Thence comes his insistence on absolute authority and unconditional obedience. In the hands of a loveless, unjust or mulish pedagogue this method automatically is transformed into a dangerous tool of destruction, for the teacher holds all power and enjoys all rights. For two generations a whole literature of accusation—and perhaps of revenge—has dealt with these failures and the mischief they have wrought. Perhaps this is why too little has been said about the blessings of the method and its remarkably high average of successes (which has been equalled by no other) when exercised by good and conscientious persons.

The wise educator of this type knew nothing of the "rights of the child". He knew only that the child had a right to be loved, to firm, clear guidance, and to a share in all the treasures of tradition. But is this not a good deal? He knows also, and does not think it tragic or regrettable, since he himself has passed through the same thing, that all formative training must cost the growing human being grief and the effort of self-conquest. Therefore he demands a great deal.

Imperceptibly, little Thérèse grew into the old, dignified and lovely forms of a truly "well brought-up" child. The aims of her education should not be underestimated; they were reverence and order, self-control and adaptability, consideration and modesty, tact and good bearing, grace and poise.

The marks she received for her work every day alone determined whether Father could take his "Benjamin" out in the afternoon—he too bowed to the pedagogical strictness of his grown daughter. And Pauline was unbending. A "no was a no". "It is a wonder to me how you managed to bring me up so lovingly without spoiling me, but you certainly did", Thérèse wrote gratefully twenty years later. "You never let me off with a single little fault, and never went back on any decision you had made, though you never rebuked me unless there was a good reason." The imaginative child's fear of the dark was overcome by gentle ruthlessness; she was sent to fetch things from dark rooms on the other side of the house until she could do so without being frightened. "In her childhood", Pauline said thirty years later, "we thought it very important to train her in humility. We carefully avoided praising her. We literally told her that she was ugly." [44] When a servant made a complaint against her, she was reprimanded as a matter of principle. In order to teach the child submission to all adults, Thérèse had to ask pardon of the offended servant.[45] And since she always took for granted that her home was the measure of all

[44] 2 S., 307.
[45] Petitot, 44.

things, she long afterwards considered the flattering words of strangers sheer nonsense because Papa and Pauline had never said such things about her.

She was given direct instruction very young, as is still done in French families; the thought is that school must not lay the cornerstone of "education", but build on foundations already laid in the family. There was nothing unusual in Thérèse's already knowing the alphabet while her mother was still alive, and soon learning to read under Pauline's tutelage. By the time she was four or five she was being given lessons in the morning, and schoolwork in the afternoons was part of the day's routine. Gradually "distribution of prizes" such as are held in schools was instituted. The whole family assembled in the decorated room, and Father, in his easy chair, read out the marks in various subjects and gave the prizes for excellent work—books and bouquets. "Though I was the only competitor this did not mean that I was let off easily", Thérèse wrote; "I was never given a prize unless I had really deserved it. How my heart used to beat when my report was read out.... I used to think the Day of Judgment must be just like that."

It was natural to the way of life of the Martin family that Thérèse learned to read first such words as "heaven", that religious instruction permeated the entire day. There was much talk—perilously blunt and overpowering talk, we may feel nowadays—of the most intimate concepts of religion. Aspects of the faith were discussed with that boldness which is customary in devout families, and which outsiders find so hard to digest. Thérèse would come into the house, hot and tired. "Oh, Pauline, how thirsty I am!" And Pauline would reply: "How would you like to save a poor sinner by giving up your drink?" With a heavy sigh the child nods. The big sister is so touched by this willingness that after a while she comes to Thérèse with a glass full of water. Puzzled, Thérèse asks whether she will not harm the sinner if she drinks after all. No, Pauline suggests; first you gave him the merit of your sacrifice; now you can also help him by your obedience.

At the age of six or seven Thérèse went to the seaside for the holidays for the first time. In the evening the family sat on the beach, the child deeply moved by the wonderful sight of the setting sun drawing a golden path of light across the waves. Pauline told her that it was an "image of the path to Heaven when grace lights up the way". In a child ridden by the spirit of contradiction such religious education would undoubtedly have aroused resistance. Thérèse responded to it as she had responded to her mother: with unconditional trust born of unconditional love. "I cannot remember", Mother Agnes said during the trial, "that she was disobedient to me a single time. In all things she asked for permission, and when I refused she sometimes cried, but she obeyed without ever insisting on having her way."

This religious training was not confined to pious words and poetic images. Pauline placed great value upon clear, pure dogmatic instruction, and with amazing pedagogical skill sought to make the truths of dogma comprehensible to the child. As a teacher she presented a happy contrast to the attitude so widespread at the time: condemnation of questions and pondering on the part of a child as examples of forwardness and dangerous doubts.[46] Thus, one day, Thérèse brought to her her scruples about divine justice: was glory in Heaven fairly distributed? she wondered. "You [Pauline] sent me off to fetch one of Father's big glasses and had me put my little thimble by the side of it; then you filled them both up with water and asked me which I thought was the fuller. I had to admit that one was just as full as the other because neither of them would hold any more. That was the way you helped me to grasp how it was that in Heaven the least have no cause to envy the greatest."

Thus Thérèse lived a happy, fulfilled and sheltered child's life.

4. THE MENACE

We seem to be regarding an idyll as peaceful and charming as any poet could imagine, and so this childhood of hers has usually been interpreted. It may seem strange to those who take this view that Thérèse herself speaks of this stage in her short life as the saddest and felt it as a break with her true self, which began during her fifth year and lasted until she was fourteen. But a closer look will plainly reveal the dark, troubling tone which runs, persistent as a shadow, alongside the sunny picture of the "little queen".

"My gaiety all went after Mother died. I had been so lively and open; now I became diffident and oversensitive, crying if anyone looked at me. I wanted to be left alone and hated meeting strangers. It was only in the intimacy of my own family, where everyone was wonderfully kind, that I could be more myself." [47]

---

[46] Compare the following passage from the obituary letter of Sister Marie Martin. As a schoolgirl in the boarding school of the Salesian Nuns Marie once said to her beloved aunt and teacher, Mother Dosithea: "It seems to me that a great deal is repeated in the Gospels, and our composition teacher always says we should avoid repetitions.... Thereupon Aunt put on a stern, almost outraged expression, and replied: 'Do you mean to find fault with the Word of Our Lord?' And I, who had only intended to confide in her, was plunged into shame at my idea, and thought: Never again will I tell her anything like that, since she makes such a fuss about it."

[47] S.S., ii.

At first the move to Lisieux plainly did her good; the shock seemed to be overcome. "Everywhere else I felt lost, and used to cry and miss Mother, but there my little heart opened out and I could greet life with a smile." "Everywhere else" meant her old house in Alençon, where the absence of her mother was tangibly felt. In the new environment of Les Buissonnets, a house that as yet held no memories, the harsh outlines of grief soon faded. Hence it is understandable that Thérèse considered the sole cause of the change in her to be her mother's death. However, the longer we study what we have been told about Thérèse's growth, the more we are forced to realize that this event only released something that had slumbered from the beginning, like a hereditary disease, deep within the merry nature of the "little princess". Under her mother's strong protection this tendency may never, or only much later, have come into the open. As things were, it was now painfully exposed. Thérèse seems to have been one of those nervous, oversensitive children for whom life itself represents an almost overwhelming burden, even under the most favourable conditions.

The average person usually conceives of a "nervous" child as skittish, restless, ill-behaved. But the term covers other traits as well, such as we encounter in Thérèse's case: early maturity in regard to moods and emotions of sadness; excessive vulnerability to humdrum, trivial hurts; low physical resistance; enormous need for protection; fear of strangers and strangeness. Even a healthy child experiences terrors, vexations, burdens ranging all the way from the routine obligation to attend school to the loss of beloved members of the family. But normal children are only temporarily affected by these things; they recover quickly, come to terms with them. In a "nervous" child the same causes produce states of exhaustion from which a return to equilibrium is very difficult; they produce long-lasting depressions reminiscent of melancholia or agitation that may terminate in hallucinations. This is by no means to say that an emotional life of this sort is inferior or morbid; frequently it goes hand in hand with superior talents. But it approaches the highly fluid boundary between health and sickness and contains a certain susceptibility to serious disturbances. When a child shows such signs, the adults in charge must watch over it alertly.

The change in Thérèse's character after the death of her mother seems to us the first signal suggesting such a disposition. The elder sisters, after all, had lost incomparably more, and more consciously, than the youngest. Their grief may well have been deeper and more painful; yet none of the four showed similar reactions. So sudden and long-lasting an emotional disturbance would certainly be understandable in a child for whom the mother's death meant exposure to the mercies of strangers, whether good or bad, or some other crucial change for the worse in her accustomed mode of life. But this was not the case with Thérèse. On the contrary, we see the entire family engaged in sheltering the child, by an overwhelming outpouring of affection and tender care, from all sense of loss, and in compensating her for her sorrow. Thus the tremendous shock to her whole being which Thérèse nevertheless experienced points to a dangerous, abnormal sensitivity. It may well be that, as the last child of an already ill and exhausted mother, she entered the world with a certain deficiency of vital powers.

Many minor, easily overlooked features of her childhood support this assumption. So, for example, Thérèse tells about the importance to her of Pauline's nightly judgments on her behaviour during the day and emphasizes that any answer but "Yes" to her question "Have I been good today?" would have resulted in her crying the whole night through. Such a reaction on the part of a child between the ages of four and seven cannot be simply set down as one of the "signs of early saintliness". Rather, it is the mark of that morbid excess of conscientiousness which later became for the growing girl, as she herself put it, "a veritable martyrdom". How little this attitude has to do with "perfection" becomes manifest from Thérèse's treatment, when she was mistress of the novices in the Carmel, of young nuns who similarly took their faults too seriously. With what freedom and composure the mature Thérèse knew how to master these difficulties which she had experienced so early in life. We would be indulging in false deference if we attempted, since we are dealing with a saint, to justify or even elevate every trait she displayed during her growth. There is no reason to read into these sorrows of childhood solely the preciousness and singularity of a chosen nature, when in reality they indicate grave rents in the basic fabric of the child's personality. When Monsieur Martin fished and the child sat silently by his side, watching the clouds, the water and the flowers, listening to the murmur of the wind and snatches of martial music from the town, her heart was not filled with the deep pleasure of childhood, but with a gentle, restive, almost adolescent melancholy: "My thoughts used to become very deep then, and though I had no idea of what meditation was my soul was really lost in prayer.... Earth seemed to me a place of exile and I dreamt of Heaven."

When she unpacked the basket the motherly sisters had put up for the two anglers and found the lovely jam "gone a miserable pink and sunk into the bread", this seemed to her a symbol of transitoriness and disappointment: "This made the earth seem a sadder place than ever and I was quite convinced that one would never find unclouded happiness this side of Heaven." Sunday is a holiday that always returns, but even at seven the child experienced, every Sunday evening, the heart-wrenching passing of beauty: "After Compline my happiness gave way to a certain pensiveness. Tomorrow I would have to go back again to my daily routine, and my lessons; I felt an exile again and longed for Heaven, my true home, where it would always be Sunday."

The thoughts to which such moods gave rise, her way of linking things quite naturally with religious themes which were, after all, the prevailing and almost the sole content of her play, her conversations and of the life of the grown-ups around her—this was surely edifying and testifies to the piety of her environment, which directed her imagination along such lines. And certainly, mysterious and sudden fits of melancholy on the part of children are fairly common. Nevertheless, such sadness over—of all things—a stale jam sandwich must strike us as strange.

At this time there also occurred that mysterious and, in a far narrower sense, "strange" experience which has entered the literature on Thérèse under the name of "the prophetic vision"—when she saw her father with his face veiled. "This all took place in a short space of time, but it made such a vivid impression on me that the memory of it is just as real to me as the vision itself. . . . You [the sisters] told me to think no more about it; but how could I do that? This strange vision kept coming back to me, and I often tried to lift the veil which hid its secret, while in my heart I was sure it would be lifted entirely one day."

God alone knows how often and how deeply the frightful vision occupied the little girl's mind when her sisters thought her absorbed with her toys, with her books or in prayer. Their command "think no more about it" was obeyed by Thérèse to the extent that henceforth she maintained complete silence about the vision. More than this, she could not do. And so she had to deal all alone with the perplexities and anxieties that now pursued her for a full ten years. For it was not until ten years later that her father's illness provided the interpretation of the premonitory vision.

At the age of eight and a half Thérèse entered the Abbey school of the Benedictine nuns in Lisieux, as a day pupil. Céline had already been attending the Abbey for some time, and Léonie had been a boarding pupil there since the family's move to Lisieux.

Entering school is always a crucial experience for a child, and most crucial for those who have never associated very much with children their own age. Moreover, the French schools do not divide classes into age-groups, but according to the standing of the pupil, which is determined by the entrance examination. Marie and Pauline had taught Thérèse well and carefully, setting for her the rather high standard which is so often applied to the later children in a family. Thérèse was placed in a class of girls several years older than herself; the eldest of them was fourteen.

This was her first step into the human world and her second great, unshared trial. The tremendous resistance she soon experienced, from outside and from within, came from a number of causes. Hitherto she had lived in her monastically isolated parental household, as if it were an island. All persons who did not belong to the family were no more than vague shadows gliding past outside the enchanted walls of Les Buissonnets—more unreal to her than the characters in her fairy tales and legends.

In this isolation, and in the peculiar spirit of her household, the "little queen" had really developed into the princess who felt the pea through all the mattresses. In spite of her firm, even strict upbringing, her emotional constitution lacked, as it were, a protective skin. In her home environment her excessive sensitivity was judged to be a "weakness", but scarcely a "fault", let alone a failure or a sign of inferiority. Those about her were doubly concerned to spare her all strain, all contact with raw reality. Her sudden introduction into the bustling school life of some sixty older girls, sturdy, loud and to some extent distinctly rough children from the small town and the countryside round about, was terribly upsetting.[48] Thérèse was familiar only with the muted, considerate ways of her father and sisters. For the first time she became acquainted with boisterous rudeness and naughtiness. Never in her life had she seen bad manners, never heard vulgar expressions. What is more important, never had she experienced a deliberate act of unfriendliness. She had never witnessed an uncontrolled outburst of anger, never heard nasty talk about others, never heard an impertinent reply. It was characteristic of her nature that all these things were experienced as a shock. For Céline had come from exactly the same sheltered milieu, yet seems to have adjusted herself to the school without difficulty, with that philosophical unconcern of healthy children who let others be different from themselves without feeling that their own natures are challenged. But, significantly, Thérèse could not adjust herself to it all; she was so constituted that every blow left a wound. After all, the girls' school was no worse and no better than any other: a vanity fair in miniature, a reflection of the human condition within the smallest frame. Here as everywhere there was a good deal of fresh, joyous, healthy activity, and alongside of it the unpleasant aspects: ambition and jealousy, mendacity and defiance, conceit and envy, inquisitiveness and gossip.

---

[48] Marguérite Léroy, a fellow pupil in the Abbey who later became a nun there under the name of Sister Mary of the Rosary, speaks of "the contrast between the exquisite delicacy of the mutual understanding and the forms of piety in her home, and the composition of the boarding school, which at that period included a considerable number of extremely common pupils..." (1 S., XV, 160).

For Thérèse, all this meant her first close, virtually physical contact with the *reality of sin*—she who had hitherto known only small, inadvertent, strictly condemned and eagerly corrected faults and imperfections. Her innocent heart was alarmed and suffered unspeakably when she discovered for the first time that the class would profit by the teacher's absence to do all kinds of mischief, that children would dissimulate, and that they would deliberately break rules.[49] As yet she had no inkling of obedience which was just a matter of form, which was only skin-deep. For her, all duties were deeply ingrained in conscience. No wonder that she took far too seriously what was probably innocuous misbehaviour on the part of her fellow pupils and suffered as if she had become an accomplice to real wickedness.

Moreover, this strange, incomprehensible and confusing world turned with hostility towards the "new girl" who so timidly held aloof from it. For she, in spite of being the youngest, not only maintained her place among the older girls; she attracted attention, carried off prizes and distinctions from under their noses. Monsieur l'Abbé called her "his little doctor" because of her intelligent questions and clear answers. No wonder that she was envied and decried as a teacher's pet. Since she often spent her free Thursdays at home—her frequent headaches were already beginning—but scarcely ever missed a class, the rumour spread among the children that on such afternoons her elder sisters helped her to prepare her brilliant lessons for the following day, especially the compositions. And this "unfair competition" naturally aroused great indignation.[50]

Another element in her unpopularity was her shyness, her obvious touch-me-not discomfort with her surroundings. Children are quick to notice and slow to forgive one who keeps apart from them; they sense the alien, the aristocratic temperament that cannot adjust itself to them, as well as the helplessness of one who does not know how to defend herself. Thus this ugly duckling in the hen yard was thoroughly pecked at and plucked. The other children were not necessarily particularly ill-willed. But anyone who has been in a boarding school knows how ingeniously cruel girls of this age can be towards one another. Theirs is not the forthright roughness of boys, which can easily be met with the same weapons. Rather, with feminine keenness they discover all the weak spots in their victim and stab away at these weak spots with a good pretence of innocence. That is all the more the case if the general enmity of a group towards an outsider is deliberately organized by one member of the group. The fourteen-year-old girl in the class had probably been "left back" one or

[49] Laveille, 112; 1 S., ii, 64.
[50] Laveille, 113.

more times and perhaps belonged to the fairly common type in whom mental dullness is joined to physical strength and a certain superiority obtained by age. Such girls often have an astonishing influence upon their younger fellow pupils. This one did and seems to have felt the scholastic triumphs of the new girl as a personal affront. She organized a little campaign of torments in which many of the other girls participated, and which of course remained wholly invisible to the teachers.[51] Thérèse, who had hitherto experienced nothing but fairness, kindness and candour, was utterly baffled and helpless in the face of such behaviour. She had never learned to practise caution or to be mistrustful, never learned to defend herself. Now she saw herself betrayed on all sides, found herself deeply and incomprehensibly wounded anew every day.

The result was that she lost track of her real self. Her talent, and still more her diligence, enabled her to surpass the others. She could retain what she was taught easily and well (only memorizing was painful to her), as the jealousy of the other girls made plain. The teachers liked and praised her. But at the same time she felt herself, for the first time in her life, rejected by others, "counted, weighed and found wanting". For the first time she failed completely in an art which had never been discussed at all in her home, and which all the others seemed to have mastered naturally: the art of self-assertion, especially in the competitive games which were played during the recreation hours, such as croquet and badminton. She was clumsy, a burden to the side she played on; none of the leaders wanted her in their team. Whenever she shyly betrayed a little of her own inclinations, she encountered amazed indifference, and probably mockery as well. Yet this world must simultaneously have exercised the ambiguous, painful attraction for her that the unattainable always has for the outsider. The high-strung person who has been excluded from the group, who knows himself to be different, often has the keenest consciousness of the magic that emanates from the uninhibited, self-assured, untroubled vitality of those who are "normal". Anyone who has ever lived among a group of young people understands this. Thérèse tasted to the full all the bitterness of the others' judgment of her. "I did not know how to play like the other children, and I was not much fun for them, but I did do my best to join in, even though it was never any good."

Thus the little princess of Les Buissonnets became in her own eyes— and so, gradually, in reality—what she was in the eyes of the others: boring, awkward, unsociable: an ugly duckling. "Something like a veil spread over all her rich gifts from God", admits Céline, who ordinarily presents

---

[51] S.S., iii; Laveille, 113.

Thérèse in the most glorified light. "In company no attention was paid to her. The reason she was so overlooked was her great shyness, which made her irresolute and paralysed her in everything she attempted. In fact she constantly called forth unfavourable judgments because she said almost nothing and always let others speak. At this time she suffered from constant headaches. But her extraordinary sensitivity and delicate conscience were the chief sources of her sufferings, which, incidentally, she bore without complaint."[52]

Since she could not achieve inconspicuousness by adjustment, and since being conspicuous was embarrassing and shaming to her, Thérèse henceforth deliberately sought the camouflage of retirement. "She now developed a fondness for hiding", Céline again informs us;[53] "she did not want to be observed, for she sincerely considered herself inferior."

"Often the intelligence of other children was praised in my presence, but never my own; from that I concluded that I had none, and I resigned myself to this lack."[54]

Thus Thérèse was lonely, plunged into that bitter and humiliating loneliness which is not self-elected, but imposed by others. It lasted two full years. Then she ventured for the first time to look for a friend among the girls. On her free days she became more and more attached to Marie Guérin, the younger of her two cousins in Lisieux, "because she always let me choose my games", Thérèse comments significantly. In speaking of this she chooses to conceal something we learn from the testimony of the maid Marceline, later Sister Josepha of the Holy Cross, at the trial: that this little cousin was a sickly and spoiled child whose humours Thérèse endured with touching patience and love.[55] At least, however, Marie had a taste for the kind of play which would have been impossible with the other girls at the Abbey. Within the shelter of their home gardens the two girls would play at being anchorites, as the great Teresa had once played with her brother. Harmoniously, they tilled the little field which supplied their needs; they sat in contemplation in front of their "cell" and practised perfect silence for hours. They even walked in the street

---

[52] I S., 67.

[53] I S., 55.

[54] *Esprit*, 165, from unpublished notes. In the first edition of this book we raised the question of whether these unpublished notes might not be the expunged passages of *The Story of a Soul*, for which corrections had been substituted. For it seemed to us surprising that Thérèse should have written down private notes on her youth other than the autobiography, since she always considered such journal-keeping a danger and a temptation to vanity, advised her novices against it, and composed *The Story of a Soul* only on express orders from her superior. This question has now long since been answered affirmatively.

[55] I S., ix, 60–62.

with closed eyes, to shut out all distractions from the evil world—and upon one such occasion stumbled over some packing cases in front of a shop, creating a considerable mess, as Thérèse relates. We can feel how she must have enjoyed this quiet, dreamy game which accorded so much better with her nature than the rough and tumble of the school playground.

During those years Thérèse was moving, unknown to herself, along the dangerous path of the outsider and eccentric. At this formative age the roots of deep emotional defects might easily have become established. Similar causes give rise to such defects in many healthy persons and cause them trouble all their lives. Bitterness and self-pity, delusions of being slighted, inferiority feelings, might easily have settled in her consciousness as permanent attitudes. That Thérèse passed by all these dangerous precipices, that her heart lost none of its sweetness and honesty, its innocent friendliness and devotedness, is nothing short of amazing. Embedded in this rather frail disposition of hers, with its susceptibility to serious disturbances, was an ultimate core of indestructible wholesomeness; in the deepest substance of her soul she was immune to all the dangers inherent in her nature. Indeed, the solitary struggle, guided by conscience alone, of this core of her personality against a menace she did not understand, but in some strange way clearly grasped, seems to us to be the true theme of this period of her life. We shall try to demonstrate this.

The family had no inkling of the special difficulties of Thérèse's development. In those days, in general, no one was especially inclined to worry much about the psychic life of a child. A well-behaved child in a good Christian family simply *had* to be "happy". To whatever extent Thérèse was different from the others, these differences, it was taken for granted, were signs of being better and more blessed. In this particular situation, however, such confirmation of her idiosyncrasies by her near and dear was exactly what the child needed. Every evening she plunged into the family circle as if it were a healing spring. "Fortunately I could go home every evening and then I cheered up. I used to jump on Father's knee and tell him what marks I had had, and when he kissed me all my troubles were forgotten. . . . I needed this sort of encouragement so much"; the "little flower" had to thrust its tender roots deep down into the specially prepared soil of its beloved home, because only there could it find its necessary food. How significant it is that she told her father of nothing but the favourable side of school life, nothing but the praise and good marks, for which she was rewarded with a "bright little silver coin" to put in her money-box for the poor.

She said nothing at all about her other experiences at the Abbey. Her *petite mère* Pauline heard not a word about her troubles, nor Céline, who was after all attending the same school, making her way cheerfully and energetically, and who was always ready to support and defend her timid little sister whenever she noticed that such chivalrous action was needed.[56] But Céline was in another class; she saw little, and Thérèse did not tell her. Thérèse held her peace, as she had done at the age of four when something went wrong. Only the autobiographical notes written at the end of her life informed her sisters of what had been taking place before their eyes.

How can this silence be fully explained? The pride of a finely tempered nature, which led her to think her defeats and griefs somehow deserved, was probably one factor in her reticence; also that curious feeling for boundaries and separate spheres which frequently makes children consider life at school another existence which should be concealed from their parents. Perhaps, too, the little queen was unwilling to admit at home the ignoble part she played at the school. But at the same time Thérèse was also remaining silent now as she did later, out of submission to adversity, out of unwillingness to seek mitigation or escape. In purity of will she was already making sacrifices "for God". She was motivated also by a deep, unconscious humility; sensitive as she was to her own suffering, she did not regard it as worth talking about. Above all, she kept silent out of love, because she did not wish to burden sympathetic hearts with the knowledge of things which she felt to be as incomprehensible and essential as fate. And while an end might have been put to some of her trials—as, for example, the persecution by the oldest girl in the school—this could be done only by Thérèse making complaints and bringing punishment upon the other. In such a case she remained silent out of that dignity and desire to spare the other which children call being a good sport.[57]

She also did not do what many children would have done: make amends for the painfulness of her position among her fellow pupils by seeking preferential treatment from her teachers. With her good marks, that would not have been difficult. Her class teacher has expressly declared: "She accepted being overlooked without objection, and when she was neglected she did nothing to call attention to herself. This was all the more remarkable since in her family she was constantly the centre of loving regard."[58]

Here at school, it seems, Thérèse learned to choose and love the veil she was henceforth never to lift entirely: the guise of smiling graciousness, of apparently effortless silence which betrayed none of the struggles going on beneath it. The way to perfection was long and steep on this

---

[56] *S.S.*, iii.

[57] I *S.*, 57.

[58] Sœur de St François de Sales, O.S.B., teacher at the Abbey of Lisieux, I *S.*, ii, 156.

road also, and marked by many breakdowns. The tension of the double life and the daily self-conquest gradually placed such a strain upon Thérèse that her delicate health gave way. Her tears flowed more and more readily; going to school became more and more difficult.

In October 1882 Pauline took the veil. That very fact is an indication of how successfully Thérèse had maintained silence even towards her dearest sister, her *petite mère*. For it is inconceivable that Pauline would not have postponed her entrance into the Carmel a little longer if she had had any intimation of the dangerous crisis her little sister and charge was going through.

Their separation was in itself no surprise; even during their mother's lifetime it had been openly and often discussed, as in other families the marriage prospects of daughters are talked over. Among Thérèse's earliest memories was of her saying eagerly, when such conversations took place: "Then I will go with Pauline." In a child's fashion she had imbued the unknown Carmel, which later became associated with Bible stories about the prophet Elijah and his adventures with raven, juniper bush and the cake baked on coals, with romantic conceptions of hermits and caves. Often she had secretly dreamed that some day she would go with Pauline "to a far-off desert". Perhaps her games with Marie Guérin were a reflection of such fantasies. In all such plans she and Pauline were inseparable. Now, one day, she gathered from a conversation of the two elder sisters that the day of parting was close, and that it would mean irrevocable separation: that Pauline was leaving her and all of them, just as her mother had left them by dying. This blow struck at the roots of her being; nothing harsher could have come her way. For day after day, deprived of words, she had drawn the strength to endure only from the sheltering presence of those she loved. "I look upon it as a great grace", Thérèse wrote in retrospect, "to have been able to bear a trial which seemed quite beyond me."

On the painful evening after that revelation, Pauline had a long talk with the child, and attempted to explain to her the life she had chosen. That talk was crucial in arousing in Thérèse the longing and the resolve to live this selfsame life in the Carmel. We would be inclined to explain this "call" in a nine-year-old child as a passionate desire to recover in this way her "little mother", to go where Pauline was going. But Thérèse assures us that this was not so, and we have no choice but to believe her; she tells us that out of her child's sense of being abandoned there burst forth the longing to unite herself irrevocably with the sole fidelity that is permanent. "I felt that Carmel was the desert in which God wished to hide me too. I felt this so intensely that there could be no doubt about it. This was no childish dream, nor the enthusiasm of a moment. It had about it the certainty of a divine call." Pauline took it seriously—in contrast to Marie—so seriously that she took her little sister along, accompanied only by Marie Guérin, to introduce her to the Prioress. Thérèse's own account of the stratagem she employed to force her innocent cousin to leave her at the proper moment, so that she could speak with the Prioress quite alone, is not without importance. It shows how much purposive feminine guile there was in the little girl, along with her pure-hearted simplicity, upon an occasion when she *wanted* to have her way. Thus it throws light upon her customary docility and obedience.[59]

Mother Marie de Gonzague, of whom we shall subsequently have much to say, listened benevolently and with friendly gravity to the "secret" of this youngest aspirant to the Order whom she had ever seen. With that deep, good breeding which so quickly won hearts to her she explained to Thérèse that she did not receive nine-year-old postulants; the minimum age was sixteen. Thérèse had already been ardently counting on entering at the same time as Pauline and making her First Communion in the convent on the day of Pauline's Clothing—this dream reveals how much a child she was, for all her precocity. Now she returned home with a new disappointment.

That Pauline did not simply vanish from the face of the earth, but could be visited in the convent, made the matter only so much the worse. The half-hours in the visiting room became pure agony for Thérèse. There was her little mother in a strange, uncomfortable room, behind a heavy grille, always in the presence of the whole family and, as the Rule prescribes, of a supervising nun. And naturally the entire visit centred around Papa and the big sisters, while Thérèse, hitherto accustomed to unlimited heart-to-heart talks with her sister, received at most two or three minutes at the end of the visit, crumbs of the affection she had formerly had. "I spent those few minutes crying, and went away heartbroken." On top of all this was her unavoidable knowledge that Pauline was completely happy in this separation and wanted nothing else. This rubbed salt upon her wounded spirit and strengthened her conviction that she had lost Pauline for good and all.

[59] "I told Marie that as it was such a privilege to see Reverend Mother we ought to be very good, and that the polite thing to do would be for each of us to confide in her; that would obviously mean that first one, then the other would have to go out for a while. Marie was not very happy about it as she hadn't anything to confide anyway, but she accepted what I said, and I was able to have my private talk with Mother Marie de Gonzague."

The dreadful sense of the unreliability and fragility of all the apparently secure and sustaining elements of life, this feeling which had clouded the edges of her consciousness like a phantom shadow since the death of her mother and had been reinforced and corroborated with terrifying frequency by so many small and large experiences, now broke overwhelmingly into the open. "In a moment I saw what life is really like, full of suffering and continual separations, and I burst into bitter tears." Her reason, still so childish in spite of all her brightness at school, could not resolve these riddles, which her heart nevertheless had to deal with, alone and silently. "The weight of this suffering caused my mind to develop much too quickly, and it was not long before I was seriously ill."

In these words Thérèse herself gives us the key to understanding of the childhood disease to which she soon afterwards fell prey.

Towards the end of the year 1882—Pauline had entered the convent on 2 October—her headaches became incessant, but bearable enough for Thérèse to continue attending school. Around Easter Monsieur Martin went away for a few days with the grown-up daughters, and the two smaller children stayed at the home of the Guérins. One evening Thérèse was sitting alone in her uncle's room. He talked with her about her mother, for he had always been very close to his now deceased sister. Suddenly the child began to cry so violently that Monsieur Guérin was alarmed. After all, six years had already passed since the mother's death, and he had had no suspicion that his recollections would touch a still open wound. He began talking about holiday plans to divert his niece. But it was too late. The fit of tears was succeeded by headaches of frightening violence, and in the evening Thérèse had an attack of shivering resembling fever chills. Madame Guérin did not dare to leave the child alone; the attack lasted all night. Next day Thérèse's father was recalled by telegram. He found his little queen in an alarming state of "intense overstimulation". Aunt Guérin did not let her leave the house— perhaps she was kept in bed. For the present, however, neither convulsions nor mental wandering occurred, as Marceline Husé, the Guérins' maid, expressly testifies.[60] Unfortunately, we have no further description of this stage of the disease; we may assume that the symptoms already listed—painful headache, shivering, weeping and violent agitation (*surexcitation*)—persisted. After a week there was a remarkable pause; then the disease entered a new phase.

In the middle of March Pauline was due to take the habit. Thérèse obstinately insisted that she would get up for the ceremony and would be

[60] 2 S., 104.

well; God would be merciful upon her, for her sister's sake. "I was sure that God would console me by letting me see you again on that day— that the feast day would be cloudless. Surely Jesus would not give pain to His Bride, by leaving me out; my illness had caused you enough suffering already." No one in the household believed in the possibility of so rapid an improvement. On the morning of the ceremony, however, Thérèse awoke completely calm and strong, as if cured. She was actually allowed to get up and accompany the family, felt quite normal, sat happily on her sister's lap and playfully hid under her veil. That evening she had to go to bed early, and next morning the sickness began anew, with such violence that her family seriously began to fear for her reason, and even her life. Long comas and dull periods of weakness continually alternated with fits of great agitation. The child screamed and shrieked in extreme fear, contorted her face, rolled her eyes, saw monsters and nightmarish figures everywhere, sometimes failed to recognize members of the family, was shaken by convulsions, twisted her limbs, tried to throw herself out of bed and had to be forcibly restrained. Marie narrates: "She had frightful visions which froze the blood of all who had to hear her cries of despair. A few nails on the wall suddenly appeared to her as big, charred fingers, and she screamed, 'I'm afraid, I'm afraid!' Another time my father sat down by her bed. Thérèse regarded him silently; she had spoken very little all through this disease. Suddenly—as always, it happened in a flash—her expression changed; her eyes fastened on Father's hat, and she uttered a horrible scream: 'Oh, the big black animal!'" Once Léonie left the room briefly while Thérèse was lying quiet; when she returned she found Thérèse lying on the floor between the wall and the bed. She had thrown herself head-first over the high railing, but lay on the stone floor "without a scratch".

These outbreaks lasted altogether from the middle of March to 10 May. "The crises followed one another without pause", Léonie relates. Her account seems to be particularly valuable because she tells only what she saw, without attempting to interpret. "The attacks came several times daily", the maid, Marceline, says. "In the intervals she was extremely weak; she could not be left alone." The physician, Dr Notta, whom Marie describes as a *savant*, diagnosed the disease as St Vitus's Dance, or chorea, as Jeanne Guérin testified during the trial.[61]

This nervous disease of childhood strikes girls more frequently than boys. It usually occurs between the ages of eleven and fifteen, lasts on the average from six to twelve weeks, and is followed by recovery in the

---

[61] "*Le docteur qui la soignait, appelait cette maladie Danse de St Guy*" (2 S., 145).

majority of cases. Delicate, anaemic children of weak constitution are especially subject to it. The doctor prescribed water treatments, showers, massages and compresses, according to Léonie and Marceline Husé, but these did not seem to help. Violent cases of chorea may end in death, and in some circumstances mental health is affected even if the patient comes through. Consequently, the family's anxiety increased daily—all the more, perhaps, because the sisters were already beginning to doubt the doctor's diagnosis and to view the uncanny disease as a diabolical attack upon the child. Thérèse herself informs us that during the attacks, and even when she lay in apparent comas, she was fully conscious, able to understand every word and even the whispers of those about her. Hence she observed that her family was coming more and more to believe that only a miracle could save her. She heard her father instruct Marie to write to Paris and ask for a novena of Masses to be said for her at the church of Our Lady of Victories. A statue of the Blessed Virgin stood in the room; it was May, and Thérèse frequently turned her eyes in fervent pleading towards the smiling countenance. Here she must find aid. But this week, too, passed without improvement. The following Sunday Thérèse suffered an attack of unprecedented violence; she screamed in agony for Marie, but did not recognize her sister when she came in and spoke tenderly to her. When Marie tried to give her something to drink, she screamed in terror: "You want to poison me!" The sisters sensed that a frightful climax in the disease had come. Helplessly, they fell to their knees before the altar. And Thérèse, too, in some strange fashion "conscious" in spite of her ravings, fixed her wild eyes upon the statue and inwardly joined passionately in their prayers.

Anxiously looking back to the bed, Marie saw the child's eyes clear, wholly tranquil, blissfully radiant; Thérèse recognized her at once and smiled at her in the midst of tears. Thérèse was cured. The very next day, she resumed ordinary life.

Thérèse herself says of her cure: "Suddenly the statue came to life,[62] and Mary appeared utterly lovely, with a divine beauty I could not possibly describe. There was a wonderful sweetness and goodness about her face, and her expression was infinitely tender, but what went right to my heart was her smile. Then, all my pain was gone. Silently two big tears trickled down my cheeks, tears of complete and heavenly happiness. Our Lady had come to me! 'How happy I am,' I thought, 'but I must not tell anyone or this happiness will go away.' When I lowered my eyes, I recognized Marie at once."

---

[62] This phrase, *La statue s'anima*, is not found in the *Manuscrits Authentiques*. Thérèse wrote only: "*Tout à coup, La Ste Vierge me parut belle.*"

That Thérèse's recovery was a miracle seemed plain as day to this devout family. Such an explanation was in any case most natural to their way of thinking. It is therefore curious that aside from Marie none of them seems to have been told anything specific about the matter. Marie had caught Thérèse's transfigured expression and immediately afterwards took occasion to ask her what she had experienced. "At the sight of her bearing and her ecstatic look I immediately understood that she had seen Our Lady herself", she said later during the trial—a statement as typical of the piety of the family as Céline's similar comment: "At the sight of the sudden transformation which took place in her bearing, and of the expression in her eyes during this ecstasy, I had not the slightest doubt that she had perceived Our Lady. I was so convinced of this that I cannot remember ever having urged her in any way to tell me what seemed to be so obvious." [63] Evidently this means that Céline did not hear of the miracle from her sister directly. Léonie knew nothing about it until she read *The Story of a Soul* after Thérèse's death.[64] The same holds true for the Guérin family.[65] We have no evidence that Monsieur Martin was informed. Perhaps, with a kind of devout jealousy, Marie permitted only a very small group of religious ladies associated with her sister Pauline in the Carmel to share in the exciting secret.

Whatever the organic basis of Thérèse's illness may have been, we share the view of Father Petitot that the collapse was produced by "various causes, among them excessive psychic tension". There can be no doubt that Pauline's departure underlay the disease. The oversensitive and in many respects precocious child experienced the death of her mother as an appalling upheaval of the foundation of her life. An abyss formed in the ground on which she stood. Then Pauline stepped into the gap, a miraculous re-embodiment of her mother, and gradually restored the child's lost sense of security. Pauline's vigorous training taught Thérèse to suppress her emotional problems in many respects, such as her fear of darkness—but these were by no means abolished.

The inner rent did not mend. That fateful conversation with her uncle revived acutely the image of her mother and all that was connected with it at the very time Thérèse was passing through a new crisis produced by the same cause: abandonment. "In every great separation lies a germ of madness; one must guard against spreading and cultivating it by brooding", comments Goethe. But that is precisely what ten-year-old Thérèse did, with a

[63] I S., viii, 93.
[64] I S., xviii.
[65] I S. ii, 115.

child's obstinacy and defencelessness. Later on, she became conscious of the connection. All witnesses agree that the illness represented an eruption of overwhelming anxiety fantasies. Repeatedly, and graphically as the gestures of an actor, everything Thérèse experienced and did in the course of the disease represented emotions of extreme terror and forsakenness. The familiar room became strange and uncanny to her. "My bed seemed to be surrounded by frightful precipices." The most innocent objects became transformed into hideous gargoyles; her screams and writhings expressed feelings of pursuit and desperate attempts at flight—flight even into self-destruction, as when the child flung herself head-first to the stone floor in a moment when she was left unguarded.

She failed to recognize Marie, the other members of the household, even her adored father. It was as if they were not there; they did not count, offered no protection, vanished utterly in the face of the devouring horror—and were even felt to be a part of it: "They want to poison me!" Father himself brought a horrible monster to her bed. This too clear-sighted child had long known that her father was himself weak and menaced, he himself marked out as a victim. Pauline alone offered protection, not only because she was Thérèse's own, self-elected "little mother", but because she really was in her whole being an image of their deceased mother. And Pauline had now been taken away also, transported to some incomprehensibly remote place. That accounts for the strange temporary "cure" on the day Pauline took the habit. Such a cure can easily be interpreted as "hysterical"; we can understand it when we consider that for the child, who had not yet completely succumbed to her disease, here was an opportunity to take refuge in the powerful protection of her sister. But after the ceremony, when Pauline was "finally" lost, all barriers went down; the disease opened an assault against her life.

Here was a case where the cure proceeded directly from "the one thing needful". The child had been cast into the outer darkness, but now other sheltering arms cradled her and offered her protection, that love which is also power. When Mary smiled at her, the spell of fear was broken. A mother had returned to her, was given to her again, and one greater than her departed mother or her maternal sister—the Holy Mother appeared before her bodily.

What actually wrought the transformation no one can decide. Perhaps, at the sight of the sisters praying before the altar and before the familiar statue of Mary, the child's vital faith evoked, by inner illumination and force of imagination, this consoling vision out of herself, just as her tormented spirit had previously transformed the familiar objects of the room into images of horror. Or perhaps God's mercy made use in this way of the unique forces of the child's soul to shatter the spell of fear. Or perhaps it was actually needful to dissolve the limits of earthly reality and grant the child a moment's insight into that other reality which awaits us after death.

To her dying day Thérèse herself was convinced that she had seen Mary herself. She was, to be sure, no less convinced that her sickness was caused by diabolic possession. She took this attack on the part of the devil in a purely physical sense and gave a curiously naïve reason for it: the devil's jealousy over Pauline's entrance into the convent, raised to a pitch of rage because he foresaw "all we were going to do against him in time to come" and so "wanted to vent his fury on me". However, she continues, "the Queen of Heaven was keeping faithful watch over her little flower... ready to calm the storm just when the frail and slender stem was in danger of being broken forever." In other words, the devil wanted to kill her in order, at least, to prevent her entrance into the Carmel, since he could not exterminate the entire family.

We would prefer to see the daemonic influence elsewhere. The assault of the Evil One, we believe, was not expressed in the child's convulsions and grimaces (just as we cannot agree with the prim sisters in seeing a special divine dispensation amid the symptoms of possession in that Thérèse, even during the most violent writhings, never exposed herself in an unseemly manner). Rather, the devil's onslaught should be perceived in the uncanny struggle that must have gone on in the unconscious depths of her soul. Christians know that daemonic influences upon man's psychic life exist. They know, too, that in a "wholly natural" neurosis, in any severe affection of the nerves or the psyche, the sick person is weakened and more dangerously exposed to the eternally alert, knowing and sharp-eyed adversary of his salvation. Periods of illness are times of intensified vulnerability of the "soul" in both the religious and the psychological sense of the word.

A crisis which produces a state of confusion and agitation in body and soul, which attacks simultaneously a person's alertness, confidence, presence of mind and powers of resistance, can at the same time—while the state of the disease remains unchanged—*also* mean a grave temptation, a diabolical invitation to discouragement in the face of life. It can lead to stifling inhibitions, to erroneous interpretations of the self, to lifelong hypochondria about one's "weak sides"—all attitudes which may later on hinder radical, heroic commitment. And we may well assume—many events from the lives of saints seem to confirm this—that the demons discern a lofty vocation in a person much sooner than do human beings, and bring to bear their power against him.

Certainly little Thérèse, in that restricted region of her soul which was illuminated by the radiance of consciousness, had wholeheartedly "renounced" her *petite mère*, had gladly surrendered Pauline to the Saviour as

His bride, and was proud of this sister's dedication to God. After all, sooner or later she would be following her. But the psyche consists not only of this upper stratum; it extends downward into dark regions into which even adults seldom obtain clear insight. To what extent little Thérèse had, in the depths of her self, really renounced her beloved sister, how intensely possessiveness had "taken possession" of her heart, is revealed clearly enough by her own description of the agonies she suffered in the visiting room at the Carmel. How could this have been otherwise? Anyone who understands his own psyche to even a slight degree knows well how long it takes, and what profound transformations are necessary, before such a release of someone else is really complete, not only determined on. The heart's tendrils, once they have grown closely around another person, cannot be ripped by a mere act of will. That is all the more true the more the relationship is founded upon dark, elementary sources of being. Thus "on the surface", in the transparent world of her religious ideas, Thérèse resigned herself to her sister's profession, recognizing it to be good; but in the dark, speechless abysses of the blood all the forces of nature rebelled, immoderately and irreconcilably, against this deprivation. (We shall have occasion to mention frequently how extraordinarily powerful the physical bonds were in this family.) And the turmoil within her soul became so overpowering that it ultimately broke out, found expression in neurosis.

In constant reiteration, in ever more emphatic form, Thérèse expressed by a whole language of gesture one and the same emotion: "I want Pauline, I must go to Pauline; I don't want her to be away; I can live only with her; I will fall sick, go mad, die without Pauline; none of you can help me; I don't want any of the rest of you to help me." She could not understand herself, of course (how could we expect her to be capable of such understanding?); she was terrified by the incomprehensible forces that overwhelmed her. From all her sisters' whisperings (which, as we have seen, she heard even during her apparent comas), she had to assume that the most horrible of all fates had come upon her: diabolic possession. Nevertheless, we believe that a decision must have taken place deep within her when, in the midst of her direst distress, the saving grace of the vision of Mary shone upon her. We believe that at this point Thérèse was confronted with a temptation, for all that it was hidden in the unplumbed depths of the soul. For here she was confronted with alternatives, and the second of these alternatives was the perilous one. She could accept the offered comfort, the new support and protection. That is, she could abandon her wild despair over what she had lost, could really carry out the unendurable renunciation within the core of her ego, could release the hand of Pauline and reach across the irrevocable gulf for the hand of the Blessed Virgin. Or—and this was the other possibility—she could cling to her despair, could hold tight to her neurosis, could maintain her protest, stubbornly persist at all costs in the sinister attempt at blackmail which this disease represented.

Such decisions take place not by deliberate processes of thought, but far below the strata of thoughts and words, by a lightninglike opening or closing of the core of being.

Precisely here we see the child destined to be a saint: not that the miracle happened to her, but that she obeyed it. Thérèse held on to that capacity for undeviatingly following a straight line which had characterized her from the beginning, which was always to be the mark of her personality. She did "the right thing" and did it as she had learned to do, in simple obedience, without even thinking of other possible courses. Perhaps this very simplicity of hers defeated the diabolic assault; she could not be corrupted because the proposal, the demand and the insinuation were not even "understood". Against the simplicity and wholeness of this little girl who was sick unto death, the diabolic ruses were aimed in vain. Thérèse yielded to the forces of the disease with fearsome "docility". Her whole nature wrenched out of joint, she screamed and wept, stood on her head and writhed in convulsions. She was beyond all human aid and almost insane with fear because her state of abandonment was so incomprehensible to her. And yet, through all this, her submissive heart clung, uncomprehendingly and tormentedly, but prayerfully and trustfully, to God.

In this case, too, she learned the lesson that was later to be enunciated again and again in her spiritual message to the world: that grace can do anything, grace offered, vouchsafed out of pure mercy, not to be won by any degree of struggle; that acceptance of and dependence upon this grace is man's crucial "act" which will save him gloriously when all toil and effort, all exercise of will in renunciation, cannot help him to overcome his innate nature. To be sure, she did not yet consciously know this, would not know it for a long time to come. But she had experienced it; this lesson had entered her very being and could no longer be expunged.

5. TEMPTATION TO SAINTLINESS

The miraculous cure had taken place on 13 May. On the following morning Thérèse resumed her normal life. "Neither nervousness nor irritability lingered", says Marie.[66] But this remark is obviously guided by the

---

[66] 2 S., 287.

desire to leave no doubt of the thoroughness of Thérèse's recovery. During the next month there were in fact several brief spells of agitation and weakness, but no real relapse such as the doctor had feared.[67] There remained, however, a constant danger in Thérèse's overdelicate, oversensitive, vulnerable nature; there remained an amazing struggle of the mind for control of her physical and psychic constitution.

We might expect that the sign of divine beneficence she had received would confer a new gaiety and security upon Thérèse. This did not happen. The four years of intensified religious development which now followed produced painful crises of growth.

At first her solitude deepened. This child, who believed that she had been persecuted by horrible demons for ten weeks and had been cured by the smile of the Blessed Virgin, felt more isolated than ever from her rowdy classmates in the Abbey. Such experiences would make anyone stand apart. What kinship had she with these companions whose lives consisted exclusively of school, games, prizes, punishments, quarrels and friendships, enthusiasms and petty vanities? She took refuge more than ever in studying, reading and keeping silent. And within her beloved family itself a new source of painful loneliness had been created. We will remember that Marie, by dint of her threefold authority of maternal eldest sister, of godmother and of faithful nurse, had persuaded Thérèse to reveal her vision. Nevertheless Thérèse knew perfectly well that she had done wrong to yield to this urging. Marie thought it good to initiate Pauline and the Carmel into the secret; soon afterwards she took Thérèse to the convent, and the wonderful event was dramatically told to the Prioress and the nuns. The recipient of such grace was gaped at and showered with questions prompted by pious curiosity. What did the Mother of God look like? Was she carrying the Child Jesus in her arms? Was she accompanied by angels? The questions were of the kind which sprang from imaginations nourished by the devotional painting of the times. "Our Lady was very lovely, and I saw her come towards me and smile"— Thérèse could say no more than this, but she was well aware that the nuns were unsatisfied and even disappointed. Some of them regarded her with doubt and disapproval as if to say: if the child really has had this vision, as she claims, she ought to be able to describe it in greater detail. Had, perhaps, fancy and a desire to be important played a part in her "vision"? Thérèse herself no longer knew whether she had described her experience accurately; for a time she even doubted its reality. But one thing she grasped fully: it had been wrong of her to betray the secret. Her

---

[67] 2 S., 131.

insight at the moment of the vision had been valid. If she had maintained silence, as she had then intended to do, her happiness would have remained unclouded; now it had been transformed into painful bitterness. "For four years the memory of that unforgettable favour caused me nothing but pain", she writes. "... Our Lady was allowing me to go through all this for my own good. I should probably have become vain about it if it had been otherwise; as it was, all I got was humiliation, and I could only regard myself with contempt."

Three months later, during the school holidays, her father took her on a short tour of their relations and friends. Everyone knew that the child had been seriously ill, and everyone made an effort to entertain and coddle this pretty, bright and modest girl. Thérèse had hitherto known only the cloistered simplicity of her home and school. The villas and gardens, the merry, pleasure-loving French style of life which was cultivated in most families of their circle—except hers—seemed to her the very essence of worldly magnificence. No wonder the child at first enjoyed the unconstraint and festiveness; no wonder, too, that in her inherited austerity and the puritanical character of her upbringing she later recoiled from these things as from sin itself. The rustic parties and small gatherings of these solid provincial business men must have been innocent enough. Yet all her life they were to remain in Thérèse's memory as a torrent of pleasures surrounded by all the seductive lures of the "world". The touching narrowness of her understanding, and at the same time her idiosyncratic way of seeing all things more than life-size, of experiencing good as well as perils with exaggerated intensity, can be found in her account: "*I began to see something of the world. . . .* I was entertained, pampered, and admired; in fact, for a whole fortnight my path was strewn with flowers. But those words of the Book of Wisdom are only too true: 'The bewitching of vanity overturneth the innocent mind.' When you are only ten your heart is fascinated very easily and I must admit that I found this kind of life charming. The world is able to combine so well the search for pleasure with the service of God, forgetting death . . ." And so on. These observations conclude with the supposition "I think Jesus wanted me to see something of the world before He came to me for the first time, so that I might choose more surely that path in which I would promise to follow Him."

It is highly typical of the devout mind of those times that Thérèse should all her life have seen "the world" as an alternative to the convent only in this particular manner and in this light—never in terms of the life her parents had lived. In general it may be said that the fixed formulas and figures of speech employed by that kind of piety seldom spring from a direct view of objective reality. Rather, all too often they seem to be clichés drawn from the inventory of a rigid tradition.

Thus this holiday, intended by her father as a distraction, led only to an intensification of her brooding and isolation. Almost exactly a year after her cure Thérèse made her First Communion and soon afterwards received the sacrament of Confirmation. Both ceremonies were high points in her already markedly developed religious life.

Thérèse was in her element in the atmosphere of the preparatory period, which was saturated with suggestions, instructions and ardour. Pauline presented her with a notebook in which she was to enter daily her "sacrifices" and "acts of virtue"—a tried and true method of spiritual training similar to the "chaplet of virtues" which Marie had once given to the four-year-old Thérèse. The notebook itself was a labour of love; the giver had decorated its pages with flowers, some signifying the various virtues: roses for acts of love, violets for acts of humility; bluebells, daisies and forget-me-nots. For each flower there was a special prayer. Perhaps it was from this that Thérèse imbibed that "style" which was later so to characterize and distinguish her saintliness: to conceal from others and from herself elements of pain and harshness under sweet pet names. We shall have occasion to remember this when we discuss her doctrine of "scattering flowers".

The notebook reverted to Pauline when it was filled up; she kept it and was able to produce it at the beatification trial. After three months it contained "evidence" of 818 sacrifices and 2,773 "acts". Possibly we may also see here one root of that habit of excessive self-observation which burdened Thérèse all her life.

During the last week before the ceremony she moved into the Abbey to make her retreat. These days of silence and prayer were sheer delight for Thérèse, who found herself for the first time in a wholly cloistral community. Rapturously, she took part in some of the Offices of the nuns, attracting attention because of the big crucifix Léonie had given her, which she wore on her belt like missionaries in pictures.

The day of her First Communion was an experience of pure spiritual bliss without shadow or disturbance. The piety of the time, remote as it was from the Liturgy, understood Communion, and especially First Communion, as something almost apart from the Mystery of the Mass, exclusively as a ceremony of meeting (in fact of "wedding", as the devotional books were wont to say) of the individual soul with the Saviour within the sacrament. Thérèse's experience was in terms of this pattern, but she drew from the stereotype its fullest content. The child experienced all the emotional storm and rapture of passionate surrender, of a true union with God. In retrospect Thérèse for *the first and only time* feels sincerely prompted to employ the language of bridal mysticism, the language of the Canticle of Canticles, of the Office of St Agnes and the visions of

Mechthild and Gertrude. In the account of her Profession she employs the traditional conventual formulas, but here they sound original and full of content: "How lovely it was, that first kiss of Jesus in my heart—it was truly a kiss of love. I knew that I was loved, and said, 'I love You, and I give myself to You for ever.' Jesus asked for nothing, He claimed no sacrifice.... On that day it was more than a meeting; it was a complete fusion. We were no longer two, for Thérèse had disappeared like a drop of water lost in the mighty ocean." The other children, seeing her face streaming with tears, pitied her and assumed that thoughts of her departed mother or of her sister, who was making her profession that same day, were weighing so heavily on her spirits. "It was beyond them that all the joy of Heaven had entered one small, exiled heart, and that it was too frail and weak to bear it without tears."

It is characteristic of the peculiar blunting of perception which daily contact in a family so often produces that Marie, her teacher and guide who had to a great extent by now replaced Pauline and aided her in her spiritual preparation, should have said to Thérèse on one of the following days: "I am sure that God will always carry you like a little child, and not make you tread the path of suffering." Thérèse's companions in the convent made the same assumption as long as she lived. But for all her uncritical submission to her elder sister, the child felt that in this regard Marie was mistaken. Her heart had long known that there was "many a cross in store" for her. And she craved them as high-spirited young persons have always craved trial and tribulation. She wrote: "Suffering began to attract me; I found charms in it which captivated me without my yet fully understanding it. I felt another great desire, to love God alone, and find my joy only in Him. Often during my thanksgivings I repeated the passage from the *Imitation*: 'O Jesus! unspeakable sweetness, turn earthly consolations into bitterness for me.'" And she adds: "These words came to my lips without any effort. I said them as a child recites what someone it loves has prompted, without fully grasping what it means." Of her Confirmation she says laconically: "On that day I was given the strength to suffer." Céline has related in detail that at the time Thérèse appeared to her more ardent and more carried away, if that were possible, than at her First Communion. "My sister, ordinarily so tranquil, was no longer herself; a kind of rapture and intoxication broke out through all her reserve. One day, during her preparation, when I expressed to her my surprise at this, she told me that she understood the effect of this sacrament to be a complete taking possession by the Spirit of Love. There was such an impassioned quality in her words, such a flame in her eyes, that I left her deeply moved, permeated by the impression that something supernatural was taking place here, and the memory of this remained with me." [68] It seems to us that this last sentence must be taken with some caution; Céline, one plainly feels, is most liberal in producing recollections which tend to show that there was always "something special" about her sister, whereas the other witnesses stress Thérèse's inconspicuousness during those very years. Nevertheless, this statement is valuable as additional proof of the earnestness and ardour with which Thérèse surrendered to the great religious experiences of that year.

Thus her life turned inward with increasing intensity. Nevertheless the child, now eleven, at last attempted to forge some connecting links with the real world around her. Gradually she overcame her timidity in the face of the noisy, rough activity of the school, which had once so horrified her. As she grew up, she sought friendship and understanding outside the family for the first time. But as soon as she found a friend, she experienced the fickleness of the human heart. The holidays interrupted the newly formed alliance. During the long weeks of vacation Thérèse looked forward to seeing her friend again, but in the interval the other girl forgot her and reacted with astonishment and coolness to Thérèse's warm greeting. Thérèse had never possessed the active temperament which would allow her to woo others and fight for their affection, to force the dubious to take a stand, and to attempt to hold those who were slipping away. Bitterly hurt, she withdrew: "It was the last time I sought affection as fickle as hers." So deep had this first friendship of childhood been, and so unswervingly loyal was she to herself and therefore to everything she had ever included in her life, that thirteen years later, recalling this first disillusionment, Thérèse had to add: "But God has given me such a faithful heart that once I love I love for always, so I went on praying for her, and love her even now."

As yet she could not reconcile herself out of hand to her loneliness; at this age the heart craves companionship too strongly. Since friendship with her classmates had failed, she sought personal attachment to one of the teachers, of the kind she saw all about her. The girls were at the age for "crushes", which can assume at times complicated and sordid forms, but more frequently pass into a lasting, happy relationship of trust and respect on the one side and maternal sympathy, guidance and stimulation on the other. But this effort, too, failed. "I could not attach myself to anyone", Thérèse says simply. This means, for one thing, that no attention was paid to her. This quiet little creature with tearful eyes appeared to be a thoroughly "good child", quite without problems; she was not

---

[68] I S., vi, 61.

the sort to attract a personal or even merely pedagogical interest on the part of her teachers, as did other pupils whose presence was more attractive or who aroused the teachers' sense of responsibility because they were problem children. But Thérèse's failure to attach herself to anyone lay also with herself. In the conflict between her longings and her inhibitions, the braking forces won the upper hand. "It was a happy failure and saved me a lot of pain", Thérèse exclaims, retrospectively interpreting this experience. "I thank Our Lord that He let me find nothing but bitterness in human affections. I should have been caught easily, and had my wings clipped.... Our Lord knew that I was far too weak to face temptation; He knew that I would certainly have burnt myself in the bewildering light of earthly things, and so He did not let it shine in my eyes. Where stronger souls find joy but remain detached because they are faithful, I found only misery."

The fact that Thérèse was so lonely, so entirely left to her own devices, seems to us one vital proof that at that time not a soul sensed the future saint in her. This must be said forthrightly, for we read again and again of the "stigma of election", of the supernatural aura which glowed about her, inspiring reverence in everyone, and similar fictions. The legend of her childhood is already well developed. When a woman asks for a lock of the child's hair and "carries it away like a relic", or when an old lady, seeing the child in a procession, prophesies, "If she lives she will become a great saint",[69] we should not attach much meaning to such tales. We know how readily such judgments are made at times in devout circles— especially in retrospect. We recall, for example, a girl of about four who showed a great preference for leafing through the lavishly illustrated edition of the *Imitation of Christ* which lay beside her father's desk. It contained all sorts of remarkable pictures of monks, hermits, devils; for chapter decorations there were dragons, death's-heads, festoons of roses, victory palms, goblets and similar fascinating things. It is hard to imagine a child who would not have been enthralled by such a picture-book. But when the girl entered a convent fifteen years later, her family promptly interpreted this childish sport as a symptom of early saintliness: "Even at four no plaything was as dear to her as the *Imitation*;... she looked through it for hours, and wept when anyone wanted to take the sacred book away from her."

We know well that apart from her father and sisters, the persons "in charge" of Thérèse during her childhood saw nothing special in her: neither

---

[69] Laveille, 95.

her relations,[70] nor the nuns who taught her, nor the priests who frequently visited the Martin home. As her enthusiastic biographer expresses
it: "The nuns probably sensed how precious was the treasure entrusted to
them, but they did not recognize its full value."[71] It is both touching and
comical to see how her teachers later, when their almost forgotten pupil
suddenly stood in the limelight of the world's curiosity, made an effort to
unearth something significant out of their memories in response to official as well as private questioners. But with the best will in the world
they could find nothing of importance. "She did nothing extraordinary,
but she did everything extraordinarily well" is a typical judgment in retrospect. Of a similar nature is the reply of an aged nun to a pilgrim:
"From the moment I first saw her I was struck by her heavenly look, her
air of distinction and her majestic bearing." Had it not been for Sister
Thérèse's meteoric rise in the ecclesiastical sky, neither of these statements would ever have been made. One teacher noticed that Thérèse
never used a prayer book in church. She thought this a sign of insufficient attentiveness and gently admonished her to conform to the regular
order of things.[72] Another teacher once asked her what she did with
herself during her free afternoons at home. "Sometimes I go and hide
myself in a little corner of my room which I can shut off with my bed
curtains, and... just think", Thérèse replied. "But what do you think
about?" the teacher asked laughingly. "'About God,' I told her; 'about
how short life is, and about eternity... and... well... I just think.'"[73]
The teacher, who after all belonged to a contemplative Order herself,
seems to have seen nothing but humour in this confession. Afterwards
she was fond of teasing her pupil by asking her whether she still "thought".

It struck no one that Thérèse was revealing an unusually early and
independent talent for meditation. Pauline alone firmly believed that her
sister had the beginnings of a religious vocation. But during this period
her influence upon the child was no longer so strong and decisive. Marie
was Thérèse's principal guide. At home, at any rate, Thérèse was not
elevated by force to a child prodigy. Everyday life at Les Buissonnets was
already so saturated with religious ideas, feelings, habits and conversations
that no one thought it at all unusual for the youngest sister to assume the

---

[70] The statement by her elder cousin Jeanne, who also saw her daily, leaves no room for
doubt: "Never would I have suspected, at the time, that she was so saintly. She was exceptionally impressionable and wept for no cause at all...; she was not communicative and
spoke very little. Since she frequently complained about headaches, I imagined that this
affliction made her so serious" (2 S., 145).

[71] Laveille, 114.

[72] Laveille, 114; 1 S., ii, 152.

[73] S.S., iv.

general cast of the family. Rather, any deviation from this style of life would have attracted attention.

Marie, for all the limitations of her overconservative mind, was a sober and sensible guardian—more so than one would expect from her behaviour after the miraculous cure. She looked askance upon all signs of singularity, setting restraints upon the child's zeal rather than encouraging it. When she was preparing Céline for First Communion Thérèse, then seven, was eager to listen in on the instructions. Marie sent her away.[74] According to the regulations of the Diocese of Bayeux, First Communicants must have completed their eleventh year during the year of admission to First Communion. Hence Thérèse, because she had been born on 2 January, did not have her turn until a full year later than other children her age. She was very sad about this, and when she chanced to meet the Bishop with his Vicar-General on the way to the railway station in Lisieux, she wanted to run after them and ask for a dispensation. This must have been shortly after the vision which cured her of her illness. Marie said no to this; she would not hear of Thérèse receiving exceptional treatment. Pauline in the same situation would probably have acted differently.[75] Marie also refused her request for permission to practise meditation for half an hour every day; in the end, however, she let Thérèse wheedle a quarter of an hour out of her. "I did not permit her more than that; I thought her devout enough, and filled with so sublime an understanding of heavenly things that I became anxious about it." [76] Therefore Thérèse asked an older schoolmate, the prefect of the Children of Mary at the Abbey, to teach her how to meditate.[77] Probably little Thérèse had already gathered that the members of this devout organization were obliged to practise this mode of prayer daily.

Marie may have been the only member of the family who sensed the dangers of religious precocity. She had the most vigorous, down-to-earth temperament among the five sisters; for all her own devoutness, she fell less into the spiritual clichés which dominated all of them. It was Marie too who opposed all talk of a premature entrance into the Carmel, although she had no doubts about her sister's vocation; whereas Pauline wholeheartedly supported her youngest sister in this ambition.

But inner destiny, determined by nature and grace, was stronger than all the protective walls that those concerned for her well-being tried, consciously or unconsciously, to erect around the child.

---

[74] Laveille, 99.
[75] Laveille, 124.
[76] I S., vi, 24.
[77] Laveille, 114; I S., ii, 159.

Scarcely a year after her First Communion, two years after her cure, Thérèse once more plunged into an extremely dangerous psychic state which was to last two more years. "This is the second sorrow of the soul", writes Henry Suso, who, so rich in all experience, has passed through these deep waters also, "that a person ponders what should not be pondered." "What a martyrdom! It lasted about two years, and no one could possibly understand what I had to go through unless they had gone through it themselves", Thérèse writes. "Every single thought and even my most commonplace actions became a source of worry and anxiety. I used to enjoy a momentary peace while I unburdened myself to Marie, but this used to cost me a lot because I thought I ought to tell her absolutely everything, even the wildest of my fancies. But this peace only lasted about as long as a flash of lightning, and I was back where I started. At least I made Marie practise wonderful patience!"

Marie was able to cope with the situation. She took over treatment of this "illness" with as sure a hand as if it were mumps or measles. Probably the matter did not seem much different to her. The sisters' matter-of-fact statements that Thérèse at this time "suffered from scruples" sound as if they were speaking of some childhood disease, although there is also a certain undertone of respect—for not every child catches scruples, only one who is marked out by grace, one of the elect, precociously devout and filled with extraordinary passion. In the minds of these people who practised and discussed the spiritual life, the *vie dévote*, like connoisseurs, such a phenomenon was just one of the predictable but unpleasant incidentals which could affect anyone—just as, say, a traveller in certain parts of the world must not be surprised at encountering vermin. And there was a tried and true treatment for the affliction. "Thérèse's scruples" seem to have been an ordinary subject of discreet conversation among the Martins and the Guérins. Even such an outsider as Léonie knew all about it. And when Thérèse once happened to cry more than usual, her big cousin Jeanne assumed, half in irritation, half with forbearance, that she was having *"un gros scrupule"*—does not this "fat scruple" sound exactly like a hideous insect? Marie, also, did not take the matter too seriously. "On the eve of confessional days her anxieties doubled. I let her tell me all her supposed sins. Then I tried to help her by explaining to her that I would take all her sins (which were not even imperfections) upon myself. I allowed her only to charge herself with two or three sins in the presence of the priest, and I told her which these must be. She was so docile that she obeyed me to the letter."

There are genuine and there are invented scruples. The second type are more common: they consist of various temporary attacks of exaggerated anxiety and insecurity in a person's religious life, in regard to sins, obligations, requirements of conscience. Most of them can be traced to a particular source, to false, one-sided or twisted religious ideas, to ill health which goes hand in hand with lasting spiritual exhaustion and confusion, to the imposition of unexpected responsibilities which cannot be shouldered. There is also a kind of chronic scrupulosity which is the expression of innate or acquired emotional rigidity and intellectual poverty, and which reveals itself in warped moral judgments upon oneself and others.

Thérèse's scruples were of a different sort. Given the nature of her religious training it can scarcely be assumed that crude misunderstandings of the nature of sin, commandments or punishment would have given rise to such torments of doubt. No sinister, frightening picture of an eternally wrathful God who lies grimly in wait for man's errors then gleefully closes the trap upon him and subjects him to damnation—no such misconceptions troubled her heart and sent her imagination fleeing down confused paths from an inescapable judgment. Nor did she find herself suddenly confronted by the complex demands of obscure tasks, forced to immediate decisions and, in childlike inexperience, rendered utterly perplexed and helpless. Nor do we find in this clear, simple and open mind any of that petty crankiness from which spring the scruples of those who are emotionally limited and obtuse. What Thérèse describes, in the few but precise and comprehensive lines she writes on the matter, are "genuine" scruples, the spiritual illness brought about by obsessional ideas and obsessional fears, which rise out of the fateful overshadowing of the soul in open contradiction to her bright, healthy mind and becloud her clear vision with dark mists. Her unwholesome mode of life was also a contributory factor: her keeping to her room, her excessive studiousness, her complete lack of diversions, of company, of physical outlet. (With the aversion that children of her type naturally have to all vigorous movement, Thérèse contrived to abstain from the rough-and-tumble games of the other girls during playtime.) At home no household work was required of her, not the slightest help in cleaning, not even care of the flowers in her own room. On top of all this was the natural strain of oncoming puberty, her solitary brooding over her two frightful experiences: the vision of her father with covered face and the diabolic disease. There was also her troubled conscience over the secret she had betrayed.[78] In other children these years of pre-puberty exhibit the so-called

---

[78] The *Manuscrits Authentiques* inform us of a highly important detail which was not published in *The Story of a Soul.* "Long after my recovery [from chorea] I believed that I had expressly arranged matters so as to be sick [*j'ai cru que j'avais fait exprès d'être malade*], and this belief became a veritable martyrdom for my soul. I told Marie, who with her customary kindness did her best to soothe me; I talked about it in confession, and my

"negative phase", the impulse towards criticism, the spirit of contradiction, the first pains of breaking with the hitherto complete identity with the parents. It may also be that in Thérèse these stirrings did not find their natural channels—her blind attachment to her blood relations lasted all her life. Instead, they turned with tormenting questionings against her own being.

Perhaps a third circumstance throws some light upon the significance of this stage in her life—and thereby upon the religious character of her generation. Thérèse can almost name to the day the time when the "ugly disease", as she sensibly calls her condition, broke out in her. It was while she was making her retreat for her "second Communion", as the anniversary of the first is called in France—a day celebrated with great ceremony. We will not be going far wrong if we link this with another factor which appears in *The Story of a Soul* in another connection, but refers to approximately the same period.

"As I was no good at games, I would have spent most of my time reading", Thérèse writes. She developed a craving for reading as do all talented, lonely and shy children who live inwardly. Marie, who was aware of this passion, felt obliged to place strict limits on the amount of time Thérèse might spend with her beloved books. Obedience in this matter cost Thérèse greater self-sacrifice than anything else that was demanded of her, for she adhered strictly to the time allowed and would stop reading even if she had come to the most engrossing passages. Together with devotional reading, the child was given chiefly romantic historical novels which inflamed her imagination. "I must admit that... I did not always grasp the realities of life." Her head was filled with the deeds of patriotic heroes, especially the Crusaders and Joan of Arc (of whom she remained all her life an enthusiastic admirer); she identified herself, like all children of her age, with the adored characters and burned with the desire to imitate them. In one hour of such excessive enthusiasm "Jesus taught me that the only glory which matters is the glory which lasts for ever, and that one does not have to perform shining deeds to win that, but hide one's acts of virtue from others and even from oneself so that 'the left hand does not know what the right hand is doing'." This insight, which broke through the horizon of her years and clearly outlined the figure of the future saint, was strange enough; altogether amazing, it seems to us,

---

confessor, too, tried to reassure me by telling me that it was impossible to simulate a disease to the extent that I had had it. God, who undoubtedly wanted to purify and above all humble me, let me keep this secret martyrdom until my entry into the Carmel. There the Father of our souls swept all doubts from me with a wave of the hand, as it were, and since then I am entirely tranquil about that."

was the response which her child's mind gave to this "illumination": "I was sure that I was born to be great—*que j'étais née pour la gloire*—and began to wonder how I should set about winning my glory; then it was revealed to me in my heart that my glory would lie in becoming a saint, though this glory would be hidden on earth." "I have always considered this one of my life's greatest graces, for God did not enlighten me then in the way He does now", Thérèse says expressly. Thus this was a serious inner experience, not merely one of the innumerable pious thoughts which daily filled her head, drawn as they were from things she had heard or read, or from her own speculations. It was an inner communication, falling into her soul like a seed that was to sprout only slowly and painfully.

In itself there is nothing startling about this illumination. Ever since she had been able to think Thérèse had absorbed with her daily bread the idea that every person in her immediate surroundings could, should, must become a saint. This, to be sure, did not carry the same meaning as being canonized. But becoming a saint was to her as natural an ambition as wealth, beauty or a fine career to others. It was, so to speak, the normal goal of her devout family. Moreover, the people around her had very definite and unshakable conceptions of the paths which led to saintliness. Here, to be sure, we encounter a curious paradoxical aspect of their piety: the contradiction between official and literary theory, and private practice. By theoretical standards "the saint" was not a particular human being led to personal spiritual perfection by a unique action of grace. He was a pure type, a super saint, a pure abstraction, the embodiment of innumerable features of historical saints. He was the geometrical locus of all ethical perfection. He possessed all virtues in the highest degree, had discarded all faults and even all weaknesses—the possibility of sins was not even thought of. He had utterly purged himself of all human inclinations and ties. He was poor as Francis, ardent as Ignatius, profound as Teresa, wise as Benedict, innocent as Agnes, loving as Magdalen, unworldly as Simon Stylites, capable as Vincent de Paul, mild as Francis de Sales, and austere as the Curé d'Ars. And he was to be imitated in every point, and without qualification. He was not seen as an inaccessible ideal, but as the standard of perfection.

An echo of some of these dreams can still be heard when Thérèse, much later in life, speaks of her "vast desires" (*mes désirs infinis*): "I feel the call of more vocations still; I want to be a warrior, a priest, an apostle, a doctor of the Church, a martyr—there is no heroic deed I do not wish to perform. I feel as daring as a crusader, ready to die for the Church upon the battlefield.... I long... to go to the ends of the earth to preach Your name, to plant Your glorious Cross, my Beloved, on pagan shores."

And how characteristic that in this list of all imaginable types of saintly lives, even the lay path of the "Christian soldier", she does not mention that of wife and mother.

No one questions the natural premises of such an image of perfection. Its partisans speak and write as though everything were possible to everyone, as though "iron will" sustained by grace could magically transform lambs into lions and hens into eagles. It is a grave and anxious question, which we can barely refer to here, how many souls may have missed their truly assigned completion in voyaging towards this chimerical perfection. All intelligent spiritual guidance within the Church must take into account, as Francis de Sales and many others taught with incomparable firmness and clarity, that every Christian has his own unique way to "perfect maturity in Christ". But the bulk of popular devotional literature set up a standardized sanctity and extolled innumerable infallible recipes, methods and special devices for achieving it.

On the other hand, however, it is difficult to think of an age more lavish in its distribution of the glorious appellation of "saint". *Petite sainte* was a common epithet, especially in groups moulded by conventual education. No especially great achievements, no medieval penances, were needed to win this title; a certain puritanical style of life, considerable time spent in spiritual conversations with priests and other religious-minded persons, devout reading and meetings, strict rejection of all "vanities" in appearance and occupations—these were sufficient to prompt admiring, yet half-mocking, members of the family and friends to speak of "our little saint". How quickly priests of impressive demeanour were canonized by the whispers of the pupils (and sometimes the teachers as well) in boarding schools. In this language and by such standards a charitable lady soon became known as "another St Elizabeth"; a hard-working student, "a St Stanislaus", or even "a St Aloysius"; a nice acolyte, "a St Tarcisius"; an eager promoter of Church concerns, a "St Paul". For every category there was a saintly label, as in the old days there was a patron saint for every craft. To be sure, this custom betrays the extent to which names once representing awe-inspiring human destinies had become decorative clichés.

Even without such somewhat pompous analogies to the great typical saints, fellow human beings were viewed under this aspect and classified accordingly. Ever since Thérèse had been able to think she had heard her aunt in the convent referred to only by the affectionate nickname "our holy maiden" (*la sainte fille*). She knew that both her grandfathers had died "like saints"; that Mama had been a true saint, and Papa was a living saint. Later she was to continue this usage without embarrassment, as innumerable passages in her letters demonstrate.

The letters her deceased mother had written to the elder sisters at boarding school were guarded as the most precious of family treasures and read silently and aloud again and again. They repeat with many variations the one desire of Zélie Martin's heart: that all her children would be saintly. "I ask the Holy Virgin that all the little girls she has given me may become saints, and that I may be permitted to follow their destinies from close by; but they must be better than I!"[79] "I should like to be a saint; it will not be easy; there is much chopping to do, and the wood is hard as stone.... I suppose I should have begun earlier, when it would have been easier, but better late than never."[80] "How often I say daily: O God, how I wish I were a saint! And then I nevertheless do not do what they did."[81]

Many years later, in 1887, Marie, after taking the habit, wrote in exactly the same tone to her father: "O you best of all Fathers who have given to God, without reckoning, all the hope of your old age, to you belongs the glory which does not pass. Yes, most beloved of Fathers, we will glorify you as you deserve to be glorified (*nous te glorifierons, comme tu mérites être glorfiée*) by becoming saints. Anything less would be unworthy of you."

There was, thus, nothing at all strange or alarming for Thérèse in seeing the combination of glory and sanctity as part of her personal future. What seemed new to her were only three things: in the first place, that she would be a *great* saint; in the second place, that "her" glory would remain concealed—at this time it still seemed to her perplexing and strange that this should be so; and thirdly, as she touchingly puts it, that this matter of becoming a saint was going to be difficult and painful. For: "I did not realize in those days that one had to go through much suffering to become a saint."

This sentence appears to us particularly characteristic of the epoch. After all, everyone knew so well what a saint looked like and how he behaved; it really wasn't such a difficult business; it was simply a matter of living up to "our way of life". How often Madame Martin related in joyful, maternally proud letters that one or the other of her girls in prayer "looked like an angel", or looked "like a little saint" at First Communion. She averred that the infant Thérèse "will be good; one can already see the germ of it; she talks of nothing but God." The baby was taught to recite pious little verses, and "at the last words, 'up above in the blue firmament', she turns her eyes upward with an angelic expression. We

[79] Piat, 166.
[80] Piat, 191.
[81] Piat, 129; to her sister-in-law.

never tire of having her repeat this, it's so charming! There is something so heavenly in her look that it quite carries us away." [82] And the big sisters, going all the way as young girls will, demand even more than Mama. From one letter we learn that Madame Martin had to check Marie's zeal to raise Céline to perfection all too sternly and quickly: "I told her that it is unreasonable to discourage her so" (by demanding everything or nothing); "that it is impossible for such a small child (seven years old) to become saintly at one blow, and that she must let trivialities pass." [83]

Certainly we sense the unsoundness of the attitude, exemplified by Marie's zeal towards her sisters' perfection. Such signs of saintliness can be evoked all too easily.[84] How could Thérèse, so willing and eager in all things, so anxious to win the approval of her elders, so bent on imitating them to the fullest extent—how could she have failed to seek to please them in this realm first and foremost?

At this point Thérèse encountered a wholly unconscious, highly dangerous temptation. The weight, the persuasiveness, the well-nigh irresistible character of that temptation can be measured only by someone who has succumbed to it at least for some part of his life. This temptation was, namely, to don the costume of "saintliness" which was offered to her ready-made, to fit herself to it and to confound it with reality.

Young girls in particular, with the extraordinary flexibility of their natures, with their imagination, sensitivity and adaptability, with their intense desire to please—to please even on the highest plane and only the best and most respected of persons—with their capacity for imitating and adjusting themselves to an ideal type, are supremely susceptible to this danger. The make-up of piety, if we may put it so, is no more difficult to learn than the cosmetics of athleticism, sophistication or intellectuality. Only it is incomparably more dangerous because these latter poses need go only skin-deep, while the former, if a pose, can affect the deepest strata of being.

The spell of this projected wish-dream can affect persons at various stages of age and development and can last for a very long time. Identification with an ideal ego causes least harm if it occurs at puberty, when the unfinished personality is still, so to speak, playing with various possibilities of self-development as if these were roles and costumes. At such

---

[82] Piat, 183.

[83] Piat, 172.

[84] At the same time this rigid stereotype involved complete blindness to all religious growth outside the pattern, as the long, tragic misunderstanding of poor Léonie most clearly indicates. "Saintliness" either had the well-known features or was given no credence at all.

a time the attachment to the imaginary figure does not go too deep and is shed like a snake's skin, without any great shock, during one of the numerous "castings" characteristic of that age.

It must be said that Thérèse Martin was literally predestined, by nature, education and environment, to take this unfortunate by-path. Her genuine precocity, her uncommon psychic burdens, her strong intellectual grasp of religion and her boundless readiness to obey and to act should already have laid the foundation stones for some such airy structure of false "self-sanctification", for an imaginative anticipation of true sanctity. And who among her family would have noticed the imperceptible shift in emphasis? All would have been too happy about the visible fruits, the high number of self-conquests recorded in her notebook, the customary pious conversations and good works, the tears at the Communion grille.

Such self-deception would of course have been only a pause on a true way. The wonder was that in the incorruptible purity of her nature Thérèse passed it by, did not fall prey to the tremendous temptation of the "projected image". She could not but have felt this temptation to believe she had achieved a pinnacle of devoutness of which in fact she was not yet capable. She was constantly being offered the palm of sainthood. Yet she resisted the enormous pressure, withstood it without crippling or straining her nature, without self-deception. In this successful resistance, not in the high statistics of her acts of virtue, not in the ecstasies she experienced during Communion, we see the token of her growing sanctity.

God stood by her. Perhaps she would nevertheless have given way to complacency. As it was, this all too easy smug satisfaction with herself was constantly being "crowned with thorns" by a merciful hand. One great and terrible school of humility was spared her: sin. But in the school of weakness where we learn the same lesson, only more mercifully, little was granted to her without heavy payment. From the beginning of her spiritual career Thérèse had to learn how great was the difference between self-appointed "accomplishments" and those imposed upon one, how well all of us know how to make the first kind compatible with our abilities, so that we emerge from the test with flying colours—and how unyieldingly the other kind expose the true limits of our "virtues". Not that she indulged in any theoretical consideration of the subject; a child can experience the reality, of this bit by bit, in her whole being. "Thérèse possessed a will of iron", her sisters unanimously testify—precisely the quality that the pedagogues and ascetics of her day considered the magic wand for winning saintliness. And yet it turns out that the most conscientious efforts, the most burning zeal in prescribed, advised and self-sought exercises, does not suffice to master even the most ridiculous faults, the commonest contingencies.

Thérèse could pour out bucketfuls of reverential tears; she had seen the heavens open and the smile of the Blessed Virgin. But she could not, simply *could not*, manage what the most average, worldly and superficial of her fellow pupils managed without any difficulty: to accept a harsh word unperturbed, smile in the face of mockery or reproach, master her feelings at receiving a poor mark. She described this weakness with humour and sternness: "I made myself almost unbearable by being far too sensitive, and nothing that was said to me seemed to help me overcome this tiresome fault. . . . I used to cry as much over little things as big ones. For instance, I very much wanted to practise virtue but I went about it in a very funny way. Céline used to do our room because I had not learnt how to look after myself yet and did not do any housework—but occasionally I used to make the bed or go and fetch Céline's little plants and cuttings from the garden if she was out, just to please God. As I said, it was 'for God alone' I did these things so I should not have expected any other reward; but I did, and if Céline did not seem surprised or thank me for what I had done, I was far from pleased about it, and showed it by crying. If ever I hurt anyone's feelings by accident, instead of making the best of it, I was so disconsolate that I made myself ill and that made things worse. Then if I got over the first mistake, I would begin to cry because I had cried."

Once, during the summer holidays, her Aunt Guérin gave her a pretty sky blue hair ribbon. Promptly, she self-tormentingly interpreted her pleasure in this as a sin and could not rest until she had rushed off to confession that very evening—which meant, of course, that someone had to sacrifice the time to take Thérèse to town, for morality would not permit a young girl to take a step across the street alone. Undoubtedly, she afterwards became conscious of scruples over the trouble she had caused others and began to ask herself whether she could not have been more considerate and waited until the next time the family attended church. But then, could she have gone to sleep with such a sin on her conscience? The familiar windmill began to turn; Don Quixote, once he set out on his hunt for perfection, was bound to be whirled through the air.

During those same holidays a significant little incident took place. Marie Guérin, the younger of the two cousins, liked to make a good deal of fuss over her headaches and other ills, and she was then regularly pitied and coddled. Thérèse, as we have seen, had headaches every day and seldom showed her discomfort. But one evening she was tempted to try the other course. She huddled in an armchair, began crying and answered

her aunt's and cousin's questions with Marie's formula, "O my poor head!"
But this attempt to win sympathy missed fire. Since she was ordinarily so
controlled about her physical ills, no one would believe that this was the
real trouble. "Aunt... treated me as if I were a grown-up, while Jeanne
reproached me in a pained tone of voice, though very gently, I must
admit, because she thought I was guilty of lack of simplicity and confidence in my aunt by hiding the real reason for my tears."

This sadly comic tale, which Thérèse with gracious self-irony compares to the fable of the donkey and the dog, shows with great clarity
how excessively strong was her urge to win attention and be comforted;
it could break through all the inhibitions imposed by her natural and
ascetic reticence. The occupations Thérèse preferred at school, during
the playtimes which she found so dreary, point in the same direction.
Under the tall old linden trees in the grassy inner courtyard of the Abbey
she picked up dead baby birds and gave them "an honourable burial in a
little plot of ground which I turned into a cemetery". Or else she discovered a social talent in herself: she could tell stories so well that the
other children, and even some of the bigger girls, gathered around her to
listen. But this pleasure did not last long; the authorities on principle
discouraged group-forming for anything but the prescribed common games,
and recreation hours were supposed to be for exercise and not for sitting
around. These episodes, too, show that Thérèse felt at ease only in pastimes in which she herself was the centre of attention. The games in
which an individual counted only by conforming, and his achievement
represented only a victory for his team, had no attraction for her.

We hear also that Thérèse was extremely tormented by ambition in
school—not because she was so ambitious for herself, but because she
had resolved always to make Papa happy by bringing home the best possible marks. A "good" instead of "excellent" even in a single subject produced a veritable storm in a teacup over "Papa's disappointment".[85] We
may assume that the child conceived the effect of her imperfections upon
the Heavenly Father in much the same terms and worried about it with
the same intensity. And let us not forget that her first dream of sanctity
had at first been nothing but a direct transposition of a wholly earthly
craving for fame and had to be corrected by her "inner illumination".

All this makes for no very pleasant picture. From an unbiased point of
view Thérèse displayed an unusual degree of precocity, such as is fairly
common in youngest and sickly children. Given such a disposition, the
constant self-observation and introspection which were part and parcel of

[85] I S., ii, 58.

a particular method for promoting piety could only be harmful in the beginning—all the more so since every small failure was set against that ideal image of absolute sanctity we have already discussed. Since she had learned to view her own actions as all-important elements in sanctifying herself, she could blame any failure only on her own inadequacy, her own lack of sufficient effort. Must she then pray more, record more acts of virtue, make more "sacrifices"? And must she then face more defeats, more tears, be more of a burden upon others? The more she strained, and the harder she tried, then the more incomprehensible and depressing were her failures, the more complex and malignant became her entanglement in scruples, the more poisoned by fears and doubts her whole life. "Every single thought and even my most commonplace actions became a source of worry and anxiety."

The question of freedom, responsibility and grace had always concerned her deeply in her religious instruction. When such subjects were discussed, the usually shy and silent child became conspicuous by her lively and persistent questioning.[86] Most of all, her teacher reports, she was intrigued by the apparent contradiction between infinite mercy and human freedom. Even at nine she could not accept the idea that unbaptized children should be barred from the face of God. Now this outlook, intensified by her passion for goodness and propriety, produced an exaggerated longing for security: as a First Communicant she prayed that the Saviour would take away her freedom of will, "the liberty she feared". We feel the sense of giddiness that overpowered her when she contemplated her own weakness and the justice of God, the giddiness which must inevitably overpower anyone who has not yet grasped the third thread of this unfathomable complexity: grace. For five years the way of this girl, outwardly so placid, passed between abysses of obsession; on one side false dreams of sanctity, on the other, gulfs of despair. That her foot nevertheless did not stumble was not due to any trancelike sureness, but to highly conscious, toilsome watchfulness. On the day of her First Communion she scribbled down only three resolutions: "I will never lose courage. I will say a *Memorare* every day. I will take pains to humble my arrogance."[87] "My arrogance"—none of those close to her even guessed its existence, as many expressions of amazement at this and similar confessions were later to indicate. Yet Thérèse, with astonishing certainty, recognized this arrogance as the root of her difficulties. How lonely her struggle must have been, since no one but herself was aware of the actual enemy. She had only one weapon, but this was the weapon with which

[86] I S., ii, 146.
[87] I S., ii, 96.

she won triumphantly all the battles of her life: her fidelity to the demands of conscience; her resolution to do what was right and necessary here and now, and to do it at all costs. For the schoolgirl Thérèse such fidelity to conscience meant simply obedience: to do good as she had been taught, to carry out whatever was legitimately required of her. That alone was some firm ground underfoot; that was the strait way amid the glittering reflections that floated about her, tempting and frightening her. That she saw, affirmed and performed this obedience is a sign to us of the indestructible soundness of her nature at its inmost core; a soundness that could not be impaired by any strains which she herself or others unwittingly imposed upon it.

Thérèse's obedience carried her safely through those imperilled years. By virtue of it alone she escaped the attitude which might have turned her scruples into a fatal disease of the soul: that obstinate self-will which engenders blindness of the spirit. So precisely did she obey Marie's commandments and prohibitions in regard to confession that her confessor himself never learned anything about his "patient's" scruples. "He must have thought me freer of pangs of conscience than any other soul, although I was suffering from them to the highest degree."

Thérèse may have concluded, since she was apparently not taken seriously (and for young people it is so terribly important that they be taken seriously), that her beloved elder sister "did not understand" her. But Marie's was the power to decide and command, and so Thérèse obeyed, whether she felt that she was understood or not.

This same simple, tremendous obedience governed her entire life. On what it cost, her own account, so fulsome in some respects, so curt in others, does not waste a word. We can piece together only from the testimony of others the real extent of her "goodness", and the enormous achievement it represented in her childhood and youth, for all that it may have seemed so innocent and unimportant. It is obvious that the true danger of such a psychophysical condition consists in a tremendous egoism. The person suffering from his own nature, "overladen with himself", Henry Suso has put it, whose emotional constitution is a mass of sore spots, is just as much inclined to unrestrained exhibition of his griefs, to immoderate demands for consolation, patience, sympathy and consideration on the part of his fellow human beings, as he inclines to indifference towards the joys and sorrows of others, to stubborn evasion of all demands of duty and of his surroundings. He tends to be lenient towards himself, self-pitying, fecund in excuses for his failures, moody, depressing to all who must live with him. Given a psychological crisis, even the most mature adult will exhibit some of these reactions, the more so if this state lasts for years.

The sisters agree unanimously that during this period Thérèse showed not the slightest alteration in her "goodness", her conscientiousness and loving kindness. In school she continued to be "extremely punctual and regular". Her teachers noticed nothing at all—no slackening-off in her work, no moodiness, no ostentatious behaviour, though they were able to observe her all day long, since she was a day boarder. One teacher does remember that Thérèse, caught telling an answer to another pupil and reprimanded with the words "Thérèse is being naughty", burst into "unquenchable tears" and for two solid weeks was inconsolable. "Whenever she met me, she threw herself into my arms and began crying again, and sobbing: 'I did wrong and led others into sinning!'"[88] One teacher remarks that at the time she had "been tempted" to see in Thérèse's behaviour "exaggerated conscientiousness and the signs of an unstable and overscrupulous state of mind".[89] "In the midst of her physical and spiritual sufferings she was never rebellious or troublesome", the objective Léonie testifies.[90] "I suppose she cried easily, but never did she make the slightest resistance, the slightest fuss, about any request or assignment." "She got sick every winter, suffering from bronchitis with violent fever and shortness of breath. But she persisted without complaint in her ordinary routine until she could do so no longer, and resumed her duties as soon as the first signs of improvement appeared."[91] "She was often very sad, but she never complained", says Céline. "Her state of depression never, never in the slightest, kept her from performing the smallest duty. I myself [Céline was her inseparable companion during these years] in all this time never observed an outbreak of temperament, an uncontrolled word, a failure in virtue. She kept a grip on herself at every moment, and in the smallest things."[92]

In this severe trial Thérèse behaved basically exactly as she had during the uncanny illness and demonic temptation of her now passing childhood: she tasted the bitterness, ugliness, humiliation and discouragement of her state with every fibre of her nature. She could not turn to flight or retreat—who can escape from himself? She could not abridge this trial, could not deceive herself; she had to make her way through it. With the peculiar submissiveness of her helpless, exposed state, she had to "swallow" everything, suffer everything her own state did to her and imposed upon her. She had to cry and become agitated and disgrace herself, she

---

[88] I S., ii, 139.
[89] Ibid.
[90] I S., ii, 89.
[91] I S., xii, 1.
[92] I S., ii, 68.

had to be confused and wretched and inconsolable. She could not harden herself, could not brush everything aside, could not divert herself; neither humour nor defiance came to her aid. She could not medicate, as it were, her swollen and inflamed emotions. She was well aware of the painful change in her disposition, yet she could do nothing but accept it as a sick person must accept the rash spreading all over his body. The charm of her childhood had faded; "everything was obscured by diffidence and oversensitivity"; she thought herself, with some justification, "unbearable". Conscious of how troubled and troublesome she was, she became slow, inhibited, almost paralysed. She even gave the impression of being stupid and retarded. "Her teachers recognized her talent, but in the world she was considered awkward and incompetent. It is true that she gave ground for such opinions, since she said scarcely anything and always let others talk." With gentle chiding, kindly Uncle Guérin delivered the opinion that her conduct was a direct result of interrupted education, since for reasons of health Thérèse had to give up attending school.[93] How, with her ambition and her pronounced sense of the fitting, she must have felt such reproofs!

But all such manifestations are in fact no more than the distortions produced by a disease which the affected person "cannot help". At that time the foundation stone for Thérèse's "new doctrine" was probably laid, the doctrine of the Little Way, which meant a break with her contemporaries' theory of perfection. Thérèse learned by experience that all human efforts towards self-sanctification are highly questionable and in themselves impotent, given even the "strongest" of wills and the best of intentions; that all our running takes us nowhere, that nothing avails us but the grace of God. Reduced to its ultimate core, the child Thérèse experienced then, in child's measure, the same temptation as the monk Luther during his years in the cloister. Little Thérèse came out of this temptation with her "way of spiritual childhood". Ten years later she would be teaching her novices "to accept and *to love* our imperfections", not "to work to become saints, but to give joy to God",[94] to expect more from grace, the more we are aware of our own weakness and see it to be inescapable and ineradicable. She renounced completely the pasted-on mask of a conceptual ideal ego as well as the defiant posture of a sinner reconciled to his sinfulness. She boasted of her weakness like the Apostle, and sang the mercy of God who lifted this very weakness up to himself "as upon eagle's wings".

[93] I S., ii, 67.
[94] I S., ix, 21.

As yet, however, this solution was still far from Thérèse's mind; it did not yet even glimmer on the edges of her troubled consciousness.

So we see her passing through these dark years like any adolescent amid the tempests and crises of maturing—disharmonious and clumsy, foolish and a little silly, trying the patience of herself and others. But underneath all this wretchedness, like the seed under masses of snow and the storms of spring, the destined heart grew undeviatingly towards sanctity.

When Thérèse was thirteen her father decided to take her out of school at the Abbey because her scruples "ended by making me ill". The family probably hoped that Thérèse's emotional state as well as her health would improve if she lived entirely at home once more.

To "round off her education", as people put it in those days, she was given private lessons, which she describes with a touch of humour. Twice a week Papa himself accompanied her to a "highly respectable" lady. The rather curious lessons had a double aspect: "I learnt a lot from her while at the same time I came into close contact with the world." That is to say, the lessons took place "in her old-fashioned room" where the teacher's mother also sat and received a string of visitors. The pupil in the corner, "nose in my book", listened with one ear to the babble of conversation, which sometimes touched on the "lovely young girl" whose hair, they remarked, was "very beautiful". No doubt Thérèse heard a good deal of town gossip. On such days she "did not learn much". The flatteries did some good to her self-tormenting temperament, but at the same time they served as grounds for fresh scruples. Thérèse was no longer the little girl who could simply ignore people's praise of her because she received no such praise at home. She became concerned about her vanity when she realized how greedily she devoured all such signs of others' favour. She thought herself imperilled and in need of special protection and asked to join the Congregation of the Children of Mary at the Abbey. That meant spending two afternoons a week at her old school, in order to attend the prescribed meetings and conferences. This was hard for her, since she had rapidly become a stranger there since leaving the school. She had no friends at the Abbey, no teacher who was especially fond of her, and sat alone and silent through the afternoon, busy with some sewing. No one addressed a word to her or paid any attention to her. After the obligatory meeting she usually knelt alone in the chapel until her father came for her.

She suffered from this loneliness, but she was already coming to recognize that its source lay more in herself than in any unfriendliness on the part of others. "Here, in the silence, I found my one consolation:

Jesus, my only friend. I could not open my heart to anyone else; conversations with other people—even about heavenly things—seemed tedious." When her loneliness became too oppressive, she consoled herself with a verse from "a beautiful poem" her father was in the habit of reciting: "The world is but a ship, and not thy home."

In October of that year Marie entered Carmel, four years after Pauline. Thérèse must have harboured a child's blind hope that this long-impending event would somehow be postponed still longer, for the separation again struck her a sudden, annihilating blow. "As soon as I knew what she had decided to do, I cried just as I did when you [Pauline] went, and resolved that I would take no more interest in anything on earth." Marie had never been her *petite mère* like Pauline, but still she had been "my last support... who used to guide my soul". Above all Marie had given her invaluable support and aid in the protracted struggle with her scruples. Nor could any further substitute for Marie be found in the family. Léonie was already twenty-three, but she was remote from her youngest sister in all respects. Thérèse's intimate friendship with Céline did not begin until later; one gathers that the latter, a healthy, sturdy and high-spirited girl, did not know how to deal with the strange, confused character of her younger sister at this time. Father could not help at all; perhaps the sisters were already feeling it necessary to spare him all burdens.

In her distress Thérèse no longer dared to seek some asylum upon earth for her abandoned heart. Such asylums, she had learned by bitter experience, were always being lost again. With childlike trust, which nevertheless held the wisdom born of grief, she chose her four brothers and sisters who had died young to be her friends and protectors. Were they not closely related to her, and in Heaven, so that they could not be taken from her again? Out of all the sufferings of awakening maturity the indestructible child in Thérèse suddenly rose again. "I turned my attention to Heaven and had recourse to those four little angels who had gone on ahead. They never had had to bear scruples, so I thought they would be sure to take pity on their poor sister still suffering on the way. I used to talk to them with all the simplicity of a child, reminding them that I was the baby of the family, the one upon whom our parents and sisters had showered most love and tenderness, and that they would surely have done the same if they had stayed on earth. I could not see why they should forget all about me just because they had gone to Heaven. On the contrary, they could delve into divine treasures and could easily prove that one could still love up there by getting me some peace. I did not have long to wait for their answer! Peace soon filled my soul." The consciousness of being "loved, not only by those on earth, but by those in Heaven too", comforted her tormented spirit. "From that moment my love for my little brothers and sisters in Heaven grew deeper. I loved to talk to them about the miseries of exile and tell them how much I longed to join them in our eternal home."

The melancholy flagging of her will to live, her attitude of profound joylessness towards life, had therefore not been banished by this illumination, but rather intensified. It required, as Thérèse herself calls it, a "Little miracle" to bring about the healing of her soul.

6. LIBERATION AND BLOSSOMING

"Second conversion", which opens the way to the next higher stage of religious existence, is a commonplace in the classical theory of the dynamics of the inner life.

Religious development very seldom proceeds along a straight, gently rising and uninterrupted line. After a person has crossed a certain plane, he comes to a border, comes up against a wall. To enter the new segment of his way he must "jump" this wall or be carried over it. By "conversion" we generally mean only the first, fundamental "turning to God", the return from unbelief and sin to penitence and faith. And we tend to assume that this is all that is necessary. The linguistic usage obscures the fact that this "conversion" is only a beginning, though a crucial one; that a heart which has turned resolutely to God must constantly repeat, deepen, renew the decision. The earnestly striving Christian again and again enters periods of darkness and flagging faith when only a new impetus, a rending of the invisible cords that hold him fast, can save him from sliding back again into the "unconverted" life. The earnest Christian in particular constantly comes up against a boundary, finds that he has reached the limits of his previous religious experience and cannot simply continue straight on. His customary forms of faith, hope, love and prayer cease to serve, and he must seek new ways on which new depths of his own soul may open up, be plumbed and taken possession of.

"Now our salvation is nearer than when we came to believe." [95] The Scriptures plainly draw the stages in this growth of faith in the disciples of Jesus, from the first call and the first act of emulation to the achievement of "maturity in Christ" in the Pentecostal fulfilment through the Holy Spirit. [96]

Thérèse experienced the grace of her "complete conversion" on Christmas night, 1886.

---

[95] Rom 13:11.

[96] Cf. Garrigou-Lagrange, O.P., *Les trois Conversions et les trois Voies* (Éditions du Cerf), Juvisy, 1932.

The ostensible cause was so insignificant and almost ridiculous that in recounting the story we must be very careful not to enlarge upon it or ornament it unjustifiably. For here we see yet another instance of that essential trait of our saint: the ability to receive and to comprehend the divine in the banalities of everyday life.

Monsieur Martin had come home with his daughters after Midnight Mass. It was not French custom to have a Christmas tree or presents; the giving of gifts was reserved for January, New Year's Day or Epiphany. However, on Christmas night the children would find their shoes filled with sweets and little gifts. Thérèse was actually past the age for this, but in her case the elders could not give up this little festivity—"so you can see I was still treated as a baby", Thérèse comments. Perhaps Thérèse continued to place her shoes by the fireplace with a secret desire to please her father, for "Father used to love to see how happy I was and hear my cries of delight as I took each surprise packet from my magic shoes, and his pleasure made me happier still."

But this particular Christmas Father was cross for once, and while the girls were taking off their coats he said with audible irritation to Céline: "Thérèse ought to have outgrown all this sort of thing, and I hope this will be the last time." [97]

Céline knew her sister well enough to expect a torrent of tears of disappointment and injury. "Don't come down again just yet", she whispered to her; "you'll only cry if you open your presents now in front of Father." But "I was not the same Thérèse any more; Jesus had changed me completely." She held back her tears and tried to stop her heart from pounding. And, wonder of wonders, she *succeeded*. To her own amazement she ran down the stairs as if nothing had happened; laughing, she knelt by the fireplace and unwrapped her surprises as jubilantly as ever, "looking all the while as happy as a queen". Céline "thought she must have been dreaming".

That is all. Nothing more, and nothing less, had happened than the tiny jolt which breaks the wrapping of the bud and releases the blossom. It was as sudden, as radical, as irrevocable as almost all invisible, soul-stirring "miracles" of rebirth.

Thérèse instantly understood what had happened to her when she won this banal little "victory" over her sensitivity, which she had borne for so long as an inescapable yoke, as a law of her nature. She had been vouchsafed a freedom which all her efforts had been unable to win. A long, painful period of growth lasting almost ten years was now over; a task

---

[97] Such is the sisters' version. According to Thérèse's own account, the remark was even more trivial; her father merely said: "Fortunately, this will be the last year."

which had caused her infinite toil and agony had at last been completed. Ushered in by an utter triviality (behind which, nevertheless, stood divine grace), the transformation of a fairy tale took place; the spell was broken, the hideous mask fell away, revealing the beauty that had been secretly forming during the long years of servitude.

"The Divine Child, scarcely an hour old, flooded the darkness of my soul with radiant light." Thérèse had regained for ever the strength of mind she had lost at four and a half. "That glorious night the third period of my life began, the loveliest of all, and the one in which I received the most graces. In one moment Jesus, content with good will on my part, accomplished what I had been trying to do for years. I could have said what the Apostles said: 'Master, we have laboured all night and have taken nothing.' Jesus was even more merciful to me than to them, for He took the net in His own hands, cast it into the water, and pulled it out full of fishes, making me too a fisher of men. Charity took possession of my heart, making me forget myself and I have been happy ever since."

The whole of this section is a veritable hymn of joy and thanksgiving that can be fully understood only by one who has himself, in some fashion, experienced such an abrupt step out of darkness into light. Thérèse had learned a new lesson, added another foundation stone to the structure of her future "doctrine". There is no liberation, she had learned, in an attitude of rigid earnestness towards the ego with its vices and sorrows, nor is there any in the noblest intention to combat one's own bad impulses. Rather, freedom is found in resolutely looking away from oneself, in forgetting self and turning one's concern towards others. And the fact that a person can cast himself away from himself reveals again that being good, being able to be good, "victory", is pure grace, a sudden gift at the predestined hour. It cannot be coerced, and yet it can be received only by the patiently prepared heart.

Thérèse had now really found herself, found herself again. And what she found was the completion of her beginnings, of which we spoke at the outset. The "little queen" reappeared. Only now she was mature, grown-up, strengthened. Gaiety and an overflowing, outpouring love, warmth and clarity, a lighthanded ease, replaced the tormented tension of the will which had marked the outgrown stage. Her morbid sensitivity took flight as though an ugly boil had burst. "My tears were dried up at their source, and after that I hardly ever cried again. By becoming little and weak for love of me, He made me strong and full of courage, and with the arms He gave me, I went from one victory to another, and began to 'run as a giant'."

Her nature blossomed forth like a garden in springtime. Hitherto, the constant struggle with herself had filled her mind, had consumed the forces of her intellect and her heart in the wretched but necessary activity of sheer enduring. Now, with the burden thrown off, her repressed gifts, like rose-trees forced unnaturally to earth for the winter, shot up and sprouted mightily.

"Freed from my scruples and oversensitiveness, my mind grew. I had always loved everything noble and beautiful and now I had a great thirst for knowledge; not satisfied with what my governess was teaching me, I began to study other subjects by myself and learnt more in a few months than I had ever done at school." It is a pity that at the time she was writing down the story of her soul, she saw in this fine youthful urge nothing more than "vanity and vexation of spirit". From Céline we learn that the subjects she chose for herself were history and the natural sciences[98]—the two great passions of the late nineteenth century, a breath of which had even penetrated through the Chinese Wall erected by the *émigrés de l'intérieur*. In these studies alone young Thérèse inhaled for a moment the "spirit of the times". The family must have felt ill at ease about this, for Céline only mentions it in order to add immediately and zealously that Thérèse quelled her "too impetuous thirst for knowledge".[99] She was now permitted to determine her study timetable independently and assigned herself—as Marie had once done to repress her passion for reading—only a limited time for her favourite subjects. This she would not exceed.

Thérèse seems to have had so keen a gift for observation, and so genuine a joy in discovery and understanding, that we can only regret that she did not fall into the hands of a capable and sympathetic teacher at this time. In judging her writings we must never forget that she attended school only for five years, and that the "final polish" was restricted to that one year in the old-fashioned parlour where her teacher's mother entertained her friends. Her self-instruction, though practised with such enthusiasm, cannot have lasted even that long. In the convent she told her novices, making use of a vivid "practical application", how she had once been given a kaleidoscope, and had taken apart and studied the baffling toy with the skill and objectivity of a boy, until she discovered the principle of its construction. "I admired this object very much, and I

[98] I S., xiii.

[99] Cf. the remark of her pious biographer: "Only her craving for knowledge frequently outran the teacher's programme: *surely a dangerous disposition*, had not God concerned Himself for this young soul, who nevertheless saw Him as the end of all wisdom" (Laveille, 154).

wondered what could produce such a charming play of colours. One day, after examining it gravely, I saw that it was simply a few bits of paper and wool, cut up quite at random and mixed together. I went on with my investigation, and saw three mirrors in the inside of the tube. Then I had the key to the riddle. This has become for me the symbol of a great secret. As long as our actions, even the smallest of them, do not fall away from the focus of Divine Love, the Holy Trinity, symbolized by the three mirrors, allows them to reflect wonderful beauty. Jesus, who regards us through the little lens, that is to say, through Himself, always sees beauty in everything we do. But if we left the focus of inexpressible love, what would He see? Bits of straw... dirty, worthless actions." [100]

Pauline reports that once, when they were together in the convent, Thérèse had a conversation with her about marriage and told her that "by observation of plants and birds" she had independently, and without saying a word about it, obtained clear ideas about procreation. "But," she added, "it is not the knowledge of these things which is evil; God has made nothing that is not very good. Marriage is very beautiful for those called to it; only sin distorts and taints it." [101] When we consider how in that great age of prudery the whole realm of the sexual constituted a dire taboo for a young girl, how all curiosity in this direction was branded as in itself immoral, and how daughters were usually "enlightened" only shortly before marriage (and many not even then), this little confession betrays a considerable degree of intellectual boldness and honesty. She began writing verse and learned to paint.

Her new maturity affected not only the growth of her intellectual powers; it also transfigured her physical being. Her inner happiness made Thérèse lovely and radiant and restored to her the striking charm of her early childhood. The gaiety and overflowing spirits of that blessed period of her life also returned. Once again Thérèse became the "sunshine of the family". "She was amiable and kind; one felt good in her presence", Léonie testifies without envy. [102] "She was very clever, witty and full of fun; she had a special talent for imitating accurately the voice, intonation and manner of other persons; but never, so far as I know, did this little amusement degenerate into mockery; it never gave rise to the slightest unpleasantness. She knew exactly how far she might go, and kept these bounds with perfect tact." [103]

[100] *C. S.*, 286.
[101] I *S.*, xvi, 2.
[102] I *S.*, ii, 98.
[103] I *S.*, ii, 102.

Now once more the sunniness of her temperament struck people, instead of her former tearful irritability. Or rather, it was there without particularly attracting attention, for this unvarying serenity seemed natural and spontaneous, as if she could not be otherwise. "The consistency of happy disposition was so plain and *seemed* so natural", Léonie comments in the same place, "that one would have thought the continual self-conquest cost her nothing at all." This passage is important, for we can be as easily deceived as many of her contemporaries were. We must not forget that the new life still cost her "continual self-conquest". The conversion had not removed all her difficulties at one blow.

Many years later, shortly before her death, Thérèse was asked foolishly "whether she had ever known difficulties". She replied emphatically: "I certainly have! I have had to fight every day, every day of my life!" The elimination of morbid oversensitivity did not obliterate that natural sensitivity which was part of her character. Her nature had never been "easy"—for herself. Precisely at this time, when the old, strong spirit of her childhood awoke once more in all its spontaneity, when she was sure of herself, enterprising, directed outward, no longer hampered by shyness and anxiety—at this time it became by no means easy to continue in her unconditional, unquestioning submissiveness in all things great and small. Nevertheless, she did not change course.

Father Pichon of the Society of Jesus, friend and confessor of the Martin family for many years, and one of the priests to whom Thérèse opened her soul, expressly testifies: "She did everything her sisters asked with the greatest willingness, submitted in everything, even if it were only to moods; she herself had no moods, never expressed a wish, did all that was wanted. At the same time she was by no means a placid and dull person; rather, she was extremely lively and probably would have had her moods and special desires, if she had allowed herself to have them. Never did I see this child show vexation or ill humour." [104] "Her obedience, for ever serene, simple and without objections, especially struck me. Never did I see her resist, question or even hesitate over an order, a recommendation, or even an expressed wish on the part of her father or her sisters; and I always admired the ease, the charming grace, with which she was able to overcome herself in order to adjust herself to everyone and everything in her home." [105]

At this time it must have come hard for her to remain faithful to the "veil" she had once chosen and which she now understood in an ever-deepening sense; hard now that the veil was not a cloak of invisibility

[104] 2 S., 228.
[105] 1 S., ii, 125.

wrapped about herself, that its purpose was not only to hide griefs and defeats, but positive elements as well, the sparkle of a young, awakening personality. It means a great deal that we find Léonie saying: "She did not know what rich capacities of body and soul God had given her." Or: "She was very pretty, but she alone seemed not to be aware of it. In all the time we lived together at home I never saw her looking in the mirror." There can scarcely be any doubt that this was all deliberate on Thérèse's part. Her self-oblivious manner on which her sister's opinion was based was a conscious thing. Indeed, with more insight, the elder sister says elsewhere: "My sister Thérèse says in her autobiography that she was by nature proud; she controlled this disposition so well that without her having written it, it would never have occurred to me." [106]

"What particularly impressed me about this child was her simplicity, naturalness and innocence; ... it seemed especially remarkable to me in a girl of that age that she made absolutely nothing of herself, referred nothing to herself, sought in no way to make herself important, completely forgot herself, did not stress or display any of her many good points. She was shy and retiring and never thrust herself forward."

"She was very careful to let her sisters shine. One had to observe her closely to realize that she was very bright indeed. For a long time I was not aware that she possessed genuine talent for poetry. Her father and her sisters would have been most eager to bring her out and place her in the limelight, but she carefully arranged always to be noticed as little as possible." This is again Father Pichon. [107]

This grace, this ethereal effortlessness with which, henceforth, she was to master all the difficulties of her character and temperament, the "veil of the smile", is Thérèse's own special note as a saint. She knew too, in retrospect, that it was a new element which had come to birth since her conversion. But she never mentioned—if indeed she knew—that it was simultaneously the fruit, ripened at long last, of unending effort. "Until my fourteenth year I practised virtue without finding consolation in it. ... Now the practice of virtue became attractive, and seemed to come more naturally. At first, my face often betrayed my inward struggle but little by little sacrifice, even at the first moment, became easier; Our Lord promised that 'to everyone that hath shall be given, and he shall abound,' and every time I made good use of any grace, He gave me many more."

The liberation of conscience showed most deeply and richly in liberation of the heart. "Charity took possession of my heart." Thérèse had had "a loving heart from youth on", in the phrase of Henry Suso. We are

[106] 1 *S.*, xvii, 33–34.
[107] 1 *S.*, ii; 2 *S.*, 229.

already familiar with her excessively tender attachment to her parents and sisters. The other members of the household also received a share of her love. Marceline Husé tells of entering service in the Guérin family when she was only thirteen. Someone informed little Thérèse that the new maid was homesick, and the seven-year-old child "made it her special task to console me by all possible signs of affection".[108]

Léonie, so often slighted and hence sensitively observant, stresses that Thérèse "exercised the most tactful care not to embarrass or sadden anyone. I was able to observe this trait in connection with something that concerned me very personally. I was at that time twenty-three years old, but extremely behind in spelling and other subjects because I had always had great difficulty in learning. Thérèse was ten years younger than myself and went to the greatest pains to help me fill these gaps in my education. Even at that time I admired the tact with which she did this for me without embarrassing me in any way, and with the most unlimited patience." [109]

Marceline tells of a walk with Thérèse at the time of her First Communion. They passed some workers whom they heard swearing blasphemously. The child instantly excused the men and spiritedly explained to the young maid that they could not look into the hearts of these people and therefore had no right to judge them; moreover: "They have received far fewer graces than we and are unfortunate rather than guilty." [110]

Like every good child, she was eager to give to the poor, and she was early trained to do so. Her father and sisters preferred to have her give the alms for them. When Thérèse was six years old, she met a poor old man on crutches while out on a walk with her father. She thought him a beggar and asked her father for something to give him. But the old man shook his head with a sad, wry smile, refusing to take the proffered coin. Thérèse wanted to offer him her cake, but she did not dare, for fear of offending him again. This encounter affected her so deeply that she resolved on the day of her First Communion to offer special prayers for the unknown man, because she had heard that all requests on that day were granted. Nor did she forget—a full five years later!

Now this good, carefully nurtured disposition was strengthened.

The members of the household were conscious of the warmth that radiated from her. "The servants, too, were fond of her because everything about her was peace, goodness and friendliness", Léonie says. In an age of blunt class feeling, when in general employers scarcely troubled

[108] I S., x, 62.
[109] I S., ii, 102.
[110] I S., ii, 110.

their heads over the inner life of the servant class, the following little item shows keen and sympathetic insight: "I felt very sorry for the servants who had to wait upon us at large parties. If they ever had the misfortune to do something awkward, I saw the mistress of the house turn a stern, condemning look upon them, while the poor folk blushed with shame. And I thought: How the difference that exists here on earth between masters and servants proves that there is a Heaven in which each receives his place according to his inner value, where we may all sit at the banquet of the Master. And what a Servant will wait upon us then, since Jesus Himself has said that He will 'go among us and will serve us'. That will be the moment for the poor and the little folk to be rewarded in more than due measure for all humiliations." [111]

Now something else was added to this simple natural kindliness and goodwill: the religious love of men which includes not only our neighbours, those who think like us, and the "good", but also strangers, the remote and the wicked. Writing of her Christmas grace Thérèse noted that Jesus made her "a fisher of men". She discovered her "spiritual zeal".

This phrase, too, is somewhat embarrassing to our modern sensibility. Spiritual zeal is not the same as the craving to rule and direct the consciences of others. It is not the nobler impulse of spiritual sympathy which leads one to perform certain works of mercy. It is not the pedagogical nor the pastoral impulse to teach, to improve and to cure, which springs from insight into the wretchedness of spiritual poverty. The particular form of Christian charity we mean here makes use of these pure and strong natural inclinations, but it is different from them. It is by no means allied to the attitude of the Pharisee who prays: "I thank thee, God, that I am not like the rest of men" and then proceeds, with a consciousness of superiority, to toss a few crumbs of virtue, cleverness and ability to the dogs under the table. The person inspired by spiritual zeal has little or no desire to proselytize or be a propagandist. He does not desire the conquest and subjugation of others and the strengthening of his own party. He does not take growth in power and sheer numbers as his supreme concern. For that is purely political zeal, though in a good cause, and the "converts" are not personally important; they are mere "material", mere instruments and auxiliary troops. Such an attitude has nothing in common with the salvation of souls, with the love of the servants of God. Spiritual zeal is nothing less than cooperation with the saving love of Christ for man.

Saving love: that is to say, this love regards man as endangered, exposed, as dwelling on the brink of doom; it deals with man as a "sinner". The

---

[111] *N.V.*, 8 August.

zealous person has been reproached for this very attitude, as though it were offensive arrogance to consider one's neighbour in this light. But the reproach is valid only when such a person actually forgets to include himself in this category of the distressed and the endangered, under the formula "We poor sinners". If his attitude is not a deprecatory verdict on "the others", but rather acknowledgment of the situation of all humanity, then this phrase means no more than the simple and incontestable fact, known to every Christian, that before God man is in a fallen state, and that his salvation or damnation is an uncertain and fearsome matter. Saving love affects not so much the how and what a person is, but what can betide him. Its fires are nourished by contemplation of the Ultimates: Death, Judgment, Heaven and Hell. In the face of the frightful and inescapable gravity of these things, much else fades to naught. While merciful love contemplates and aids man "on the way", in his manifold troubles, needs and desires, saving love regards only his final destination. Whether a given man knows his destination and prepares for it—this is the sole question asked by saving love. Apostolic zeal is, properly, an attitude of exclusive and unconditional fervour; for that reason it may so easily seem one-sided, primitive and even fanatical; for that reason these shortcomings are so often closely associated with it. But how can anyone who beholds himself and his brothers for ever drifting in a feeble boat on the ocean of eternity be polite, pleasant and ready for a thousand pastimes? Zeal is not indifference to ordinary human life—though that is the charge brought against it. It is an anxious love which is willing to stake everything in order to save. It sees man not only as the most burdened and imperilled being in Creation, but also as the most precious. The person inspired by spiritual zeal is concerned with souls above all. He remembers at all times the immortal, eternally valid being in every man, and this is more important to him than all the visible aspects of the man. To be sure, it is significant of certain periods that the term "soul" was understood primarily in a negative sense, as a protest against the value and meaning of man's physical being and everything involved with it. That was because a highly unchristian, time-bound, materialistic misconception of the body was joined to the Christian view of the soul—as though the word "temple of God" had never been spoken, as though there were no eleventh article of the Creed, as though the destiny of man's body were not to be resurrected in glory and conformed to the body of the King of Glory. And as though a man could save or lose his or another's soul without the body's participating in the same eternal destiny!

This second part of the One Truth was veiled from the eyes of believers of the late nineteenth century; it did not even enter their field of vision. But these believers understood profoundly the breathtaking reality of the "soul" and responded with a "zeal" for which we can have nothing but respect. (And we may ask ourselves what right we have to criticize such zeal so long as we only point out its inadequate premises and misguided methods, while doing nothing ourselves for the cause we recognize as so essential.)

The Christian, who has been made cognizant of man's ultimate end as either salvation or damnation, learns not only from contemplation of man's being and destiny, not only from the "last things", but above all from the figure of his Lord who came to seek and redeem what was lost. "His" Christ is the Good Shepherd who searches for the lost sheep until He finds it; He is the Master of the Apostles, who made them fishers of men; the Friend of the publicans and prostitutes, who was sent not to the just but to the sinners, not to the well but to the sick; He who called for the millstone upon the neck of the Tempter and wept over Jerusalem.

Above all, however, saving love lives by the sight of the Crucified Lord.

The bitter suffering and death of Jesus is to the Christian not only the measure of the value that God places on the sinner—"God so loved the world that He gave up His only-begotten Son so that the world might find salvation through Him"—but the measure also of man's forlornness, and of the urgency of the danger which made needful such a way of salvation.

Hence there is a deep correspondence between zeal and that devotion which re-lives the Lord's Passion. As the latter grows, so proportionately does the former. The Christian who has grasped the reality of the "Precious Blood" is fervently anxious that the sufferings of the Saviour on the Cross will not be lost on any of us. Out of dual concern for man and for the price that was paid to redeem him there grows that impetuous, restless love which filled the Apostles, driving them on from act to act. In the saints who embody that concern, it takes two basic forms; some direct that zeal more to the "honour of God", others to the "salvation of man"; but in both forms the coming of the Kingdom of God is sought.

Young Thérèse came within the spell of this mighty fire as soon as God, as she says, "lifted me out of my narrow world".

One Sunday, as she was closing her Missal, a picture of the Crucifixion slipped out from between the pages, just enough to expose a pierced and bleeding hand. A strange new emotion swept over Thérèse: the mysterious initiation into the reality of the "bitter Passion" which according to the testimony of all spiritual teachers is the door to a deeper realization of the Christian life. With a pang she realized the terrible fact that Christ's sacrifice is rejected and forgotten by innumerable souls. "It pierced my

heart with sorrow to see His Precious Blood falling, with no one both-
ering to catch it, and I made up my mind, there and then, to stay in
spirit at the foot of the Cross, to gather up the dew of heavenly life and
give it to others."

Thus she expresses her new experience in the traditional, thoroughly
worn-out bombastic metaphors of her devotional books. But how can
this be spoken of, if not in metaphors? Are not these images, in spite of
their crudeness, the most reverent clothing for inexpressible realities?

"The cry of Jesus as He died, 'I thirst', echoed every moment in my
soul, inflaming my heart with burning love. I longed to satisfy His thirst
for souls; I was consumed myself with this same thirst, and yearned to
save them from the everlasting fires of Hell, no matter what the cost."

A new mystery of infinite significance dawned upon her, one with
which she had indeed been familiar since her childhood, when Pauline
would suggest that she renounce a drink of water "for a sinner". But
now she grasped its vital meaning for the first time: that the Christian
really and truly can save souls, in conjunction with Christ. Certainly he
cannot do this through his own power, by mere instruction or example;
but he can help to carry out the redemptive work of his Lord, by intercessory prayers, love and suffering "in the name of Jesus".

Thérèse soon learned how real and effective her new impulse was. In
June 1887 a criminal case of more than usual horror was filling the imagination of newspaper readers: the "Pranzini case". An Italian—a habitual
criminal, thief, receiver of stolen goods and procurer—had committed in
Paris a sensational robbery and triple murder of a lady, her maid and a
child. He was caught in Marseilles trying to sell the jewels he had stolen
and was condemned to death. The newspapers reported that he waited
for his execution in obstinate cynicism, rejecting all efforts on the part of
the prison priest.

Naturally the daughters of the Martin family were not allowed to read
the newspapers, not even the clerical and royalist *Croix* to which their
father subscribed. Nevertheless, the Pranzini case was discussed even at
table, and probably also in her teacher's parlour, where the lively conversation used to disturb her studies.

From her father's sombre remarks and from the general sensational whisperings about the famous criminal, who also seems to have been a Don
Juan of the lowest and most corrupt sort, Thérèse grasped only one key
fact: here was an incredibly guilty human being facing death and judgment, a man who was in absolute peril of Hell, a person upon whom the
Blood of the Lord was wasted if he died unrepentant. As though he were
the first and only person in the world to be in such sore straits, Thérèse
threw her own heart into the scales. "I longed to save him from this final

tragedy." Love which asks not the natural worth of the other, but evaluates him only by the price that has been paid for him, turned for the first time towards a particular "poor sinner". For the first time Thérèse tested the power conceded by God to those who knock; for the first time she ventured, with the boldness of childhood, an unconditional appeal to the Pure Mercy which is capable of all things. "But though I did use every spiritual means in my power", she writes—these will have been the traditional means of prayer, fasting and good works—"I knew that by myself there was nothing I could do to ransom him; and so I offered for him Our Lord's infinite merits and all the treasures of the Church. Needless to say, deep down in my heart I was sure that he would be reprieved, but I wanted some encouragement to go on in my search for souls, so I said very simply: 'My God, I am sure You are going to forgive this wretched Pranzini, and I have so much confidence in Your mercy that I shall go on being sure even though he does not go to confession, or show any sign at all of being sorry; but because he is *my first sinner*, please give me just one sign to let me know.' He answered me to the letter."

Thérèse did not feel that she was being disobedient when, henceforth, she looked in the newspaper for the items on Pranzini. The execution approached, but there was no word of any change of heart on the part of the criminal. On the morning after the execution, Thérèse unfolded the newspaper with pounding heart and skimmed rapidly through the repulsively copious description of the horrible process. On the very scaffold the murderer had rejected the priest; then, strapped to the board, when the executioner's assistant was already holding him by the hair, he "asked the priest for the crucifix and kissed it three times".

Eyes filled with tears of overwhelming emotion and gratitude, Thérèse ran to her room. She never forgot her "first sinner", her "first-born" as she sometimes would say. With characteristic faithfulness she asked permission, while in Carmel, to offer Masses for him when her relations would donate money for Masses.

"It had been the sight of the blood flowing from the Sacred Wounds that had given me my thirst for souls. I had wanted to give them His Precious Blood to drink and to wash their sins away, and here was my 'first-born' pressing his lips to His wounds. What a wonderful answer! After this, my desire to save souls grew day by day. Our Lord seemed to be whispering to me, 'Give Me to drink', as He did to the woman of Samaria.... But the more I gave Him to drink, the greater grew the thirst in my poor little soul, and I felt this burning thirst as the sweetest of rewards."

There was nothing warped about this zeal, no shadow of that morbid mania in many decorous people to sniff about in the sins of others, and in general in the filthier gutters of life, with rank curiosity and an un-mistakably pleasurable shudder. With equal sympathy and joyousness, Thérèse turned her attention upon unsensational innocent things. She had always liked visiting the poor; now she added spiritual alms to her material gifts. Shy as she was, she tried to strike up conversation with workmen who came to the house, in order to have the chance to say a word to them about God. An unbelieving woman worked for the Mar-tins by the day, perhaps in the laundry or the garden. Thérèse, reports Céline, could obtain nothing from her but a promise to wear a medal of Our Lady around her neck. Happy that she had won this much from the woman, Thérèse took her own medal from its chain to give it to her. One wonders whether, after she had complied with this whim of the pretty and friendly daughter of the household, the woman ever gave the matter an-other thought. Such youthful missionary efforts, supported by no knowl-edge of psychology or experience of life, are scarcely likely to have made any very deep impression. But they did serve to nourish Thérèse's own zeal.

With children she had more luck. Theirs was a world to which she had the key. "Children delighted Thérèse's whole heart", Léonie declares.[112] "Never will I forget her angelic smile, and the caresses she lavished, es-pecially, upon poor children. These were her favourites, and she missed no opportunity to tell them about God; at the same time she suited every-thing she said, with charming grace and presence of mind, to the level of their understanding. I must add that no matter how neglected or dirty such children were, she was not thereby inclined to be more cautious or sparing in her kindnesses and caresses. Since she also had a distinct pref-erence for beauty, and kept herself very clean and neat, this devotion in her dealings with the poor can only have sprung from solid virtue."

So the unfamed sister speaks. And behind her praise of the youngest sister's virtue is hidden the fact that Léonie herself at this time not only cared for children, but tended a sick, utterly neglected old woman, cleansed her bed of vermin, provided her with her own linen, washed the body herself when the woman died, and conducted her to the grave. What a tale the family would have made of such a work of mercy by any other of the sisters. But in connection with Léonie no one thinks to mention it, and even Thérèse completely ignores this example of her elder sister.[113]

In *The Story of a Soul* Thérèse herself recalls with particular pleasure two little girls, less than six years old, whom she looked after while their mother was ill. "It was at this time that Our Lord gave me the consola-tion of a deeper understanding of a child's soul. . . . It was a real joy to see

[112] S., ii, 104.
[113] Obituary letter, 1941.

the way they believed everything I told them.... Innocent souls like these, I thought, were like soft wax, ready for any impression, evil ones, unfortunately, as well as good. I understood what Jesus meant when He said: 'It were better to be thrown into the sea than to scandalize one of these little ones.'"

We can feel in this and the following sentences her growing preoccupation with the significance of religious education—perhaps also the possibility of her own choice of a vocation.

"How many souls might reach a high degree of sanctity if properly directed from the first. I know God can sanctify souls without help, but just as He gives the gardener the skill to tend rare and delicate plants while fertilizing them Himself, so He wishes to use others in His cultivation of souls. What would happen if the gardener were so clumsy that he could not graft his trees properly, or knew so little about them that he wanted to make a peach tree bear roses?"

Reflecting on childhood, she records a personal recollection which vividly evokes the bright, freshly observant child of those years: "This reminds me that among my birds I had a canary which used to sing exquisitely, and a young linnet of which I took very special care, having adopted it from its nest. Poor little captive, deprived of its singing lessons and hearing only the joyful trilling of the canary from morning to night, it tried one day to follow his example; no easy thing for a linnet to do! It was delightful to watch the efforts of the poor thing whose soft voice was not made for the vibrant notes of its master, though much to my surprise, it did succeed and began to sing exactly like the canary. You know who taught me to sing when I was young, Mother, and whose voice enchanted me."

7. DECISION

In the language of the *émigrés de l'intérieur* and their successors, "choice of vocation" for girls could mean nothing but the decision between marriage and the convent. In Thérèse's youth no other possibilities were considered; moreover, even here freedom scarcely existed, since the selection of a husband depended more upon the parents than upon the girl.

It is difficult for us to realize today how naturally these groups who bore so deeply the impress of piety took it for granted that every Catholic girl had only these alternatives, yet imagined that she actually had a "choice" to make, a rational decision by a girl between sixteen and twenty which would fix the course of her whole future life.

In this connection the story of Thérèse's eldest sister, Marie, is highly instructive. In spite of personal piety and her convent education, this dry, strong-minded girl had long had a distinct disinclination towards the religious life. But long before Marie Martin herself showed the slightest desire to enter the convent, her Carmelite sister as well as her confessor "worked on her" in all sincerity to bring her to make the decision. She yielded finally, as she might equally have yielded to the impetuous and determined wooing of some suitor: without any especial interest, certainly without enthusiasm, almost without emotion, simply in the belief that her confessor was proclaiming the will of God, and in her readiness to obey that will unconditionally.

With Thérèse the case was different. We will recall that when she was only nine, when Pauline entered the convent, she had felt inner certainty that she was destined to share the lot of her beloved sister. Given the utter radicality of her love of God, the only possible decision was to give herself entirely to God for ever. The conception that such devotion could also be manifested "in the world" was and remained unknown to her. In this she was wholly the child of her time—and wholly a child; untouched by any experience of her own, she simply repeated credulously what had been taught her by the important persons around her, and what was "in the air" in the pious circles to which her family belonged. It is remarkable that the life of their own parents was not felt, by any of the daughters, to be a model worth following; probably their mother's urgent desire to see them all in the convent—a desire which the elder sisters remembered and which the father must frequently have repeated—obscured the example she herself had set. Thérèse never had the chance to broaden her conception of "Christians in the world" beyond the pattern which had been handed down to her; in this respect she remained permanently at the stage of a pious adolescent of her era. It is therefore all the more remarkable that she was the first since Francis de Sales, the first in three hundred years, that is, to show a "way of perfection" that could be followed by the layman.

Nevertheless, it seems as if Thérèse in this significant year 1887 for the first time had a glimmering that "the world" might not be merely what she had been taught: a sink of corruption, a snare and a delusion for the unfortunate soul, an outlying field of the Church, a reservoir of transitory and illusory sham values. It is as though she had sensed that the created world were after all greater and more glorious than the limited circle of the "pious life", and perhaps not so altogether unworthy of its Creator. Certainly no wish to take possession of these unexpected splendours arose in her. But she did feel a certain nostalgia which she energetically and consciously rejected as a temptation. How else can we understand the curious phrase with which she concludes her account of her mental and spiritual awakening: "As I was so impetuous this was *a very dangerous moment* in my life."

That is all she says—she who can give such a fulsome account of the smallest temptations inside the convent. But it is one of the peculiarities of her book that she speaks of little things and is silent about big ones—not because she confused their importance, but because she made a careful selection of what she wished to bring to the fore.

The great danger she alludes to can, in the context, mean nothing less than that her rejection of the world, her indifference to "earthly" things, and even her melancholy longing to be free of them, was being shaken by her dawning insight into the unsuspected glories of the created world. Hitherto she had taken for granted that she wanted no part in the world. Such an attitude, moreover, corresponded with her temperament. But now: "I had always loved everything noble and beautiful and now I had a great thirst for knowledge." She was too honest, too direct in her responses, to disregard these new impressions. No stubborn negation would help her here—only a more intense affirmation of a deepened attachment to God.

Thus that remarkable sentence about her "dangerous moment" continues expressly: "*But* God had fulfilled in me that prophecy of Ezekiel." And there follows, with a truly amazing, almost medieval ingenuousness the passage in which the prophet speaks of the choosing, the glory and the unfaithfulness of Jerusalem in the image of the young beauty whom the king raises from lowliness and adorns: "Behold, he saw that the time for love had come for me; he swore to me and entered into a covenant with me and I became his. He spread his garment over me and washed me with water and anointed me with oil. He clothed me with fine garments and put a chain about my neck. He fed me fine flour and honey and oil. Then I was made exceedingly beautiful in his eyes, and was advanced to be a queen."

"This is just what Jesus has done for me, and I could apply every single word to myself", Thérèse stresses. But she contents herself with explaining what "fine flour, honey and oil" mean to her—the books which nourished her soul during this critical period. Her "fine flour" was the *Imitation of Christ* of Thomas à Kempis, "the only book which did me any good, because I had not yet discovered the hidden treasures of the Gospels". Not until after she entered the convent did she begin to read the Scriptures. The *Imitation*, however, she always had with her; she knew every word of it by heart—Thérèse, for whom memorizing had always been a trial in school! "Much to everybody's amusement... my aunt would often open it at random and make me say by heart the first chapter she came to." This preference is indicative of the essential sobriety of Thérèse's piety, even at that period of extreme enthusiasm. Thomas à Kempis is, in form and content, distinctly the wisdom of age, the last harvest of a wholly matured and tranquillized soul, one that has outgrown all fantasy and brooding, all dreaming and deception. This wisdom become simplicity created for itself a language so gentle and economical, so careful and precise, that as a rule young people, beginners, are disappointed and imagine they are reading platitudes and truisms.

She received "honey and oil", however, from another book, the only one she mentions besides Thomas à Kempis: lectures by an Abbé Arminjon on *The End of This World, and the Mysteries of the World to Come*. It is a book that forms a startling contrast to the "fine flour" of the *Imitation*.

In a footnote to his volume of letters (no. 186), Abbé Combes supplies a table of contents of this book, which can no longer be located—so we learn from all the works on Thérèse we have consulted. From the biographical point of view, this is a regrettable loss. For the influence this book exercised upon Thérèse in that crucial year of her spiritual growth seems to have been enormous. The nuns of the Carmel of Lisieux had lent the book to Thérèse's father. Thérèse, "contrary to my usual custom, for I was not in the habit of reading Papa's books",[114] asked permission to look at it. "The reading of this book likewise became one of the greatest graces in my life."

Ten years later she still recalled vividly how she "read it sitting at the window of my schoolroom", and "the impression it made upon me was too sweet for me to describe.... All the great truths of religion, the secrets of eternity, gave me a joy which was no longer of this earth."

We know that there is a special "providence of books" which in the most astonishing fashion brings to each of us the right book at the right moment (for every book that is important to us has its own moment). We know, too, that the period of intellectual awakening has its own laws in regard to discovery and stimulation. The substance is slumbering in the maturing mind itself; one's reading often acts only as an initial spark. A good many of us owe to a sentence or a picture in a wholly unimportant or even stupid book a decisive impulse which spiritual and secular classics have failed to give us—the impulse which enables us to force open the door to treasures that nourish us long after the initial impetus has been forgotten.

Perhaps this is what took place between Thérèse and that vanished volume of sermons which seems to have made so little impression on her contemporaries that it was never reprinted or even thought worthy of preservation in a library, not even one of those monastic libraries which continue to grant shelf-room to the dustiest of didactic works.

[114] *M.A.*

Perhaps this was not a contemporary book at all. It may have been a relic of an earlier generation, spume from the subsided wave of Romanticism. To the grown-ups in Thérèse's milieu it may have seemed strange and indigestible, queer and overcharged, to be lent only with discretion to such firm believers as Louis Martin, to whom it could do no harm.

The chapters were as follows: "1. On the End of the World and the Forewarning Signs. 2. Persecutions by the Antichrist and the Conversion of the Jews. 3. On the Resurrection of the Body and the Universal Judgment. 4. Of the Place of Immortality and the State of Transfigured Bodies. 5. Of Purgatorial Fire. 6. Of the Eternity of Punishment and the End Awaiting Evil. 7. Of Eternal Bliss and the Supernatural Vision. 8. The Christian Sacrifice, Means of Redemption. 9. *Of the Secret of Suffering in Its Relations to the Life to Come*" [our italics].

The eighties of the last century [the nineteenth] looked askance at eschatology and apocalyptic visions. Léon Bloy was still an unknown and isolated figure, and when he spoke of such things his voice went unregarded like the blabber of a madman. His books would never have entered such houses as the Martin family's. Such subjects were as remote and taboo to the end of the century as they had been close and exciting to its beginning. They were now thrust under the surface, were held more or less in distrust by strict theologians, and espoused only in such circles as went in for voices, visions, apparitions and prophecies, small groups of brooders and dreamers, rather than the solidly orthodox bourgeois. One wonders how such a book happened to find its way into the Carmel at Lisieux.

That such a table of contents would have appealed strongly to the imagination of fourteen-year-old Thérèse is certainly understandable. But it led her much farther than the novels of chivalry which were so dear to her. How strangely this sort of thing compares with the Martin household's sober, practical, daylight Catholicism which ran firmly in well-worn grooves and was benevolently supervised by so many religious.

But Thérèse felt highly stimulated by the book. Perhaps this was her first and last encounter with a deeper and more powerful level of the Christian faith than the one in which she lived. We suspect that this book guided her spiritual way to an extent greater than we can ever positively know unless a copy can somehow be obtained. So impressed was she that she copied out lengthy passages and tucked these notes into the spiritual handbooks she most used. Two such notes have come down to us by lucky chance. Marcel Moré quotes them in his essay.[115]

---

[115] See Bibliography (II, 15).

"The man who has been ignited by the flame of Divine Love is as indifferent to fame and shame as if he lived alone and without witnesses upon earth. He despises temptations. He cares no more about suffering than if it were being endured by flesh other than his own. What is full of sweetness for the world holds not the slightest charm for him. He is no more susceptible to the onset of attachment to creatures than sevenfold purified gold is susceptible to rust. Such are the effects of divine love, even upon this earth, when it truly takes possession of a soul."

This is nothing but a condensation of the general ascetic doctrine of perfectionism—with perhaps a perceptible leaning towards stoicism. Or can the thinking of Abbé Arminjon have been somewhat coloured by the Eastern Christian doctrine of *apatheia*, the detachment experienced by sages and saints, just as other of his themes may show the influence of the German Pietists, who were so strongly concerned with eschatology?

The second note contains a view which we will instantly recognize as central to Thérèse's piety in later years. It describes God's greeting to the Blessed in Heaven: "Now it is My turn! Can I respond to the gift which the saints have made to Me other than by giving Myself now, without limit or measure? . . . Yes, it must be so: I am now the soul of their soul. I must penetrate them with My blessedness as fire penetrates iron. . . . I must show Myself to their spirit cloudlessly, unveiled, without the medium of the senses, must unite Myself with them face to face. Thus it must be, that My glory illuminate them, that it break forth and radiate from all the pores of their being, that they recognize Me as I recognize them, that they become as gods."

We may say without exaggeration that this quotation represents the principal content of Thérèse's spiritual doctrine of suffering and bliss. Here it is in a nutshell. All her life, especially in her letters, she would repeat these ideas, sometimes giving them this very wording, sometimes varying it. God Himself, not any goods or joys, will be the essential reward of the blessed, she would maintain. She would see bliss as overflowing grace, not as something to be earned; she would see it as beyond all earthly exigences and nevertheless springing forth from earthly existence. Above all, would not her thoughts almost constantly revolve about "the secret of suffering in its relations to the life to come"? Certainly she mentions Arminjon only very rarely—but then Thérèse was not given to quotation.[116] She had not the slightest historical interest in the sources of her

---

[116] In Letter 186 Thérèse advises Céline to lend this book, as a kind of panacea, to an acquaintance for whose salvation they were both concerned. (Incidentally, with an access of feminine craft as amusing as it is revealing, she gives Céline precise instructions on how to get the book into the young woman's hands without the knowledge of her husband or her aunt and without any recommendation, apparently by sheer chance.)

insights; whatever she took in, she assimilated so completely that henceforth she could bring it forth as her own. This fact has undoubtedly contributed a good deal to the widespread legend of her being directly inspired by Heaven. Moreover, Thérèse's frequently expressed expectation of an unprecedented persecution of Christians, which would permit her the grace of martyrdom, probably stems from this same source. Perhaps, too, it is responsible for the Christmas play, cited in detail by Moré, which she composed at Christmas 1894 for the convent community. In it the Child Jesus appears among angels; the Angel of Judgment calls for the day of vengeance and the impending annihilation of the impure world of fire. The Child Jesus, however, proves to be the herald of peace and reconciliation: Have not the devout and the faithful daily consoled Him by their simple glances of love for the blasphemies of the unbelievers? Is it not right for them to be glorious in their heavenly home now—"will I not make gods of them?"

This too may well show the direct influence of Abbé Arminjon—not only the last sentence, but the entire playlet.

She now embraced the religious life with an extraordinary degree of passion, even more intense than at the time of her First Communion. This was the familiar state which the teachers of mysticism call "consolation"; later on she was to become more familiar with the antithesis of that state, "desolation", or "spiritual night". Now she experienced what Willibrord Verkade in his *Unruhe zu Gott* has called *"infatuation towards the Divine"*.

This experience which lasted for months was counterpoise enough to the "magic of the world" of which she was beginning to be conscious; although it could not stamp out the attraction entirely, it far outweighed it. Thérèse herself speaks of being made "oblivious of everything on earth" by the "sparks which He scattered in our souls". *Our*, because since that Christmas night Céline had become her close friend and confidante again, as in their early childhood. Jesus, she says, had "bound our hearts together with ties far stronger than those of blood, and made us sisters in spirit too". The constant exchange of similar feelings and attitudes between young people can intensify their mutual enthusiasms. Thus, evening after evening, the two girls now sat in their father's belvedere, contemplating the starry heavens, talking of spiritual things and dreaming of the future.

For Thérèse, then, the "choice of vocation" was only a choice among various forms of convent life. To be sure, since early childhood she had clung to the idea of entering the Carmel. But this dream of "the desert in which God wished to hide me" had sprung up during the period when she was "under a cloud", when her whole nature craved solitude, concealment, even flight. The beginning of a new phase in her life, one full of energy and boldness, her sudden vision of new, limitless possibilities of "conquests for God", called into question the unconditional validity of the contemplative ideal.

The "thirst for souls" was not the centre of Thérèse's life; that was clear. But were there not innumerable ways to save souls? We will recall Thérèse's strong concern, during this period, with the importance of religious education, her growing love for children. Even in the convent she had a deep and never fulfilled longing to tend the sick. Petitot reports a significant fact: "On the journey to Rome a fellow traveller lent Thérèse the magazine of a Missionary Order. She took the magazine with great delight, but then gave it to her sister, saying: 'I don't want to read it, because I have *too wild* a longing to be a missionary. What would happen if I were to feed it by such pictures! I want to be a Carmelite, after all!'" [117]

Sometimes she revolved still other daring plans. She had somehow learned of the existence of "fallen women", girls who lived by indescribable, inconceivable sinning, the lowest of lost souls, the dregs of humanity according to the standards of middle-class morality; and she had learned also of institutions which would take in such persons if they wished to escape their lives of vice. Thérèse seriously played with the thought of smuggling herself secretly into some such institution (what would her family have said!) in order to live, unknown and despised, among the poor "penitents". To all appearances one of them, she would "tell them about the mercy of God". Even the priest of the institution would never learn of her innocence: "I would have told him that before entering I had made a general confession, and had been forbidden to repeat it." [118]

"I did not dare talk about my inmost feelings at that time. My way was so straight and obvious that I did not feel I needed any other guide but Jesus. I thought of spiritual directors as mirrors which faithfully reflect Our Lord for others, but in my case He did not have to use such a medium; He could act directly."

Céline eagerly confirms these recollections of Thérèse, with the clear intention of showing that her sister was the beneficiary of special illumination and closeness to God: "She knew so exactly what she had to do that she had no need of asking anyone." [119] According to the prevailing convention in those pious circles, for whom the confessor stood as an almost overpowering representative of the Holy Spirit, it might

---

[117] Petitot, 134.
[118] *C. S.*, 261.
[119] 2 *S.*, 205.

have seemed an unwonted and possibly dangerous sign of independence that so devout a girl as Thérèse had no actual *directeur*. Most persons had such a permanent spiritual guide to whom they regularly reported, laid bare their souls, and tendered unconditional obedience. But let us not forget that precisely this sort of relationship linked Thérèse with Pauline. She saw her sister every week or two; their conversations "revolved constantly around the love of God and the practices and customs of the spiritual life", as Pauline testifies. And during these months, of course, the two also talked about Thérèse's vocation to the Carmelite Order. It is significant that Thérèse's declaration of her inability to talk about her inmost feelings is contained in the chapter addressed to Pauline. The spiritual ties between herself and this sister who guided her were already so close that Thérèse could no longer distinguish between her sister's influence and her own impulses. She had, at the time she wrote, probably long since forgotten that she also frequently consulted, in person and by letter, the common confessor of all the sisters, the Jesuit Father Pichon. She not only discussed her spiritual states with him, but also expressly asked his advice about her vocation and all the steps she must take in connection with it.[120]

Looking back upon this period of her life, Thérèse applies to herself the verse of St John of the Cross:

> I had no guide, no light
> Save that which burned within my heart,
> And yet this light did guide my way,
> More surely than the noonday sun
> Unto the place where waited One
> Who knew me well.

This "place" was the Carmel. In her heart of hearts the decision remained unaltered and inevitable. It is time for us to explain something of the form and content of the life embraced by this name.

8. THE CARMEL

From the earliest days of the Church people have "withdrawn from the world", have left behind everyday modes of life and normal social arrangements in order to live apart, either alone or in communities, and devote themselves to God. This impulse, arising from many motives, fed by a multiplicity of currents, carried out in innumerable variations, has

---

[120] Father Pichon in the trial; 2 S., 159.

one fundamental, underlying element: the attitude which we may term "singleness of mind"—exclusive and unconditional dedication of all one's forces and all one's actions towards a single goal. We recognize the operation of such an attitude in many areas of human life; usually it remains in force only for a limited period, but it may fill an entire lifetime. It can be found among scientists, artists, soldiers, great statesmen and mothers. Everyone who is "obsessed" by his calling thereby demonstrates that he indeed has a call.

This type of complete devotion is also present in the religious life. We must stress that it is not the only valid, certainly not the only "perfect" form of true religious feeling. Every baptized person is required to love God and cling to Him unconditionally "with his whole heart, with his whole soul, with his whole mind, and with all his strength". Normally the test of the Christian life is to be found precisely therein: that this devotion is preserved through all the involvement, complexity and variety of ordinary life with its requirements, demands, duties and cares. Such devotion interpenetrates the Christian life "as the soul the body".

Nevertheless, from the days of the Apostles on there have always been persons in whom the basic human urge "to be alone with the Beloved" (which G. K. Chesterton has brilliantly called the primary and infallible test of love) has asserted itself. Love, that is, claims its right to forget all else for the sake of the One; to communicate with God not in the midst of the world's complexities, but apart from them; to make God the chief concern, the sole object of all thinking, all speech, all action. The monk takes, as it were, a lifelong furlough from ordinary human life. Yet he does not negate that life or reject it. He still sees the life of the world as consonant with the order established by God—but he takes leave of it in order to be alone with God. His "flight from the world" is dual in character. It partakes of "renunciation"—that is, abstention from all diversions—and of "disdain" for earthly things, not out of vainglory, but because the forces of longing and desire within him are already fully occupied with something else. "There are persons", says Möhler, the famous theologian of German Romanticism,

> upon whom God has conferred a spiritual eccentricity. In them the urge towards the divine, the holy and the eternal is so strong and vital that only a very weak thread ties them to the finite and the temporal. The true spiritual nature of man, his essential kinship with God, merges so strongly in these persons that their fleshly nature dwindles almost to nothing even while the soul is still clothed in flesh. They do not actually make a conscious decision to cut utterly their ties with the finite in order to be freer to bind themselves to the eternal. Refraining from marriage, taking the

sparsest of food and drink, holding aloof from earthly pleasures, is for such persons scarcely a means to attain a higher realm. Rather, they are already in that higher realm, and *because it fills their whole soul, satisfies all their desires, earthly matters cease to interest them.* Their abstinence happens of itself; their outward mode of living is *a consequence* of their spiritual eccentricity, not a means to achieve it.[121]

The various types of monastic Orders differ from each other in the greater or lesser stress given to the two elements—renunciation or disdain.

In the "freedom for God" which is thus gained, or, to cite Möhler again, in the "withdrawal of the soul into its own depths, thereby achieving unhindered contemplation, untrammelled exaltation, unselfishness and unwavering candour", manifold possibilities for the service of the Highest unfold. The ultimate standard remains always the imitation of Christ. Thus the monk can devote the time gained by renouncing the world primarily to imitation of the Lord in prayer, to the solemn act of communal worship. He becomes a member of a body of persons whose vocation it is to praise God. Conscious of the Church's mission "to pray continually and not be discouraged", he becomes the spokesman and deputy of the petitioning people. He can dedicate to the Lord that leisure time which is the highest treasure of the elect. He can devote his time to the service of truth, to seeking out truth and preaching it; he can spend his time in the realm of religion and in the more general realms of the mind: in scholarship and education, in missionary work and pastoral care. The history of the Church and the history of Western culture, of which the history of the monastic Orders is an integral part, provide evidence enough of these activities. The monk can lead an active life by practising that helpfulness and charity through which Christ manifested His love for mankind. Indeed, we know how many communities carry on corporal and spiritual works of mercy.

These aspects of monastic life can be understood and appreciated by the standards of ordinary common sense, which asks that institutions serve a useful function. Though the genesis and underlying reason of monasticism may not be understood, at least the visible benefits, the so-called "good works" which the Orders have practised and continue to practise, can be prized.

Understanding becomes considerably more difficult when the Order in question is one of the few special ones—like the Carmel—which have dedicated themselves expressly to the work of vicarious penance in imitation of the suffering Lord and to contemplative prayer.

---

[121] Johann Möhler, *Gesammelte Schriften und Aufsatze*, ii, 166, as quoted by P. Anselm Günthör, O.S.B., *Möhler und das Mönchtum* (Weingarten, 1942).

This type of prayer is not only "intercession" in the ordinary sense of the word; one might also say that the intercession of a contemplative, praying for the world, is so effective because more is involved. Contemplative prayer, which requires intensive preparation, for the practice of which a whole human life scarcely suffices (an enormous remove from the lowly and common variety of daily prayers)—such prayer represents in itself the perfection of the soul, the transformation of man in intercourse with God, and reaches its peak in a union which is the preliminary and image of the eternal union with God after death. Only he who has thus been mastered by God, or one who is at least on the way to that perfection, is a "focus of divine forces", an open door for the effective entrance of God into humanity. All mystical doctrine is concerned with the description or analysis of this prayer. All mystical doctrine agrees that such saturation of the soul by the divine is a pure gift of grace which can neither be acquired nor earned. Nevertheless, it comes only to him who, though lowly and useless, "has done everything that was incumbent upon him". He must toil with pure, persistent ardour over that aspect of prayer which lies within his scope as a human being. For prayer is not simply a gift; it includes recollection, meditation, impetration and patience; above all it is a hard work of penance. For true prayer the soul must be purified of all which hinders, beclouds, distracts and weakens the influx of the divine.

Contemplative prayer is not an end in itself; it is a means and an instrument. It strives against all subjugation to the created world; it is a struggle for freedom, so that there will be room for God. "He who would properly receive the honoured guest must hold himself in sheer seclusion from created beings" (Suso); he must become empty, practise renunciation.

One who chooses the life of prayer as a "vocation" consciously chooses a life under the aegis of suffering. This does not mean suffering as self-torture, as the fakir's record-breaking accumulation of pains and mortifications. It does not mean deliberate violation of the beauty, joy and simplicity of peaceful living. The voluntary suffering in such a life is primarily acceptance of what comes along; it is no more nor less than the necessary measure of grief and tribulation which afflicts the most commonplace human lives.

In the course of centuries of experience in the ways of the spirit and the intellect, however, certain ascetic practices have been found to promote the growth of spiritual freedom and power: solitude, silence, fasting, deliberate breaking of the domination of physical and emotional instincts, regularity, strict discipline and routine. This kind of suffering the ascetic takes upon himself. And the suffering is redoubled inwardly by the echo, so to speak, of the objective rigours, in the body and soul of the penitent. He experiences pain and toil, hunger and cold, weariness and dullness, solitude and temptation, injury to the feelings by constant submission and humility, inward dearth from renunciation of family, marriage, friendship, mutual relationships, outside stimulation. Finally he experiences the most mysterious and deepest suffering of all, which must accompany the inner purification of the soul: what the spiritual teachers call dryness and desolation, the dark night of the soul, in which they see a shadow of Christ's sense of desolation on the Cross and a foretaste of the fire of Purgatory. All who have had the experience testify that such sufferings of the soul incomparably exceed all rigours of the body and mind.

These sufferings conceal, like so many growing, concentric rings, an innermost core which alone gives meaning to them: the Christian attitude of devotion and obedience. This attitude makes all these "exercises" (as the term "asceticism" denotes) ethically significant and gives them religious worth. It is Christian love alone which elevates into a sacrifice what would otherwise be merely a hardship.

Suffering which flows from the exercise of love thus acquires a new dignity, a new force. Not only because it becomes the fuel of love, which feeds upon it, but also because it represents man's participation in Our Lord's Passion. Christ suffers in the man who has given Him room within himself. Just as the "I am alive; or rather, not I; it is Christ that lives in me"[122] has become reality, so, too, the phrase of the Apostle comes to life, "with Christ I hang upon the Cross". And as in the Passion of Christ, this "freely consented" suffering of the member of Christ is adoration of the Father, is obedience and devotion rising out of the hapless, the god-forgetting world, as a redeeming and atoning sacrifice.

The suffering of the Christian is united to the suffering of Christ in the mystery of the Mystical Body. This is expressed in the profound words of the Apostle from the Epistle to the Colossians: "I am glad of my sufferings on your behalf, as, in this mortal frame of mine, I help to pay off the debt which the afflictions of Christ still leave to be paid, for the sake of His body, the Church."[123] It is not as if the sacrifice of the Son of Man were insufficient for the redemption of the world; rather, these sufferings are, as it were, an extension of the Passion of Christ carried on in the souls of the just. Thus Erik Peterson explains the utterly inexplicable in his exegesis of the Epistle to the Philippians: "The heart of Christ Jesus

[122] Gal 2:20.
[123] Col 1:24.

is Love which is effective in the martyrs, in the saints.... The grace of Love, which is awakened in the hour of martyrdom as a witness for Jesus Christ, is imparted to the Church. *The Church, which participates in the grace of the martyr, participates also in the love of the martyr, in the kindling of the heart of Jesus, so that there comes an overflowing of Love in the Church.*"

The martyr represents in the purest and most significant fashion, by his terrible death, this initiation into the suffering and sacrificed love of Christ.

Those who have followed other paths of atonement have always seen martyrdom as the "real" fulfilment of the sacrifice to which they have offered themselves and have therefore longed for it with all their heart, although they know that the blood testimony depends upon special divine election. They have, moreover, always understood their own forms of suffering devotion as a kind of "sign language" expressing readiness for martyrdom. Even in the Early Church the life of an ascetic was considered a "substitute" for martyrdom; since the supreme sacrifice was no longer being demanded by the outer world, it was being offered in another form, and voluntarily.[124]

That there may come "an overflowing of love in the Church" is the concern and the goal of all "atonements" practised by the monk or any other believer.

---

[124] This word "voluntarily" may be disputed. Is not all the Christian's suffering before God obedience by its very nature? Must not the Christian prove himself by steady submission of his own will to the will of God, which thus tries him? Is, therefore, "voluntariness" not just another word for "self-will", and does not such a self-willed "choice" deprive the suffering of its real value? To this we may reply that there is a kind of voluntariness which is self-will and arrogant importunity. Indeed, the Church has always condemned the seeking of martyrdom, self-assertive grasping after "heroism", as sternly as it has glorified obedient sacrifice of life. But there is a form of affirmation of a vocation which unites supreme free will and supreme obedience. For "vocation" is not coercion; it always presupposes the freedom of man, who may flee from it or respond to it. The destinies of the prophets of the Old Testament clearly testify to this, as does the story of the rich young man in the New Testament. Many doctors of the Church emphasize that even Mary, at the moment of the Annunciation, was free to say yes or no, and that her reply, "Behold the handmaid of the Lord; let it be unto me according to thy word" (Lk 1:38), therefore represented simultaneously an act of perfect obedience and perfect freedom of the will. To be sure, again and again young people will be carried away by the glory surrounding an ideal, will overestimate the measure of their own strength, and will force themselves to some sacrifice which it is not their destiny to make. The wholesome disillusionment they experience in no way annuls their right to make such decisions. For those who persist on the way they have chosen have always known themselves to be "called", though often called very much against their wills and inclinations; and the freedom of their choice is nothing but obedient submission to the divine call which asks of them precisely such a form of devotion.

Because "the charity of most men will grow cold as they see wickedness abound everywhere";[125] because innumerable persons do not fulfil
their duty of adoration and obedience, in imitation of Christ; because
innumerable souls have lost the seed of the Word of God, have crushed it
or smothered it, intentionally or unintentionally—therefore these lovers
may "bear fruit a hundredfold". With the "kindling of the love of Christ"
in their hearts, they are constrained to make up for, and if possible to
more than make up for, all that the others have neglected.

How does that actually take place? How can one person be deputy for
another before the face of God? How can one "pay" another's debt, not
merely by external actions but as though he were that person, and not
only as a fiction but in fact? How does God go about "calculating" the
balances? These are all questions for theology. Hitherto, astonishingly little has been said on the subject in theoretical terms, and this little is often
more in the nature of polemic aimed against error rather than patient
explication. But the believing and loving heart need not wait until slow
reason has limped along in its path, for the path is not illuminated by
reason, but by the light of the enkindling flame which Christ cast upon
earth. Atonement has been offered by men and experienced as a reality,
since the deacon Stephen collapsed under the hail of stones crying out
for the forgiveness of his murderers.[126]

Although these experiences have, for the most part, been expressed
only in stammering figurative language, this is no proof—as some scorn-
fully maintain—that behind such an attitude is nothing but vague emo-

---

[125] Mt 24:12.

[126] In the second-century *Didache* (ii, 3) we already find: "The teaching of these words
is this: Bless them that curse you, and pray for your enemies; yea, pray for them that
persecute you." In connection with this we find (in the appendix to the edition of the
Didache by L. A. Winterswyl, *Die Zwölfapostellehre*, Freiburg im Breisgau, 1939, pp. 14 ff.)
the following commentary: "Moreover, the Didascalia, a Church canon of the end of the
third century, which supplemented the Didache, orders the regular weekly fasts and the
great Easter fast to be held for the sake of the unbelieving Jews. 'Therefore, when you fast,
pray and plead for those who are lost.... On these days you shall all fast, the whole time,
especially those who come from the pagan peoples. For since the people [the Jews] did not
obey, I [in the *Didache* Christ is introduced as speaking to the Apostles] have liberated
them [the pagans] from the blindness and the error of idols, and have taken them in, so
that by your fasting and the fasting of those who come from the pagan peoples, by your
service in these days when you are praying and pleading for the error and the downfall of
the people, your prayer and plea will be accepted by My Father in Heaven... and they
[the Jews] *will be forgiven everything they have done to Me*. Therefore I have said to you before
in the Gospel: Pray for your enemies, and it will be well for those who mourn over the
ruin of the unbelievers. Therefore know you, dear brothers, that we must keep our fasts at
the time of the Paschal Feast *because the brothers did not obey*.'"

tion and a grievous lack of intellectual clarity. Rather, the poverty of the language is great when it attempts to deal with so deep, so delicate and hidden mysteries as those of divine grace and human love. The saints, in speaking of these things, have made no attempt to deliver generally valid theological definitions. Rather, they have expressed—often clumsily—the intent and concern of their own hearts.

We "know" only this much: that atonement is not a judicial process in the strict sense. It springs from love, a plea not merely in word but in deed. The suffering in which this plea is embodied is, since it is "offered up" for the sinners, an act of love which, before God, testifies to the earnestness and fervour of the petition.

The suffering and the prayer of atonement are, together, the second great mode of expression of religious zeal, as evangelizing and the care of souls are the first. The first mode is imitation of Christ in His preaching and His labours for the conversion of sinners; the second, imitation of Him in His passion and death. It is so essential, and the roots of both modes of imitation are so closely intertwined, that every genuine missionary and pastor has always known that his work is related to that silent and hidden form of activity as digging and sowing is related to watering and cultivation. Upon both activities God alone confers fertility.

Therefore the monasteries, which conceive the work of atonement as a common task and as the predominant aim of every individual, play as large a part in the general struggle for the Kingdom of God and the salvation of the world as the labour of the missionaries.

"We must stand shoulder to shoulder in order to press forward", Teresa of Avila cried at the time of the schism when she was building her convents as "divine forts" behind the line of battle. Her nuns were to pray like Moses during the Amalekite battle. "Heresy rages, the Sacrament is desecrated, a tremendous conflagration is consuming Christendom. Jesus beholds Himself once again condemned to death. It is our task to make atonement and to guard the Gospel of Christ by loyal adherence." [127]

The Order of this great Spanish saint embodies this vocation purely and precisely. "*Zelo zelatus sum pro Domino, Deo exercituum*—I am consumed by zeal for the Lord God of Hosts" was the motto of these nuns who, almost alone in the West and in modern times, kept alive the spirit of the "desert".

For the Order of Our Lady of Mount Carmel, "Carmel", as it is called for short, actually traces its lineage to the tradition of the earliest Christian hermits. To this day it reveres the prophet Elijah as its "father and

[127] Quoted from Reinhold Schneider, *Philipp II, oder Religion und Macht* (Munich, 1935), p. 165.

leader". In the caves and clefts of Mount Carmel, in which this mightiest man of spirit of the Old Testament sought refuge and fought his battles with the servants of Baal, there settled in the days of the primitive Christian Church anchorites who sought to escape the world and find God. A sixth-century pilgrim's account mentions monasteries at this holy spot, near the caves of the prophets Elijah and Elisha. In the thirteenth century St Brocardus requested a Rule for his hermits, which was given to him by the Patriarch of Jerusalem and confirmed by Pope Honorius II; the Rule is related to that of the Basilians of the Eastern Church. At the time of the Crusades the Order was exterminated in its homeland by the Saracens. The original monastery was destroyed, and the band of monks martyred. However, the branches which had meanwhile sprung up in the Western world grew and spread. The Order, previously devoted only to contemplation and penance, like all Eastern monastic Orders, assumed a new and active aspect. Innocent IV included it among the preaching, militant mendicant Orders; like the Franciscans and Dominicans, the Carmelites henceforth took on missionary and pastoral work and engaged in studies.

In the sixteenth century the great Teresa of Spain and her disciple and brother in spirit, St John of the Cross, reintroduced the original spirit of the desert within the Order, which had grown slack and forgotten its origins. The reform brought about a fresh flowering and greater expansion. But the storms beating about the Church as a whole, and even more, perhaps, the cumulative parching of the spirit of prayer within the Order, once again annulled its great promise. It was severely weakened in France by the Revolution, in Germany by secularization, and in Austria by the anticlericalism of Joseph I.

The general aspect of this Order displays features of the East and of the West. The major part of the day is occupied in prayer, common worship, the Divine Office, spiritual reading and meditation; the nuns devote between six and seven hours to these duties. The rest of the time is assigned to the tasks necessary for any community, and to needlework. As in the old cloisters in the desert, this needlework is supposed to be crude and simple; it must not "absorb the mind too much and prevent it from thinking about God";[128] it must not be mere "occupation", but should help to support the poor community, which apart from this work, may derive its subsistence only from alms. "The rule about work is to be conscientiously observed: namely, that whoever wishes to eat should also work, as the holy Apostle Paul did, who worked with his own hands", the Rule

[128] Rule, 9, 82.

declares.[129] And again: "Each nun shall endeavour to work so that by her work she also earns livelihood for the others."[130] As in the old monastic colonies, this work was to be performed, not in common rooms, but by each nun separately in her own cell.

In still other aspects life in the Carmel has the character of the "desert": complete silence, separation from the world, inviolable seclusion—that is to say, lifelong enclosure, without any exceptions, within the walls of house and garden. Intercourse with the outer world by letters or visits is to be restricted to a minimum. The silence in the convent itself is broken only once or twice a day, during the recreation hour after meals.

The strictness of physical asceticism is also characteristic of the primitive Church in the East. Abstinence from meat is lifelong; exceptions are made only in case of illness. On fast days—which the Carmel observes considerably more often than the rest of the Church—eggs and dairy foods are also forsworn. Even on non-fast days there are only two meals daily; in winter the first is eaten at 11:30, in the summer at 10:00. As late as the time of our St Thérèse the convent went unheated all the winter, except for the community room, which was scarcely used. This stricture has since been relaxed because later generations have been unable to bear this hardship.

Poverty is observed with a strictness that the layman would scarcely expect in any Order outside the Franciscan tradition. None of the nuns is allowed to have a wardrobe or a chest in her cell, to keep the smallest possession, or to introduce anything into the room for adornment. They sit upon stools without backs; in chapel they kneel on the bare floor whenever the liturgical order does not prescribe standing or sitting. The Rule expressly requires the Prioress to watch conscientiously and "wherever she observes in a nun an excessive attachment or preference to any thing, whether it be a book or a particular cell"—what else could there be?—"or anything else at all, she must at once deny the nun this thing".[131]

The beds are to have no mattresses, only straw pallets, for "experience has shown that such a pallet is sufficient even for the feeble and the sick."[132] The Carmelite habit, because of its weight and its crudeness, is itself almost an instrument of penance.

These regulations, however, are only the fence which encloses the space and leaves free the area in which inner growth is to take place.

---

[129] Rule, 9, 85.
[130] Rule, 9, 84.
[131] Rule, 7, 63.
[132] Rule, 8, 76.

It is no poetic exaggeration, but simple description, when Thérèse calls this life a "life of death". Anyone who really carries out this existence in spirit and letter must see it as a foretaste of death, of the radical and irrevocable parting from all things that make life rich, sweet and attractive. It is a venturing into death in the hope of receiving a new, mysterious life from the hand of the Lord.

"The servant of God", Céline Martin said at the trial, "confided to me the reason for her preference [for Carmel]: she chose this vocation *in order to suffer more* and thereby to win more souls for Christ. To a nature such as hers it seemed harder to work without ever seeing the fruits of her own efforts" (as she would have in educating the young, in nursing the sick or in similar occupations), "to work without encouragement or distraction of any sort whatsoever, to devote herself to the most toilsome of all labours, that of overcoming one's own nature. This life of death, more fruitful than any other for the salvation of souls, Thérèse wished to choose for herself. In particular she entered the Carmel in order to pray for priests and to make sacrifices for the concerns of the Church."

At the ecclesiastical interrogation which precedes every canonical taking of religious vows, the candidate must solemnly testify before the bishop or his representative as to the motives which finally and decisively led her to enter the Order (this regulation is intended to forestall as far as possible vows taken from coercion, persuasion, thoughts of economic security and other inadequate reasons). Thérèse declared: "I have come to save souls and above all to pray for priests."

This resolve was only the completion of the readiness which had blazed up in her soul at the time of that first encounter with the Crucified: "I yearned to save sinners from the everlasting fires of Hell, no matter what the cost." No matter what the cost—once again we see that determination to take no half-measures which Thérèse herself, with charming seriousness, read into the "basket story" of her childhood: "I saw that one could be a saint in varying degrees, for we are free to respond to Our Lord's invitation by doing much or little in our love for Him; to choose, that is, between the sacrifices He asks. Then, just as before, I cried: 'I choose everything.'"

9. ROME AND THE WORLD

Thérèse now strove towards this goal stubbornly and consciously. She had recognized it, and now she wanted to realize it, not in any vague fashion, not in dreams of the future, but at once, in the here and now. She determined to enter the gates of the Carmel of Lisieux on the anniversary of her "conversion", at Christmas 1886. She could not wait, although she knew that the Lisieux Carmel—as yet the Rule did not prescribe any age limit for entrance—required attainment of the civil majority. She would ask for a dispensation—she who always sought not to attract attention, to be obscure in the crowd. She who was ordinarily gently submissive to all orders, to all regulations, waged her campaign with an impatience and a self-assertive bluntness which can only arouse our astonishment and throw a surprising light upon her ordinary submissive obedience. Was this the obscure urge of those marked for early death, who unconsciously know that they have little time to lose? "The divine call was always so urgent that even if it had meant going through fire, I would have cast myself in to follow Him."

Pauline alone supported this desire of hers. Marie, who even in the convent was as down-to-earth and unromantic as ever, refused to hear of it. Thérèse's visits to the convent, in which the one sister urged her on and the other dampened her ardour and advised against early entry, became more and more difficult for her. Even before the tribunal which decided Thérèse's beatification, Marie still defended her viewpoint: "I resisted her vigorously and stubbornly because our sister was too young and because I feared the great grief it would be to our father, since Thérèse was the true sunshine of his life."[133]

Father Pichon, the well-known Jesuit who had won Marie for the convent, and in whom Thérèse now confided, declared "as his considered judgment" in favour of Thérèse's early entry.[134] (It is typical of Marie that even this decision on Father Pichon's part could not quell her objections.) The Prioress, who had previously been encouraging to Thérèse, suddenly frowned upon the idea. Céline was for the time being excluded from the discussion, to spare her, as long as possible, the grief of parting; since the two were so close at this time, this silence was very hard for Thérèse. The two had long since agreed that the Carmel was their ultimate goal. Informed at last, Céline enthusiastically supported her sister's cause and generously granted her precedence "like the martyrs of old, who used to say farewell with joy to those who were chosen to go into the arena first".[135] Céline wanted to stay with their father for the while. Léonie, at this time, had entered the Poor Clares and returned home again, because the excessively austere Rule of this Order was too much for her unstable health. It is very strange that *The Story of a Soul* does not

[133] I S., iii, 45.
[134] I S., iii, 77.
[135] S.S., v.

even mention this setback; we learn of it only from marginal comments of her biographers.[136]

But all these crosscurrents were insignificant compared with the bitterest difficulty of all: speaking out to her father. He was ageing rapidly, had already had his first light stroke, and was ill from a venomous insect bite. Thérèse knew very well what she would be doing to him if she declared herself. She was the darling of his heart, the "Benjamin" of the house; the bond between Papa and herself was unique and irreplaceable. Now she was going to deal him the worst blow since the death of his wife. He had still not recovered from the sorrow of the sudden parting from Marie; and although he must be expecting Thérèse to choose the cloister, he was not prepared for separation so soon.

At Pentecost Thérèse decided to tell him the truth. All day long she prayed to the Holy Spirit for the proper words and asked the Apostles, whose work she was about to share, for strength. Her account of the decisive conversation between father and daughter, as she gave it in *The Story of a Soul*, has such simplicity and beauty that it merits quotation in full.

It was in the evening, on coming home from Vespers, that I found my chance. Father was sitting out in the garden with his hands clasped as he drank in nature's loveliness. The setting sun's last rays were gilding the tree-tops where birds were singing their evening prayer.

There was a look of Heaven on Father's noble face, and I felt sure his heart was filled with peace. I sat down beside him, not saying a word, but there were tears in my eyes. He looked at me more tenderly than I can express, pressed my head to his heart, and said: "What is it, little queen? Tell me." Then, to hide what he was feeling too, he rose and walked slowly up and down, still holding me all the while close to his heart. Through my tears I told him about Carmel and my longing to enter soon, and then he too began to weep, but never said a word against my vocation; only that I was still rather young to make such a serious decision. When I insisted, and gave him all my reasons, his upright, generous heart was soon convinced. We went on walking for a long time; my heart grew light again, and Father dried his tears, talking to me just like a saint. Going to a low stone wall, he showed me some little white flowers like very small lilies; then he picked one of them, and gave it to me, explaining how carefully God had brought it to blossom, and preserved it till that day. So striking

---

[136] Flor., 101; Laveille, 194, note; obituary notice of Sister Françoise-Léonie. There is a more detailed discussion in Piat. From this it is evident that the family, who otherwise sang the praises of each daughter's vocation with pride and emotion, rejected this ambition on Léonie's part; they were, in fact, repelled and coldly astonished at her presumption, because she did not at all fit in with their conception of a chosen spirit. Thérèse mentions the matter in the *Manuscrits Authentiques*, but only on a note of pity.

was the resemblance between the little flower and little Thérèse that it seemed as if I was listening to the story of my own life. I took the flower as if it were some relic, noticing that when Father had tried to pluck it, the roots had come out too, but quite undamaged, as though destined to start life again in some other and more fertile soil. Father was doing just the same for me by letting me be transplanted to Mount Carmel from the lovely valley which had been the scene of my life's first steps.[137]

Now Thérèse thought she had won the game—just as once before, at the time of Pauline's taking the habit, she had hoped to celebrate her own First Communion behind the grille at Carmel. Matters did not proceed quite as rapidly as she hoped. Thérèse's biographers are fond of dwelling on the "tremendous difficulties" she had to overcome in order to make her way into the convent.[138] Let us qualify this somewhat. Description of such obstacles, with the whole wicked world apparently conspiring to keep the chosen soul from reaching the goal of its desire, the heroism required to break through the resisting wall—such accounts are, in a certain type of edifying literature, as much part of the stereotyped story of a vocation as in the average novel are the perils encountered by a pair of lovers before the happy ending.

On closer scrutiny we must see Thérèse's trials as wholly natural and ordinary. Above all there is none of that element which makes such a struggle a cruel one: ill will on the part of the opponents, and real conscientious doubts on the part of the person concerned. Thérèse had to contend only with the established order of things, with the objection by the ecclesiastical authorities that she was far too young. In this struggle, to be sure, she ran her head against and through the wall. It is quite understandable that her uncle, Monsieur Guérin, was at first horrified by his brother-in-law's consent. In his temperamental French way he swore that he would never be a sponsor to such reckless plans which he thought would be equally harmful to the cause of religion and to the well-being of his favourite niece. This intense opposition on his part broke down within four days. Thérèse attributed his sudden change of mind to her fervent prayers, her uncle to his own prayers for illumination. And the touching words which this worthy man addressed to the girl were in spirit much like her father's: "Go in peace, my dear. You are a little flower whom Our Lord has chosen and wants to gather for Himself. I won't stand in the way." He, too, sensed that a special religious destiny ruled in

---

[137] *S.S.*, v.

[138] This legend even found its way into the historico-liturgical breviary lesson in the Office of St Thérèse.

this case, that it had to be judged by other than usual standards, and he reverently withdrew his own opinion.

From the Carmel itself, however, there came an unexpected refusal. Not only from Marie—Thérèse was already accustomed to that; but the Prioress, who had hitherto wavered between yes and no, suddenly took her stand squarely behind the convent Superior, who categorically refused to consider Thérèse's entry.

Poor Canon Delatroëtte. In most books on Thérèse his role is that of the "villain", the rough, heartless, dry pedant, who alone did not sense the breath of the Holy Spirit and the blessedness of this chosen child, who would have blocked a saint from reaching the door to her mission and her happiness—and this when he could not even refer to official regulations, but had only his own obstinacy for authorization. But can we blame him for his objections, even though he may have expressed them somewhat intemperately?

Canon Delatroëtte, after all, knew what the Carmel was like in reality. He knew the ideal Carmel of the Rule, which required an extremely high degree of spiritual and physical sturdiness; he knew also the actual character of his convent, where at times the atmosphere was often thoroughly earthly. He knew best of all what a burden it would be for all concerned if a young person should enter upon such a way of life too soon, too thoughtlessly, too poorly equipped. He knew better than anyone else the curious, complicated, unstable character of the Prioress who might today receive an unusual candidate with open arms and tomorrow regret the whole matter.

In a small town, moreover, nothing escapes the eye of the neighbours. Canon Delatroëtte probably knew—and if he did not already know, all the pious souls in Lisieux now informed him—that little Thérèse Martin was a spoiled, overdelicate baby of the family, a true little princess, whose health was certainly not to be relied on—had she not had to leave school early because of overstrain and constant headaches? Had she not suffered a curious nervous breakdown only a few years ago? Monsieur Martin, of course, was goodness and piety personified, but undoubtedly he was somewhat too weak. He could not withstand all the whims and fancies of his troupe of daughters. Had not one of them just returned from a convent because she did not fit in? And really, how overindulgent their father was. Not six months ago he had spent two days taking his eldest daughter all the way to Calais, merely because she had expressed the wish to be first to greet her confessor on his return home from Canada. How could the spiritual director of the convent burden his house with the consequences of such upbringing, with a starry-eyed adolescent who was used to having her every wish fulfilled on the spot? Moreover, she already had two sisters in the Carmel. Two sisters were more than enough in a community which was not supposed to number more than twenty heads; three blood sisters would almost form a faction.

Already, two of the sisters were tugging in different directions. "Marie did all she could to stop me", Thérèse says, and at the trial Pauline emphatically repeated this charge, with the gentlest note of upbraiding. Who can say whether Sister Marie of the Sacred Heart, as she was now called, did not simply hide behind the authority of the convent's superior—she would scarcely have had many other ways to express her opposition. Pauline, now Sister Agnes, was not idle either; she remained as clever and purposeful as ever. It was probably she who kept trying to win over the vacillating Prioress; she may also have persuaded the older, more influential sisters in the convent to put in a good word for Thérèse's cause. How otherwise could it have happened that Mother Geneviève, the aged, highly respected founder of the Lisieux Carmel, spoke up on behalf of the unknown girl when Canon Delatroëtte visited her sickroom one day.

Was it really "remarkable doggedness in clinging to his own ideas" or "jealous overestimation of his authority"—these are but some of the phrases employed in condemnation of him—or was it not simply the natural reaction of a straightforward, conscientious, somewhat rigid man when he suddenly responded to all the warning and pleading whispers by bursting out: "I keep hearing about this girl all the time! To listen to you, one would think the salvation of the convent depended upon the entrance of this child. The world isn't going to come to an end on her account. Let her stay with her father until she is of age! *And besides, do you think I have made my refusal without having prayed to God for illumination?* I want to hear no more of this matter!" [139]

It seems to us to bespeak a high sense of fairness, and by no means narrow-minded self-righteousness, that the Canon concluded his brief and cold conversation with Thérèse and her father by offering the hint: "I am only the Bishop's delegate, of course, and if he gave you his permission to enter, I could not prevent it."

Father and daughter took the hint at once. But it was autumn before they were able to make the journey to Bayeux. Thérèse was hopeful, although apprehensive also; she had never visited anyone without one of her sisters, and now her first call was to be upon no less a personage than a bishop. She was to plead her cause before the Bishop and his Vicar-General. With a touching, chivalrous loyalty and steadfastness, Louis Martin

---

[139] Laveille, 159.

supported his little daughter. Her decision had struck him hardest of all; both of them knew how deep and incurable the wound was. But had not this new ordeal also bound them together in a new and inexpressible intimacy? How rightly the daughter had described her father; his "upright, generous heart", so like her own, would not hesitate to fulfil the will of God, once he had recognized it as such. Now the two, each embarked on a course of equal sacrifice, were resolute, inflexible allies. Thérèse, with the indestructible confidence of her age, once again thought that the visit to the Bishop would make everything turn out all right. This exalted shepherd would certainly receive more illumination from the Holy Spirit than others had; his paternal eye would swiftly perceive the genuineness of her vocation; his powerful hand would sweep away all obstacles.

Her father let her hope, although he himself was more doubtful. Not for nothing had he associated with ecclesiastical circles all his life. At any rate, in case they failed, he had already conceived a new plan. On 4 November a French pilgrimage was going to Rome; Monsieur Martin had taken tickets for himself and his two youngest daughters. Was this the reason he had postponed the conversation with the Bishop until All Saints' Day? We do not know.

Louis Martin knew that Mgr Hugonin, Bishop of Bayeux, was a mild and genial person, scholarly, opposed to complications and agitations. Moreover, he was an old man, accustomed to leaving the burden of official duties to his hale and efficient Vicar-General. The latter was Mgr Révérony, a former military chaplain, for many years a curé, devout, quick-witted, knowledgeable about human beings. It was quite possible that in Bayeux also little Thérèse Martin's desire to enter the Carmel at the age of fourteen would not be hailed with delight; pastors with a wide experience in the ways of the world do not always take a favourable view of mystical ventures and exceptional states; every saint in the history of the Church has had to contend with this. Such may well have been Monsieur Martin's thoughts. And now there once more awoke, after long years, the young Louis Martin, the dreamer who had sought the salvation of his soul among the glaciers of the Great St Bernard. At the same time there was aroused the insuppressible independence of the French Catholic even towards the highest and most legitimate powers; this is stronger, because innate, than all the "émigré's" acquired, lamblike, pious submissiveness to clerical authority. If the Bishop and the Vicar-General would not consent, there was still the Pope. They would go to Rome. The Holy Father, thought this pious romantic, has always recognized those marked out by destiny; he will not say no to the child of my heart.

In the fifth chapter of her book Thérèse has described with humour and grace the audience with Mgr Hugonin. Her account is vivid down to the last detail; we can sense (as we can even more in the following chapter, describing the trip to Rome) how she desired to entertain her beloved elder sister by narrating these adventures which turned out so well in the end. The note is similar to that long ago struck by her mother when she wished to amuse Pauline at boarding school by recounting the doings of the "little monkey".

For this journey Thérèse had put up her hair for the first time—a symbol for being "grown-up". A photograph of that period shows a fresh, firm, girlish face, almost rectangular beneath her excessively unbecoming coiffure. The familiar flowing locks are combed sternly back and up, piled in a hard little chignon on the top of her head. This picture is worlds away from the all-too-familiar portraits which show Thérèse with thin, ethereal features and a dreamy expression. Her true face has the quality of a hazelnut; it is vigorous, tensed, concentrated around an invisible core, almost tough in its astonishing poise, with a resolute, straight mouth, stubby nose, stubborn chin; but this impression of toughness is contradicted by eyes full of profound life, clear and filled with a secret humour.

The grown-up coiffure failed to accomplish its purpose. In spite of her effort at forcefulness, Thérèse looked like a four-year-old child in a stubborn mood; she resembled far more her first picture taken at three than any of the portraits of intermediate stages. Looking at this picture we understand why she believed she had found her way back to the personality of her early childhood.

So she may have looked at the venerable gentlemen with grey, glowing, unfrightened eyes; nevertheless, the conversation was very difficult for her. Her father deliberately remained in the background. If Thérèse felt so sure of herself, she would have to advocate her own cause. "Until now, I had never had to do more than answer questions others put to me, and now I should have to explain why I wanted to enter Carmel and prove that my vocation was genuine."

The Bishop and the Vicar-General were friendly, gracious and noncommittal. They talked of waiting; they told her that she ought to stay with her father a while longer. To their surprise, the father spoke up resolutely on his daughter's behalf; like her, he seemed eager for the separation. In all modesty and respect he even dropped the remark that they intended to take part in the pilgrimage and that his daughter "would not hesitate to speak to the Holy Father if permission were not granted before then". But the Bishop and his assistant seemed well aware that Roman bureaucracy was even slower moving than that of the French provinces, so that this somewhat blunt hint failed to make much of an impression. The Bishop praised their zeal, remarked that Mgr Révérony would be representing him on the pilgrimage, and said that he could come to no decision in the matter until he had spoken with the Superior, Canon Delatroëtte.

Alas, now the grown-up coiffure did not help her, any more than her ladylike little hat "with two white wings".

Hitherto Thérèse had valiantly retained her composure, although she felt like an ant in the solemn rooms and in the armchair before the fireplace, "so vast that it would have held four of my size with ease". But the prospect that her fate would be dependent on the hostile Superior was too much for her; her tears began to tumble down, in spite of the Vicar-General's previous warning not to make a display of her "diamonds" before His Lordship.

The Bishop patted the overwrought girl as if she were a small child and urged various consolations upon her: all was not lost; he would speak to the stern Superior the following week, when he would be going to Lisieux. Meanwhile, instead of weeping, she should be looking forward to the trip to Rome: "It will confirm you in your vocation." And he promised that she would receive his answer in Italy. His Lordship, with the greatest kindness, saw his visitors to the garden gate; and the Vicar-General praised Louis Martin's readiness to sacrifice his daughter. Nevertheless, Thérèse and her father knew they had accomplished nothing. As far as the authorities in Bayeux were concerned, the matter seemed settled. After all, Thérèse had not exactly given proof of a high degree of maturity.

Now Rome loomed before her eyes; she would appeal to the Holy Father.

The party of pilgrims with which they set out four days later was characteristic of the church life of the whole era. Mgr Laveille, who personally took part in it, has provided us with many illuminating details.

The Italian controversies with the Church were a thing of the recent past. In Catholic circles indignation over their outcome still raged: Church property had been confiscated, the theological faculties at the universities had been abolished, many monastic Orders and congregations had been dissolved, secular schools and civil marriage instituted. The picture of the Pope as the "Prisoner in the Vatican" was still new and full of pathos. Foreign bishops made a point of sending sizable bands of pilgrims to Rome from time to time; these were both declarations of loyalty to the Vatican and protest demonstrations against the oppressors of the Church.

Mgr Germain, Bishop of Coutances, was considered the most passionate "ultramontane" in the French episcopate. Since the jubilee of Leo XIII's ordination was approaching, he was anxious to lead an especially imposing pilgrimage to Rome and organize a conspicuous act of homage in the Vatican. Thus it turned out that in addition to the Martins, who had their own reasons for going, the group was made up almost exclusively of representatives of the old royalist Catholic society of France. The political overtones of the pilgrimage were very plain, and almost the entire Norman nobility was present. "In order to gain more participants," Laveille says candidly, "the intended pilgrimage was to be arranged not only as an act of piety towards the Holy Father, but also as a lavish pleasure trip."

An efficient travel agency managed the programme. The pilgrims were put up "only in first-class hotels". There were carriage trips and guided tours in all important cities—arrangements which, in those days, when travelling conditions in Italy were generally bad, would appeal even to the travel-shy French. The whole affair was surrounded by the magical aura of a grand social event and therefore attracted the public who cared for that sort of thing. Perhaps only the two young girls from the small town found it curious that the rest of the group manifested no specially devout mood, although the cars were decorated with religious emblems and each compartment bore the name of a saint. Monsieur Martin, who from his young manhood had associated the idea of a pilgrimage with hymns and penances, also regarded this parade of vanities with some discomfiture. If there were nothing special to be seen from the windows, he thought the time could be best spent "in joint praise of the Most High". Instead, the pilgrims played games, read novels, and flirted with one another. When the old gentleman refused an invitation to play cards and voiced his opinion on the regrettable lack of prayerfulness among the pilgrims, one of the younger men retorted: "It's a good thing there aren't many more Pharisees about." Typically, Louis Martin was not offended, bore no grudge, and made a point of bidding good-bye to the rude young fellow with especial cordiality. For Thérèse this and a good many other incidents gave rise to the observation: "How interesting the study of the world becomes when one is just about to leave it."

This four-week pilgrimage offered Thérèse a first wide and colourful encounter with the "great world", with the *saeculum*. Now, with far more justice than during that holiday trip in her childhood, she might have written: "The world is able to combine so well the search for pleasure with the service of God."

Unfortunately, here too she encountered "the laity" only in the most superficial way, saw only idleness, social ambition and vanity. For she was seeing people in the peculiarly irresponsible situation of travel, released from everyday reality and the burdens of ordinary life. Such a situation was ill suited to add to her child's conception of the life of Christians.

Thérèse had prepared herself for disturbing and confusing impressions during this journey. We can imagine what such a trip, a whole month long, down all of Italy, in the company of nothing but priests and aristocracy, must have meant to these two middle-class girls who had never seen anything beyond the narrow circle of boarding school and small town, except for modest visits to seaside resorts. Now "the world" in its most exciting sense was awaiting her, with all its unsuspected wonders and abysses. In the centre of that world, however, stood the Holy Father's white throne, irradiated by mystic rainbows of countless sanctuaries, but surrounded also by a world containing Pranzinis and murdered ladies, freemasons and godless persons who kept the Pope a prisoner—that whole world of "sinners" which Thérèse wished to redeem. This was all the tempting splendour which Satan had shown to the Saviour from the mountain top: "Come then, all shall be thine, if thou wilt fall down before me and worship." [140]

Even more distinct in Thérèse's mind than this upwelling of ideas, was the conception that Italy, although the land of the most glorious Christian monuments, was also the land of the most perilous "pagan" art. In the Abbey, and in her home also, there were thick volumes which could only be looked at with caution; certain pages always had to be turned over quickly, unseen.[141] What sights would she see on the many announced guided tours through museums and galleries? "I knew nothing about evil, and was afraid of finding it", Thérèse writes. Then she adds with touching lack of equivocation: " 'To the pure all things are pure.' The simple and upright see no evil because it does not exist in inanimate things, only in impure hearts, but I had not found that out yet." Thus the pilgrimage brought her this insight, although she does not dwell upon it. Céline, on the other hand, recounts as if she were relating a miracle: "She commended herself to St Joseph and daily prayed to him to shield her. And in fact, nothing ever offended her eyes, neither in the public squares nor in the many museums we visited!" [142] How, one may ask, could her eye have been offended by classical art or Michelangelo!

This experience disposed of one of her worries. At first, however, she underwent a wholesome disillusionment. It was in regard to the uncritical, almost touching respect for titles and old names so typical of conservative and monarchistic groups. This is not simple snobbery; rather it sprang from a wish-dream, into which many factors enter, of a "higher life". This dream transfigures everything which glows with even the most distant reflection of crowns and courts. We read that Thérèse's eldest sister, in spite of her puritanical upbringing and unbending character, was

[140] Lk 4:7.
[141] 2 S., 304.
[142] 2 S., 398.

fond of sunning herself in the radiance of the proud old names borne by her fellow pupils and went out of her way to make friends with them.

Four weeks of association in the narrow confines of a party of travellers is more instructive to a sharp-eyed young person than a whole library of critical books. "Céline and I found ourselves mixing with members of the aristocracy; in fact the pilgrimage seemed to be made up of them, but we were not impressed and looked upon their high-sounding titles as nothing more than the vapour of smoke. The words of the *Imitation*, 'Do not be solicitous for the shadow of a great name', were not lost on me, and I realized that real nobility is in the soul, not in a name."

This was one disillusionment. The other concerned the nimbus which surrounded every priestly soutane as far as the *émigrés de l'intérieur* were concerned. The words in which Thérèse describes this experience are discreet, gentle and reticent, far removed from irony, accusation or superiority. But in their terseness they let us read much between the lines: "Up to then, the principal aim of the Carmelite Reform was a mystery to me; I was quite happy to pray for sinners, but the idea of praying for priests seemed surprising because I thought their souls must be crystal pure. But I grasped my vocation while I was in Italy, and this alone would have made the journey worth while." But she promptly adds placatingly, as if in anticipation of unspoken questions: "I met many saintly priests that month, but I also found out that in spite of being above angels by their supreme dignity, they were none the less men and still subject to human weakness. If the holy priests, 'the salt of the earth', as Jesus calls them in the Gospel, have to be prayed for, what about the lukewarm? Again, as Jesus says, 'If the salt shall lose its savour, wherewith shall it be salted?'"

It is also of some importance that on this journey Thérèse for the first time associated with young men. In her brotherless existence, masculinity had hitherto been represented only by her father, her Uncle Guérin, and various priests. Now she had her first and only experiences—troublesome and tempting ones. In Bologna a student boldly jostled against her on purpose—an experience which often befalls blonde girls in Italy. Then he took her in his arms and carried her across the street. However, a single look on her part was enough to make the young gallant let her go and retreat in embarrassment.

Céline declared at the trial that one of the young men in the pilgrimage group fell in love with Thérèse ("developed a tender affection for her"). Shyly and without speaking, but making his intent quite plain, he paid court to her; probably he thought her older than she was. In spite of her inexperience Thérèse became aware of it at once—and it was hard for her to produce the "icy reserve" which her biographers have so praised.

"It is high time", she confessed privately to her sister, "for Jesus to remove me from the poisonous breath of the world.... I feel that my heart is easily caught by tenderness, and where others fall, I would fall too. We are no stronger than the others."

The sixth chapter of *The Story of a Soul*, in which Thérèse describes her trip to Rome, is the longest and most detailed in the book; it is, so to speak, the *pièce de résistance* of the modest narrative. Nevertheless, it leaves open a good many questions about her actual experiences. As we have said, her intention is clearly to give her sister, for whom she was writing, some impression of the wonders Pauline was unable to experience. Perhaps Thérèse based her account on letters she wrote during the trip, as in the first section she used letters of her mother's. The chapter begins with a long preface, with detailed, loving descriptions of landscapes, moods, minor events, descriptions of fellow voyagers. Then it is as if the writer recalled that for Carmelites even entertainment must refer to divine things, as prescribed in the Rule for the visiting room and recreation hour: "They should comfort and cheer one another in reverent and pious ways." Perhaps, too, the living flow of description was checked by an inward call to order, a reminder that she wished to tell of nothing but the story of her vocation. At any rate, there is a marked contrast between the terseness and stiffness of the second half of the chronicle and the volubility and vividness of the first half.

We wish we knew whether Thérèse was so full of impatience to reach Rome and the Holy Father, so single-minded in her aspiration, that she really absorbed only those impressions which had a direct bearing on her dream of entering the convent. Given the extreme concentration of her personality, that is not out of the question. Or did she, as a nun, deny herself the pleasure of summoning up once again her less spiritual impressions?

It is understandable that in Paris she should have had eyes only for Notre-Dame des Victoires, the ancient church which contained the original of the Madonna who had worked her miraculous cure. At the feet of the Madonna she received assurance that the vision of her childhood had been a reality; and at the same time she was given peace after the years of bitter self-reproach for having disclosed her secret. But did she really see nothing in Padua but the tongue of St Anthony, to the exclusion of Donatello's figures; in Bologna only the body of St Catherine, which for all her veneration still struck her as somewhat gruesome and mummylike; in Rome only the Colosseum, the catacombs, and the Pope; in Assisi only "the places hallowed by St Francis and St Clare"; in Florence only the body of the Carmelite St Magdalene de Pazzi? Did the benignity of this or that prelate really loom larger for her than the shades of Dante and Savonarola? Did she actually fail to encounter either Giotto or Fra Angelico, Leonardo or Michelangelo? Did no breath of vanished antiquity brush her wide-awake mind, which had been so thirsty for knowledge? Was her sole "artistic" experience really the Campo Santo in Milan—the pompous, expensive, modern tombs with their statues in pathetic poses, which she lauded as incomparable masterpieces? "Here a child casts flowers upon its father's grave, and one forgets that the frail petals are of marble as its fingers seem to let them fall; there a widow's fragile veil, or the ribbons in a maiden's hair, appear to tremble in the movement of the breeze." It is not improbable. Milan stands at the beginning of her account, and the later stages of the journey are dismissed with great brevity.

We wonder, too, how Thérèse responded to this land thronged with the myriad shadows and figures of history as is no other. She had, after all, spent half a year studying history of her own accord out of sheer fascination with it. Had this curiosity, at the time she wrote, already become so empty to her that she preferred not to revive it; or did she omit any reference to history out of affectionate consideration for her sister, who was not interested in such things? The little description of Venice in the early part of the chapter is genuine and charming, filled with awe and a melancholy sense of the city's past. Céline recalls that on this trip her sister, especially in Rome, fell into a state of rapture over "the splendour of the buildings, the perfection of the pictures and sculptures, not to speak of the harmony of the language." "How beautiful Italy is!" she wrote to Marie Guérin. "I never imagined that we would see so many splendours." [143]

Perhaps, in order to arm herself against the "dangerous" allure of breadth and richness which poured in upon her, she deliberately strewed the thought of transitoriness like ashes over every impression. "I am glad I went to Rome, only I can see why some thought Father took me on this pilgrimage to change my views about the religious life; a vocation not so secure might have been shaken.... I saw splendid monuments, studied treasures of art and religion, and, most wonderful of all, stood on the very soil that the Apostles trod, the soil bedewed with martyrs' blood; and from its contact with these sacred things, *my soul grew strong*, while I learnt the emptiness of things that pass."

She yielded more easily to impressions of nature, to God's masterpieces rather than men's. She was carried away by the ride through Switzerland with its mountains, glaciers and vast views. In these passages we feel clearly how on the threshold of departure she drank in with keen, alert and

[143] 2 S., 591.

thirsty faculties every smallest sensation; how her responses were intensified and painfully deepened by the peculiar mood of leave-taking. Ten years later she could recollect not only the snow-covered mountains and the waterfalls, the lake in the "crimson of a setting sun" and the toylike villages with graceful spires, but also the "giant ferns" and the "purple heather" which she saw flashing past the window of her train deep in some lost valley. These sights made her think of Heaven—and certainly not because she was forcing her thoughts in the direction of piety. Her mind functioned in this way. Like Cardinal Newman, Thérèse had belonged from childhood among those for whom the invisible world is always a reality near at hand, as though the veil separating them from it is thinner than for ordinary mortals. It was not that the thought of the hereafter overshadowed all this beauty, opposing it and dimming her pleasure in it. On the contrary, Heaven and earth shone radiantly out of this spectacle, as inseparable as the sun and its mirroring lake. "I can't say what an impression the magnificence and grandeur of these scenes made upon me; it was a foretaste of Heaven's wonders."

Confronted with this amplitude, this tremendous freedom, she also thought of the restraint and dreariness of the exile which she was seeking, which she was coming to Rome to plead for. No adolescent illusions obscured her vision of what was awaiting her and what she wanted. "Then I thought of the religious life as it really was, with its restrictions and its little hidden sacrifices every day, and I saw how easily one might become so taken up with oneself that one might forget the glorious purpose of one's vocation. I thought to myself: 'Later on, in the hour of trial, when enclosed in Carmel, I shall only be able to see a little corner of the sky; I will look back on today and be encouraged: the thought of God's majesty and greatness will put my own small troubles in their place. I will love Him alone, and not make myself unhappy by being taken up with trivialities now that I have caught a glimpse of what He has reserved for those He loves.' "

In her account, the visit to Loreto in the province of Ancona naturally takes a place of honour. For Thérèse and Céline, everything they saw there was genuine: the chamber of the Annunciation; the bowl used by the Infant Jesus. Joyfully, the sisters received Communion in the Casa Santa itself, from a friendly priest, while the rest of the band of pilgrims docilely attended the service in the basilica. In an exalted moment they surreptitiously scratched a little plaster from the wall of the Holy House, to take it home with them as a priceless relic, and still more as a promise of the many mansions in the Father's house: "For His house will be all our own for ever and ever", Thérèse writes.

Rome in the eighties, which the pilgrims reached late at night, was very different from contemporary Rome, far more like the Rome shown in the pictures of Gregorovius. Thérèse was delighted by the timelessness and age of the Campagna, where they spent their first day, whereas the centre of the city disappointed her: "The hotels and shops take one back to Paris."

The places of the martyrs naturally attracted her most strongly. At that time the excavations had not progressed very far. When the travellers reached the Colosseum they found to their disappointment that the floor of the ancient amphitheatre was buried under some twenty-six feet of rubble. At one spot a part of the former pavement had been exposed; beyond a barrier yawned a shaft the height of a house. Once more the child in Thérèse broke impulsively through all maidenly restraint, and she cried to Céline: "Follow me, there is a way through!" Recklessly, the two girls clambered over the crumbling stone where the excavators had been working—a considerable accomplishment, for we must remember the costume of the eighties with its ankle-length skirts and whalebone corsets, and the fact that the two were completely without practice in athletics. After a first warning cry their father looked on smilingly, with male pleasure in a prank. Perhaps he would have preferred to join this unscheduled climbing party.

At the bottom of the mass of rubble the girls found the small spot marked with a cross where the blood of martyrs had been shed. With pounding hearts they knelt and kissed the holy soil. "I asked the grace to be a martyr too for Jesus. At the bottom of my heart I felt that I was heard."

In the catacombs Thérèse found something she had not expected: a friend. With all the directness and intimacy of a living person, the holy martyr St Cecilia spoke to her soul. It was as if she had seen her; she felt the presence of the royal Roman virgin of whom we know so little and so much: the clear, high-spirited, bold profile which glows so compellingly for us out of the laconic accounts we have, a face fearless and noble, sustained by inner melodies, conveying courage and purity to all those she loved. "I likened her to the spouse in the Canticles, finding in her the 'choir in an armed camp', for her life was simply a magnificent song amid the greatest of trials. This did not astonish me, because 'the Holy Gospels lay ever on her breast', while in her heart reposed the Spouse of Virgins."

For six days the tireless guides led the pilgrims on foot and by carriage from church to church, through palaces, galleries and museums, in defiance of the bad weather. "It was a veritable race", writes Mgr Laveille, who participated in the pilgrimage as a young abbé; forty years later an audible sigh of relief that he survived the expedition can still be heard between the lines. "At the most venerable spots the guide often left us only a brief time for prayer. Then it rained continually, and the domes and obelisks stood out gloomily against a sky of grey clouds."

On 20 November the pilgrims foregathered at the Vatican for the act of homage. "For six days we looked at all the principal wonders of Rome; on the seventh I saw the greatest of them all—Leo XIII", Thérèse wrote with that Latin pregnancy in expression which she occasionally achieved.

First of all the pilgrims attended the Papal Mass; reverently Thérèse watched the frail, grey-haired Pope who, leaning upon two chaplains, yet with wonderful presence, went up the steps of the altar. "Fear not, little flock, for it hath pleased the Father to give you a kingdom" was the text for the day. Thérèse saw the words as a good augury for her own cause.

The French pilgrims went in to the audience by dioceses. Coutances, which had initiated the pilgrimage, came first; then came Bayeux and finally Nantes. The bishops of Séez and Vannes had come to the side of the Pope. The Pope sat in his raised throne, listening benignly to what each bishop had to say about the individual kneeling before him; after each pilgrim kissed his foot, he held out his hand to be kissed, addressed a few words to the pilgrim, blessed him, and had a memorial medal handed to him. Group after group entered the hall in suspense and left it in joy. When the turn came for the Bayeux pilgrims, Mgr Révérony, representing his bishop, introduced Monsieur Martin as the father of two Carmelites. The Pope laid his hand in blessing upon his head. As this happened, the Vicar-General may have recalled the remark of the old gentleman who was now kneeling so reverently before Leo XIII: "She will not hesitate to speak to the Holy Father if permission is not granted before then."

At any rate, as the next little group, in which were the two Martin sisters, approached the throne, Mgr Révérony announced in a loud voice that he absolutely forbade anyone to speak to the Holy Father. Pale and quivering under the black veil worn for the audience, "heart beating wildly", Thérèse darted a questioning look at her sister. "Speak!" Céline whispered.

The next moment Thérèse was kneeling before the throne. She kissed the white shoe as all the others had done, but when the Pope held out his hand to her, she raised her streaming eyes to look into his face. "Most Holy Father, I want to ask you a great favour." The Pope bent his head until his face almost touched the veil, while his piercing black eyes looked into hers. "Most Holy Father," Thérèse said tremblingly, "in honour of your Jubilee, let me enter Carmel at fifteen!"

This was downright disobedience. Before the Pope could reply, the Vicar-General stepped forward. "Your Holiness," he said, "this is a child who wants to enter Carmel; the superiors are already going into the question."

"Very well, my child," the Pope said, "do what the superiors decide."

This was the Holy Father's only possible reply, and it was the only one Thérèse had not counted on. In her dreams the Pope floated ethereally above all petty regulations. She did not suspect that it is precisely the task of the highest office to guard the prescribed order of things. Beseechingly, she clasped her hands upon the Pope's knee and spoke to him as directly as if he were her own father: "Holy Father, if you said yes, everyone else would be willing." Leo XIII gave her a quiet, searching look, and then said emphatically: "Well... Well... You will enter if it is God's will."

Thérèse wanted to speak once more, but the episode had already lasted too long. The noble guards at the side of the throne ordered her to move on, and since she remained on her knees, they pulled her up and led her away. Mgr Révérony, dismayed, himself aided them. At the last moment the Pope silently and gently laid his hand on Thérèse's lips—was this to close them, or was he offering her the kiss of the hand which she had missed, in order to show her his favour in spite of what had happened? His eyes followed the tearful girl to the door.

That was all. It had been an impossible scene, a horrid breach of etiquette, an open act of insubordination—Mgr Révérony would certainly say all this to the Bishop. And Thérèse's venture, this whole trip to Rome, had been an attempt to write in water.

It speaks well for the tact, as well as the tactics, of the Vicar-General that he did not refer to the embarrassing incident by so much as a word, though he saw Thérèse and her relatives often in the next two weeks. Moreover, he remained perfectly polite when Monsieur Martin "reproached him gently" for not helping Thérèse through her "ordeal". He never gave any sign of disapproval, irony or disfavour—not even during the expedition to Assisi, when Thérèse lost a buckle of her belt, missed her carriage while searching for it, and had to ride home in the Vicar-General's carriage. Thérèse sat, embarrassed and intimidated "like a squirrel in a cage" among the important gentlemen; Mgr Révérony made a point of drawing her into the conversation. He talked with her, with deliberate kindness, about the Carmel and promised to support her. Thus he made her understand that he regarded the scene at the audience as a slip which he tactfully preferred not to take seriously. Thérèse probably understood that he attached no meaning to it, but at the same time she felt that she had lost her game at the moment when she thought she had won it—just as she had done when she cried in front of the Bishop. She placed no value upon her generous opponent's conciliatory phrases. "I had lost all confidence in mankind, and was depending only on God." This phrase probably refers principally to the Pope; she had placed all her hopes in him, and he had disappointed her profoundly. She does not waste another word on this subject.

We wish we could know what Leo, the aged, wise prelate with so deep a knowledge of men, thought of this encounter with a pretty, fearless girl who wanted to beg so curious a favour of him.

Thérèse's dramatic plea to the Pope is no proof of her ardent, intrepid nature, as modern interpreters would like to make it out. Nor was it the result of a sudden heavenly inspiration, as others have interpreted the incident. Rather, her words to Leo XIII were the obedient execution of a tactical plan prepared carefully beforehand. The plan had been framed at the Lisieux Carmel, and Thérèse's course of conduct had been prescribed to her in a letter, down to the very words she was to speak.[144] The plan was devised by Mother Marie de Gonzague—such a plan was, indeed, quite typical of her—who here, for the first time, intervened forcefully in Thérèse's life. The aged founder of the convent along with Sister Agnes had considered everything carefully. Father Pichon, too, had been informed and approved the plan. Thérèse's regular confessor, however, was left out. "She thought", Father Piat says expressly, "that God and her Little Mother sufficed as guides for her." Thérèse was, it is true, very frightened, but she took refuge like a little nun in the law of obedience. "I do not know how I am going to do it.... Really, if God had not taken over all this, I wouldn't know what to do." The wish of her sisters—Céline, too, enthusiastically supported the plan—was, to her, identical with the will of God, although this time her father seems to have known nothing about the origins of her determination. Consequently, the depression and disappointment that afterwards overcame her referred only to the dignitaries of the Church, not to the Carmelites who had set her to this deed. The child felt that the Pope was more likely to err than her sisters.

All Thérèse's pleasure in the journey was now over. Although she put a good face on the matter, if only in order not to spoil her father's and Céline's enjoyment, her heart was filled with inconsolable sadness. In Pompeii alone the mood of the ruins suited her own. She longed "to walk alone amid the ruins and ponder how transient all things human are", but there was no chance for even a moment of heart-easing solitude. She was eager now for the trip to come to an end. The cold luxury of grand hotels, the everlasting carriage drives, the shallow-minded company bored and depressed her—now that there was no beckoning purpose behind it all. And longing for the Carmel gnawed at her. "I should have been a thousand times happier under a thatched roof with a hope of entering Carmel than I was in the midst of gilded apartments, marble staircases and silk hangings, while my heart was in anguish. I learnt from

[144] Piat, 283, 294–97.

experience that joy does not reside in the things about us, but in the very depths of the soul."

They went home by way of Florence, Pisa, Genoa and the Riviera. Thérèse wastes not a word describing these places; only the southern coast of France moved her strongly. But "my fairy land faded, leaving no regrets, for my heart was set on far more wonderful things".

After the failure in Rome her father seems to have given up hoping for a miracle. Even before they reached home he proposed to his sad little daughter, by way of consolation, that they go on a pilgrimage to the Holy Land. But Thérèse was tired of sightseeing. She wanted no consolation prizes; she wanted her dream, and in defiance of all the facts she continued to wait with unshakable confidence for the gate to the convent to spring open on Christmas Day. On Pauline's advice she wrote once more to the Bishop of Bayeux, respectfully reminding him of his promise—in spite of anything the Vicar-General may have reported. And every day she rushed to meet the postman, certain that there would be an answer for her. Not for a moment did her will waver, that "patient, indestructible will" which Nietzsche saw as a decisive trait of quality in human beings; not for a moment did she ask herself whether God might not have proclaimed His will in some fashion contrary to hers, whether humble submission might not be in order.

Christmas came and went; nothing happened. On New Year's Day Thérèse learned, in the visiting room, that the Bishop's approval of her immediate entry had arrived on 28 December. But now the Prioress wanted to postpone her entrance until Easter. The idea was to mollify Canon Delatroëtte, who otherwise would feel rudely overruled. Moreover, Pauline felt that it would be better for her sister not to plunge first of all into the Carmelites' severe Lenten fast.

Thérèse was not informed of these reasons. This last postponement struck her harder than any refusals by Bishop and Pope. That the "Ark" itself now refused to take in the "dove" which was free to fly to it was incomprehensible to her. Inwardly, she had broken completely with her whole past, torn out her heart by its roots. She was already homeless in her old house. For a moment she was inclined to spend those unexpected three months before her final departure as a diverting and pleasant breathing spell before entering upon the life of penance. She was tempted to enjoy for one last time the innocent pleasures and freedoms which "the world" at home still offered to her. But she overcame this understandable temptation—which in a single revealing flash shows us how little the austerities practised for so long had really become "natural" to her as yet. Instead, she heroically resolved to make use of this respite as a time of serious preparation for her sacrifice. Already she was so sure of her principles that she did not try—though this would have been characteristic of her age, and likely after the powerful impressions of heroic saintliness she had brought back from Italy—to apply the painful mortifications of the saints to herself. With an amazing independence of mind she once again chose the "veil": "My mortification consisted in checking my self-will, keeping back an impatient word, doing little things for those around me without their knowing, and countless things like that. By these little things, I made ready to become the Spouse of Jesus, and I cannot tell you how I grew in abandonment, humility and other virtues, as a result."

3

THE DESERT

1. ABSTINENCE OF THE HEART

On 9 April 1888, Thérèse entered the Carmel at Lisieux. Her departure from home was agony and bliss both together. "To part is to die a little"; every separation is something of a foretaste of the ultimate and irrevocable leave-taking. "How heartrending these good-byes are", Sister Thérèse wrote in retrospect.

> Just when I would have liked to have had no notice taken of me at all, everyone spoke to me most tenderly! It made me feel the sacrifice of parting all the more. Next morning I had a last look around at Les Buissonnets, the charming cradle of my childhood—then I was off to Carmel. I heard Mass surrounded by those I loved as I had been the evening before. At the Communion, when Jesus had come into our hearts, their sobbing was all I could hear; I did not cry at all myself, but as I headed the procession to the cloister door, my heart was thumping so hard that I wondered if I were going to die. It was a moment of agony which must be experienced to be understood.
>
> I kissed the whole family, then knelt for Father's blessing. He knelt down too, and he was crying as he blessed me.

In the midst of this moment's solemn emotion there sounded the dry voice of Canon Delatroëtte, still adamant, from the open gate: "Reverend Mother, sing a *Te Deum*. On the orders of His Lordship the Bishop I give to you this fifteen-year-old child whose entrance you desired. I hope that she will not disappoint your hopes, but I want you to remember that you alone bear the responsibility if things turn out differently from what you expect." [1]

This fierce introduction seems to have made more impression upon Thérèse's relatives—who recall it twenty-four years later with obvious indignation—than upon Thérèse herself. She does not mention it, of course, and possibly did not even hear it. Her heart was too full of pain and rapture.

[1] Laveille, 195.

Then the doors of Carmel closed upon me. The two darling sisters who had each been a mother to me embraced me first, then my new sisters, whose devotion and tenderness are beyond anything those in the world can guess.

My dream was at last realized, and peace flooded my soul, a deep, sweet, inexpressible peace; an inward peace which has been my lot these eight and a half years. It has never left me, not even when trials were at their height. Everything here delighted me, our little cell most of all;[2] it was as though I had been transported to our far-away desert. But my happiness, I must say again, was a calm happiness.

Tranquil, unruffled by the slightest wind, were the waters on which the little boat was sailing under a sky of cloudless blue. All my trials had found an ample recompense, and profoundly happy, I kept saying over and over again: "I am here for ever now."[3]

From her childhood Thérèse had dreamed of the "desert" to which God would some day lead her. Now she had entered the desert, and the law of the desert took hold of her, made its mark upon her, and at last consumed her. For she was granted that which is given to the favourites of God: to succumb without reservation to her chosen vocation, to become wholly and purely part of it. It is difficult to trace her path through that mysterious country, as difficult as the attempt to paint the gleam of a candle in the noonday glare—so utterly does the outline of the wavering figure dissolve in the shimmering distances, in the blazing, abstract light.

The outer framework of those nine brief years in the convent can be rapidly described. On 9 April 1888, Thérèse Martin entered. On 10 January 1889, after a probationary period somewhat longer than the usual, she was given the habit and received the name: Thérèse of the Child Jesus. A month later her father suffered his second stroke and had to be taken to a sanatorium. On 8 September of the following year Thérèse took her vows; the ceremony of "taking the veil" followed on the twenty-fourth when she added to her name in religion, "and of the Holy Face", a title which was to become increasingly important in the development and character of her inner life. About this time Thérèse was employed as sacristan, whereas previously she had been given domestic duties in the laundry and the refectory. In December 1891 a severe epidemic of influenza broke out in the convent, and three of the nuns died. Thérèse was then eighteen; although she escaped with an extremely light case, it may be that then, overstraining herself in caring for the other sisters, she contracted the disease which was later to prove fatal.

[2] The custom of the convent prescribes the word "our" instead of "my" even for all objects of personal use, as a constant reminder of the nun's vow of poverty.

[3] S.S., vii.

In the summer of the following year she began her "artistic" dabbling with verse and painting, which much impressed the sisters in the convent. In February 1893 Marie de Gonzague, under whose régime Thérèse had entered, completed her term as Prioress. The convent elected Mother Agnes of Jesus, Thérèse's elder sister Pauline, to succeed her. One of Pauline's first official acts as new Prioress was to assign her twenty-year-old sister the task of "assistant to the Novice Mistress".

Next July her father died, after having been taken to the convent parlour to speak with his daughters during a brief spell of mental clarity. Shortly afterwards, Céline—now relieved of the burden of care for her father, which she had borne with such devotion—joined her three sisters in the convent. In December of that year, on the orders of her sister, the Prioress, Thérèse began writing down the recollections of childhood which form the first part of *The Story of a Soul*. A year later she gave the manuscript to Pauline.

In the spring of 1896 Mother Marie de Gonzague was re-elected Prioress. On Good Friday Thérèse coughed blood, the first manifestation of the consumption which rapidly led to her death. In June 1897, at the request of the Prioress, she wrote the second part of *The Story of a Soul*. On 8 July, in a state of complete collapse, she was taken to the infirmary. At the end of July she received the Last Sacraments, but the slow and painful process of dying lasted until 30 September. On 4 October she was buried in the town cemetery of Lisieux.

Between these dates lies the path of one human being from piety to sanctity, from beginnings to perfection, from obedient practice of set exercises to the breakthrough of a new, creative form of Christian life.

The law of the desert!

In all probability Thérèse would have been able to reach maturity by passing through all the pleasures and pains of experience and loving contact with the things of the world. In her last year "in the world" she had become conscious of this other potentiality of her nature. But her vocation was already too solid and clear for this alternative to become a temptation. She was drawn too strongly by the mystical image of the ascent of Mount Carmel, the holy mountain of solitude, and of the meeting with God. She obtained what she wanted, obtained it immeasurably more deeply, richly, mercilessly, than she had ever dared to hope, although never more than she had innocently longed for and accepted in advance.

In looking back upon her own beginning in the convent, Thérèse continues: "It was no mere transitory happiness, no passing illusion of one's first enthusiasm. Illusions! Thanks to God's mercy, I had none at all; the religious life was just what I expected it to be. No sacrifice took me by surprise." Here she is referring primarily to the hardships which are a normal part of convent life.

The saint's first biographers dwelt, with lavish exclamations of praise and admiration, astonishment and pity, on the physical hardships prescribed by the Carmelite Rule. The standards by which they measured this type of "suffering" were, of course, the lush middle-class standards of the turn of the century. Thérèse's contemporaries, living at the height of a long-since-vanished hedonistic culture, were tremendously impressed by such tangible "sacrifices" as straw pallets, fasting, vigils and rough clothing. Such austerities evoked from them a shudder of respectful awe. To the bourgeois devoted entirely to security and comfort, it must have seemed the apex of heroism for a young girl of good family to prefer such a life of privation to all the promise of a "brilliant match". Given the pronounced class feeling of the period, it was really considered a humiliation for a well-born Mademoiselle Martin, daughter of a prosperous and respected retired business man, to sully her tender hands with washing floors and sweeping stairs.[4]

Modern biographers of Thérèse have taken the same attitude, but in an even more extreme form. Some have gone so far as to represent the Lisieux Carmel as a kind of spiritual concentration camp in which pietistic furies "made a little saint struggle agonizedly for ten years", without a finger being lifted in her behalf.

It is highly interesting to see two very different threads of source-material being spun out side by side in connection with this question. Hitherto, we had only the first thread, consisting of statements by Thérèse's sisters. Now, by way of correction and supplement, we also have Thérèse's letters. These have significantly changed the picture.

Thérèse's relatives were convinced beforehand of her heroism, and physical suffering was to them an integral part of heroism. Hence they saw what they wished to see. During their extremely frequent visits the family observed, with a curious mixture of edification and indignation, that Thérèse looked pale and worn, and they became quite upset over the bad food she was receiving in the convent. "I can still see her with her pale face, but so happy because she was able to suffer something for God" (Céline).[5] "Since she was seen to be so patient, always uncomplaining, this child was served all the remnants of meals, instead of being given especially strengthening food, which was what she needed. It frequently happened that she had nothing on her plate, but a few herring heads, or

---

[4] As a matter of fact, the Carmelite Rule is the very opposite of detrimental to the health; readers will be astonished to see the extremely advanced ages mentioned in the obituary letters on Carmelite nuns. Eightieth birthdays and celebration of the golden anniversary of a nun's Profession are far from rare in the Carmelite convents.

[5] 2 S., 208.

reheated left-overs that had been standing around for days." This is Céline again—though here she could only be repeating statements by her elder sisters, since at this time she was still living at home. Léonie speaks in a similar vein, though more briefly and soberly, as always—and she, too, is repeating things she could know only from conversations in the convent parlour and in the family: "As far as food and recreation are concerned, she was kept on short rations and treated sternly by her Mother Prioress." [6]

What must have been Thérèse's feelings as she sat in on such conversations. She tried gently to appease her elder sisters' indignation, without offending against respect for them by contradiction. But her corrections were only taken as corroborations: "Then Thérèse, with angelic expression, was in the habit of comforting Pauline; she assured her that she was not unhappy, that she received all she needed to eat" (Céline).[7]

We must add that postulants and novices are strictly separated from nuns who had already made their Professions, even in a small convent. We can only think that Pauline suffered from a virtual obsession that the child of her heart was always being treated too harshly. For years she had exerted all her influence in order to direct Thérèse's choice of vocation towards her convent and to bring about her entrance at an early age. "I confess", she said at the trial with complete sincerity, "that for my part I did everything I could to draw her to our house—once it had been decided that she wanted to enter the Carmel—because I saw that she was a little saint and could bring great blessings upon us." [8] Now she had attained her goal, but for the time being her sister was entirely out of her hands. Possibly she was tormented by a sense of responsibility, coupled with the genuine maternal feeling that no one but herself could see, understand and satisfy the child's real needs.

Pauline saw the outward sternness that the Prioress practised towards the youngest novice directly and indirectly—we shall discuss this in detail in a moment; she saw Thérèse's pallid, worn face, which might have come about from many causes, and she came to the conclusion described above. That conclusion has remained as posterity's verdict.

Thérèse's letters provide us with an entirely different picture. They show us how carefully the superiors treated this frail young postulant, how many exceptions they made in her case, and literally forced her to accept. Thérèse herself, to be sure, expressed no wishes of her own; but her father, aunt and sister outside showered her with attentions and gifts. The Prioress not only tolerated this, but obviously approved of it. She even permitted

[6] 1 S., 32.
[7] Ibid.
[8] 2 S., 160.

Thérèse, following Pauline's suggestions, to write requests to her relations outside. These were instantly granted. "Sister Agnes thinks I must have fur-lined shoes, the kind I have so often seen you wearing in the winter. If Aunt could buy them for me, I would be very glad. Jeanne could try them on; her foot is just the same size as mine.... If I could get the shoes this afternoon, I would be really pleased. You cannot imagine how completely they take care of me here in Carmel; they're always pressing me to eat something and to warm my feet." [9] The editor's footnote assures us somewhat shamefacedly that Thérèse wore the shoes only two months, up to the time of her Clothing, and that the last sentence was only a *boutade familière*, not to be taken literally. Nevertheless, he admits that "because of her extreme youth she was the object of very particular solicitude on the part of her Mother Prioress and her Novice Mistress during her postulancy". Of course it must be remarked that the somewhat more ample but still frugal diet which she was allowed did not always agree with her; her digestion was not easily adjusted to it. That was the cause of the frequent stomachaches which caused her such great embarrassment.

Moreover, the letters indicate that this solicitude did not cease with the end of Thérèse's postulancy. Only the manner changed. A conspiracy of love and anxious tenderness both within and outside of the convent kept watch over her. Those who loved her made unceasing efforts to soften the self-chosen hardships of the Carmel by a thousand alleviations both large and small.

This fact may in itself have been one of the most painful of trials to Thérèse. Certainly she was young and came from an easy, comfortable life. But what mountain climber wants a maternal chorus of lamentations and sympathy to accompany the natural and necessary exertions of his ascent? Healthy and unspoiled youth has always felt that coping with physical challenges, especially honourable ones which have been self-chosen, is more a sport than a "cross". Of course Thérèse's generation, especially the feminine half of it, and especially in France, had scarcely an inkling of the sporting point of view. But Thérèse was, at least in her own feeling about herself until shortly before her breakdown, possessed of "iron health".[10] And she had yearned all along to prove herself in hardships.

Her family, however, was of the opinion that the Carmelite life in itself offered more than enough hardships, and they vied with each other in spoiling their darling as far as possible.

---

[9] Letter 44, sent in November 1888 to her cousin Marie Guérin.
[10] Letter to Céline of 19 August 1894.

For her affectionate father she still remained, even after her entrance, the little queen for whom nothing was too good or too costly. He heaped surprises and gifts upon her, some of which the whole convent shared in, some of which were for her alone. Fish were a large item—Monsieur Martin was in the habit of giving a considerable part of his catch to the convent whenever he went fishing. And after his illness the Guérin family generously assumed responsibility for this gift.

"Oh, how good you are to your little queen; scarcely a day passes that she does not receive some gift from you!" Thérèse is writing[11] after her first three weeks in the convent. And soon afterwards: "Thank you for the fish, dearest Father. Thank you, thank you; you give us so much that I am forced to thank you only in general, but every single thing is a special pleasure in itself."

"The postman of the Child Jesus is very kind; I send him all kisses and caresses. I drink the wine he gives me with delight, and as I do so I reflect that it comes from the cellar of the Child Jesus."[12]

"Happy New Year, my darlingest king; thank you for spoiling us with all the luxuries" (*gâteries*—how often this word occurs!) "which you have given us this week and all through the year."

The letters follow in close succession, expressing thanks for lavish gifts on birthdays and feast days, for the New Year and for convent festivals, for cakes and baked goods sent on no special occasion, for "an avalanche of huge onions, plums and pears", for apples and cherries, for fabrics, candles, flowers to decorate the altars which Thérèse had charge of, for chocolate, tonics and medicines.

"If you knew how much pleasure your monster of a carp gave us; it made lunch last half an hour longer. And Marie of the Sacred Heart [her oldest sister] prepared the sauce for it; it was marvellous, tasted literally like worldly cuisine.... But it does not always take such things to give one an appetite. Not me, anyway; I have never eaten so much in my life as I have since I have been in the Carmel..."[13]

In fact, Monsieur Martin, with tireless fancy, one day hit upon the idea of presenting his Carmelite daughters—who were required to abstain from meat for life—with three water hens: "One bird for the Diamond, one for the fine Pearl, and one for Papa's Little Queen."[14] For waterfowl, according to the ascetic gastronomy of the Middle Ages, were not regarded

---

[11] Letter 25.
[12] Letter 45.
[13] Letter 33.
[14] Letter 45.

as warm-blooded creatures, but as fast-day food. We can imagine the sensation this present aroused in the convent.

For his youngest daughter's Clothing, Monsieur Martin sent the most amazing surprises: an artificial melon which burst to scatter a rain of sweets; champagne; and precious lace for the bridal dress. "Your little queen is absolutely crushed under the weight and splendour of your presents; it's easy to see that a king is offering them to his queen." [15]

For Thérèse's sixteenth birthday her aunt sent a "splendid package of spice-cake" for the entire convent, and the Prioress mentioned in the refectory that the sisters owed this pleasure to Thérèse.

"Embrace the whole family lovingly for me, and thank them for all the *gâteries* that have been sent to me, in such quantities that I am afraid I have forgotten to mention some things", Thérèse writes to her cousin years later.[16] And again: "My uncle spoils his Carmelites; they do not need to fear that they will starve." [17]

Madame Guérin seems now and then to have sent Thérèse sizable sums of money for the support of the house—for example, as a "fee" for a painting done by her niece. Thus the girl found herself having to assume the part of benefactor of the convent. "I really must laugh when I consider that thanks to my darling relatives I am actually supplying the whole community with fish!" [18]

Both sets of facts—Thérèse's strict treatment and Thérèse's coddling—do not contradict one another. Rather, it would seem, there is a clear connection between them. On the one hand the Prioress certainly did not deplore this abundance of highly useful gifts which poured into the convent on Thérèse's account. None of the numerous letters of thanks was written without her knowledge and consent, and she was quite capable of gracious gestures to show her appreciation. Thus, for example,[19] she had a hair embroidery in the fashion of the times made from Thérèse's clipped locks for Madame Guérin's feast day; the design was of a lily stalk above a cross. On the other hand, it is quite understandable that Mother Marie de Gonzague, who possibly recognized Thérèse's vocation more fully than anyone else in the convent, felt that this very toleration of *gâteries* obligated her to emphatic sternness in other matters. Later on, no one understood this intention better than Thérèse herself. She expressly and fervently thanked Mother Marie de Gonzague for it. The other nuns,

[15] Letters 38 and 53.
[16] Letter 115.
[17] Letter 150.
[18] Letter 60.
[19] Letter 112, November 1891.

however, must have regarded this shower of gifts with very mixed feelings. Of course they shared in the spoils; but we can imagine what interpretation small-minded and envious sisters must have put upon this never-ending series of exceptions and special privileges. The story of the herring heads and the leftovers may very well be based upon a crude, unauthorized attempt at pedagogy on the part of the nuns who worked in the kitchen; they may have wanted to show this pampered little novice in drastic fashion what real monastic fasting meant. Of course it may, too, have been altogether harmless in origin, based on confidence in the sound appetite of the young. A child, after all, could be given food that old, invalid or sick nuns could not tolerate, just as in many families the youngest child or the one with the biggest appetite will have all the leftovers pushed his way. Thérèse was, after all, the only adolescent in the convent.

She herself was probably torn between gratitude and embarrassment. Subordinating her own feelings and desires, as always, she responded to the family's loving intentions with charming letters of gratitude, redoubling by her letters the joy of the givers. On the other hand, we may see in this initiation the origin of her own rule of conduct: never at any cost to ask for a dispensation, exemption or relief. As we shall discover, she carried out this principle with steely energy and consistency. In a long, silent struggle, which nevertheless never offended against charity, she acquired a certain independence for herself, and the right to obey her rule as she thought it should be obeyed. In this may be found the key to the merciless sternness towards herself which she displayed during her illness, and which led to her early death. A struggle against uncomprehending love may, in some circumstances, be even harder than against baleful persecution.

It may be that she was glad when, occasionally, she had to go really hungry, or when for a time she suffered daily stomachaches, and when she became ill from a particular dish of beans which was a staple item of diet. At such times she may have felt herself a proper Carmelite in a penitential convent.

We shall have much more to say later on about Thérèse's asceticism. The sufferings of the body were not the least of those she was required to endure. But before her illness filled the cup to overflowing, no more was imposed upon her by her environment than what is borne by every Carmelite. An inevitable part of the "desert" is extreme simplicity in the satisfaction of physical needs. The Carmel was still far from the standard of the early hermits, who lived on roots and slept on rocks. Far more significant was the aspect of her "imprisonment" which Thérèse had very consciously taken upon herself: the renunciation of the living things of nature. For all her small-town origins, Thérèse was, perhaps because of

her youth, perhaps because of the unspoiled simplicity of her receptive
temperament, very close to the things of the earth. Having to live without meadows and flowers was probably the greatest ordeal imposed upon
her in the convent. The promise she had given herself on that journey
through the Alps, to remember the glories of the created world when her
soul threatened to wither in her self-chosen confinement, must have returned to her again and again. Frequently she consoled herself, as she
admits in a letter to Céline,[20] with the verse of St John of the Cross, who
was so akin in spirit to her:

> In my Beloved I have the mountains,
> Lonely valleys and groves,
> Strange islands,
> Rushing streams,
> The whisper of sweet breezes.

Her repressed homesickness burst forth in strange and touching little
gestures. When her sisters expected that her dreams must be solemn and
inspired, she confessed: "My dreams are usually about woods, flowers,
rivers and the sea. I am nearly always with children, or chasing butterflies
and birds I have never seen before." The poem she put into the mouth of
the Maid of Orleans in prison transparently expresses her own emotions
as a young prisoner:

> The voices said so: see, I am a captive.
> From Thee my help will come, from Thee alone, my Lord.
> My aged father I left, for love of Thee,
> My vale of blossoms, with sky so blue and pure.
> Left the fields, left my dearest mother,
> And showed the soldiers Thy banner of the Cross.
>
> Behold my wages: a gloomy prison cell,
> Reward of toil, the price of tears and blood!
> Never again shall I see the places of childhood,
> The meadow laughing in its floral radiance....
> Never again gaze on the distant mountains,
> The silvery peaks, dipped deep in cerulean blue,
> Never again hear the trembling vesper bells
> Breathing sweet dreams through the pure breezes....
>
> In vain in these prison nights I look for the star
> That hung in the sky at evening, bright and low,

[20] 15 August 1892.

The arbour that gently wrapped me in the spring,
When guarding the flock I lay and slept.
Here when I fall asleep amid my tears,
I dream of scents, of the sweet morning dew,
And dream of the magic of woods and vale and fields—
But roughly the clank of my chains awakens me.

It is moving to see how the Lord consoled His child tenderly, again and again, precisely in this respect. From childhood on Thérèse had loved snow, and for her Clothing she wished, as children wish something for their birthdays, that it would snow. The warm, damp January seemed to quash all such hopes. But during the ceremony the weather suddenly changed, and as the procession left the chapel, the cloister quadrangle gleamed snow-white before her eyes. Blissfully, Thérèse recognized in this a greeting from her Lord. She had a similar experience when the longing for flowers, the greatest pleasure of her girlhood, painfully assailed her. It was her task to decorate the statue of the Child Jesus in the cloisters, and one day she was overcome with distress. Would she again have to make do with artificial flowers, when she so delighted in "corn-flowers and poppies and big daisies"? That same day an unknown benefactor brought a large bouquet of field flowers to the gate. She still missed one favourite, the corn cockle; but when she "wished" for it, this flower, too, soon materialized in the bouquet, "all smiling, to prove to me that in little things as much as in big ones God gives even in this life a hundredfold to those who have left everything for love of Him".[21]

The renunciations of the heart, however, pierced her to the depths. First came the parting from her beloved father. Soon thereafter God Himself undid the firm though tender ties which still linked these two in spite of all walls and bars. The lax customs of the Lisieux Carmel permitted weekly visits from the family and frequent letters. At her Clothing on 10 January Thérèse was vouchsafed the joy of having her own father lead his little queen, radiant in the richest of bridal gowns, from the door to the chapel altar. Thérèse had only a year to enjoy the sweetness of his visits and of constant exchanges between them. A month after the ceremony her father was struck down by the shattering cerebral haemorrhage. For five years the daughters knew him only as a living corpse, first among strangers in an institution, then at home under the care of Léonie and Céline. Thus he had been taken away from her in a different and terrible way, could no longer be reached by any call, by any expression of love. The nest of childhood had been finally destroyed.

[21] S.S., viii.

General monastic tradition has always required, by way of mortification, repression of the natural ties of blood. Those who take the way of renunciation must first free themselves from the tyranny of this tie and its overpowering claims upon human nature. The object is to attain sufficient detachment so that one can "possess as though he does not possess" in this respect as in all others. This attained, one may turn again to blood relations with purified love, pure concern and responsibility. It is strange and yet understandable that human nature often finds the first part of this task easier to encompass than the second. It may be that the calls of blood are so imperious that those who venture to free themselves from these calls can, thereafter, find salvation only in fleeing beyond them entirely. It may also be that, frequently, a purely human and purely rational urge to liberate the self from instinctive feelings will utilize, and even hide behind, the religious impulse. Perhaps this is the explanation of the harshness, almost the savagery, which the ascetic so often displays in this struggle—a harshness going far beyond the measure permitted by Christian charity. In any case, in spite of all the shock to our feelings, there is also a curious appeal in the strong words in which Christ demanded the abandonment of father and mother for His sake: "He is not worthy of Me, that loves father or mother more." [22] "Follow Me, and leave the dead to bury their dead." [23] "Who is a mother, who are brethren to Me? Then He looked about at those who were sitting around Him, and said, Here are My mother and My brethren! If anyone does the will of God, he is My brother, and sister, and mother." [24]

We know from many examples in the lives of the saints how this call was obeyed, and kith torn from kin violently and painfully. There was Francis of Assisi before the bishop's tribunal, tearing the clothes from his body and laying them at his father's feet: "Henceforth I shall say only: Our Father who art in Heaven." There was Elizabeth of Hungary brokenheartedly parting from her own small children, whom she could not very well take with her into the Franciscan life of poverty, and with tears and prayers striving for the grace to quell even her unquenchable longing for the abandoned children—until she was able to utter those striking words: "Now I love my children no more than other human beings." And although in her case these words certainly meant, "Now I love all who are entrusted to me as much as I do my own children", such an utterance is still frightening. Thus, too, Jane Frances de Chantal won victory over her maternal heart when, obeying the mysterious call from

[22] Mt 10:37.
[23] Mt 8:22.
[24] Mk 3:33–35.

beyond, she departed from her castle, stepping over the body of her son who in despair had thrown himself down before the threshold. Thus the Swiss peasant Klaus von Flüe left hearth and home, wife and ten children, to dwell in a lonely cell in the rocks, there to pray and do penance for his country.

Such incidents are well known and have called forth emotions ranging all the way from horror to glorification. Who can presume to judge in an individual case? Such deeds were often the outcome of error, but they often sprang from genuine spiritual destiny, from a mission to accomplish the extraordinary. They might be forced and unnatural, the work of men; they might be a sign from God, announcing His unconditional mastery and His claim to a devotion that rightly takes precedence over all human devotion and all human ties. Again and again in history it has happened that He who is the Lord demands of men yet alive this leave-taking which is an anticipation of death, so that in their poverty and emptiness they appear before Him like the dead, so that they may be "with Him" all the more. And it will continue to happen again and again.[25]

Those who receive such a call and answer it are not inhuman. They are marked souls who must call forth in us fear and awe, reverence and perhaps painful sympathy. And if they offend us also what does it matter? Everything that exceeds average humanity offends those who cannot understand it.

Thérèse was not one of these extraordinary souls. Strange as it may sound, she was not at all capable of such sacrifices. She was really and truly not heroic in this sense, not heroic on such a scale. It was with purest self-knowledge, without a trace of creeping humility, that she so often and so consciously contrasted herself with the "great souls" and counted herself among the "little souls". In her relationship with the family, this becomes very plain.

For Thérèse her family remained an absolute value which could not be shaken, gainsaid, conditioned by anything, anything at all. It was simply

---

[25] Cf. Romano Guardini, *Liturgische Bildung*, Epilogue, p. 89: "That it is a fearful thing to fall into the hands of the living God; ... that the Lord may come any moment, like a thief in the night; ... that the sword can come between husband and wife, between mother and daughter; that men can become the foes of their nearest kin—these and many other of the words of Jesus and His Apostles apply here. What it means is this: Any moment the call of God can force men to discard the finest, soundest, apparently most necessary order. Every moment God's fearful purity can shine clearly, and then we see our sins with new and with such inexorable clarity that all earthly values become ridiculous. Any moment God's infinite glory and sweetness can pour into the soul, and then everything that is called worthwhile on earth, property and toil and everything, becomes 'as ordure'. All this is so, and the life of every saint shows us such upheavals."

a component part of her existence, from which she could not free herself, towards which she could obtain no perspective. The authentic French sense of family was there in her blood, more deep-seated than any passion could ever be. We may say: in this respect alone she was wholly a creature of nature. Her father, her sisters and herself were almost a single living organism. In fact it is scarcely imaginable that the Martin daughters could have chosen different convents—except for Léonie, the outsider.

For Thérèse it was beyond dispute from the beginning that Céline, the fourth of their band, must enter the Lisieux Carmel as soon as she was freed by the passing of their father. It is at once touching and astonishing to see how clever, persistent, passionate and unyielding she is in the dozens of letters in which she worked for Céline's entry. How her indignation flared when at last the question became acute, since her relations and fellow nuns alike understandably wondered whether four sisters and a cousin in a convent of twenty nuns might not, after all, be somewhat too much of a good thing. Every fourth nun a member of a single family! Even their revered and exceedingly benevolent confessor, Father Pichon, seems to have held this opinion. He suggested that Céline join him in Canada. But on this one question Thérèse would yield to no one's authority. She simply could not imagine that God would deny her so intense and deep a desire. She agreed with Marie that their "dearly beloved" Father Pichon was in this case simply mistaken in daring to make such proposals to them. If Céline did not have the courage to refuse, Thérèse offered to do so for her. "I shall not be at loss! I am absolutely set on it." Nevertheless, she thought Father Pichon was only a pliable instrument testing Céline for her ultimate sanctification, and therefore Thérèse was not angry with him. "Listen to what I tell you: never, never, will Jesus separate us.... It is impossible for Jesus to deceive a child like you." And then, out of the depths of her heart, she cried: "My heart is breaking..." (because Céline was thinking of surrendering her plan to enter the Lisieux Carmel in obedience to her confessor's desire). "I have suffered so hard, so much, for you that I hope to be no obstacle to your vocation. Has not our love for one another been purified like gold in the smelting furnace?" [26]

It is striking to see how little she was perturbed, in this regard, by the unequivocal consensus of opinion in all the monastic and devout literature with which she was acquainted. Never, in any of the edifying books which she had read and meditated on from childhood, could she have discovered a word about the inherent value of creatural order, the reli-

[26] Letters 146 and 147.

gious import of natural things, the holiness and importance of blood ties—
ideas that *can* be found in books nowadays. Instead, she undoubtedly was
acquainted with the classical instruction material for novitiates, the Jesuit
Alfonsus Rodriguez' *Practice of Perfection and Christian Virtues*, which probably formed part of her daily reading and meditation for years. Rodriguez
devotes a whole section to "inordinate affection for kindred". With many
examples from the lives of the saints and quotations from doctors of the
Church, he directs the true religious to avoid journeys to his home, visits
from relations, and even correspondence with his family. There is praise
for a monk who, after fifteen years of separation, threw a packet of letters
from parents and brothers unread into the fire, without even looking at
the seals or signatures. Rodriguez stresses that even eagerness of producing spiritual fruit in the souls of relations should be regarded as a temptation and fought against; that the religious should especially guard against
engaging in the affairs of his relatives. A separate chapter describes "other
evils and losses" resulting from attachment to kin, as well as the means of
avoiding such attachment. It is pointed out that "this temptation is apt to
disguise itself not only under the appearance of piety, but of that of duty"
as well.

"For the sake of God we have left house and home and kin. Now we
would leave them entirely. We would forget them, so that we may be
entirely free and unhindered to think all the more upon the Lord, to love
Him more fervently and serve Him more faithfully." Thus Rodriguez
sums up the classic ascetic doctrine in regard to kindred.

Thérèse had imbibed virtually with her mother's milk the usual devaluation and condemnation of "nature". We will recall Céline's words: "The
chief virtues I saw practised at home were the observance of the holiness
of Sunday, and contempt for the world." Yet it never seems even to have
occurred to Thérèse that her family, too, was by its very nature a part of
"the world", that it belonged in the sphere of the blood, the earth, of
unredeemed created life, and was subject to the same judgment as everything else. She was confident that *her* ties with *these* relatives, at least,
were subject to grace. Was this confidence due to her conviction that
they were all in common doing the will of God and therefore lived on
the new plane of the Kingdom of God, as "father, mother and sisters"?
Or had the common religious principles which filled their whole consciousness, and which were so taken for granted, simply obscured the
extent to which this "supernatural" community was after all determined
and held together by ties of blood?

God could, of course, demand physical separation; just as He had called
her mother to Heaven, He had called Pauline and Marie into Carmel.
Each time the deep pain could be endured only by obedience and by

loving the sacrifice. He could also lift the little white flower out by its roots, with a wrench that nearly cost it its life, and place it in the stony desert of Carmel. That, too, Thérèse accepted obediently—far more than obediently, with tears of gratitude and bliss. But that physical separation could, and even should, also involve inward parting, a cooling and silencing of feelings, a mortification and death of blood-knit unity—that concept simply did not exist for her. In this case as in so many others the ineradicable imprint of her family remained untouched by all later influences. Thérèse resisted, with all her gentle, inflexible obstinacy, any such stricture. Where things were against her nature, "she was incapable of being taught". She was deaf in that ear. "I do not understand the saints who did not love their families", she says quite candidly. "I love Théophane Vénard because he was a little saint, because he loved dearly the Mother of God and his own family." And with emphasis: "I too love mine very much." "My heart does not leave you for a moment", she wrote to Céline from the convent.[27] "If oceans separated us, our souls would remain united." [28] Heaven remained always for her a reflection of Les Buissonnets. Eternal bliss would be one long Sunday evening with Mama, Papa and all her eight brothers and sisters. She does, to be sure, speak joyously elsewhere of a general community of saints (and even in these cases it is noteworthy that Thérèse conceives of her place in this great Church always as that of a "child", a small daughter imbedded in the venerable band of older relations). But whenever she talks of the *bliss* of the hereafter, what comes forth is her childhood's paradise. When she dies, she sees the Mother of God, with Mama, Papa and the four children who died in infancy, coming to fetch her.

Sober and temperate as Thérèse usually was in her estimates of people, in the case of her blood relations she gloried in superlatives and exaggerations. "Is there anyone else on earth whom God can love as much as my darling father?" she writes to him without embarrassment. (The Censor of the Holy Office dubiously marked this passage.) And again: "It seems impossible to me that there could be anyone on earth saintlier than you.... Yes, you are certainly as saintly as St Louis [his patron saint] himself." [29] Her sisters remain for her "*petites saintes*", chosen souls before all other human beings, angels in human form. "Céline, do you think St Teresa received more graces than you?" she writes to her twenty-year-old sister.[30] Pauline and Marie, she assures them again and again, will sit upon

[27] 14 August 1889.
[28] 8 May 1888.
[29] 31 July 1888.
[30] Letter 65.

the highest thrones in Heaven, and the glory of their crowns will out-shine all others.

After her father's death "the ties which bound his guardian angel to earth were broken, for angels do not remain here below once their task is done. They wing their way back to God. That is why they have wings, and that is why Céline tried to fly off to Carmel." [31]

This extravagance extended even to her most distant, married relatives, as the letters vividly show. Again and again she bursts into veritable fits of ecstasy over her relatives. Each one is canonized in succession: her Aunt Guérin, her uncle, her mother's brother, her two cousins, and even her elder cousin's husband.

"Oh, my dearest Auntie! If you knew how proud I am to have relations like you! It makes me happy to see that God is so well served by those I love, and I ask myself what His reason must have been to accord me the grace of belonging to so wonderful a family." [32] Or: "Yes, my dear Aunt, I know that it would displease you if I were to tell you that you are a saint; nevertheless I am terribly tempted to." "My uncle... a saint still upon his earthly pilgrimage and filled with His divine strength.... If you knew what sweet tears I shed as I listened to my uncle's heavenly conversation. He seemed to be already transfigured." Or, in a letter to her uncle, on the occasion of a cousin's sickness: "How glorious is the crown which is being reserved for you. It cannot be otherwise, since your life has been nothing but an everlasting Cross, and God only deals so with great saints." [33] Or, to her aunt after she had given her daughter Marie her consent to enter the convent: "My uncle, who is a saint like few upon earth, and whose faith can be compared with Abraham's..." Her other Guérin cousin, Jeanne, and Jeanne's husband, she must also "count among the number of saints whom it has been granted to me to see from close up upon earth." [34]

"I too hope, my dear Aunt, to receive a good place at the heavenly banquet, and for this reason: when the angels and saints learn that I have the honour to be your daughter, they will not make me grieve by placing me far from you. Oh, truly, I was born under a lucky star, and my heart

[31] *S.S.,* viii.

[32] 17 December 1897, written for Madam Guérin's feast day.

[33] 22 August 1888.

[34] All this did not deter Thérèse from condemning these same relations abruptly and in a very decided tone as "the world" when they tried to dissuade Céline from entering the Carmel. "They judge others by themselves, and because the world is mad, it naturally thinks that *we* are the mad ones!" And: "Jeanne and Francis have chosen a way so different from ours that they simply cannot grasp the sublimity of our vocation." "They [people in the world] breathe perpetually poisoned air."

melts with gratitude towards the Lord, towards God who gave me such relatives as cannot be found again upon earth."[35]

These examples could easily be multiplied tenfold. We must remember that we are dealing here with a manner of speaking which devout circles had affected for generations, and which should not be understood literally.

To go into the desert with so passionately emotional and affectionate a nature was certainly a strange undertaking; it was quite another thing from resolutely throwing off the burden of such emotions.

We may judge Thérèse's unusual attitude in various ways, depending on what our own is: as a touching weakness which, precisely because it was a weakness, offered a special opportunity for her to prove her saintliness; as a natural limitation of her simple nature which remained within its national, petty bourgeois, girlish bounds and could no longer be remoulded by inner growth; or as a proof of outstanding independence of mind in opposition to the current spiritual fashions. In refusing to bow to these fashions, it might be said, she achieved a refreshing victory of "naturalness" over all crankish ascetic ideals.

Whatever view we elect, we must not forget that Thérèse entered the convent at an age at which (in her case) the second birth into the world, the liberation from the "extended womb" represented by the family—which is certainly one of the processes of maturing youth—had by no means been completed.[36] She was still a part of the warm enclosure of her sheltering home, of the compound organism known as "the Martin family". The violent parting, taking place prematurely as it did, may have been the cause of Thérèse's remaining spiritually at this stage for the rest of her life. On the other hand, every word that the sisters spoke or wrote about their canonized youngest sister proves that in them, too, religious emotion was inseparably connected with the ties of blood.

In the light of all this we can more easily see what it must have meant when God Himself erected an impenetrable barrier between father and daughter. This barrier alone made real the separation Thérèse had offered for His sake. Thérèse herself was nearly shattered by it. "I am suffering very much, but I feel I can suffer yet more", the sixteen-year-old had said to the Novice Mistress shortly before, with the bold confidence of her age. But now she admitted that she had come to the limit of her strength: "I did not

---

[35] Letter 189, November 1896.

[36] Conversely, of course, it fairly frequently happens—the acts and pronouncements of youthful saints should be examined for this—that the labour pains of this liberation, common to all adolescents, and the extremes of renunciation by which such youths hope to accelerate it, may prematurely be confounded and equated with genuine ascetic renunciation in the spirit of the Gospel.

say I could suffer more when I learned that. I can find no words to express our anguish, and I am not going to try.... My desire for suffering was fully realized!" And she wrote to Céline, who was now living at home: "Now we no longer have anything to hope for on earth. The lively freshness of morning is gone, and nothing is left to us but to suffer." The ceremony of her taking the veil after her Profession was "veiled in sorrow" because a temporary improvement in her father's condition, which had raised her hopes that he might be present, proved to be illusory after all.

The letter of 23 September 1890, in which Thérèse again poured out her heart to Céline, was for all its bravery an outburst of bitter weeping in which her whole two years' schooling in self-control was washed away:

> Oh, Céline, how can I tell you what is going on in my soul! What wounds there are. But I feel that they have been inflicted by the hand of a Friend, by a divinely jealous hand. All was in readiness for my espousal, but didn't you feel that something was lacking to the feast? It is true, Jesus had already contributed many jewels to my wedding gift, but one more of incomparable beauty was needed, without a doubt—and today Jesus gave me this precious diamond.... Papa is not coming tomorrow! Céline, I confess to you, my tears flowed... they are still flowing as I write; I can scarcely hold the pen. You know how ardently I wished to see our dearest father this morning; ah well, now I see clearly that it is the will of God that he should not be here. He has permitted that simply to test our love.... This test today is suffering that is hard to understand. A joy had been tendered to us, it was possible, was natural, and we held out our hands. Then we were not permitted to grasp this longed-for comfort. No human hand has done this to us, but Jesus!

Then, through her stunned child's lamentation, there came the flash of insight: "Jesus wants me as an orphan; He wants me to be all alone with Him, so that He may be united with me more intimately." But this deprivation still cannot be borne without hope of redress: "And in the eternal home He will give back to me these so innocent, so legitimate joys, which He denies me in exile."

"... *Ces joies si légitimes!*" Thérèse does not give up a single iota of her claim. As these touching words make perfectly plain, she considered such family happiness her legitimate due from God, and in the future life He would not simply grant it to her as a gift, as a grace, but give it back to her, "*rendre*", as something that is inalienably her own, which He is only keeping in trust for her for a short while.

Two years later a letter to Céline expresses the same feelings with undiminished emphasis. The pain has not been blunted by any habituation to the facts. "Now three years have passed since the time our hearts were still unbroken, since happiness here upon earth still smiled on us. Then Jesus looked down upon us, and all things were changed into an ocean of

tears, though also into an ocean of grace and love. God has taken from us
the one we loved with such great tenderness. Did He not do so in order
that we may be able to say, really and altogether truthfully: Our Father
who art in Heaven?" (It is strange to see this prayer, which St Francis of
Assisi placed like a sword between himself and his physical father, used
here in such a context.) "How consoling are these divine words! What
horizons they open before our eyes!"

There is a kind of spiritual maturing which illuminates suffering by
growing insight, softens it by perspective and reflection, reduces it to its
just proportions, until at last it is assimilated and thus overcome. Such
maturing is not given to everyone. Many a person is compelled to hold
his heart unswervingly and unprotected in the consuming flames until it
is burned out or has become fire itself and can endure the now related
element. In this way, too, the overwhelming and confusing power of suffering can be overcome.

Thérèse belonged to the second category. Her years of enduring this
grief, which was never alleviated by habituation, over which no healing
scar of adjustment formed, worked a deep transformation upon the child
that she was. After her father's death in July 1894 she could write: "Even
now, Father's three years of martyrdom seem to me the most desirable
and fruitful years we have ever had, and I would not exchange them for
the most sublime ecstasies. In face of such priceless treasure, my heart
cries out in gratitude: 'Blessed be Thou, my God, for the days wherein
Thou hast afflicted us.'" And to Céline she wrote: "Our darling father
makes us feel his presence in a way that moves me to the depths of my
heart. After a death lasting five long years, what bliss to find him again,
just as he used to be, and still more fatherly."

No, it was surely no little thing to carry so overflowing, so inexpressibly attached, so unshielded and sensitive a heart, out into the desert. But
among other things this pilgrimage has surprisingly shown us that not
only the born hero, the despiser of pain, who is always in command of
his emotions, can take such a road, and is called to it. It can also be
sought out by the weak victim of his emotions, by one who was raised in
a hothouse, and early wrapped in cotton wool.

The desert had swallowed up her father. But Thérèse's two, soon three,
sisters lived together with her under the same roof, closer and if that were
possible more affectionately linked with her than ever before. Thus we
might almost be tempted to think that fate, or in more Christian terms,
God's merciful providence, spared her the ordeal of complete separation.
A good many of Thérèse's contemporaries saw the situation in this light,
her family in the world regarding it with complacency, her fellow nuns
not infrequently with envy.

Thérèse's description of how she was greeted at the gate of the convent suggests the jubilation she felt at first at this reunion after long separation. But let us not forget that this sentence, too, was written for her beloved Pauline, as a kind of hasty, affectionate requital after nine years of deliberate, underlined alienation.

For Thérèse viewed it as anything but a dispensation of fate that she was able to live in the same convent with her sisters. The joy of seeing them again was one thing. This joy was a gift; it was permissible to accept it, and to express it. But after all it was only the greeting at the gate; once inside, each must go her own way again. Her sisters did not see this obligation with equal clarity. They felt no embarrassment about their naïve, passionate family feeling; they had imparted it to Thérèse and were even more filled with it themselves. It seemed to them natural and so ordered by God that, following Thérèse's entrance, their old maternal rights and duties should be revived, only upon a higher plane. For now, they would come together once more as spiritual sisters in a family group within the larger family of the convent. But they had reckoned without Thérèse.

It is impossible to overstate her inward ties to her sisters. Thérèse went much too far in modesty, subordination and gratitude towards her maternal sisters; she felt herself almost their product. Jeanne Guérin was not alone in her impression that "Pauline entirely formed her, imprinted upon her the stamp of all virtues." This was the general opinion of the family. Ever since Thérèse could think, Pauline had been her ideal. In this attachment lay, undoubtedly, the human roots of her vocation for the Carmel. Her separation from her elder sister had produced that childhood illness which had literally threatened her life. Later on, Pauline continued to guide, from the convent parlour, Thérèse's budding vocation for the Order. And Thérèse obeyed blindly. In the convent, too, her "little mother" continued to be the measure of all things. "You were always my ideal, and I wanted to *be just like you*; so, seeing you paint charming miniatures and write beautiful poetry, I thought how happy I would be if I too could paint, write poetry and do some good to those about me." [37] So reverent is she of Pauline that she quite forgets that at home she had possessed a "pretty poetic talent", as Father Pichon reported at the trial, and that her pleasure in painting was very great even as a child. It was, in fact, so great that she felt her voluntary withdrawing from Céline's drawing lessons to have been the greatest sacrifice of her youth. After a pause lasting for several years, Thérèse's artistic impulses awoke once more in

[37] *S.S.*, viii.

the convent, and she wrote a large number of poems. She seems to have regarded this resurgence as a special grace, an almost miraculous answer to her plea that she might be like her "*petite mère*".

After Pauline's entrance, Thérèse partially transferred her feelings of passionate attachment and dependence to Marie. "I loved her so much that I could not live without her gentle companionship." During the last two years of her life outside the convent there had then developed her renewed intimacy with Céline; together with her child-mother relation to her two big sisters there was now her love for her third sister. This relationship was, indeed, her sole experience with the storms and tensions of adolescent friendship. We may say that Thérèse poured out all the wealth of feeling of her gifted heart, all her precocious sensibility, upon these sisters alone. This excess of emotion never became "detached", in both senses of the word, from its first objects.

But the Carmel was the desert. And if the Lord had called four sisters to it, His purpose was not that they might find themselves cosily together again (this privilege was reserved for Heaven), but that each might, for herself, fulfil her vocation in Carmel as if she were alone. Thérèse had made her renunciation once and for all; she was not minded to retract an iota of it, just because the nearest available Carmelite convent happened to be at Lisieux. From the first day she began her struggle to win and keep her distance from her sisters. She fought with infinite gentleness and tenderness, but unflinching determination.

Biographers who insist on seeing the Prioress only as a tormentor of the saint, and those also who accuse her of intriguing hostility towards the Martin sisters, might look to the letters to see how this woman did everything humanly possible to relieve Thérèse's loneliness—even though Mother Marie de Gonzague was herself by no means pleased to have so many members of the family in her community. "The only fault Thérèse has are her three sisters", she is reported to have said to a priest.

Nevertheless, right at the start she turned the postulant over to her eldest sister Marie, who was to teach her how to follow the Divine Office—a lengthy business which allowed them to be together a great deal. Later she appointed Thérèse assistant to Mother Agnes in the refectory. And when cousin Marie Guérin also entered, she employed the two together in the sacristy. Since the Prioress herself placed little value upon silence and strict adherence to the Rule, this was literally an invitation to intimacy. Sister Marie understood it as such without the slightest embarrassment. "I often tried to intercept her, to say a word which I thought would be useful to her", she reports in her simple, straightforward fashion. But Thérèse was resolute in her strict observance. "Sometimes I used the pretext that I wanted to teach her the Office of the Day.

But after three weeks she sent me away, saying: 'It would be very nice to stay with you, but we are no longer at home.' " [38]

Pauline had no better luck. During their work together in the refectory, Thérèse adhered strictly to the rule which forbade all superfluous talk during work. "How I suffered then, dear Mother. I could not open my heart to you and it was as though you knew me no longer", she ultimately confessed, but only on her deathbed. Even lively little Marie Guérin, "the elf", was tamed by Thérèse. "We must be very careful not to indulge in any needless talk", she wrote to her aunt as late as 1896. "Because for every necessary sentence we think of a funny little rhyme which then must be saved for the recreation hour."

Thérèse never asked permission for special conversations, although she could easily have received it, since the Rule permits spiritual conversations which serve to enlighten and mutually inspire the nuns. Thérèse sanctioned such conversations for many other nuns, but never requested any for herself. Later, when Pauline became Prioress, Thérèse was not only entitled, but in duty bound to have a frank discussion with the Mother Prioress. The Rule called for an hour of spiritual direction once a month. In Lisieux custom had long since broken down this regulation; the nuns came to the Prioress every week for consolation and instruction. Thérèse alone observed the prescribed interval. She saw her sisters only in the hour of common recreation after the main meal. At such times she would sit down beside whomever she happened to be near, or beside a nun whom she had observed to be downcast, tired or out of sorts, and hence in need of cheering, disregarding the tacit and sometimes expressed sensitivity and even jealousy of her sisters, who considered such conduct almost a demonstration of lack of love.

When Pauline was ill, she petitioned her favourite sister to come and see her. "Have the other sisters visited you?" Thérèse gently retorted. "No? Then I must also deny myself this."

"We must apologize to the others for our being four under one roof", she was in the habit of remarking. Even during her last illness she was concerned to impart some of this spirit to her sisters. "When I am dead, you must be very careful not to lead a family life with one another. Do not tell each other anything without permission, not even news from the parlour, and ask for permission only when really useful and not merely distracting matters are concerned." After Thérèse's death, one of the nuns asked Marie why she had not sought to be with her blessed sister more frequently. Marie replied sadly: "Alas, how could I

[38] 2 S., 330.

have done so? I wanted to, but in her conscientiousness she did not want to speak with me." [39]

In her Epilogue to *The Story of a Soul* Mother Agnes stated: "We may also say that it was impossible to tell whether she loved her sisters more than the others." An older sister, who was not particularly partial to Thérèse and watched her sharply, testified: "I have observed that her sisters showered great attentions upon her, but she herself was completely free of these family ties."

In other respects also the Prioress was most generous in granting Thérèse the opportunity to foster these family ties. The amount of correspondence Thérèse was permitted was an astonishing privilege.

In other Carmelite convents the regulations permit a single letter annually to the closest relations, a visit from relations once in three years. Thérèse has left 214 letters from her period in the convent, and these are certainly not all she wrote. (In one, for example, she mentions five letters written the same day, of which only three have been identified.) Those to her sister Léonie—to whom she wrote least of all—have been preserved only in part. Similarly, Father Pichon, her spiritual director, did not keep her letters. From the first year of her novitiate, in which separation from the "outside world" was, if possible, enforced more strictly than at any other time, twenty-seven letters are preserved; from the second year, thirty-one. And on top of this her relatives came to see her in the parlour every week!

From the fourth year on (1891) a distinct self-limitation begins. The total number of letters drops to six or seven and then rises again from ten to sixteen. In her last year her correspondence reaches its peak figure of fifty-three letters in the year (long after her father was dead and both Céline and cousin Marie had entered the same convent). This large number undoubtedly reflects her feeling that she was taking farewell; almost a third of the letters are to members of the convent. During her father's illness the Prioress gave express permission for Thérèse to write to Céline every two weeks, "in order to support her". She was permitted to write to her father even during the retreats, those days of strictest withdrawal before special spiritual events. On such days more rigorous rules of silence prevailed even within the house.

"I am in retreat now, and so letter-writing is not really allowed, but our Mother is permitting me to send you a word anyway, in order to thank you [for the bridal gifts which had arrived; Thérèse was permitted to look at them as soon as they came, rather than wait the three days

[39] Laveille, 269.

until the retreat was over]. And then, after all, writing is forbidden during retreats in order not to ruffle the silence of withdrawal. But how could the silence be ruffled by writing to a saint?" Even the editor of the volume of letters calls this an altogether unusual exemption.

The generous correspondence privileges which Thérèse received from the Prioress were not limited to the family outside the walls. In most Carmelite convents it is customary for the sisters to tuck notes, requests for a book or tool, important information, or something of the sort, into the doors of others' cells. These notes were in part a continuance, in part a relaxation of the obligatory silence. Personal matters—a plea for forgiveness, a word of consolation—might also be included in such notes. In Lisieux there seems to have been a great deal of such intraconvent correspondence. Thérèse was allowed to write to her sisters, whom she normally saw every day, even during retreats, both her own and those of others. In other words, the authorization for spiritual exchanges was not cancelled even for those three- or eight-day periods. Out of the three days before Thérèse's own taking the habit—days which, in the language of the convent, the sister was supposed to spend like a hermit in the desert—seven letters have been preserved (including the one to her father). From this we may judge what heroic renunciation Thérèse had to summon up, of her own free will, in order to make relatively little use of this always available opportunity.

Her letters to her three sisters are among the most original, intimate and moving documents she left to posterity. They are veritable love letters, ardent, passionate, sentimental—so much so that the reader is almost pained to see such intimacies exposed to the public gaze. In these letters she allowed herself from time to time to requite these sisters, for whom her love remained unaltered, with some small measure of the trust and affection they poured out to her.

Pauline alone, as was so often the case, understood the inner discipline her sister was obeying, and she supported Thérèse silently and reverently. Although it hurt her no less, and perhaps even more, when Thérèse in the course of their joint work in the refectory made it clear that her *petite mère* was this no longer, Pauline did nothing to change the situation. During her period as Prioress she made no objection when Thérèse did not avail herself of the opportunities for conference. When as a novice Thérèse asked her permission to make her oblation to Merciful Love, of which we shall speak later, Pauline granted the request without any further inquiry. And with the same apparent indifference she accepted her sister's report, shortly afterwards, of her one real mystical experience during her years in the convent, an ecstatic rapture while making the Stations of the Cross. But Pauline preserved all these things in her heart.

In the spring of 1896 a plan was conceived for sending Pauline and Céline to the Carmelite mission in Saigon. Later Thérèse herself was picked for this transfer. Presumably Mother Marie de Gonzague wanted to break up the clique of sisters. Nothing came of this; but we can imagine what the impending lifelong separation meant to Thérèse.

During her last illness Thérèse kept unerringly to the discipline she had set for herself. Then, however, something new took place, which removed the bars: the awakening consciousness of a mission urged her to deposit her spiritual bequest in the listening, receptive, almost imploring hearts of those who loved her best.

Thus the sisters' common road in Carmel was above all a way of pain. There was the perpetual need to oppose an inner detachment to their outer proximity, to impose discipline and silence upon their undiminished feeling for one another, to check mercilessly the rash tempests of their hearts. To the Prioress rather than to her sisters Thérèse made the reticent but highly informative confession which is to be found in the ninth chapter of her story:

> You know, too, that Jesus has offered me more than one bitter chalice through my sisters. David had good reason to sing: "Behold how good and how pleasant it is for brethren to dwell together in unity", but this unity is impossible on earth without sacrifice. I did not come to Carmel to be with my sisters; on the contrary, I saw clearly that their presence would cost me dear, for I was determined not to give way to nature. How can anyone say that it is more perfect to cut oneself off from one's family? Has anyone ever blamed brothers for fighting side by side in battle, and for winning the palm of martyrdom together? It is no doubt true that they encourage one another, but the martyrdom of one affects them all.
>
> It is the same with the religious life, which theologians call a martyrdom. A heart given to God loses none of its natural tenderness; on the contrary, the more such tenderness increases, the more pure and divine it becomes.
>
> Such is the affection with which I love you, Mother, and my sisters.

During the last two years of her life two young priests belonged to her "family". In November 1895 Abbé Bellière, a twenty-year-old seminarian and subdeacon of the White Fathers, wrote to the Carmel of Lisieux—at the inspiration of St Teresa, as he said—asking for a nun who would help him in his missionary work by devoting her prayers and her penances for him and the souls that were in the future to be entrusted to him. Mother Agnes, who was Prioress at that time, came letter in hand to the laundry tub where Thérèse was working and "gave her a brother" for her feast day. Thérèse was overcome with delight. As is the case with many devout girls, a priest in the family seemed to her the pinnacle of honour and grace; for that reason, above all, she mourned so intensely the loss of her brothers who had died in infancy. Now she saw this apparently unfulfill-able longing satisfied in a miraculous manner. "It was such an un-expected answer that I felt happy as a child. I say that because I can't remember ever having been so happy since my childhood, when my heart seemed all too small to contain its vivid joys. I had not, I say, felt as happy as this for years; it was as though my heart were born again, as if forgotten chords of music had been touched for the first time."

Thérèse never met Father Bellière. Shortly after her death he went to a station of his Society in Central Africa. In the ten letters that passed between them we discern a generous temperament thirsting for spiritual heroism, but at the same time anxious and rather soft, overscrupulous and a little too conscious of the greatness of his sacrifices for the good cause.

A year later Father Adolphe Roulland (1870–1934) of the Society of Foreign Missions requested the same service of the Lisieux Carmel. Once more Thérèse was assigned the duties of "spiritual sister", this time by Mother Marie de Gonzague. "She will be a great help to you. She is the best among my good souls. She belongs altogether to God", Mother Marie wrote on the margin of the first letter Thérèse sent to the missionary. But Mother Marie de Gonzague's choice seems also to have been somewhat coloured by a tiny element of jealousy towards her rival, Pauline. Pre-sumably she did not want Thérèse to be indebted only to Pauline for the joyful gift of a spiritual brother. The Prioress even forbade her to tell Mother Agnes of this second assignment. And as always Thérèse obeyed so faithfully that she locked herself in her cell when she was writing to Father Roulland, or painting devotional pictures for him, lest she be ob-served accidentally by Pauline.

The sixteen letters which have now been published adhere, in form and content, to the usual conventions of elevated discourse. But it is quite clear that Thérèse, in spite of all her reverence for the priestly office, in both cases felt herself to be the teacher and the giver. It is she who con-soles and warns, encourages and praises, answers questions, offers corrob-oration, and instructs the priests in the meaning of her "little way". "I see how much your soul is sister to mine, since it is called to raise itself to God upon the 'lift [elevator] of love' instead of climbing the steep stairway of fear. I do not wonder that familiar intercourse with Jesus still frightens you; it cannot be attained in a day; but I am certain that once I am freed from my mortal shell I will be able to help you far more to walk in this happy path."

A strange destiny linked her still more closely with Father Roulland. On the day of her Profession, 8 September 1890, she had prayed the Lord for an "apostle's soul": "Since I could not become a priest, I wanted a priest who had the same intentions and strivings as myself to receive in my place the Lord's graces." Six years later, shortly after his ordination, Father Roulland celebrated Mass in the chapel of the Lisieux Carmel. Afterwards he was allowed to see Thérèse in the parlour; he had already been in correspondence with her. He told her that on that 8 September his own vocation as a missionary had been decided. Thérèse was happy, but not surprised. "I thought I would have to wait for Heaven to see the apostle I had asked of Jesus", she wrote to him soon afterwards. "But the Saviour has lifted a little the mysterious veil which obscures the things of eternity, and has given me the comfort of meeting the brother of my soul here in exile and working with him for the salvation of the poor heathen."

It seems to us extremely characteristic of Thérèse that she always viewed this relationship entirely as a sisterly one—not in the popular pious phrase, but literally so, just as if the departed little brothers of her childhood had unexpectedly descended again from Heaven to resume the life they had missed. The letters in no way bear even a remote resemblance to the correspondence between other such couples, the famous spiritual exchanges between holy men and women who met one another in the name of God and of divine love, but also more or less consciously as men and women in the emotional depths and tensions of genuine friendship. It is as though Thérèse could conceive and feel such affinity only within the orbit of actual blood relationship. This, too, gives us some idea of what it had cost her not to share the "increase" in her family with Pauline. In her letters to both missionaries she called herself, tenderly and without embarrassment, their "little sister". From the very first lines she wrote, she poured out her innermost thoughts and feelings as she did to her sisters. "All that is mine belongs to them." On her deathbed, she said to Pauline: "When I pray for my brothers, I only say: Dear God, give them all that I ask for myself." She set down the prayer which she wished the two to say for their sister: "Merciful God, in the name of Your gentle Jesus, of the Holy Virgin and of all the saints, I ask You to inflame my sister with Your love and give her the grace to lead many souls to Your love." The letters, in fact, read like letters to sisters who were also priests. How significant it is that Thérèse wrote to Father Bellière, who was somewhat closer to her than Father Roulland: "I see how much your soul is *sister* to mine—not: how much you are my brother in spirit."

Yet there is no immaturity behind this curious childlikeness, which in another individual might be a highly dubious trait. Thérèse was thoroughly adult and thoroughly aware that this genuine "sisterhood" was something uniquely hers. It was not intended to serve anyone as a model, certainly not as a fixed pattern to follow. With amazing candour and clarity, she warned both the Prioress and Pauline against letting any other nun repeat or continue the experiment. After her death, she thought, when the story of her soul had been widely read, undoubtedly many young priests would write to the Carmel requesting "spiritual sisters" like her. However, she warned, the superiors ought to proceed very carefully and sagely in such cases. Permission for correspondence of this sort ought to be granted very rarely, and the number of letters severely limited. There should be no question of nuns volunteering for such a task. For while the missionary would perhaps suffer no harm from such a correspondence, the Carmelite might, since her mode of life in any case exposed her to the constant danger of being too concerned with her own person. Instead of contributing to union with God, "such correspondence, however infrequent, would occupy her mind too much and to no purpose. She would probably imagine she was working wonders, when, in fact, under the guise of zeal, she had done no more than involve herself in a useless distraction.... She might even wound her soul and fall into the fine-spun snares of the Devil. Anyone might write what I write, might receive the same compliments, the same demonstrations of confidence.... We serve the Church only by prayer and sacrifice. In Carmel we must not try to buy souls by counterfeiting. And how often the fine phrases we pen, and the fine phrases we receive, are nothing but an exchange of counterfeit coins.... What I am telling you here is very important, Mother."

2. THE SOUL'S DISILLUSIONMENT

Thus Thérèse was ready to postpone her "legitimate" family joys, the eternal Sunday evenings, until Heaven, for the sake of purification, penance and atonement upon earth. But she felt she might at least count upon her new family, the spiritual community within the convent and the Carmelite Order; from these she was not barred by any interdictions. After all, the precise difference between the hermit and the religious living in a community is that the latter consciously chooses, as one of the instruments of salvation, the strength to be drawn from the example and stimulation of the others.

With great yearning Thérèse had looked forward to the "blessed Ark" of Carmel, had envisaged herself as a dove striving to reach its only proper nest there. With boundless respect she looked up to the nuns dedicated to God who had already been walking the way of perfection there for years and decades, whom she wanted to join as the youngest and least worthy of all—but one unreservedly prepared to learn, to honour and to emulate.

What she found was a community of very aged nuns, some odd and cranky, some sick and troubled, some lukewarm and complacent. The Carmel at Lisieux was anything but a collection of saints.

We need not be too surprised at that. Let us remember the atmosphere of the era among those *émigrés de l'intérieur* who condemned all "profane" life as without religious value. Let us remember the exaggerated overestimation of the monastic life, the superstitious belief in it as the sole road to salvation. Given these things, it was inevitable that a flood of persons without vocation poured annually into the cloisters. Their motives might be sincerely religious, of course, but their call inadequate. Moreover, there were other than religious motives. Throughout all the periods when monasteries and convents stood high in prestige among Christian nations, there have always been many motives for entry not of the purest, not of the most spiritual nature. Painful as it is to remember this, we must not overlook the simple historical fact. No one will deny that convents during the Middle Ages and the Baroque Age served, very much contrary to the intention of the Church, as useful asylums for daughters of the nobility and the urban patricians whose prospects of marriage were, for one reason or another, not good. A train of unfortunate consequences extending through long years of the Church's history has resulted from this. Nor should we deny the equally obvious fact that convents during the past century and a half have suffered from a similar plague. Here, as in other areas, the course of evolution spread from the topmost stratum of society down to the lower levels. In the nineteenth century female Orders and congregations—true to the trend of the times—shot up like mushrooms and were very frequently institutions for taking care of the daughters of the bourgeois and peasant classes. Certainly the matter was not approached with the crude simplicity typical of medieval practice. Earlier, there had been more loosely organized women's communities founded on a spiritual basis, but making no special claims upon the religious life of the individual—the Béguines, for instance, and various other sisterhoods. These had provided a frame of reference, a home, and a measure of economic security to single women who would otherwise have been unprotected and unemployed. By the nineteenth century, however, these sisterhoods had dropped away. Part of the surplus of women in Church-minded circles, who would have been the proper material for such organizations, found their way into the convents proper. Thus it turned out that many girls sought and found in the religious Order a sheltered life relieved of burdens, a kind of continuation of their home circumstances, rather than an austere climb to the pinnacle of religious development. There prevailed, moreover, the comfortable conviction that this choice was in itself the ethically highest and most meritorious decision which could be made; the nun was *ipso facto* elevated far above ordinary mortals. For girls of peasant or petty bourgeois origins taking the habit meant a tremendous social rise—this remained the case almost to the present day. Such girls could not hope to climb so high by marriage; whereas to be a nun was virtually equivalent, in the eyes of Catholics, to culture and status. Then again, since piety in general had taken its character so much from the monastic ideal, the step from the "world" to the Order did not seem especially great.

In conclusion, then, such "external" reasons for entering a convent existed side by side with the "vocational" reasons, just as marriages of convenience existed side by side with marriages for love. And who, in the end, can say that nuns who originally entered convents for such "superficial" reasons may not have yielded good fruit pleasing to God?

Nevertheless, it may still seem strange that so strict an Order as the Carmel should have attracted persons of dubious vocation. We must, however, remember the importance of priestly guidance and the pseudomonastic concept of obedience prevailing in devout circles. In addition, especially in Latin countries, sentimental enthusiasm with a strong tinge of religion was far from uncommon. In the close atmosphere of the "Catholic ghetto" pride and ambition often turned to the field of religion, which was the only one open. Out of such sometimes morbid impulses arose strivings for record achievements, for the glory of saintliness.

The institution of the novitiate was supposed to act as a sieve. But the mesh of the sieve had gradually become too large. The active Orders, by virtue of their efficiency and their well-merited repute, took charge of more and more schools, hospitals and other social establishments. The urgent necessity for meeting the increasing demands on their labour force could not but influence the selection of candidates. In the contemplative Orders, on the other hand, the danger arose from the diminishing number of candidates. For lack of choice, prioresses were chosen from the existing community which was often mediocre enough. Such prioresses guided the convent by softened, lowered standards and adjusted everything more and more to the steadily dropping average.

There is no doubt that the considerable number of such members threw a heavy burden upon the convents and were a severe trial to those with genuine vocations. Where such persons were in the majority, the meaning and aims of a community could well be distorted.

During the eighties of the [nineteenth] century a remarkable mixture of all the above-mentioned types was to be found in the Carmel at Lisieux. The nuns came from that withdrawn Catholic France we have described, from families in which there prevailed a similar deep, living, unquestioning piety such as dominated the Martin family. The obituary letters of the convent are a mine of information on this score. They tell of devout parents who joyfully raised many children for Heaven—and for the convent. In one case two out of six children, in another three, chose the religious life. The sister of one Carmelite had ten children; as in the Martin family, four of these died young, and of the survivors, two became nuns and one a priest. Many of the sisters had acquired from their mothers the habit of daily attendance at Mass and fear of "worldly amusements"; they had early exchanged a semimonastic life in the "world" for the Carmel. One, a sturdy peasant child, when first she heard about the sufferings of the martyrs was so impressed that she cut away her toenail with a pocketknife; she wished to train herself for such a trial of her faith. Another reports that "as a child of a few months she wept at the sight of a crucifix" and could not go to sleep at night without a rosary; her mother did not permit her to look into the mirror or to talk about her clothes. More than one had been tormented as a child by religious anxieties and scruples, like Thérèse. One had lain awake weeping for many nights out of fear that she was unworthy to make her First Communion. More than once we hear of a pious mother praying, from the time of her child's birth on, that it will have a vocation to the cloister. Even parents with only one daughter persisted in this hope and encouraged the girl when she seemed to lose heart at the prospect of parting from them. In the case of only one lay sister, who entered after Thérèse, do we hear of a hard, unsheltered life; the young woman was an orphan who had been knocked about in the "wicked world" and been made to work as a servant, until her spiritual director sent her into the refuge of Carmel. The advice and even the command of priests almost always played a crucial part in the decision to enter, just as the will of the parents did in the marriages of other girls.

The convent Thérèse entered was not an old-established house with a great tradition, hallowed by the memory of saintly predecessors. In 1838 two nuns from the Poitiers Carmel had been sent out to found the house at Lisieux. One of them, Mother Geneviève of St Teresa, was still living when Thérèse entered; she was then eighty-one years old and very ill. The first six sisters had put up for a time in a straw-roofed hut by the brook. Then had come a first small house on the Rue Vivarot. In the course of forty years, interrupted again and again by the poverty of the small community, the convent buildings had grown; the chapel took seven years from the laying of the cornerstone to the consecration. When Thérèse entered, the second wing, containing the cells and sickrooms in which she was to live and die, had been standing only ten years. The whole structure was a red brick building in the shape of a horseshoe, with a small, slate-roofed dome, the different wings connected by cloisters. It was plain and sober, like the dreary square brick tenements then being erected in countless numbers in all the cities of the continent. Its appearance might well have disappointed anyone who associated something romantic and picturesque with the name "Carmel", as the individual houses of this Order are called in memory of their common origin, the mysterious mount of the prophets in the East.[40]

Of recent origin, unformed, without a character of its own: such was the community inhabiting this house.

In the years Thérèse Martin spent there the Carmel of Lisieux averaged twenty-five members.[41] Almost all of the sisters came from the petty bourgeois and artisan class; only a few were originally country girls. The Prioress and Thérèse's Novice Mistress were of Old Norman nobility. Probably the Martin sisters alone represented the new class of the rising bourgeoisie.

These origins and this leadership emerge clearly in the complement of the small community. There were women whose piety was simple, taken for granted, who unquestioningly pursued the aims set before them by the prescribed means. As far back as their thoughts could reach, they had been familiar with the realities of the Church, with prayer, penance, self-sanctification, zeal. At the same time all, without exception, bore the mark of the "exiles in their own country". Raised behind artificial walls, cut off from the intellectual life of the age and from the shaping forces of ordinary reality, even before they entered the convent reared in an atmosphere of monastic, or rather puritanical, narrowness and timidity, they unconsciously suffered from intellectual and cultural undernourishment.

The convent should have been able to give them everything they needed for the perfection of their natures. It could put them in touch with a wider sphere of the mind. It should shape and refine their characters by means of the incomparable schooling of the liturgy. The ancient tradition of monastic asceticism, the Rule of St Teresa, which had stood the test of centuries, could serve to deepen their spiritual lives—for that charming and brilliant woman had had immense knowledge of human nature. Finally, their whole beings could be impelled by the tremendous impetus

[40] Only the convents are so called; the monasteries of the Order are simply known as "Carmelite Monasteries" (Communication from the Carmel of St Joseph, Wien-Baumgarten).

[41] According to the charter a Carmelite house without income should not number more than fourteen, otherwise twenty-one; during Thérèse's lifetime about thirty sisters are mentioned; considering the four or five deaths and six entries, we arrive at the above-mentioned average. In France the custom differs from that in other countries where the Order is established.

exerted by a fairly small body of likeminded persons striving steadily towards a common goal.

Every monastic Order has its own distinguishing quality, which in time places its imprint upon the members of the Order. Bremond, that incorruptible and ironic critic of the all-too-human in the realms of ecclesiastical piety, which he knows so well, has described the unique character of Carmel: "A heavenly *élan*, a bold and generous zeal, heroic detachment... an indescribable degree of common sense, inner order, love full of intelligence and sweetness which reassures those who might be alarmed and discouraged by the vision of such heights of virtue.... These women are vitally receptive to all things which make the mind and heart resound; they are broad in their thinking, amazingly free-spirited, and full of charming gaiety."[42]

That is, truly, an exalted pattern, but it is not one into which the average person will develop of his own accord. For dull, scarcely awakened, anxious and narrow souls to fit into it, long, strenuous discipline is required, and, above all, wise, strong guidance. For the convent is no community of higher beings who easily triumph over human frailty; it is a group of converts and of those always in need of conversion. The novice brings into it herself, with her entire dowry of unregenerate, often somewhat tainted human nature. This is the time-honoured ecclesiastical view of it and it applies even to those with a genuine vocation. In the Benedictine Order the monk, who after finishing his probationary period makes his vows to his abbot, swears to a *conversio morum*, a revolution in his way of life—that is, to penance and improvement, insofar as he is one who has chosen the monastery because he stands in need of conversion. At her Clothing, the Carmelite responds to the priest's question, what is her desire: "The mercy of God, the poverty of the Order, and the community of the sisters." Thereupon the priest pronounces over her the Church's plea that she "may be renewed in mind and spirit, so that she may put off the old self with its acts, and be made worthy by Christ our Lord of putting on the new self, which is created after the image of God".

If this ultimate and only meaning of the monastic life is ignored, if the living spirit departs from it, there remains only a parched thicket of precepts and customs. Woe to the soul that becomes entangled in it. The barriers against the outer world—interior and exterior seclusion, silence, renunciation of secular reading and entertainment—have meaning only as fences around the sanctuary. Their purpose is to concentrate the

---

[42] H. Bremond, *L'histoire littéraire du sentiment religieux en France*, 2:137.

soul's attention, to simplify its contents in the extreme, to empty it that
it may be filled again with God's glory. Without that aim, all this abandonment of the world becomes a negation deadly to the spirit of life.
Poverty turns into dreariness and dullness, mortification into a fakir—
like end in itself, exercises into mechanical repetition, solitude into un-
fruitful loneliness. What remains is more barren than life in the world
because there is lacking even the natural fulfilment of the world's tasks,
while at the same time the conceit of perfection lulls the soul into a
deceptive smugness.

To be sure, no such nadir had been reached in the Lisieux Carmel.
Living flames still glowed amid a great deal of ash and slag. And, in fact,
the entrance of our saint fanned the sinking flames into a conflagration
that warmed the world. "The Carmel at Lisieux, I knew, included very
saintly souls", declares Prior Godefroy Madelaine,[43] whose testimony generally shows good judgment. But if we assemble and consider the evidence scattered through many sources on the nuns inhabiting the convent
at that time, the picture is on the whole not very glowing, in spite of a
few noble exceptions.

There was, to begin with the best, the aged founder on her sickbed,
Mother Geneviève of St Teresa, in many respects a fine embodiment of
the great Teresian model, an example of the most genuine religious vocation, tested and strengthened by six decades of physical and spiritual
travail. Her history reads in part like the classic legends of saints. She had
entered the Carmel at Poitiers at the age of nineteen, had borne the
burdens of a Prioress in Lisieux for many years. The nuns praised her
endless maternal kindliness; her tender, self-sacrificing care of the sick;
her heroic contempt for her own sufferings, which were accorded to her
in ample measure; her intense interior life; her childlike humility; the
almost visionary aptness of her consolations; the mysterious union with
God in prayer which sometimes led her to say to the sisters: "Our Lord
has ordered me to tell the community this. It is He who wants you to do
this, my dear daughters, not I." Two years before her death, Mother Geneviève responded to a question from her Prioress: "Mother, how should I
fear death? Our Lord has granted me the grace of not judging any human
soul. I rely upon His word: Judge not and you shall not be judged."

We might expect such a personality to have formed her nuns into a
band of souls equal or at least akin to hers. But that was not the case. Her
weakness was, as the reverent obituaries and descriptions hint as delicately as possible, "too great leniency". For all her kindliness and purity,

[43] See *Les Annales de Sainte Thérèse de Lisieux*, 1926, p. 16 (15 January).

she was not strong, was not a leader, not an influence. And perhaps this weakness went deeper than any of the accounts allow us to see. As far as we know, none of the nuns who survived her, and who had been under her rule, embodied her best traits and carried them on. A case in point is Mother Marie de Gonzague, who repeatedly alternated with her in office, and at last replaced her entirely. (In the Carmel the Prioress elected by the community serves for only three years; in exceptional circumstances her period of office may be extended to six years.) Mother Marie de Gonzague was a prime example of spiritual gifts dissipated by weak guidance, so that she ended by being untrue to herself. We can only see in her, as in a tragic mirror, the result of her superior's failings.

Then there was Mother Marie of the Angels, Thérèse's Novice Mistress: kind, tactful, conciliatory, always concerned with making peace and smoothing matters over. She was, insofar as that was possible in the most silent of Orders, wearisomely loquacious. She was the kind of person generally referred to as "touching"—a description whose slight undertone of forbearance borders on disdain. For she distinctly lacked prudence and objectivity; she was all overflowing emotions, having the best intentions in the world, but lacking "discrimination and insight into souls" (a most unfortunate lack in a Novice Mistress). She was simple-minded and limited, fluttery and distracted; this weakness provided the convent with material for jest over a period of decades. She had, however, the fearlessness of the aristocrat; she could stake her life recklessly for others, as she did on the occasion of a sudden flood. Aristocratic, too, was her feeling for her family. This could not be subdued; she remained entangled all her life in the joys and sorrows of her kinsfolk in the world. In the practice of poverty, humility and prayer, however, she was exemplary; Thérèse gratefully calls her "a perfect example of an early Carmelite"— although we must probably ascribe the phrase before this, "real saint", to the loose use of this appellation within the convent.

The other nuns, insofar as we know about them, were quite average, well-intentioned, unimportant; among them were a surprising number of odd, stunted or sick personalities. When we consider that at the time of Thérèse's entry the convent contained between twenty-one and twenty-five members there remain—apart from Thérèse's sisters—few healthy, radiant personalities.

The Martin sisters must have formed a highly special group from the first. Although Marie and Pauline were in their thirties, already mature women, they were almost the youngest. Their religious background had also been exceptional; they brought with them a pure, high, austere religious ideal. They were gifted and capable, knew how to get their way. Soon after their entry they brought in their two younger sisters and a cousin—a whole group of fresh, healthy, aspiring young people in a convent overbalanced on the side of age. When Thérèse entered as a schoolgirl of fifteen, there was a gap of a full eight years between herself and the single other novice. Next in age came her sisters, who had been mothers to her. Then the curve climbed sharply past a small group of women in their forties to a majority who were fifty and more. Four nuns between sixty and eighty-five completed the pyramid. Not until Thérèse's third year in the convent did more young girls enter.

3. MOTHER MARIE DE GONZAGUE

All others were overshadowed by the prominent and rather ambiguous figure of the Prioress, Mother Marie de Gonzague.

The tendency to legend-making has operated with particular force upon the strangely enigmatic, contradictory personality of this woman, who took Thérèse into the convent against the will of her superior, who was her Prioress for six years, who was present at her deathbed. In the commonly accepted tale she quickly assumed the typical features of the "antagonist of the saint", and almost of the wicked stepmother in fairy tales. When we add up the best-known descriptions, and the allusions strewn throughout the various documents, a strange picture forms.

Domineering and ambitious, jealous to the point of morbidity, petty and suspicious, sensitive and so uncontrolled that she gave way to outbursts of wrath, stiff and inaccessible, calculating and flattering towards outsiders, swayed by every impression of the moment, hence unpredictable and entirely unreliable in her statements and promises, demanding fawning submission, provoked by decent straightforwardness, an easy victim of flattery, inclined to abuse the powers of her office, ruthless and irresponsible towards natures more tender than her own—truly, the charges brought against her are a veritable catalogue of sins.

The few rays of light which the biographers (much against their will) allow to fall upon their portrait reveal purely worldly virtues such as competence, generosity, "a certain degree of culture and distinction", but cannot brighten the picture as a whole. Moreover, the talebearers plainly imply that they are not telling all they know; they confine themselves to hints, are reporting only what is essential, and spreading the "mantle of Christian forbearance" over the most incriminating material because, after all, the Prioress died penitent and as a sincere venerator of the saint. The mildest judgment on Mother Marie de Gonzague is to be found in Bernoville (pp. 160–67); however, it is strangely at variance with the usual representation. Bernoville maintains that Mother Marie de Gonzague was a good little nun whose sole trouble was her high office; that she was

incompetent and insecure, confused and nervous, could maintain her authority only by violent exaggerations, thus deceiving herself and trying to
create in others the impression that she knew what she wanted. This
behaviour "may have given the impression of a hard heart and a parched
spirit; nevertheless she was a good soul who loved her flock and sincerely
thought she was guiding them well. Her faults did not prevent her from
being a devout and worthy Carmelite. Had she been in a position of
obedience, these defects would have been smelted away; her incapacity to
govern brought them plainly to the foreground."

In strange contrast to these portraits is the tone of sincere personal love
and respect which invests every word Thérèse addressed to her Prioress.
The relationship of these two cannot be reduced to the handy simplifi-
cation of "sacrificial lamb and tormentor". We shall have more to say
about this.

For the present, let us remember how hagiography has always been
plagued by the desire for strong, obvious contrasts, for painting in black
and white. The glory of the "victim" shines all the brighter, the more
innocent its sufferings are, the more cruelly it is tormented. In addition,
the primitive sense of justice always demands a scapegoat who can be
blamed for the undeserved sufferings of the just, and who if possible can
be paid back for those sufferings. Hence legend loves to oppose the antagonist to the saint, just as drama loves to oppose the villain to the hero.
So it has been from the days of the martyrs, whose foes were the Roman
emperors, to the time of little Thérèse, whose foe was the wicked Prioress.

If the attributes of such a figure do not suffice, they are easily eked out.
Many a relatively harmless person figuring in the fate of a saint has thus
willy-nilly been raised to diabolic stature. The father of St Francis, the
merchant Piero of Assisi, turns out on closer examination to be a far
more human and pitiable person than the legend will have it.

Out of her forty-four years in the Order, Mother Marie de Gonzague
was Prioress of Lisieux for twenty-one years. That is to say, the entire
convent elected her as their mother and leader of the house seven times
in succession, after each of the prescribed three-year periods when she
was replaced by another. One biographer of our saint asserts with some
timidity that "certain material services" which Marie de Gonzague performed for the convent—such as the rebuilding and enlarging of the
house—had been the decisive reason for these re-elections. If that were
true, it would be a grave dishonour indeed for the convent. The statutes
of the Carmel expressly direct (chapters 1 and 13) that no one should be
taken in for the sake of her dowry. What a violation of the spirit of this
regulation if a woman as black as Marie de Gonzague has been drawn
had been entrusted with the highest office in the convent not once but

seven times—simply because she knew how to raise the money for building! Prior Godefroy Madelaine, the only witness from outside the convent who seems to have known the Prioress fairly well, and who at the same time was one of the earliest devotees of St Thérèse, takes a different view of her: "Her frequent re-election always seemed to me to confirm my impression that the sisters viewed favourably her method of administration." During the official inquiry, when Mother Gonzague was no longer living, he said of her: "I knew her quite well. She seemed to me to possess remarkable judgment. In the administration and direction of the convent she had a great eagerness for the right. As far as I could judge from dealings largely confined to external matters (*relations plutôt extérieures*), but extending over a long period of time, she made an excellent impression."[44]

Numerous statements attest that many of the nuns were passionately attached to her. More than one of the sisters, in later accounts, humbly admitted that excessive love for this woman had been the sole immoderate and egoistic emotional entanglement of their lives.

Mother Marie de Gonzague—in the world, Marie-Adèle Rosalie Davy de Virville—sprang from a respected and noble family. She had entered the Lisieux Carmel in 1860, at the age of twenty-six. Tall and stately, she was dignified and distinguished in her bearing. She may have been beautiful, for such remarkable power over the minds and emotions of people is usually linked with a certain physical magic. Her most determined critic mentions her unusually pleasant voice. Laveille concedes that she had personal charm "which she probably owed in part to her careful upbringing". She was devout in an enthusiastic, generous way, given to somewhat ostentatious, unusual penances. Of iron constitution, the austerities of the Carmelite life were easy for her, so that all her life she could have little sympathy for others' claims to alleviations.[45] She did not permit the stinging nettles in the garden to be hoed out, because she used them for mortifications. Her character was full of intense contradictions. She had an amazing range of feeling, a great capacity for absorbing a variety of experiences. Childlike, overflowing gaiety alternated abruptly with blackest melancholia; tenderest consideration for others with intolerable, haughty rudeness. Along with this complexity of emotions went an almost masculine tartness and sobriety of mind. "She seemed to me less of a woman than did the saint's sisters", remarks the English convert Dr Nimmo Taylor, one of the first active proponents of the new saint, in his account of

---

[44] I S., *Animadversiones*, 13.

[45] But we learn from several remarks in the *Manuscrits Authentiques*, which were cut in *The Story of a Soul*, that she frequently suffered from bronchitis.

his visit to Lisieux. "She was cooler by nature, less excessive ... her speech was not full of exclamation marks." [46]

A nature so full and strong needs a master more than anything. What wonders more perceptive and sterner guidance might have wrought in her. There may well have been the stuff for a great Teresian personality in this woman, similar to Marie de l'Incarnation, the proud royal nun in Gertrud von Le Fort's story *Song at the Scaffold*. It was Mother Marie de Gonzague's tragedy that the necessary discipline from without was denied her. Here we see, painfully, Mother Geneviève's limitations. Neither she nor anyone else in the convent was capable of taming this unruly, ambivalent novice. Certainly the superiors were not lacking in love and mildness; certainly the young girl did not lack good will. Indeed, she had "simplicity to the point of childlike transparency". But those in charge of her lacked the power, and probably the courage as well, to force their will upon the alternately radiant and dark personality of Marie de Gonzague. In mind and natural vigour she towered over them all and was therefore incomprehensible to them. In her case richness and strength proved her downfall, as poverty and weakness does for others.

"There is no more dangerous flatterer than inferior surroundings." This profound epigram of Madame Swetchine was illustrated in the fate of Marie de Gonzague. The situation was all the worse because no yardstick of character or intellect determined her position in the convent, only her natural advantages. These were, unfortunately, the advantages of birth and rank and the sheer forcefulness of her temperament, rather than qualities of mind and spirit. Conservative pious circles are apt to have an ingrained respect for titles and names. In the sixties and seventies of the [nineteenth] century an aristocrat in the flesh counted for far more in a petty bourgeois convent than we can realize nowadays. The superiors appointed Marie de Gonzague to the highest offices as soon as her novitiate was finished. In 1866 she became Sub-Prioress, in 1874 began the long series of terms as Prioress which lasted until her death. The superiors hoped, we are informed, that responsibility would develop her genuine capabilities and at the same time exercise a moderating effect on her "strange moods". [47] What she really needed was initiation into the hard and magnificent schooling of Carmelite inwardness, humility and self-abandonment.

---

[46] I *S.*, xx, 21.

[47] The *mémorial* devoted specially to her in the records of Thérèse's canonization plainly suggests that several of the nuns, alarmed by her uncontrolled outbursts of temperament, which none of the others could remotely understand, concluded that she was suffering from the kind of morbid emotional disturbances which nowadays would be called manic-depressive. It is no longer possible to determine the facts.

To her unchecked nature, unpurified by wise, strong discipline, domination became a poison. In this point we agree with Bernoville's portrait, although from another approach. Marie de Gonzague ruled her convent just as, "in the world", after a marriage befitting her station, she would have administered her household—as, perhaps, she had observed her mother governing her father's château. For her mother's childhood extended back to the days of the Revolution. Marie de Gonzague acted like a genuine grand lady of the *Ancien Régime*, generous and competent, self-willed and moody, totally unconcerned about the views, desires or criticisms of others. She took up favourites and dropped them again, handed out tributes and distinctions as she pleased, enchanted the nuns and repelled them again. Did not the bewildering sense of her own power, the enjoyment of her personal spell over nuns, her inevitable underestimation of and possibly contempt for the too-docile herd who so eagerly wooed her favour, and the bitter though comfortable isolation engendered by her position—did not all this critically intensify her violent oscillations between high spirits and melancholy, rather than cure it? Unfortunately we are obliged to blame her convent for having literally spoiled a rare and precious person, just as weak parents spoil a promising child.

This fact seems to have escaped her detractors. More and more, Marie de Gonzague passed beyond the sovereignty of her own self-control and the Rule of the Order. That Rule never became second nature to her. Her cat was pampered and petted more tenderly than a child. Her imperiousness developed an unfortunate secondary aspect: passionate jealousy of all rivals. In those days the office of Prioress granted its holder extensive rights over the inner life of the nuns in her charge. She could ask them for a spiritual reckoning almost as if they were in the confessional. She could determine when a nun might receive Communion and could even refuse it to her. Not until 1891 did canon law abolish this dangerous right, which was far too subject to abuse. In this field also, Marie de Gonzague is said to have acted arbitrarily, following her own stern standards without comprehension for the spiritual lives of others. She felt out of place in this convent; that is evidenced, for one thing, by her seeking in applicants (possibly quite unconsciously) the traits proper to her early environment: good manners, poise, a pleasant, cultivated voice. Thus, she took ill-suited women without any commendable qualities but these into the community and into the Chapter, which was the conferring and legislative body of the house. More than once she was later forced to regret bitterly such decisions.

We ask ourselves again and again how such mistakes were possible when a subject's Clothing and Profession (which included participation in the Chapter) were subject to the approval of this very Chapter, when the priests connected with a convent as spiritual directors and confessors must also have had to be consulted. This remarkable woman must have exerted a spell upon all who had anything to do with her, so that their objections were either lulled to sleep, or they did not dare to raise them. Her accusers would have us believe that she terrorized the nuns by scenes and simply flouted the recommendations of her spiritual counsellors—among them such honest and energetic men as Canon Delatroëtte and the Abbé Youf—and that she dispensed with the Bishop and employed her diplomatic gifts to keep visiting priests from seeing what was going on. But this is no explanation at all; rather, it raises anew the question of how such tricks were possible. True, Canon Delatroëtte did once say in his rough manner: "People would burn your convent down if they really knew you." And Mother Geneviève "contented herself with weeping and praying". Nothing more was done. Not one of the nuns summoned up the courage—or else not one thought the situation critical enough—to appeal to the Bishop.

Particular indignation was aroused in the convent by the excessively close ties that Marie de Gonzague maintained with her relations in the world. Her sense of family was precisely as naïve and unchecked as that of many of her nuns. In her it was strengthened by the self-assurance of an aristocrat, and probably also by her isolation in the convent. Supported by her status, which allowed her more privileges than others, she imposed no restrictions upon herself. Against all the regulations and customs of the Carmel, a friend came daily to the parlour and retailed to the Prioress all the latest news of her circle; later this ran around the convent as welcome gossip. The Prioress also had a dearly loved sister who was unhappily married and at odds with her daughter; this sister came to her for consolation, advice, support and a chance to talk about everything imaginable. Frequently the countess appeared with her grandchildren for a lengthy visit, and Marie de Gonzague placed the whole convent virtually at the countess's disposal, just as if she were the lady of her own château. Enclosure was maintained, to be sure; the guests were lodged in the gatehouse. But it seemed to the Prioress perfectly natural to put her nuns at the countess's service on such days—to keep her company and entertain her. All those in the house who had skilled fingers were enlisted to embroider coats of arms for her, mend her lingerie, paint mementoes and little pictures on parchment, and even freshen up and copy old, dim family portraits. Since as far as we know only the Martin sisters possessed such talents, we are probably not wrong in assuming that they in particular were charged with such tasks. These were, in the eyes of the Prioress, doubtless an honour; the nuns, however, felt it to be an outrageous and unjustified imposition. Here, it would seem, bourgeois-democratic and genuinely French instincts for *liberté* and *égalité* as against aristocratic arrogance were incongruously mingled with concern for monastic discipline and order.

Did the Prioress ever learn that "the nuns whom the countess called her friends did in truth regard themselves as merely her servants", so that the whole convent heaved a sigh when the portress announced her arrival? Marie de Gonzague seems to have had no idea of this dislike; otherwise she would scarcely have made, day in and day out, the affairs of her family the conversational subject for the recreation hour and even for her personal talks with the nuns.

Equally reprehensible was the fact that Marie de Gonzague used convent funds to help her sister out of financial embarrassments. Here, however, the Chapter shared the blame, for the Prioress had to ask its consent for every sizable expenditure. The irregularity of her conduct cannot be condoned; nevertheless, it seems to us that even these breaches indicate misapplied virtues such as loyalty, generosity and readiness to sacrifice, rather than base traits or attitudes.

No wonder, at any rate, that the discipline of the convent went to pieces under such a régime. Marie de Gonzague was not pharisaical in temper. She did not take privileges for herself and refuse them to the other nuns. During her period as Prioress the parlours were used far more frequently than the Rule allowed, and even the devoutest of the nuns gladly availed themselves of this lenient custom. Thérèse's sisters relate without any embarrassment that their relatives used to visit them every week. Prolongation of the visits beyond the permitted time limit was also taken so much as a matter of course that it struck everyone as a special exercise in virtue when Thérèse adhered strictly to the regulations. Silence was poorly observed; whenever the Prioress came out of the parlour, she would regale the curious nuns who joined her in the corridor with the latest news while it was hot from the griddle.

Like all superiors who enjoy governing, the Prioress issued many superfluous and arbitrary regulations which she herself quickly forgot. The nuns reacted to this by criticism of the usefulness or wisdom of the rules—criticism at best expressed by their tacitly ignoring the things that seemed of lesser importance to them. Such conduct naturally undermined respect for authority and religious obedience. No wonder that factions formed around the Prioress. In time, it seems a veritable movement of reform arose among the younger nuns, sprung from a pure determination to end the numerous abuses, but the sisters did not summon up the strength to make a clean contest of it. Instead, they took refuge in secret criticism and subdued resistance which led to unbearable, because unadmitted, tensions.

Mother Marie de Gonzague was not alone in letting her feelings go undisciplined. "At that time there were incessant pretexts for frictions and clashes", says Pauline.[48] Many little items in Thérèse's life betray the fact that sisterly love among the nuns was not all it should have been, that a petty spirit of mutual observation, sarcastic censoriousness and intense touchiness prevailed. During their father's illness the Martin sisters suffered a good deal from foolish and tactless talk during the recreation hour; without regard for their feelings, the Prioress and other sisters would chatter away about insane asylums, straitjackets, and the violent acts of madmen.

There is the well-known story of the time Thérèse was arranging the flowers at the bier of Mother Geneviève and was reproved by one of the lay sisters: "Oh, yes, you manage very well to move the big wreaths from your relatives to the front and keep the modest ones from poor people in the back!" Even more characteristic of the spirit of the convent, it seems to us, is that this incredibly insignificant incident was described by at least eight witnesses in tones of the greatest indignation—*thirty years afterwards!* Equally indicative of the general temper is the immoderate amazement of the witnesses at Thérèse's "extraordinary heroism"—in that she responded to this bit of rudeness with a friendly smile and moved an inexpensive wreath of moss to the front. It is also food for thought when a novice (who later, as far as we can tell, in view of Thérèse's reticence, became a friend of the saint) remarks quite casually that she was little liked in Lisieux "because I came from another Carmel".[49] Or when Pauline mentions that an ill-fitting, poorly cut habit that Thérèse wore gave the community unending pretexts for teasing and sarcasms. Or when an older nun emphasizes as a special merit in Thérèse: "I observed the servant of God's tactful humility also in that she never said a word to make us feel that we owed her gratitude for the many temporal benefits that her relations showered upon us."

This was the environment Thérèse found when, that spring day, she made at last the entry into the convent which she had so ardently longed for and fought for. Of all these things not a single word, scarcely a brief, reticent allusion, is to be found in the story of her soul. But every sentence must be read against this background, if we are to comprehend her own statements about her life in the convent. Without knowledge of the framework, her account leads us from one misunderstanding to the next.

[48] 2 S., 296.
[49] 2 S., 502.

We will remember what a shock it had been to her as a schoolgirl when she encountered a few rude and ill-behaved schoolmates. What was that compared to the new experience of discovering so many inadequacies and shortcomings, so many serious faults in the heart of the sanctuary? There is no reason to assume that Thérèse had even the faintest foreknowledge of these conditions. Indeed, it is improbable, given her pure and unconditional thirst for saintliness, that she would have chosen this convent if she had known. Undoubtedly, she would have preferred separation from her sisters, no matter how painful. That Pauline and Marie lived there was to her sufficient guarantee of the worthiness of her new home. The wound must have struck to the roots of her soul as she became increasingly acquainted with this place which was to be the scene of her "voluntary imprisonment" unto death, and as she saw that the characters of her fellow nuns had become, by long habit and isolation, unalterably set.

Young people usually respond to disillusionments of this sort with extreme bitterness, with outraged criticism and rebellion, with a haughty, defiant conviction that they know better. They will burn their shattered idols, or adopt a melancholy distrust of ideals, or of human beings in general.

Thérèse does not betray by so much as a word what went on within her during the first period of adjustment, unless we can find some such reference in the veiled, generalized sentences with which she concludes her description of the "thorns"—insignificant and almost humorous incidents—of her first days:

> I can honestly say that from the moment I entered suffering opened her arms to me, not only in the trials I have already told you about, but in others keener still; and I embraced her lovingly. I declared my reason for coming to Carmel during the solemn examination before profession: "I have come to save souls and above all to pray for priests," and when one wants to attain some end, one must take the means. As Jesus had made me realize that the Cross was the means by which He would give me souls, the more often it came my way, the more suffering attracted me. For five years[50] I followed this course, though I was the only one to know it, and this practice was nothing else but the hidden flower I wanted to offer to Jesus; the flower whose perfume none would breathe this side of Heaven.

The most eloquent document of this period, it seems to us, and one which vividly sums up the saint's brief remarks as well as her studied silence, is the photograph of her Clothing day. Thérèse stands upon the

---

[50] This phrase gives us a hint: after five years Pauline becomes Prioress, and thereafter many aspects of the house certainly improved.

pedestal of the big cross in the yard, wearing the heavy, clumsy habit in which as yet she scarcely knows how to move. Her right arm is placed stiffly around the shaft of the cross, her left arm held forward, in an equally stiff and artificial manner, with two fingers protruding out of the long sleeve—a pose apparently chosen carefully by the photographer, a visiting priest, as appropriate for the occasion.

Above this body in its strange and obviously uncomfortable pose the face of the sixteen-year-old girl looks out at us, straightforward and compelling. Her eyes, slightly closed because of the harsh winter sunlight, are smiling with a friendly roguishness, but the heavy shadows in the eye sockets speak of tears and sorrows endured. Her mouth too is smiling amiably, obviously in compliance with a request, but without constraint. But how hard is the line of the mouth between the round, full child's cheeks, how mute, reserved and uncompromising. How much resistance and independence there is in the whole face. It is full of gentleness, contains a measure of humour, and much patient, unwavering self-command. How much firm readiness for what is to come, for unforeseeable and unavoidable trials, there is here, and at the same time how much composure, patience, lack of strain. It is a great pity that this picture has been rejected by the convent as a poor likeness (*"infidèle"*), because it deviates from the usual stylized sweetness. For this reason the photograph was retouched and made into one of the well-known representations. The retouching gives regularity to the features, but erases the unusually alive expression of solitude suffered with childlike courage.

Thérèse could not look to her sisters for advice and aid precisely because they were offering their help so constantly, and with such eager intensity. Among those appointed to be her superiors, she certainly could find no consolation. The Novice Mistress's gentle incessant chatter trickled by Thérèse's needs without touching them; the Mistress had no inkling of them. The Prioress herself was above all the object of Thérèse's perplexity, and the source of her secret new sorrows.

Thérèse had already known her for a long time. Mother Marie de Gonzague had received her in the parlour when she was only nine, had spoken to her, with heart-winning seriousness, about her vocation, and had even settled on her future convent name: Thérèse of the Child Jesus. Six years later, Mother Marie de Gonzague had violated custom and used all the force of her will and the weight of her office to bring about Thérèse's entry against the opposition of superiors. Thérèse must have expected to find in her the mother she had missed since the departure from her life of Pauline and Marie—a mother, and beyond that a good angel and the guiding star for the beginning of her convent life. She brought to her an open, expectant, reverent heart, and was instantly captured by Marie de

Gonzague's special magnetism. Thérèse was affected as she had never been before by anyone not her blood relation: her feelings burst into flame; she felt intense, almost overpowering yearnings. For the first time this fifteen-year-old girl experienced the strength of the currents that run between human beings, of attraction that does not proceed from a rational esti-mate of the worthiness of the other person, even the supernatural worth, but operates like a force of nature. Thérèse had to struggle with all her might to overcome this unaccustomed attachment. Bravely, pathetically, she confesses her weakness and her victory in the story of her soul:

> I remember that as a postulant I was sometimes so violently tempted to seek some crumb of comfort for my own satisfaction that I had to hurry past your cell and cling to the banister to prevent myself from going back. A thousand and one excuses for yielding to my natural inclination pre-sented themselves to me; there were so many things to ask about. I am only too glad, now, that I denied myself from the beginning of my spiritual life, for I enjoy already the reward promised to those who fight with cour-age. I no longer feel that I must deny my heart all consolation, for it is fixed on God.... It has loved Him alone, and this has gradually so devel-oped it, that it is able to love those whom He loves with a tenderness incomparably deeper than any selfish, barren affection.

In another place Thérèse recalls a minor incident of her novitiate. The Prioress was ill, and Thérèse as sacristan had to come to her cell in the morning to deliver the keys of the communion grille. An older nun, afraid that any noise would disturb the sleeping patient, wished to take the keys from Thérèse at the door. Thérèse was consumed with eagerness for a glance at the sleeping Prioress: "I was secretly rejoicing at this chance to see you." Under the influence of this feeling, she who was so gentle, submissive and steady came very close to a serious quarrel with the sister who wanted to keep her from entering. She was able to save herself from an outburst only by hasty flight. The effort so exhausted her that she had to sit down on the stairs, heart pounding violently, "to enjoy quietly the fruits of my victory". It was a ridiculous triviality, and Thérèse related it to her own shame. "When I think back on my days in the novitiate I see only too clearly how imperfect I was. I have to laugh at some of the things I did. God is certainly good to have lifted up my soul and lent it wings." But how much light the story casts on the intensity of her nature.

At this same time Thérèse received permission to talk about spiritual matters with another novice eight years older than herself. Sister Martha— described by the saint as innocent, frank, communicative and pure-hearted, and by the other sisters as foolish, tactless and bothersome—was already at least in her third year in the Order, but still had a schoolgirl crush on the Prioress. The hour given to them for conversation seemed to her a welcome opportunity to discuss together the object of their adoration and luxuriate in their own emotions. Thérèse quickly realized that here was a person on the point of losing herself in emotional entanglements and dangerous self-deception, and that these "conversations which savoured too much of the world" could only harm the two of them. She decided to shake Sister Martha out of this unwholesome emotional muddle and spoke her mind to her lovingly, but with great earnestness. Thérèse told her "what true love really is, proving that her natural affection for you [the Prioress] was only a form of self-love, and *making known the sacrifices I myself had had to make at the beginning of my spiritual life in this very matter.*[51] Soon her tears were mingling with mine." It is remarkable that this is one of the few times Thérèse admits to having wept during her years in the convent. The struggle for emotional freedom seemed to her so vital that she confronted her companion with the alternative of giving up this attachment or returning to the world.

Not in vain had the Novice Mistress warned Thérèse urgently against such all-too-human affection, which could assail and literally devastate a sensitive and unsatisfied heart even within a convent—perhaps all the more within the convent because of the narrowness of the circle. Now Thérèse could feel herself how true this was. Perhaps, too, she had other examples before her eyes. Whence, otherwise, did she derive the surprising statement in the fourth chapter of her story: "How can a heart that is taken up with human love be fully united with God? I am sure it is not possible. I have seen *so many* people attracted by this false light, fly to it as moths do and burn their wings, then flutter, wounded, back to Jesus, the Eternal Fire, which burns without consuming." This passage is written in connection with her own experiences at school, but Thérèse can scarcely have been thinking of the youthful affections of the pupils, although these were the starting point for her remarks.

The Prioress herself did nothing to foster her youngest nun's attachment. Quite the contrary; Thérèse was probably thinking of this very rejection and the painful emotions that accompanied it when she continued her remark on the burned moths: "Our Lord knew that I was far too weak to face temptation; He knew that I would certainly have burnt myself in the bewildering light of earthly things, and so He did not let it shine in my eyes. Where stronger souls find joy but remain detached because they are faithful, I found only misery. I can't take any credit for

---

[51] In the *M.A.* Thérèse had here: "in order not to become attached to you in a wholly material way, like a dog to its master". This clause was unfortunately deleted in *The Story of a Soul*.

not getting entangled in this way; it was only because God had mercy on me and preserved me."

"He let me find nothing but bitterness in human affections"—this phrase surely does not refer only to the fickleness of her eleven-year-old schoolmate!

That the Prioress had from the beginning a full appreciation of Thérèse is indicated by much evidence. Thus, for example, she wrote to the Guérin family shortly after Thérèse's entry: "Never did I think such mature reason possible in a fifteen-year-old. There is nothing about her to chide; everything is perfect." Prior Godefroy Madelaine recalls that the Prioress always spoke of Thérèse as "my little angel". Another priest remembers the highly significant statement: "If I were to appoint the Prioress, I would select Sister Thérèse out of the whole community. She is perfect in everything; the only fault she has are her three sisters." Pauline, too, mentions at the trial[52] that Mother Marie de Gonzague "told and wrote to all and sundry all sorts of good things about Thérèse, and I will add that she did this in all sincerity".

Yet from the very first day the Prioress treated Thérèse with incomprehensible sternness. In the autobiography Thérèse recounts, half plaintively, half humorously, that "our Reverend Mother" rebuked her until her head whirled. "I could not meet her without getting some reproof or other." Thérèse was taken to task for every triviality. The Prioress, prone as she was to overlook slacknesses with a tolerance which it is difficult to excuse, allowed no slackness on the part of the postulant; nothing escaped her stern eye, neither the missed cobweb in the cloisters nor any casualness in weeding the garden.[53] "Really, this child does nothing at all. There must be something wrong with a novice that has to be sent for a walk every day." She scolded Thérèse for sleeping beyond the allotted time, though this had been prescribed by the Novice Mistress, and for her lack of skill in housework and needlework. Even the conferences, those personal talks with the Prioress for purposes of spiritual direction, which Thérèse awaited with violent emotion, with dread and with yearning, brought about no relaxation of the constant, oppressive tension. Most of the hour "was spent in scolding me, but the worst of it was that I did not know how to correct my faults; my slowness, for example, or my lack of generosity in carrying out my duties."

Thérèse speaks of hours "now and then". Mother Marie de Gonzague was in the habit of receiving her nuns for spiritual directions once a week.

---

[52] 2 S., 170.

[53] These anecdotes were not written down by Thérèse herself but inserted into the manuscript by the sisters in the course of their editorial work.

Thus the very fact that Thérèse was called to the Prioress at long intervals must have seemed a sign of disfavour.

Thérèse's older sisters appear to have been more disappointed than she herself. They had probably expected their prodigy, their "little saint", whose entry they regarded as a grace and good fortune for the entire house, to be granted a rather exceptional position from the start. They thought her youth, delicacy and grace would be cherished. They assumed that this child of grace, this little flower of the Blessed Virgin, whose vocation had come so early, would be granted honour and preference since she was so obviously a divinely chosen spirit. Such treatment would have seemed to them no more than right and proper.

When things turned out so very differently, Pauline attempted to intervene in this drama which was utterly incomprehensible to her. But she was put in her place, and with no little sharpness. "This is what happens", Mother Marie de Gonzague replied, "when two sisters are in one convent. Of course you would like to see Sister Thérèse given preference and brought forward. But I consider precisely the opposite course necessary, because her pride is much greater than others think. She has need of constant humiliation. And if you appeal to me on account of her health, I say: that does not concern you; we shall do what we think proper." [54]

Pauline was struck at her tenderest spot. What a blow this was to her may be guessed by her conduct in the parlour. She, who was always so conscientious, so punctilious and exemplary, sought consolation by airing her griefs to her relatives. Céline reports with astonishing *naïveté*: "From the time of her [Thérèse's] entry I saw her and my other Carmelite sisters in the parlour once a week. My sister Pauline especially told me about her sorrow at seeing our little sister neglected, exposed to the contradictory desires of many of the sisters, and contentiously dragged this way and that.... From these conversations I learned that the principal causes of her trials were... the tactless acts of some nuns, who abused her heroic patience;... the rather inadequate government of Reverend Mother Marie de Gonzague, whose unstable and bizarre character caused the nuns much suffering. With her, everything depended on the whim of the moment." [55]

There is not the slightest indication that at this time there had already begun that profound tension between Mother Marie de Gonzague and Pauline from which all participants were to suffer so bitterly in future years. Rather, there is much evidence that Sister Agnes was one of the Prioress's favourites. Mother Marie's support of Thérèse's early entry also

[54] 2 *S.*, 308; statement by Pauline.
[55] 1 *S.*, iii, 69.

suggests that she promoted this ardent desire of Pauline's out of fondness for her, not only for the sake of Thérèse, who was after all essentially a stranger.[56] Perhaps the initial dissension broke out over Thérèse herself. At any rate, it created a new, extremely delicate and painful complication which was to grow worse with the passing years. At this time the Martin sisters probably formed the firm conviction that Mother Marie de Gonzague did not understand and did not like their little sister. Henceforth all her conduct, in matters large and small, was narrowly observed, considered and interpreted from this point of view.

On the other hand, who can say how much of the Prioress's sharpness towards Thérèse was meant as a chastisement to the sisters who were secretly criticizing her? But this ignoble reason, for all that it unfortunately seems so obvious and likely, was neither the primary nor the decisive cause of Mother Marie de Gonzague's treatment of Thérèse.

Certainly such conspicuous and unwonted sternness on the part of a Prioress who was generally a far too lenient superior, and sternness directed towards so willing and obedient a child, would seem to call for the simple explanation: groundless dislike. We can well understand Pauline's concluding that the Prioress was moody and unreliable; had she not only a while before so warmly thrown her prestige behind the effort to get Thérèse into the convent at fifteen? To the loving sister who had always endowed the child of her heart with a halo, Mother Marie de Gonzague's charge that Thérèse was more proud than people knew must have seemed the rankest injustice.

Yet we venture to assert that Mother Marie de Gonzague was the only person in the convent who fully recognized both the inward greatness of young Thérèse, and the essential peril facing her. We venture the interpretation that such deep insight, such penetration of appearances, could have arisen only from the clairvoyance of a genuine, intense love. And we maintain that Thérèse herself understood all this.

The one person of stature in the convent, the fiery and strong, though errant and spoiled soul of the Prioress, sensed Thérèse's greater vocation. "A soul of such mettle must not be treated like a child; dispensations are not made for her sort. Let her be; *God supports her.*"[57] For that reason she knocked the girl about with a veritable lion's paw. These merciless blows would have shattered any shallow self-deception. We ought all to thank her for this conduct, as Thérèse did. It may be that the much-maligned

---

[56] In a conversation (16 July) reported in the *N.V.*, Thérèse alludes to her sorrow at the time because even Pauline "shared for a moment" the Prioress's harsh judgment of her faults.

[57] *Histoire d'une Âme*, xii.

Prioress recognized in Thérèse what she herself might have become, and that she wished to save the precious soul entrusted to her care from the fate which had been her own soul's undoing: that fate of being a favoured and preferred outsider living in the convent as a concession.

Mother Marie de Gonzague accounted for her actions to no one but God and herself; possibly, also, to her faithful adviser, Prior Godefroy Madelaine. He says: "The Prioress, who loved her deeply, nevertheless treated her with a strictness which seemed extraordinary." [58] And again: "The Prioress tested her in many ways, to raise her up to fortitude and virtue. The Servant of God suffered greatly from this severity, but to the degree that she was tried, *she felt her soul becoming free.*" [59]

As soon as the Lord once permitted the Prioress to think Thérèse proud, writes one biographer, she could not be blamed for trying to teach the novice humbleness of spirit by humiliating her. We must nevertheless ask whether the Prioress's opinion had any real basis. "God and nature do not love tenderly"—and both the divine and the natural element were present in the Prioress's love for the chosen child. For it was a long time since anyone had rebuked Thérèse. The didactic principle the sisters had followed long ago, when they anxiously avoided even the shadow of praise, had by now swung radically in the opposite direction. After her years of "darkness" Thérèse, the plaintive problem child, had become the radiant favourite of the family, of whom all were proud. The "affair" of her early vocation, the visit to the Bishop, her heroic courage during the papal audience, had woven a kind of aureole around her pretty face. And it really appears as if the family considered Thérèse's youthful humility inviolable and unshakable, so open were they in proclaiming their delight in her again and again.

The catechist of her school years in the Abbey, Abbé Domin, put the matter quite bluntly during the beatification trial: "It was my opinion (and that of many others, I believe) that she received far too much flattery and adulation from her relatives, especially from her father, who could not bear to be apart from her and continually called her 'my little queen'. It seemed to me that they were risking making her vain and preoccupied with herself, like so many other girls." Significantly, he adds: "I recall that this impression of mine persisted even after her entry into Carmel. During her novitiate I visited her once, and was considerably surprised when the Mother Prioress (!) who was present at the interview began to praise the magnanimity of the little novice. I thought to myself that it was after all not wise to praise a young person to her face in that way. I have since con-

[58] 2 S., 188.
[59] 2 S., 535.

cluded that she must have been firmly anchored in humility not to be shaken by all these praises.... The pastor of the house, the Reverend Monsieur Youf, also sometimes spoke of her in the highest terms.... This talk seemed to be simply claptrap and the consequence was that I no longer went to visit her. I always observed the greatest restraint because I found the general opinion of this child simply exaggerated and did not want to join the chorus of praises." This witness was a distant relation of Monsieur Guérin, and probably had to listen to the excessive chorus of praises in the latter's house as soon as Thérèse's name was mentioned. His sober judgment shows us plainly enough where the real danger for Thérèse lay—and how wise Mother Marie de Gonzague's educational method was in this case.

He was also correct in his view that this cult was growing rather than diminishing inside the convent. The sisters, who thought their prodigy unappreciated and neglected in the community, certainly missed no opportunity to comfort her, and make amends. They sang her praises during every visiting hour and related what the poor child had to endure, uninhibited by her presence in the room. Thus Léonie was able to say at the beatification trial that the noble virtue of her sister was nothing new to her; during her visits to the Carmel in those days she had already heard *all about it from her older sisters*.[60] The Novice Mistress describes the gradual substitution of roles in the convent: "I frequently accompanied her sisters to the parlour. Did someone need advice? The elder sisters turned to the youngest, and whatever she said was like Gospel to them."[61]

Certainly their boundless confidence in this divinely inspired child was justified, and the love and gladness, the entire lack of envy, with which the elder sisters gave their former "daughter" precedence, must be counted among the purest traits in the Martin sisters. But Thérèse would not have been human if this boundless admiration from the very persons who were still the measure of all things to her, could have passed by her without constituting a temptation. She was very conscious of her disposition towards pride. There was still in her much of the child who had been good and made "sacrifices" as much for the approval of her elders as for the love of God, and who as a First Communicant had written: "I will try to crush my arrogance."

She confesses that it cost her a great deal to accept mutely an undeserved rebuke from her mild Novice Mistress over a vase that someone else had broken—"and I had to remind myself that it would all be made known on the Day of Judgment". Entrusted later with the difficult and honourable office of guiding the newcomers, she was to write of the

[60] I S., 85.
[61] I S., x, 41.

sometimes drastic criticism she received from her novices: "At times I am
overcome by a longing to hear something other than praise; my soul
grows tired of this over-sweet food; then Jesus offers me a tasty salad,
seasoned with vinegar and spice." The Prioress was the first to develop in
her a taste for such nourishment. The Prioress also ruthlessly strove to
wipe away the traces of her "little queen" character, which was the unconscious fruit of her upbringing at Les Buissonnets.

We will recall Thérèse's own humorous report on her ignorance of all
household work, and her inclination to have the smallest practical work
regarded as a special ascetic discipline. In this matter the Prioress would
stand for no nonsense. The daughters of the middle class might at least be
expected to know how to use brooms, dusters and darning needles. In
Thérèse's slowness and lack of interest in such work she by no means saw
a sign that the child was "born to higher things", but simply a deficiency
which should be amended by strict discipline. Thérèse willingly learned
the lesson. Not until she read the autobiographical notes did the Prioress
learn that her little postulant had sacrificed her free time in her cell in
order to "carry on with my needlework without raising my eyes".

Mother de Gonzague refused to be deflected from her course by anyone. The gentle Novice Mistress, too, was inclined to spoil the child and
spare her the hardships of the Carmelite life. Thérèse relates with humour how this put her into an awkward situation at the beginning of her
life in the convent:

> Our Novice Mistress ordered me, during my postulancy, to tell her each
> time I had a stomach-ache. Now I was having them every day, and the
> order became a veritable torture. When the stomach-aches began, I would
> sooner have suffered a hundred canings than have reported it, but out of
> obedience I nevertheless told her each time. Sister Marie of the Angels,
> who had long since forgotten her order, would then say: "Poor child, you
> will never have the health to follow the rule; it is too hard for you." And
> she would go to Mother Marie de Gonzague and ask for medicine for me.
> But Mother Marie, astonished and dissatisfied with my daily reports, re-
> plied angrily: "This child is constantly complaining!... We come to the
> Carmel in order to suffer; if she cannot endure it, she does not belong
> here!" Nevertheless, I continued for a long time to mention my stomach-
> aches out of pure obedience, at the risk of being sent away. At last God
> had mercy on my weakness and granted me the grace of having my supe-
> riors lift this command to report.[62]

Thérèse suffered bitterly from Mother Marie de Gonzague's conduct towards her—probably more from the cold repudiation of her loving heart

---

[62] Laveille, 333; the Prioress's words, "*On vient au Carmel pour souffrir*", in the records of
the trial.

than from the scoldings and punishments. Only an extremely shy and general allusion in the letters of this period betrays her feeling: "How good to me is He who will soon be my Bridegroom, how divinely kind, since He does not allow me to attach myself to anything created. He well knows that if He were to send me only a shadow of happiness, I would cling to it with all my might, with all the energy of my heart, and so He denies me even this shadow." And again: "Why seek happiness on earth? I confess to you that my heart has an ardent thirst for happiness, but it also sees, poor thing, that no creature would be capable of quenching this thirst." [63]

When her soul had at last become free, as the old Prior says so finely and simply, she thanked Mother Marie de Gonzague with deep gratitude for the painful discipline: "How I thank God, my darling Mother, for such a virile and valuable training. What a priceless grace! I do not know what would have happened to me if I had become *the pet* of the Community, as those outside seemed to think! I would probably have thought of my superiors merely as human beings, instead of seeing Our Lord in them, and the heart that had been so well guarded in the world would have fallen a prey to human attachments in the cloister. Luckily I escaped such a fate." And again: "I thank you, Mother, for not having spared me; Jesus knew very well that His little flower was so frail that without the life-giving waters of humiliation she would never take root; and this priceless blessing she owes to you."

How long this process had taken, the next lines reveal—these were written in the summer of her last year of life: "*For some months now*, the Divine Master has completely changed His way of dealing with His little flower; doubtless because He thinks she has been watered quite enough already, He allows her to unfold in the warmth of the bright sun. He only smiles upon her now, and she owes this, too, to you, Reverend Mother."

When the test had been met, Mother Marie de Gonzague was not miserly with signs of respect and confidence. It is a comfort to know that at the last a relationship of unclouded friendship prevailed between the two of them. Even the Martin sisters agreed that the Prioress displayed towards the saint "much confidence; indeed, at the end of her life she chose her to be her confidante". It is unfortunate that not a single example of this has been reported. Hence we must content ourselves with the shy and yet so deeply felt statements in *The Story of a Soul*; these are

[63] To Marie, 8 January 1889.

strewn through the ninth and tenth chapters, which are addressed to the Prioress, and even more of them are to be found in the original manuscript.

"You, Mother, are the compass which Jesus has given me to guide me safely to the eternal shore. To fulfil the will of God, I have only to keep my eyes on you.... You certainly make the yoke of obedience sweet and light, but my disposition is such that I am sure that even if you were to treat me harshly, I would not act in any other way, or lose any of my filial devotion.... You did not even consider it imprudent to tell me, one day, that the Divine Master was enlightening me, and that it was as though I had had years of experience.... When I say that compliments have no effect upon me, Mother, I am not referring to the love and confidence you have shown me; that, on the contrary, touches me deeply.... I am loved here, by you and by all my Sisters, and this love is dear to me."

To be sure, this happiness, too, was clouded by new sources of distress. Not the least of these was that Thérèse had carefully to conceal from her own sisters her affection for the Prioress, in order not to hurt them. How well she succeeded can be seen from the astonishment with which the sisters "discovered" in the manuscript, shortly before her death, these tender words to Mother Marie de Gonzague, words which set them wondering. Thus, long after Thérèse's death they could interpret this affection only as "virtue" in their sense: as heroic obedience, purely supernatural deference towards the superior whom God had placed over her. "She never deviated from her faith in regard to authority. She *even* assured me that she was really fond of Mother Marie de Gonzague, and that the forms of salutation I found in her notebook: 'dear Mother, darling Mother, my dearest Mother', corresponded to her actual feelings." [64] We can imagine Thérèse's quiet little smile at this outburst of amazement. These good and zealous, but yet so puritanical, women knew of love for an "unworthy" subject only in the form of condescension. They knew nothing of the tremendous tenacity of loyalty which was not deceived by years of apparent rejection, which endured all the lacks and even the culpabilities of the beloved person, and did not abandon, in defiance of all disillusionments, what the heart had once acknowledged to be worthy of love; of a fealty that, in Dante's profound and arresting phrase, "enforces love from the beloved".

It was, of course, harder for Thérèse's sisters than for any other members of the convent to regard Mother Marie de Gonzague with forbearance. She had strongly supported the election of Sister Agnes of Jesus as her successor—whether because at the time Pauline was still one of her

---

[64] 2 S., 241.

favourites, or whether Pauline seemed to her so gentle and yielding that she hoped to go on reigning through her, is hard to say. The following comment by Dom Godefroy Madelaine[65] seems to us to add a significant element to our picture of the Prioress: "She confided to me that her character and that of Mother Agnes were not naturally harmonious, and that they caused one another suffering, in spite of a very sincere mutual respect; incidentally, she made this confession without the slightest shadow of bitterness."

At any rate, as soon as she took office Pauline began, in her firm, quiet manner, to do what she thought right. Undoubtedly there were a good many changes in the convent, and Mother Marie de Gonzague was not the person to allow herself to be suddenly excluded from government. With all the means at her command, means which unfortunately included loud complaints and open opposition to the younger woman who was now her superior, she tried to maintain her influence in the house, indeed to strengthen and renew it. Above all, she violated all the rules in openly campaigning for her own re-election. Embarrassing scenes occurred more and more frequently.

For Thérèse, the whole affair was a terrible wound. She loved Pauline more than anything else in the world; she suffered over every sorrow that was inflicted upon Pauline, over every violent and unjust word that offended her person and her dignity. After one such scene she said to the Novice Mistress, eyes filled with tears: "Now I know what Jesus suffered when He saw His Mother suffering." But at the same time she also loved the unfortunate, melancholic, and conflict-torn woman who was rending herself to pieces with jealousy and whose spasms of unbridled passion degraded her immeasurably in the eyes of the entire convent.

Thérèse stood between the two and did not dare to show to either how much she was suffering for the other's sake. It may even be that Pauline's grief gave her less pain, for she was after all convinced that her *petite mère* would only be purified and sanctified by this suffering. But Mother Marie de Gonzague was destroying her own soul. Thérèse suffered from her sin, her defiance, her rebellion, her disobedience; she suffered at the insult to the office of Prioress from one who herself had borne the holy dignity of that office; and above all she suffered at the insult to God which was taking place before her eyes. She knew very well how grave the responsibility of a leader is. "The entire convent seems to be walking on a tightrope", she is reported to have said once. "God is working a veritable miracle every moment to keep it from tumbling." It

---

[65] 2 S., 739.

may be that she really "turned pale" when she was informed, after the highly unedifying "election campaign" in the spring of 1896, that Marie de Gonzague had again been re-elected as Prioress. But if so, this alarm may well have been due more to concern for the soul of her unfortunate superior than to apprehension of further unpleasantness for the convent, or even for her sisters. With the grief-stricken concern of a loving child, Thérèse feared very much for Mother Marie de Gonzague's sanctity and integrity; but she never doubted that the Prioress would save her soul in the end, "though only as men are saved by passing through fire". Thérèse is supposed to have given as her grounds for this confidence the Prioress's great devotion to the Sacred Heart. No one knows how many of her prayers, her penances and her sufferings she offered up for this woman.

The sisters, understandably, retained little beyond the memory of the Prioress's severity. Mother Marie of the Angels, limited in many respects, but wise in the things of the heart because her own heart had suffered, has preserved for us the tenderest image of the relationship between the two. "Thérèse... with her remarkably sharp and alert mind grasped the faults which were linked with so many fine qualities in our mother, *whom we loved in spite of everything*. Since she understood perfectly well the cause of Mother Marie de Gonzague's torment, she knew, in her childlike way, how to surround her with affection, how to pacify her and to *enlighten* her. No word is more appropriate to the servant of God than this: 'Thou shalt hear the truth out of the mouths of babes.' "[66]

After that fateful election which showed the former Prioress in one fell blow how much her position in the house and in the hearts of the sisters had been shaken, Thérèse wrote "our poor mother an excellent letter which was very well received by her and did her a great deal of good".[67]

What a picture of the situation—young Thérèse like the sweet shepherd boy David easing the darkened spirit of King Saul; Thérèse, the sole confidante of a troubled woman her senior by thirty years; Thérèse "surrounding with affection" a heart tormented by jealousy (what a bitter admission of defeat, of solitude, of distrust of self and others) in order to assist it to heal; Thérèse, not judging, but deriving her right to intervene solely from her affection, undertaking the hardest and most perilous work of mercy possible: that of reproof. The task fell to her because all the others, Marie de Gonzague's companions of many years, all those who

---

[66] We find a similar statement, although in quite another tone, in the comment of Thérèse's novice, Sister Marie of the Trinity: "Thérèse suffered very much to see Mother Marie de Gonzague so blinded to her faults, and tried all means to open her eyes to the truth."

[67] Letter 170.

were obliged to correct her, could do no more than anxiously cloak her faults, or fall into attitudes of censure and hostility.

Chapters 9 and 10 of *The Story of a Soul*, addressed to the Prioress, form a single urgent, veiled lesson. Here is detailed, infinitely tactful, modest and extremely earnest instruction on all the things which the Prioress had to learn or re-learn: on true charity, on patience with the weaknesses of others, on selfless kindness, on consideration, sympathy, lenient judgment, true penance, self-control, and the high art of guiding souls, an art in which only reverent, inwardly free and humble persons can succeed. Every word is a bequest. Written almost in the form of a confession, written truly "on the knees of the heart", in a tone of appeal and yet with wonderful grace, these chapters hold up a mirror to the elder woman, Thérèse's superior. They tell her truths and bring assuagement to her wounds.

In the end, Thérèse triumphed. Her love performed the miracle of thawing out and gradually reshaping her Prioress's frozen, scarred soul. And although unfortunately we possess no details, only the fact of this conversion, when her time came to die (Marie de Gonzague died of cancer of the tongue seven years after her saintly daughter), she said with noble honesty to Mother Agnes: "My Mother, no person in this house has been so culpable as I. Nevertheless, I trust in God and in my little Thérèse; she will win my salvation." [68]

But that was still far in the future. We are at the beginning now, and Thérèse had to face all these problems alone. There was still one person in the convent from whom she might have expected wise advice: Mother Geneviève of St Teresa. Unfortunately, advanced age and severe illness had already removed her so far from the life of the community that the youngest postulant could find in her no refuge. Thérèse seems to have tried once, but Mother Geneviève was no longer capable of understanding clearly; the girl's ideas struck her as odd and bold. Just once Mother Geneviève conferred her gift of consolation upon Thérèse. When Thérèse was leaving after a brief visit to her sickbed, the old woman beckoned her back and said: "Wait, my child, I have something to say to you. You are always asking me for a spiritual bouquet; very well, today I give you this one. 'Serve God in peace and joy, and remember, our God is the God of Peace.'"

Thérèse, who was that very day in the throes of deep spiritual trials, received these words as a heavenly message. Soon thereafter the seventeen-year-old girl was privileged to be present at Mother Geneviève's saintlike

[68] 2 S., 201.

death. She died at the age of eighty-three, from an internal growth she had supported for thirty years, from dropsy and senile gangrene which took the particularly horrible form of partial, creeping decay of her toes. She had endured her fearful sufferings, which were accompanied by despondency and a sense of religious abandonment, with inexpressible gentleness. Reverently, the novice wiped the last tear of the death-agony from her eyelids and preserved the piece of linen that had absorbed this "saint's last tear" as a relic.

That was all. Nevertheless, the quietly dying old woman had exercised a strong formative influence upon Thérèse. She was always to consider herself fortunate "to have lived for several years with a saint whose example of simple and hidden virtue could be imitated.... This seems to me the truest kind of holiness and the best; it is the kind of holiness I want because it is free from illusions."

4. SPIRITUAL ARIDITY

At the beginning of the eighth chapter of *The Story of a Soul* Thérèse writes tersely: "Complete aridity—desolation, almost—was my lot."

The Church's psychology of asceticism identifies two fundamental states of the soul in its religious existence: consolation and desolation. "Consolation" signifies all those joyous, elevated, inspired moods in which intercourse with God and right action seem easy, satisfy, elate and warm. St Ignatius has defined consolation in his *Spiritual Exercises* as follows: "That increase in faith, hope and love and that inner joy which calls and draws man to heavenly things and to the accomplishment of his own soul's salvation by conferring upon his soul peace and quiet in its Lord and Creator." Desolation, on the other hand, aridity, dryness, Ignatius calls "everything that... is opposed to this state, such as darkness of the soul, confusion within it, attachment to earthly and to low things, disquiet as the consequence of various stimuli and temptations, which lead to diffidence, without hope and without love, when the soul finds itself slothful, sad and, as it were, separated from its Lord". Neither state is a sign of the religious worth or unworthiness of the person in question. Consolation does not mean inner progress or higher virtue, nor does aridity mean unfaithfulness or guilt. Both states are, so to speak, landscapes through which the Christian's way passes, alternating weathers which must be accepted and survived. The manner in which he responds to them is alone decisive. Consolation must not lead to arrogance and thoughtlessness, to complacency and laxity, nor aridity to attacks of inferiority, the relinquishing of effort, to envy and despair. Consolation is granted as a breathing spell, to encourage and strengthen; aridity is imposed to test fidelity and purity of intention. It has long been known that the beginning of the conscious spiritual life is accompanied mainly by consolation. St Paul speaks (although in several senses) of the mother's milk with which the little ones must be fed. All mystics mention the "manifold consolations with which God draws the soul of a beginner". And there has never been a saint whose path did not lie, for long stretches, through the grim desert of aridity. In both phases a great variety of natural causes and contributory factors can operate; in both phases, the soul is guided by divine grace. From the Christian point of view, both phases are as essential to the growth of the soul as changes in weather to the thriving of plants.

Young as she was, Thérèse had already passed through a wide gamut of religious experiences. The account of her childhood and her adolescent years portrays the growth of her soul in the bright sunlight of divine consolation. All the colours and tones of intense inward life, of enthusiasm, emotion and elevation, of quiet possession, sweetness and bliss, were familiar to her. From the time of her first awakening her heart responded fervently to the religious call, was irresistibly drawn by the special taste of religious joy and beauty. "As I grew up, I loved God more and more, and I gave my heart to Him often, as my mother had taught me." From the child's fourth year the lovely rainbow mounts upwards through the devout routine of life: the beloved Sundays, the feast days of the Church, the peaks of first confession, First Communion and Confirmation, to the glorious excitement of the days of vocation: "Often I was carried away, experienced veritable tempests of love."

Certainly Thérèse was also familiar with the painful response of the spirit to the manifold aspects of religion: repentance, confusion, self-castigation, the torment of her scruples. But these sufferings all sprang from a vigorous, even overstimulated and overemphasized religious feeling. They, too, were "experiences" in the sense of a lively, cognizant, sympathetic vibration of heart and mind, extending down to all the nerves and senses.

During the days of decision when she made known to her father her resolve to enter the Carmel, and when her uncle opposed her entering so early, Thérèse experienced for the first time in her life that second classical condition of spiritual life. We can sense from her description of it how new, strange and frightening she found this sudden reversal. She speaks of a "martyrdom", though it lasted only three days: "It was not until then that I understood what Our Lady and St Joseph suffered as they searched the streets of Jerusalem for the Child Jesus. I seemed to be lost in some frightful desert, or like a little boat without a pilot, at the mercy of the storm-tossed waves. I knew that Jesus was there, asleep in my barque, but the night was so dark that I could not see Him. If only the storm had broken, a flash of lightning might have pierced through the clouds; it would not have been much, but at least I should for a moment have seen my Beloved. But there was only night, dark night, utter desolation like death itself. Like Our Lord in the agony in the Garden, I felt forsaken, and could find no consolation either on earth or in Heaven. Nature seemed to share my bitter sadness; the sun did not shine during those three days, and it rained hard all the time."[69]

But on the fourth day the sun rose in the sky and in her heart.

During the trip to Rome this despondency returned after her disappointment with the Holy Father: "All... was bitterness. Jesus was silent—almost not there at all, for there was nothing to betray His presence." In a very childish image, which occurs elsewhere in accounts of mystical experiences, but which Thérèse may well have found for herself—for it corresponds to her nature—she interpreted this experience and communicated it to her beloved sister: "For some time now, I had been offering myself to the Child Jesus as His little plaything, telling Him not to treat me as the sort of expensive toy that children only look at without daring to touch. I wanted Him to treat me like a little ball, so valueless that it can be thrown on the ground, kicked about, pierced, and left lying in a corner, or pressed close to His heart if He wants.... Jesus had heard me, and in Rome He pierced His little plaything because He wanted, I expect, to see what was inside; then, satisfied with what He found, He dropped His little ball and fell asleep.... You can guess how sad the little ball was, left lying on the ground."

This time, too, the state of abandonment lasted only a short time and did not affect the profound peace in the depth of her soul.

After her entrance into the convent, however, aridity became her permanent state. In other words, when she took up a life of the most intense, exclusive religious activity, she fell—as far as her feelings were concerned—into the state which characterizes the religious condition of the "average person" almost all the time. For aridity is not a state of vigorous, though negatively directed spiritual life; it does not consist of fierce struggles, "interesting" temptations, agitating torments. It is simply weary, empty indifference. We do not doubt the tenets of religion; we do not storm like titans against the walls of the Commandments. Rather, that whole area seems remote and unreal to us; it does not arouse the least response, either friendly or antagonistic, in our minds and hearts. It is as though religion had become simply something remembered, grey, cold and unimportant. At the same time, earthly real-

[69] I S.S., vi.

ity acquires dimensions that are, so to speak, more than life-size; it threatens to overwhelm our entire mind. Against the leaden weight of such a mood one must fight, with conscious effort, to be faithful and resolute, must go against the current in order at least to carry out the "fulfilment of religious duties".

Aridity, then, is what makes the religious life either difficult or impossible for the ordinary person. Its effect is much more far-reaching than isolated sieges of temptation. Hence the ordinary person inclines to regard as truly "pious" only those whose religious life is visibly impelled by the uplifting forces of consolation—warmth, joy, interest and enthusiasm. This ardour alone, he thinks, can arouse, support and sustain a more intense degree of religious action.

One of the special demands of the monastic life is that it requires, as part of the daily routine, spiritual exercises of a type and intensity originally conceived and shaped by enthusiasm. This requirement is all the harder since the tides of consolation and aridity are by no means checked within the cloister. On the contrary, the concentrating of attention upon the inward life and the lack of diversion result in these tides being experienced far more vividly and consciously. For us a few minutes' morning and evening prayer, or participation in Sunday Mass in a state of aridity, can become a wearisome duty. How much greater the strain upon the nun when she is held to six hours of prayer daily in such a state, and when her reading and conversation are largely limited to religious matters. Those who understand prayer as only a free, creative outpouring of the heart—and this, we all tend to feel, is what it ought to be—necessarily see such compulsion as meaningless, even cruel and soul-destroying.

In fact, however, the Church views such outpouring of emotion as only one and by no means the most important aspect of prayer. The soul, like the body, must have its daily bread, whether desire or lack of it accompanies the taking of this necessary nourishment which alone gives us strength. That is certainly true of the individual's spiritual life. In such difficult periods, the individual, to be sure, can adjust his intake. But the great mission of worship and intercession which the Church as a whole performs for all her children, this most profound expression of the life of the Mystical Body of Christ, must be accomplished through all the days and nights of earthly time until the Lord returns. For the member of an Order entrusted with this task, prayer is separated from personal vacillations and spiritual needs, not in a mechanical sense, but in an austere and sublime sense. Such a person is primarily a voice in the praying Church. But what conquest of the natural, human preoccupation with one's own spiritual moods, what a depth of willingness to serve, is required for the pure fulfilment of this obligation day after day throughout one's whole life.

Of course we must not overlook the fact that the aridity of the average Christian, which in large part derives from lukewarmness and sluggishness, from unmortified natural impulses and attachment to human beings, should not be confounded with that "dark night" which the classical writers on asceticism describe as a state of purification in the seeker, and as a sign of his spiritual advance. But these two states, though so different at the root, are experienced as similar, and in their psychological effect they bear an almost perfect likeness to each other. Consequently, the ascending soul which passes into a zone of dryness feels the change as if it were a drop into real slackening and alienation from God. And the very dread that this is so constitutes one of the tormenting thorns of this particular trial.

For Thérèse this condition became her daily bread. This happened to her, moreover, in the very years of life when human beings live most intensely and uncritically by the tides of emotion. True, vital, fiery rays of feeling now and again broke through the arctic mists—but after each such flare the darkness closed more oppressively than ever around her heart. The day of her Clothing was one such gleam of spring, when Thérèse once again tangibly experienced the nearness and love of God. But immediately afterwards her desolation began again. "My dryness increased. Both Heaven and earth denied me consolation." At the same time she became aware of something which she had been prevented from discovering by her sheltered position within her family: her own innate inability to speak openly of the state of her soul to any but those persons who were closely akin to her. She felt this with particular keenness in regard to the affectionate but awkward attempts of the Novice Mistress to discover her degree of spiritual development. "I cannot tell you how good she was to me, or how much I loved and respected her; but in spite of all this, my soul did not open out. I did not know how to explain what was going on in me; words failed me, and spiritual direction became a torture and a martyrdom." One of the older nuns understood what Thérèse felt, for one day she said to her in recreation: "I don't suppose you ever have very much to tell your superiors."

"What makes you think that, Mother?"

"Because you have an extremely simple soul; however, it will be even more simple when you have become perfect. The closer we come to God, the more simple we become."

But she felt her own soul falling silent before God. "In my relationship to Jesus there is nothing! Dryness! Sleepiness! ... I cannot tell Him anything, and above all—Jesus no longer says anything to me. Pray for me that these days of retreat will nevertheless please the heart of Him who reads the depths of the soul."

At the same time the sad fate of her father was plunging her deeper and deeper into solitude. Unconsoled by a sense of the presence of God, Thérèse also had to struggle through this grief alone.

The retreat before her Profession—which at the Superior's request was postponed for eight months—should have been days of deepest meditation, of ardent preparation for the spiritual "wedding". They proved to be parched as sand. "Jesus was asleep in my little boat as usual." In a letter to Pauline Thérèse set forth her state with great clarity:

> Before our departure my Bridegroom asked me to what land I wished to travel, and which path I preferred to take. I answered that my sole wish was to attain the summit of the mountain of Love. At once many roads opened before my eyes, but so many of them were perfect that I found myself incapable of choosing. So I said to my divine Guide: You know where I want to go; You know for whom I want to climb the mountain; You know whom I love and whom alone I wish to satisfy. For Him alone I have undertaken this journey, so lead me by the paths He loves to travel; if only He is satisfied, I shall be at the uttermost point of happiness. And Our Lord took me by the hand and made me enter a subterranean way where it is neither cold nor warm, where the sun does not shine and where rain and wind may not enter; a tunnel where I see nothing but a half-veiled glow from the downcast eyes in the Face of my Spouse.
>
> My Bridegroom no longer speaks with me, and I also say nothing to Him, unless it be that I love Him more than myself. This I feel is so, for I belong to Him more than to myself.
>
> I do not see that we are approaching the mountain that is our goal, since we are travelling under the earth; yet I have a feeling that we are approaching it, without knowing why.[70]

"I thank Jesus for letting me walk in darkness; even as I do so I feel deep peace. I gladly consent to spend my entire life in this underground darkness to which He has led me; my only wish is that my gloom will bring light to sinners."[71] "I am happy, yes, very happy, to feel no consolation; I would be ashamed if my love resembled that of earthly brides who are always looking to their betrothed's hands to see whether he is bringing them a present, or into his face to catch in it the smile that delights them. Thérèse, the little bride of Jesus, loves Jesus for His sake."[72]

But on 8 September, the feast of the Nativity of Mary and of her own Profession, Thérèse once more felt consolation. "An outpouring of peace flooded my soul, that 'peace which surpasseth all understanding'." In this condition she pronounced her holy vows. The letter with special requests

[70] Letter 91.
[71] Letter 90.
[72] Letter 93.

and prayers which, according to custom, she carried close to her heart, breathes inspiration and rapture: "O Jesus, it is peace I beg of You. Peace and, above all, boundless love. Jesus, let me die for You a martyr; grant me martyrdom of soul or of body, or better still, grant me both!"

On that day "I felt I was really a queen, and I took advantage of my title to gain all the favours I could from the King for His ungrateful subjects. I did not forget anyone. I wanted all the sinners in the world to be converted that day, and purgatory emptied of every single captive." At the close of that blissful day, during which she had felt herself a chosen soul upon whom graces had been heaped, she laid the crown of roses she had worn all day at the feet of the statue of Our Lady without sadness. For a long while she stood at the window of her cell, in the early autumnal dusk, uplifted by her inner peace. She looked at the stars "and thought that Heaven would claim me before very long, that there I should be united to my Divine Spouse, happy for all eternity".

But her taking the veil scarcely three weeks later became a festival of tears. "Jesus left me to my own resources... and it was obvious that they were not enough."

Henceforth the states of darkness recurred and lasted longer. She felt "inward sufferings of all kinds". During the last year and a half of her life these states concentrated into a suffocating night of actual doubt which lasted until the hour of her death.

But when the sense of vital union with the Divine and Holy departs from the soul, when enthusiasm relapses and joy in prayer gives way to the constant experience of failure in it—what remains to the natural eye and ear, to the feeling self, as the palpable content of convent life? Aside from the romantic aspect of the nun's costume—little more than the archaic fancy-dress costume of a medieval penitent—there is nothing but a routine life of the most commonplace sort: the life of a small group living at close quarters, with all its inevitable tensions; complete submission to a rather unedifying régime; monotonous work that is never self-chosen and that provides mind and emotions with neither nourishment nor diversion. Surprising as it may seem, all this results, within the framework of an apparently special and extraordinary existence, in a cross section of the standard life of the masses, of "little people". Here are the narrow, restricted, dreary and dependent conditions of real poverty. Here is the commonplace scene of petty and dull toil. And it is not even enlivened by the battles and reverses which, by challenging men, cause them to rise above themselves. Convent life, to be sure, lacks one essential factor of ordinary life: concern for one's livelihood. But on the other hand, this deprives it of the invigorating element of struggle, which can arouse unsuspected forces in men.

We would be going wide of the mark if we were to seek, in Thérèse's life in the convent, individual instances of dramatic sufferings and "crosses", although legend has long been busy inventing them. Her life itself was her cross, not one or another event in it. It was the desert itself, not storms or dangerous beasts, that met her in the Carmel. She did not "suffer from life", as do melancholics and those who are oversensitive; but she suffered life as simple and childlike folk must, suffered the permanence and inescapability of its demands, its irreconcilable contradictions, its stubborn disharmonies, its bleak destitution—suffered all this just as millions of average human beings have suffered it.

Thérèse knew this. "Everything I do must be within the reach of other little souls also." This was her express bequest at the end of her life, when a surprising sense of her mission unfolded. We may well be astonished at the sureness with which Thérèse recognized in her own life, which seemed so far away from everyday "worldliness", the basic features of all "little lives", that is, all those not marked out for something extraordinary.

With the same sureness ordinary Catholics, in spite of habit and veil and all the gilt daubed over the "Little Flower", recognized her as *their* saint, the canonization of their own "little" lives. Here was a strangely moving encounter, one truly in the Holy Spirit. For to endure, to overcome and to profit by this life itself, this network of limiting factors which we cannot alter, this commonplace life so barren of ideals, so shabby and thwarted—that was Thérèse's task. And to do so not just anyhow, not just as a decent person, but as a matter of conscience, before God, with holiness, without seeking to escape from ourselves or into ourselves, into easier or harder tasks, into change or daydream, that was Thérèse's task, as it is ours, and in this she became the exemplar for us.

4

THE WAY

I. THE SAVING LAW

ONE THING ALONE persists in the desert, in chaos, in darkness. Shall it be called obedience, faithfulness, doing one's duty—or simply goodness, that childlike "goodness" of Thérèse's, her unshakable resolve to do what she recognized to be the right thing? For rightness alone seemed certain in this opaque and troubling world. Many names fit the quality Thérèse displays, and none quite expresses it fully.

By the time Thérèse began to speak of her "little way", of what was to be entirely *her* way, it had long since taken definite shape in her mind; its direction was clear; it was very nearly a tested "system". When she began finding it and walking it, step by step, it could not have meant much more than the resolve to cling, in this world full of mists, gossip and snares, to the one thing dependable, and to do the one thing indisputably important here and now, without let up or pause, and at all costs. She hoped that by daily, unswerving fulfilment of this unquestionable obligation everything else would be clarified; all truth would be confirmed, all falseness drop away.

The one certainly valid factor in the convent was obedience. There was the order prescribed by the Rule, that obligatory framework for the whole of life; it took precedence over all habits, all local customs, all exceptions, all examples. From the very first day Thérèse clung to that: to the Rule, to the letter of the Rule. She let others keep it as they pleased. She remained silent where silence was prescribed. She walked with lowered eyes and composed mien past the chattering, whispering little groups in the corridor, past the door of the parlour. She did not frown reprimandingly, did not raise her eyebrows in consternation or inquiry as she passed. Instead, she wore her gracious, candid smile; but no calls, no beckoning, made her pause, not even when the tall figure of the Prioress stood like a visible justification in the centre of the group engaged in irregular conversation. Thérèse asked about nothing that did not concern her; faithful to the Rule herself, she did not regard what others did wrong.

She did not refuse to receive the relatives who came all too frequently to visit; she sat in the parlour, concealed by her veil, in her corner, listening, letting her sisters talk, and remaining silent throughout almost the entire visit. So Léonie and her cousins have reported. And when the hourglass showed the end of the half-hour, she would stand up, say a friendly good-bye, and vanish silently, even though the others might still have one thing or another to conclude quickly. She came to all community duties punctual to the minute, whether these were prayers or needlework, meals or recreation. To break off in the middle of a sentence, nay, of a word and a letter, was for her not only a familiar and wise requirement of the good monastic tradition, but a habit she took for granted. The Carmel at Lisieux still preserves a note written by her which breaks off in the middle of a syllable. She observed all instructions, all of the many arbitrary orders, often scarcely meant seriously, by which Mother Marie de Gonzague undermined her own authority because no one could remember and carry out all the superfluous regulations: that this door always had to be kept closed or open, that this or that way through the convent should be taken in proceeding from exercises, that when sitting down to rest all should lean to the right or the left. Thérèse carried these orders out as they were given, earnestly, matter-of-factly, without hesitation, with unflinching conscientiousness, long after such commands had fallen into desuetude, had been tacitly passed over by the nuns and forgotten by Mother Marie de Gonzague herself. Anyone who closely observed Thérèse could have compiled from her actions an inventory of all the regulations that had ever been issued.

Thérèse never criticized, never grew indignant—never even joined with the proper-minded and zealous nuns who decried the decaying spirit in the convent and carped at the faults of the Prioress. Such restraint certainly did not come easily to Thérèse. Young people make stern demands not only upon themselves, but also upon others. She has touchingly confessed that at the beginning of her life in the convent, when she saw others acting wrongly, she often thought: "If I could give her a piece of my mind, how much good that would do—me!" Later, when both the right and the duty of rebuke were assigned to her, and she felt the full weight of this office, she thought longingly of the time when she had been able to remain silent.

But gently, obstinately, silently, she insisted on being different and acting differently. She ignored the practices of the convent, lived as if she were alone or in a community of angels. And we must ask: Was not this conduct in itself, especially since she was a novice and the youngest person in the house, the clearest and most provoking kind of criticism imaginable? When she went on this way week after week, year after year, without making the slightest concession, how could it help seeming a judgment and almost a challenge? It is easy to understand that this behaviour induced the Prioress and perhaps others to conclude that Thérèse was more proud than she seemed.

And certainly Thérèse would not have been human if she had not experienced at that time the subtlest, most dangerous, most deceptive of the temptations of pride. That temptation is the one that is so fearfully akin to our best and most high-minded aspirations and is as difficult to detach from it as the thousand-rooted creeper from a tree. It is the "Lord, I thank Thee that I am not like the rest of men." In the light of this we can again judge how wise the Prioress's sternness was; instead of allowing Thérèse to admire her own virtue, this treatment filled her with constant fear of failure and inadequacy. To be sure, who can say whether Mother Marie de Gonzague did not occasionally fight back against her youngest subject as we fight against our own pricking conscience? Perhaps the novice's calm inflexibility offended and tormented this woman so accustomed to domination and so sure of her influence. Perhaps her reproofs and punishments were occasionally aimed at shattering this unassailable self-assurance and self-righteousness. All this may have been so and would certainly have complicated in the extreme Thérèse's silent struggle both for her own freedom and for the Prioress's soul. But in the end Thérèse won. By the time Thérèse died she had shaped her small group of five novices along her own lines by means of an inexorable guerrilla warfare against all slackness and tepidity. A few years afterwards the entire convent was remodelled in her image, which year by year shone forth more brightly. This metamorphosis was so unexpected, so difficult to accomplish, and so profound and enduring, that the nuns recognized it to be the first and greatest miracle after her passing.

Even on her deathbed Thérèse was tormented by the thought of all the easy-going negligence in the convent, by the lack of understanding of the meaning of perfect obedience. "Alas, how little faithfulness to the Rule there is", she said to her nurse during the long vigils. "How few souls there are in the convent who do nothing carelessly, who do not say to themselves: this way is as good as any other; I am not expressly charged to do this or that; after all, it is no great evil to talk here, to give way there, and so on.... How rare are the souls who do everything *as well as they possibly can!*"

Thérèse's obedience was not merely a meticulous observance of regulations. Nor was it the bowing of the weak before the strong, a degree of conformity and adaptation carried as far as necessary, but with inner reservations. To her, obedience was complete and pure submission to the authority of God as represented by her appointed superiors. Monastic obedience has a mystic significance that goes far beyond order and justice, though these elements, too, play a part in it. Through it the "free" soul imitates the submission of Him who was obedient to the point of death on the Cross—obedient not only to the will of the Father, but to the will of men also. Consequently monastic obedience calls for perfect inner submission, submission without a trace of repressed defiance, without any withholding of consent. Only pure, simple and joyful acceptance of what is imposed will do, even if the order is pointless, even if it is foolish, so long as it does not obviously contradict the will of God. Nor is this a mode of perfect submission which is blind and unworthy of men. It does not demand that black be called white; it demands conscious, calm daring, the kind of courage which is prepared, in freedom, to accept all dire consequences; it demands a kind of heavenly frivolity like that of Peter when he called to the Lord to make him come to Him over the water. Out of firm confidence that the Lord would be responsible for the consequences, St Francis de Sales wrote these apparently rash words: "Blessed are the obedient, for God will not permit them to be led astray."

It was wholly in this sense that Thérèse regarded her superiors as her "compass". Neither her emotional inclinations nor her repeated disappointment over the failings of the older nuns made her waver; she trusted unswervingly in the Lord who leads an obedient soul; "even when she is sure that her superiors are mistaken, she need not fear". These words are to be found in the chapter addressed to the Prioress, and the sentence that follows it is audacious indeed when we consider that Thérèse had only a few months before witnessed Marie de Gonzague's open rebellion against the then Prioress, Mother Agnes: "But the moment she ceases to consult this infallible compass, she goes astray down barren pathways, where the waters of grace soon fail her." Neither inclination nor sense of order nor consciousness of duty alone, but faith as well, make possible such an attitude; and faith requires a struggle. "By allowing me to endure temptations against faith, the Divine Master has greatly increased in my heart *the spirit of faith* which makes me see Him dwelling in your soul, and directing me through you."

We hope that we do no one an injustice if we assume that Thérèse's own sisters' vigorous, and in many respects justified, objections to the disorders encouraged by the Prioress made such pure obedience considerably more difficult for Thérèse. She thought her sisters virtually infallible, and it is scarcely to be wondered at that their silent complaints occasionally infected Thérèse's mind, so that in moments of violent temptation she felt justified because she knew they were of the same mind. She had to muster all her moral forces to recognize temptation in what appeared to be righteous indignation. One day the countess, the Prioress's

sister, was again residing in the convent on a visit. Late in the evening
Thérèse received the order to prepare quickly a night lamp for her (perhaps she was to prepare the shade). Thérèse was already exhausted by the
day's work and an attack of fever. The protesting spirit of the Martins
flared up in her. "The devil violently tempted me to rebellion—not only
against the lamp, which cost me precious time, but against our Mother's
conduct in placing a part of the community in the service of her family.
[How we can hear the sisters' grumblings in this!] She condoned something for her relations which she would never have permitted to the families of other nuns. But I realized clearly that I was on the point of offending
God, and I implored Him, in His mercy, to still the storm. I pulled myself together vigorously and prepared the lamp as neatly and carefully as if
it were intended for Our Lady and the Child Jesus." Thus pure obedience won out over her offended feelings. "Then peace returned to my
heart, and I found in myself sincere readiness to do services for our Mother's relatives all night long if it had been asked of me. From that day on
I made the resolve never to judge whether a command was sensible and
useful, or not." [1]

After such conquests Thérèse could rightfully demand the same pure,
free submission of the novices and her fellow nuns. She tolerated no criticism of the Prioress's conduct. "It always offends God a little if we grumble a little about Mother Prioress, and it offends Him a great deal if we
complain a great deal—even if we only do so inwardly." [2] "She has at
present the sacrament of authority, and we must reverence that. If we
behave towards her in the spirit of faith, God will never permit us to be
deceived. Even without knowing it, she will always give us the divine
answer." [3] Once a young companion, perhaps somewhat too emphatically, expressed pity for her on account of the disagreements between the
two Prioresses, saying: "How you must suffer seeing your sister treated
like this." Thérèse replied in all sincerity: "Yes, it hurts me, because the
authority of Jesus is offended. But I would be just as sad about it if someone else were Prioress." [4]

From the same spirit of reverence she did not permit the novices to
criticize sermons and spiritual instruction. It was not that she imagined,
Pauline comments, that all priests could speak equally well, but she would
not permit the defects of a sermon to be discussed for the sake of entertainment. During those years (1894) the alleged "revelations" of Léon

[1] 2 S., 297.
[2] 2 S., 305.
[3] 2 S., 484.
[4] 2 S., 690.

Taxil, later unmasked as a fraud, were much discussed. He had published a fantastic story about his "conversion" and about the abominations and satanic rites practised in a Freemason's lodge. His aim was only to play upon the credulity of the devout, in which, unfortunately, he succeeded too well. The book was eagerly read and discussed even in the Lisieux Carmel. Thérèse alone firmly rejected it, after some initial enthusiasm, and warned the sisters against it. A passage in it, she said, spoke irreverently of a bishop's authority; the spirit that prompted such sentences could not possibly come from God.

This very trait indicates how little Thérèse's obedience had to do with lack of independence or lack of judgment. This twenty-year-old girl calmly opposed the common opinion of the entire convent. She had no intention of adjusting her inner life to the prescriptions of the Novice Mistress, or of accepting the highly Jansenistic views of the Prioress on taking Holy Communion rarely. At this time the general shift to frequent reception of Communion was just beginning. To Thérèse's great sorrow, Mother Marie de Gonzague, who was of the *ancien régime* in all things, would not hear of this newfangled custom and simply suppressed the efforts of the convent chaplain to bring it about. Thérèse had come very early to the conviction that the Holy Eucharist was intended as nourishment for weak and struggling souls, not as the reward of achieved merit.[5] "The Bread of the Angels must come like a divine dew to strengthen you and give you everything you need", she wrote to an anxious novice. ("Il faut que le Pain des Anges vienne comme une rosée divine vous fortifier et vous donner tout ce qui vous manque.") "Jesus does not descend from Heaven daily in order to remain in a golden ciborium, but to find another Heaven, the Heaven of our souls, in which He takes His delight." She made her plea to the Prioress with full candour, and she clung to it although she met with no understanding. "Mother, when I am dead I will make you change your mind",[6] she said. She prayed ardently for the grace that the Church might renew its former custom of permitting the faithful to receive Holy Communion at every Mass. St Joseph, the head of the household, of whom it was said that he gave to his loved ones "food at the proper times", was her special patron in this concern of hers. In Lisieux the great revision of ecclesiastical practice, which came about through the decrees of Pope Pius X, was ascribed in considerable part to Thérèse's intercession. A few days after her death a new priest came to the Lisieux Carmel and delivered his first sermon on the words "Come

---

[5] C.S.

[6] Ibid. She continued: "You will see; when I am in Heaven, there will be a change in the practice of the Church regarding Holy Communion."

and eat my bread". Soon afterwards, with the Prioress's consent, he introduced daily Communion.

We will have more to say later of the manner in which Thérèse went her own ways in devotion to the Blessed Virgin and in penance.

Precisely because she considered herself under obedience to God, she was able to take a just and sane view of the human embodiments of authority. "Oh, what poisonous praises are daily offered to those who stand in the foremost rank. What a corrupting incense! How detached from itself a soul must be not to be harmed by that!"[7] It seemed to her "a true miracle" that persons who were prominent in any way could preserve their original freshness and purity.[8]

She also had, and this is very important, a clear sense of the limits of authority. Just once she criticized Mother Marie de Gonzague, not privately as was her wont, but quite publicly. Her sister Céline and another novice were due to take their vows shortly before the election of the new Prioress, and the ex-Prioress, counting on her re-election, was determined to initiate her administration by performing this ceremony. She therefore employed all means in her power to postpone the Profession of the two young novices until after the election. Mother Agnes (Pauline) was, for her part, eager to receive her own sister into the community and was unwilling to delay needlessly the longed-for day of the girls' spiritual wedding. Finally, Mother Marie de Gonzague, who at that time was Novice Mistress, made it known that she would refuse to give her vote to the two at the Chapter meeting—the Chapter decides admission and is supposed to make this decision solely on the basis of worthiness.

This case was discussed avidly in the community, and with strong shows of partisanship. In the presence of some fifteen of the sisters, Thérèse said: "Mother Marie de Gonzague is absolutely in the wrong. It is scandalous to behave in this manner towards one's Mother Prioress, and what hurts me most about it is to see the offence to Jesus." An older nun who did not particularly favour the Martin clique, and who according to her own testimony did not fully understand the situation, assumed that family emotions were once more coming to the fore and pointed out that Mother Marie de Gonzague was, after all, Novice Mistress; it was her right as such to humiliate a novice in order to test her. Thérèse replied firmly: *"There are trials that no one has the right to impose."* The witness comments that at the time she had considered this pronouncement nothing but a display of "an all too natural sisterly love"—since the interests of Céline were concerned. We need not flatly reject this interpretation—

---

[7] *S.S.* Epilogue in French edition supplied by Mother Agnes.
[8] *Esprit*, 100.

but the nun soon perceived that Thérèse had been clearly distinguishing between general and personal views. "And I am convinced that she would have made an excellent Prioress, always proceeding with intelligence and kindness and never abusing the rights of authority."[9]

If, however, abuse of authority affected herself, Thérèse simply and willingly submitted to the decree. Thus, after years of cruel inner solitude, she for the first time found a priest to whom she could open her soul without reserve, and whom she knew to be understanding. That was during the blessed retreat of 1892, when Father Alexis, a Franciscan from Caen, restored to her the peace of her soul. But the Prioress, possibly pricked by jealousy, forbade her a second conversation with this priest. Without complaint, her face serene, Thérèse did her work in the sacristy while one sister after the other went past her into Father Alexis's consultation room. Nor did Thérèse attempt to resume this interrupted relationship, even by correspondence.

Her fellow nuns might not understand her, might see her conduct as timidity, exaggeration, pretentiousness or even arrogance. But Thérèse had the consolation of knowing herself to be in accord with the great tradition of the Order, with its founders and with the deceased nun who had established the Lisieux Carmel. She expressed her secret knowledge of this ultimate accord in a curious and moving manner. Only twice in her nine convent years did Thérèse have "significant" dreams. The first time was shortly after the death of Mother Geneviève. Thérèse dreamed that the deceased nun was in the midst of the sisters, giving each of them something that had belonged to her. "And when my turn came, she was empty-handed. I thought there would be nothing for me, but she said three times, looking at me tenderly: 'To you I leave my heart.' "

And in May of the year before she died, Thérèse dreamed that she was walking in a gallery with the Mother Prioress. Suddenly she saw three Carmelites approaching in heavy mantles, their faces concealed by the long Carmelite veil, and she understood that they came from Heaven. She thought: "If only I could see the face of one of these Carmelites I would be so happy!" The tallest of the three advanced towards her, Thérèse fell to her knees, "and then to my joy she raised her veil, or rather, cast it all about me". Thérèse recognized her at once as the Venerable Mother Anne of Jesus, the beloved companion of Teresa of Avila and founder of the Carmel in France, of whom Thérèse had never consciously thought. "Transfused with a gentle light", the saint pressed the kneeling girl to her heart and promised her that God would come for her soon. Then Thérèse

[9] I S., Animadversiones, 22.

ventured to ask: "Answer me something more, Mother; does God want anything more from me than the little things I do for Him, and my desires? Is He pleased with me?" Then the Venerable Mother's face shone with a new light, "and her expression appeared to me incomparably more tender. 'God asks no more of you,' she said, 'and He is pleased with you; very, very pleased.' She took my head between her hands, and I cannot possibly express how tender were the kisses that she showered on me."

Between these two dreams lay Thérèse's life in the convent: nine years of complete obedience with deep consent and simple fidelity to the ideal of the Order as represented by its saints.

2. THE STRUGGLE FOR LOVE

Once the confusing and deceptive veil of appearances has been penetrated, and reality recognized and credited, religious obedience demands faithfulness to that reality. The love commanded by the Gospels requires first and foremost faithfulness towards an invisible reality in spite of the outward appearances which mask and veil it.

The commandment of love, too, provided something fixed, a beacon amid the ambiguities which now so largely constituted Thérèse's world. What she saw about her was anything but attractive or elevated. How could she trust her eyes and ears alone? She was still the same girl who had been so good at the dangerous art of witty imitation. We can still feel her pronounced sense of the ridiculous in her description of the peculiarities of old Sister St Peter: "Should the devil draw my attention to the faults of any one..." Like so many persons whose emotions are strongly centred on their own families, Thérèse did not naturally possess a great deal of warmth and sympathy for "strangers". All the personal love she had to give had long since found its objects. The spiritual zeal with which she turned her attention to servants, poor children, and unfortunates drifting far off in the sea of the world, could easily—alas—be combined with extreme coolness of feeling. It is quite possible to seek another's salvation without being really concerned about the other as a person. We will recall how inaccessible Thérèse had been among her schoolmates in the Abbey school. She had attended it for five years without forming a friendship, without drawing closer to any of the teachers. Certainly we cannot say that she was a person with a gift for community life. Had she established a family of her own, on the other hand, all the treasures of her heart would, as wife and mother, undoubtedly have poured forth of their own accord, inexhaustibly.

Since those half-forgotten ordeals of her early schooldays she had been surrounded by exquisite courtesy, by tenderest consideration, by persons who exemplified for her the highest ideals and the finest conduct. We would expect someone with her disposition, accustomed to such a milieu, to respond to the motley group of her fellow nuns with sensitivity and nervousness. Thérèse's sharp eyes saw the pettiness, the limitations, the spitefulness, the crudeness and the intractability of those around her. Her nature rose up against all that was dreary, unwholesome, warped. But this was the way the world was, and her task was not only to endure it, but to love it. The precept was inexorable and unequivocal: "All ought to love one another mutually in the same way as our Lord Jesus Christ so often commanded His Apostles." [10] Behind this stood the whole weight of the divine command: "I have a new commandment to give you, that you are to love one another; that your love for one another is to be like the love I have borne you." [11]

Obedience to this commandment is hard, harder than the first kind of obedience, which requires only submission of the will and understanding, not doing violence to one's own heart. It would have been easier to flee the demands of the troublesome, disappointing community into a new, self-chosen solitude so deep that other human beings would become insubstantial shadows, who could have no impact upon her, towards whom she had no responsibility. But such an escape would have meant disobedience and would have caused her to miss her goal. What sort of solitude with God would that be, if one's brothers and sisters were excluded? The desert is not a void—if only it were! It is filled with companions of the way who are themselves like personifications of its stony aridity. And the command is not to evade them, not to glance past them, but to welcome them, receive them, accept them into one's own life. There is no wall behind which one has the right to withdraw from them. Here and now these persons, these very ones, must be accepted, cared for, served, consoled. That, at the least, is positive and right, whatever else may be uncertain. They are our neighbours, assigned to us by God. For, mystery of mysteries, He wishes to be recognized and loved in them. Why does He not provide clear mirrors which will joyously and beautifully reflect His image? He alone knows that. But He knows.

Thus young Thérèse set about mastering this hidden reality of God in her fellow human beings. For "every artist is pleased when his works are appreciated". At times she may strike us as a pilgrim in the desert, digging with bleeding fingers into the hostile, dead sand, deeper and deeper, until at last the living spring of water wells up, filling the hollow, reflecting the sky above. She has told us plainly enough that this love did not at

[10] Rules and Precepts, Chapter iv, 44.
[11] Jn 13:34.

all come to her as the result of a gregarious, undiscriminating temperament, or out of any innate pleasure in community life. Nor did it spring from the kind of "social talent" possessed by a good many of the great humanitarians of her century. According to her own testimony, she arrived at a full inward understanding of the precept of charity only during the last two years of her life. In other words, previously, *for almost her entire life*, she had practised love of neighbour solely out of obedience.

"I had concentrated on loving God, but in loving Him I came to realize the meaning of those other words of His: 'The kingdom of heaven will not give entrance to every man who calls Me Master, Master; only to the man that does the will of My Father who is in heaven.' ...I set to work to discover how Jesus had loved them. I found that He had not loved them for their natural qualities, for they were ignorant and taken up with earthly things; yet He called them His friends and His brothers and wanted to have them with Him in His Father's Kingdom; He was ready to die on the cross to make this possible, saying: 'This is the greatest love a man can shew, that he should lay down his life for his friends.' "

Now her struggle to attain to this kind of love began, a hidden, inexpressibly wearisome struggle. "Meditating on these divine words, I saw only too well how very imperfect was my love for my Sisters; I did not really love them as Jesus loves them. I see now that true charity consists in bearing with the faults of those about us, never being surprised at their weaknesses, but edified at the least sign of virtue." The lowest stage of such charity, Thérèse discovered, was justice not inspired or nourished by beauty or patent attractiveness. One must not judge; one must think leniently of others. In order not to let oneself be misled by lack of charity or by one's own temperamental bent, one must calm oneself by charitable thoughts towards those who provoke and repel one. "Should the devil draw my attention to the faults of any one of them... I call to mind at once her virtues and her good intentions. I tell myself that though I may have seen her fall once, there are probably a great many other occasions on which she has won victories which, in her humility, she has kept to herself. What may appear to me to be a fault may even be an act of virtue, because of her intention." Had not Thérèse herself learned by experience how easily people misjudge. She mentions the time she was asked to help in some task she was eager to do. In order to check her impetuosity, and to give her neighbour a chance to take her place, if that should please her, she folded her needlework slowly. This slowness was interpreted as laziness, and "the whole community was left with the impression that I had acted according to nature." Thérèse adds: "I cannot tell you what I gained from this incident and how tolerant it made me." She repeats in reference to herself, and with a fine pride, the words of

St Paul: "It is the Lord's scrutiny that I must undergo." But then she must also grant to others the same right and leave judgment to the Lord alone. Time and again she repeats to her novices: "We must always judge others lovingly, for what appears to our eyes as neglect may often be in the eyes of God an act of heroism. A sister who has a headache or is undergoing spiritual trials is accomplishing more when she does half her work than others who are sound in body and soul when they do all of theirs." And when the others protested against the habits of the mentally ill sister who worked in the laundry room, Thérèse exclaimed: "Oh, let her be. If only you knew how much we must forgive her, how much she deserves pity. It is not her fault that she is not better endowed by nature. She is like a poor clock that must be wound up every quarter of an hour. Do have pity on her! How much we must practise kindness towards our neighbours!"

The neurotic portress drove all her assistants to despair by her everlasting nagging, her thousand quirks, her reiterated instructions and prescriptions. "Out of love we must let her keep her idea that she is benefiting us by all her good advice. And after all, she is really giving us an opportunity to practise patience." During her novitiate Thérèse herself assisted at the door and also felt as if she were "pierced by a thousand pinpricks", until at times she thought she could not go on. But when her successor took exception to the old woman's crotchets, the good sister said indignantly: "What is the matter with you? Sister Thérèse of the Child Jesus never talked to me that way!"

Justice towards others often mitigates anger and moral indignation. But only too easily it may also put to rout the courage to deal with imperfections. The hardest of insights is recognition of the unalterability of human dispositions and traits: "Lack of common sense and lack of delicacy, the extreme touchiness of certain people"—all the things that make community living so difficult. "I know perfectly well that such defects are so deeply rooted as to be beyond all hope of cure." But when we are confronted with persons physically ill, do we stop at this perception? A great humanitarian and pastor, Dominik Ringeisen, a German contemporary of Thérèse's whom she never knew, considered it especially good training for all of us to deal with the gravely ill, because we behave towards them as we really ought to behave towards all other human beings.

Thérèse came to the same conclusion: that lenient judgment alone is insufficient. "I see above all that charity must not remain hidden in the bottom of our hearts, for 'a lamp is not lighted to be put away under a bushel measure; it is put on the lampstand to give light to all the people of the house.'"

Thus, we must untiringly aid human beings whenever we see them suffering. And human weaknesses and defects are forms of suffering, if only because they usually drive away the love of others. Even in the convent such nuns were the loneliest: "One treats them as the courtesy of our religious life demands, but one keeps out of their way for fear of saying something unkind."

What is the conclusion? Are not such nuns the poor man who has fallen among thieves and now lies by the wayside, disfigured by ugly wounds?

> I must seek out the company of the Sisters who, naturally speaking, repel me, and be their Good Samaritan. Often a single word, a friendly smile, is enough to give a depressed or lonely soul fresh life. Nevertheless I do not always want to practise charity merely to bring consolation. I would soon be discouraged if that were so, for something said with the best of intentions may be taken completely the wrong way; so in order not to waste my time and trouble, I try to do everything to give pleasure to Our Lord, and to follow out this Gospel precept: "When thou givest a supper, do not ask thy neighbours to come, or thy brethren; it may be they will send thee invitations in return, and so thou wilt be recompensed for thy pains. Rather, when thou givest hospitality, invite poor men to come, the cripples, the lame, the blind: so shalt thou win a blessing, for these cannot make thee any return. And thy Father, who sees what is done in secret, will reward thee."
>
> A spiritual feast of gentle, joyful love is all I can set before my Sisters; I do not know of any other, and want to follow the example of St Paul, rejoicing with all those who rejoice. I know he wept with those who weep, and my feasts are not always without their share of tears, but I always try to turn them into smiles, for "it is the cheerful giver God loves".[12]

We can only quote extracts from the two wonderful chapters which develop this doctrine of charity. These chapters must be re-read and meditated on again and again.

Step by step Thérèse felt her way forward, finding the path solely by the light radiating from the Lord's own words. For there is no hint anywhere that this subject was treated in regular instruction at the convent. "I turned to the Gospels again, where Our Lord explains clearly His New Commandment: 'You have heard that it was said, Thou shalt love thy neighbour and hate thy enemy. But I tell you, Love your enemies, pray for those who persecute you.'" She goes on to say that there are no enemies in Carmel, but there are natural attractions and repulsions. And the latter may well have a bitter taste indeed because they have no right to flourish in the convent atmosphere. There were also sisters whom "we would take pains to avoid meeting". Thérèse interpreted the commandment to mean that "it is this very Sister I must love; I must pray for her

---

[12] *S.S.*, x.

even though she shows no sign of loving me". If, however, we are tempted
to anger towards someone, there is only one way for us to regain our
peace: to treat him like a benefactor. "We must pray for this person and
ask God to reward him for the very distress he inflicts upon us." [13]

Thérèse practised unremittingly all her own recommendations. Many
witnesses testify that during recreation hours she regularly (but with a
casual air, as if by chance) sat down beside the cross and difficult sisters.
She even shared the rare, cherished days of a retreat—which each nun
was allowed to devote once a year to quietest meditation and to speaking
her heart to intimates—with a stupid and tactless novice.[14] After her collapse, although she was on the verge of total exhaustion and had been
exempted from all physical work, she offered to help the mentally ill sister of the laundry room with mending; because this sister was so unbearable, the Prioress had not dared to assign any assistant to her. And how
liberally she lavished the "alms of smiling", that "unique feast" of which
she speaks. For seven years, evening after evening she helped lame, grumbling, eternally discontented Sister St Peter from the choir to the refectory, brought her stool for her, manœuvred her into it, rolled back her
heavy sleeves, and cut her bread. By these faithful little services she won,
in the end, the old woman's gratitude and confidence—but above all because she always offered her "very best smile", which gradually melted
the aged nun's frozen heart. Another old sister had her cell next to Thérèse's.
At one time she was troubled by great spiritual anguish, but did not dare
to talk to anyone about it. Thérèse, as if she had guessed this, used to
wait for her footstep every evening; then she would softly open her door
once more and greet her silently with a wonderful smile.

In *The Story of a Soul* Thérèse herself tells, with considerable humour,
of how she won the friendship of the very sister "who managed to irri-
tate me in everything she did". Her sharp, stupid and conceited personality was in every feature the opposite of Thérèse's. We are not generally
ashamed of this sort of antipathy; on the contrary, we are apt to be quite
pleased with ourselves for seeing through the other person's poses and
give him a wide berth. But Thérèse meant what she said; if she were
going to practise charity, if she were going to be a Good Samaritan, then
she must apply the principle precisely where to do so seemed almost
impossible. "And I set myself to treat her as if I loved her best of all."
Whenever they met, Thérèse prayed for her, reminding God (and herself
we must surely add) of all the virtues and merits of this unsympathetic
nun. She tried to do everything she possibly could for her, "and when

[13] *Esprit*, 83.
[14] 2 S., 279.

tempted to answer her sharply I hastened to give her a friendly smile, and talk about something else; for as it says in the *Imitation*, 'It is better to leave everyone to his own way of thinking than begin an argument.' " [15] On the days when talk was permitted, Thérèse addressed herself to this nun first and more frequently than the others; at recreation she appeared to be happy if she were able to sit beside her, and talked animatedly with her, as if the conversation gave her real pleasure.[16]

If she could not manage at all—"when the devil made a particularly violent attack, if I could slip away without letting her suspect my inward struggle, I would run away from the battle *like a deserter*." What balm for us that a saint—this saint—also met with defeats in this struggle.

But such setbacks were probably known to Thérèse alone. The entire house considered the relationship between the two a genuine intimate friendship, for all its incongruity. Good, honest Sister Marie gradually grew jealous. "After all, I brought her up," she said sadly to Pauline, "and now she likes this sister of all persons, whom I find so repugnant, better than me." [17] Marie one day actually reproached her sister and suggested that ties of blood, after all, also came from God, and that it was scarcely just to show another nun such obvious preference. Thérèse replied with nothing but an amused little smile. Céline, who regarded her sister as a model and scarcely ever let her out of sight, was thunderstruck when Thérèse one day confided this case to her in order to encourage her to similar self-conquest. "It was absolutely a revelation to me, for she had such control of herself that not a jot of her effort was betrayed; and when on top of it all she named the object of her daily struggles, I was stunned—I had always thought this sister was her best friend."

The finest confirmation of her complete victory was supplied by the very nun in question. For after Thérèse's death she said with innocent complacency: "At least I can say this much for myself: during her life I made her really happy."

This schooling in charity was at the same time schooling in implacable insight into herself. Thérèse's account contains a whole psychology of community life, a penetration of ultimate, secret, unadmitted evasions, withdrawals and barricades behind which we attempt to hide from the commandment that comes harder to us than any other.

The Lord says: "Give to every man who asks, and if a man takes what is thine, do not ask him to restore it." Nuns no longer have property, we might say; therefore this commandment does not apply to them. But

---

[15] *S.S.*, ix.
[16] 2 *S.*, 247.
[17] 1 *S.*, 18.

Thérèse probes deeper. To be sure, nothing belongs to her any longer. But still there are things she needs and is allowed to use for work: paintbrush, pencil, penknife. When she sits down to work and finds one of her tools missing because someone has "borrowed" it without asking, she is as vexed as if the property were her own and must "take strong hold of myself to resist demanding them back with asperity". Hence these words of Jesus are also directed to her; she must not *demand* these things back as if they belonged to her. Rather, she must ask humbly for them, as if the return of them depended entirely on the other person's charity. And if she receives them, she must accept them as a gift, with surprise and gratitude. And what if it is refused, and in addition she is asked to surrender something else which she needs? "If a man would take away thy coat, do not grudge him thy cloak along with it." Indeed, it is not enough to respond only to requests: "I must go beyond their desires, and show myself very honoured, and only too glad to offer my services. If something which I normally use is taken away, I should appear happy to be *rid* of it."

But suppose necessity forces one to refuse a request. Then there are ways to refuse so graciously what we cannot give that the refusal gives as much pleasure as the gift. To be sure, such conduct does not make life easier; people have no compunctions about approaching those who are always ready to oblige—to approach them and, let us say it candidly, to exploit them. But should we avoid those who are only too ready to ask help, after the Divine Master has said: "If a man would borrow from thee, do not turn away"? We should rather be careful not to look harried, tired or remote, since such expressions fend off those who might wish to ask something of us. A nurse, Thérèse taught her novices, ought deliberately to go near the sickroom, so that she will be called. She ought to respond promptly, promise to come back, show herself pleased, as if the patient were doing her a favour by making a request. "Oh, believe me, to think about lovely, sacred things, to write books, to describe the lives of saints— all that is as nothing compared to responding kindly to a call. I have practised that, and I have experienced the peace that radiates from it." [18]

While Thérèse was writing this chapter about charity, she herself was amply tried. She was already severely ill and spent most of the time sitting in the garden. Writing wearied her enormously; she could scarcely assemble her thoughts. Pauline observed her treatment of the novices who in passing pestered her with questions and talk. Thérèse never asked to be left undisturbed, never asked them to postpone a conversation; she referred neither to her condition nor to the importance of her work. Every

[18] 2 S., 391.

time a novice came up to her chair, she quietly laid her pen aside and closed the notebook, giving the sister a kind, encouraging smile. "I am writing about sisterly love," she said to Pauline, "and at the same time I have the opportunity to practise it. Oh, Mother, love is everything in this world. We love God only to the extent that we practise it."

With unsparing frankness, Thérèse continues her confession: "It seems hard to lend, hoping to receive nothing; it is much easier to give outright, for once we have given anything away, it no longer belongs to us. When someone comes to us and says, full of assurance: 'I need your help for a few hours, but don't worry, Reverend Mother has given permission, and I will repay the time you lend me,' we know perfectly well that she never will, and feel very much like saying: 'I will *give* you the time'; it would gratify our self-love, for it is so much more generous to give than merely to lend, and we would make her feel that we do not think much of her services."

Free time is almost the only thing a Carmelite has at her disposal, which she can "lend" and give away; therefore it is also each nun's jealously guarded property. Thérèse was spendthrift about this possession; she allowed herself to be so overburdened with tasks that she had scarcely more than a quarter hour now and then to put her own verses down on paper. She was always busy with needlework or brushwork, or composing verses "to order".

There is, however, still other, more intimate property which we can administer generously or stingily. When the Lord commands us to give to him who asks and to let what is ours be taken without asking for it back, He is not only referring to money and goods. "One's most intimate thoughts, the children of one's heart and mind, are riches which one clings to as one's very own; no one has any right to encroach on them." This sounds as if the vital, deeply rooted possessiveness of the French nation had been driven back to a last redoubt which it was determined to defend all the more tenaciously.

If, for example, I tell one of the Sisters of some enlightening thought that came to me in meditation, and if she makes it known as if it had come to her, it would seem as though she had taken something that was mine. Or again, if in recreation someone whispers something amusing to her neighbour, and this is repeated out aloud without acknowledgment, its author feels as if she has been robbed. She may say nothing at the time, but feels her loss, and seizes the first chance she gets to make known, delicately of course, that it was stolen from *her* treasury of thoughts.... I think it is true to say now that through grace I am as detached from the spiritual goods of heart and soul as I am from earthly goods. If any thoughts or words of mine should happen to give pleasure to the Sisters, I am only too glad that they should treat them as their own property. Such thoughts, after all, do not belong to me, but to the Holy Spirit, for has not St Paul assured us that "without the Spirit of Love we cannot even call God Father"?

So thoroughly did Thérèse hold to this communality of spiritual property that many of her poems were composed on assigned subjects, as though even language and the gift of expression were no longer her property, but a tool to be put to the service of others. This probably explains the tastelessness and stiffness of so many of her poems, alongside a few which render genuine, deep feeling and clear thoughts in an unpretentious but graceful form.

This was hard schooling, *labor improbus*. "Nor have I found the practice of charity always so easy." Thérèse knows very well that this kind of love is anything but "natural"; in this respect she is entirely French, without a tinge of idealism. "How much the divine teachings run contrary to our natural feelings. Without the aid of grace it would be impossible even to understand them, let alone to practise them." Only the Lord Himself can accomplish His commands in her. "It is only because You are willing to do this that You have given us a *New* Commandment, and I love it because it is my assurance of Your desire to love in me all those whom You command me to love. I know that whenever I am charitable, it is Jesus alone who is acting through me, and that the more closely I unite myself to Him, the more I will be able to love all my Sisters."

Thérèse gave Jesus room. When she described to Céline in glowing words the form of perfect charity, it was her own nature she was depicting: "It is natural to love to sacrifice everything, to give in all directions, up and down, back and forth, to squander itself, never calculating, destroying the hope of fruit by plucking the blossoms. Love gives everything. But we, alas, we give only after reckoning; we hesitate to sacrifice what is advantageous to us. This is not love, for love is blind; it is a wild torrent that leaves nothing behind in the path where it has raged." [19]

3. THE ANGEL OF THE DESERT

It is almost impossible to comprehend that Thérèse was able to achieve such magnificent surrender in the midst of constant spiritual aridity. Yet even her devotion during those years was primarily faithfulness, that tenacious fidelity which, so to speak, fed blindly on the memory of better days. There had been the experience of encountering God, palpably, when her emotions had been deeply stirred, as it were, and when her intellect had been stimulated. That remained real whether or not such an encounter ever recurred. She had seen the sun shine, and on the long subterranean

[19] 2 S., 362.

journey she would not for a moment forget that it was still there, invisible but radiating, like the real sun behind November clouds. God was suddenly gone; He had fallen silent and apparently turned away from her. Yet stubbornly, candidly, she would continue to attest her love, to act in the spirit of it, and to rely upon God's words and promises. In this she was acting as—may the figure be forgiven—she would have behaved towards her deranged father had she been allowed to tend him; she would have surrounded him daily with inexhaustible veneration and tenderness even though she never received so much as a single glance of recognition or response in return. This fidelity was rooted in the spirit, in certainty of truth, so that no encouraging pledge, no reassuring sign, was any longer required. Such devotion no longer needs "living proof"; it is life itself, like the life of nature in winter, suspended, as it were, from the animated world of imagination, from the conscious currents of the emotions, withdrawn to the deep roots, to the unconscious ground beneath the floor of experience. Such devotion is surrender to the faith once vowed, though everything else may have changed, except Him who is believed in. "Even if God should slay me I would still trust in Him"—Thérèse was very fond of these words from the Book of Job, the greatest of all expressions of hope.

Usually, however, her formulation of what she was experiencing was a quiet and modest "Jesus is asleep". He slept as He had in the Apostles' boat during the storm, slept like a friend who is weary in a friend's house, and may sleep, whereas strangers must always be entertained and overloaded with attentions. He was the child and she the toy which rolled away from the sleepy child's hand and now lay forgotten in a corner. He was the infant in the cradle whose slumber she guarded. In a thousand turns of phrase, some of them extremely childish, she consoled herself for God's silence, for the kind of silence which might have driven others, even less vulnerable, less sensitive and less yearning souls, to despair. What a demonstration of trust to leave, to forsake the good sheep in the desert while He pursued the lost one. This meant that He knew they would not run away! How fine it was that the Lord "made no fuss" about her, treated her as closest friend, in whose presence a friend may be silent for a while without giving offence. "How rarely souls let Him sleep peacefully within them. Their agitation and all their requests have so tired out the Good Master that He is only too glad to enjoy the rest I offer Him." "If my Jesus seems to forget me, He is welcome to do so, since I no longer belong to myself, but to Him. He will sooner grow tired of making me wait than I will grow tired of waiting." [20]

---

[20] Laveille, 383.

Would you sleep
While the tempest growls,
Lay your golden locks
Upon my breast.

How your smile delights me,
As you slumber gently
Bending over you, singing,
I rock you, my heart singing,
Dearest child!

Who would ever guess that these sweet verses, which seem to express the tender happiness of the Nativity, in reality sing the dark torment of her sense of abandonment by God?

On those rare, long-awaited days when she was permitted to receive the Holy Eucharist she found, to her shame, that for her thanksgiving she could find no words and no emotion. Worse than that, out of weariness and aridity she literally fell asleep. But she could still console herself with the thought that children asleep were just as dear to their parents as when awake; that doctors put patients to sleep for operations; and, finally, those most reassuring words of the Psalms: "Does not the Lord know the stuff of which we are made, can He forget that we are only dust?" Even at the last Communion in her life—for six weeks before her death she could no longer communicate because of frequent vomiting—she remained without consolation, "as though two very young children have been placed side by side and neither says a word. That is, I did say a little to Him—but He did not reply; probably He was asleep." [21]

But we would be greatly mistaken, if, misled by Thérèse's stammering and at the same time all-too-fluent language, we viewed her image of God as childish, petty, sentimental and innocuous. When she says "*Papa le bon Dieu*", the image of her own father stands behind the words; that image reflects, as a dewdrop the sun, the paternal love of Him who has given His name to all fatherhood. She employs the sentimental, romantic betrothal allegories dear to the convents of her time; she speaks in frequently embarrassing phrases of her bridegroom, who must be wheedled, treated properly, disarmed, whose weaknesses must be turned to account. "He has only two: He is blind and cannot reckon." She imitates the wedding invitation of her cousin Jeanne Guérin in a document of blatant teenage tastelessness: "Almighty God, The Creator of Heaven and Earth, and Ruler of the World, and The Most Glorious Virgin Mary, Queen of

---

[21] I S., xix, 283.

the Court of Heaven, Invite you to the Spiritual Marriage of Their August Son Jesus, King of Kings and Lord of Lords, with Little Thérèse
Martin, now Lady and Princess of the Kingdoms of the Childhood and
Passion of Jesus, given in dowry by her Divine Spouse from whom she
holds her titles of nobility Of the Child Jesus and Of the Holy Face." [22]
She speaks of the Bridegroom's jewel box, of her wedding gown which is
not yet beautiful enough for Him, and even of the empty honeymoon
journey. These and many other aspects of her religious testimony which
are hard to bear with, remind us again and again of her human limitations. Thérèse was, and in many respects remained all her life, a provincial child, a middle-class girl who had attended school for barely five
years. Vital and wide-awake as were her mind and her sense of beauty,
they had never been shaped by contact with the great models and the
masters of her national culture. Only once in all her writings do we find
a quotation from the classics which even the most average French girls'
schools indefatigably impress on the pupils. Her solitary year of self-
instruction, and the trip to Italy, could not fill in all the gaps.

The result was that Thérèse often spoke in acquired formulas and spoke
to companions who knew no other language and probably did not want
to hear any other. In the rare cases in which she went beyond such fancy
metaphors and found her own words, they were like windows opening
up upon unfathomable starry skies. Yet we cannot say that the spiritual
reading in the Lisieux Carmel was upon a low level. Those writings which
represented the tradition of the Order occupied the highest intellectual
rank. But there were also many lives and legends of the saints. Even Thérèse's
well-known statement about the shower of roses derived from a *Life of St
Aloysius* which was read aloud at table. The stories of the Desert Fathers
were naturally to be found in this Desert Order, together with the visions
of St Margaret Mary Alacoque, which is a favourite in all convents. But
it is typical of Thérèse that in this respect, too, she added virtually nothing to the intellectual stock she had brought with her from her home.
She absorbed nothing new. With astonishing tenacity she maintained her
own original mentality unaltered in spite of all influences from outside;
she resisted the most precious as well as inferior influences. This was both
her strength and her weakness. She remained faithful to *The Imitation of
Christ*. But nothing seems to have drawn her to the writing of the great
Mother of her Order, Teresa of Avila; we find only two quotations from
Teresa in all her autobiographical writings, letters, poems and conversations. However, the second classic writer of the Carmelite Order, John of

[22] *S.S.*, viii.

the Cross, made a deep impression on her spiritual life. But in him she was scarcely encountering something new; rather, she was recognizing a close kinship. With enthusiasm she read his great, and difficult, works: the *Ascent of Mount Carmel*, the *Way of Purification*, the *Dark Night of the Soul*, the *Spiritual Canticle*, the *Living Flame of Love*, and his other poems and songs. Passages from these writings are woven into everything she herself said and wrote. We may say that Thérèse, with childlike and feminine instinct, underwent the same experiences as John of the Cross and expressed simply what he expounded with masculine deliberation in his magnificently formed chapters and in the majestic language of the Spanish Baroque. In reading him Thérèse must have felt as if she were seeing a translation from her own inarticulation into marvellous rhetoric, as if she had discovered a map through her own desert. The Novice Mistress recalled at the trial that her extremely young novice had spoken with surprising maturity and clarity about the highly difficult mystical doctrine of this great Father of the Order. She had also committed to memory long stanzas of the mighty spiritual canticles.

Therefore, it is somewhat strange that this process of feeding on and absorbing the works of the greatest Carmelite mystic did not continue beyond the beginnings of Thérèse's life in the convent, although later, in the period of spiritual darkness, she gratefully remembered his instructions and found in them an explanation of her own condition. "The works of St John of the Cross have been such a source of light to me. Between the ages of sixteen and eighteen I read no one else. Later on, spiritual writers always left me cold, and still do. Whenever I open a book, no matter how beautiful or touching, my heart dries up, and I can understand nothing of what I read; or if I do understand, my mind will go no further, and I cannot meditate."

This state, too, is precisely described in the saint's works. According to him, it is one of the features of the "dark night", that inexpressibly mysterious and painful process of purification that must be undergone on the way to the summit of union with God. The way into the mysterious depths of the soul does not pass through intellectual concepts. German mysticism, too, is acquainted with this way into the "imageless" silence of everything in the created order which precedes the supreme illumination. Did Thérèse experience this? It would seem that she knew this condition only as one of the trials of the desert, as a paralysis of all spiritual faculties and expulsion from familiar abodes. But at the same time, and this was its hidden glory, she recognized it as a state of being thrown back upon the one thing necessary.

For the great and crucial discovery of her years in the convent was the Bible. It is typical of the Catholicism of her period that she had not encountered the Holy Scriptures in her devout home. Now that she was daily repeating the Holy Office in the words of Scripture and reading the Bible meditatively, this treasure of all treasures was opened up to her. Here, in the midst of her forsakenness and aridity, she found the Angel of God who led her step by step. "They supply my poor soul's every need, and they are always yielding up to me new lights and mysterious hidden meanings." "I no longer find anything in books; the Gospel suffices me. For example, is not everything contained in these words of the Lord: 'Learn from Me; I am gentle and humble of heart'?[23] How sweet not to have to learn from anything but the mouth of Jesus."[24]

Once, standing before the convent library, she said gaily to a nun: "Oh, I am very glad I have not read all these books! I would merely have racked my brains and lost the precious time I spent in loving God."[25] Here we feel plainly the influence of *The Imitation of Christ* with its condemnation of "vain and worldly knowledge". Against this counsel her brief surge of adolescent hunger for knowledge did not long survive.

But Thérèse threw herself wholeheartedly into the joys of receiving the Word of God and letting it take possession of her. It is evident from the many quotations to be found in every page she wrote and every reported conversation that she worked diligently to acquire a thorough knowledge of the Scriptures. Frequently passages are not quoted with perfect accuracy; in other words, they have been cited from memory. She knew the Gospels almost by heart; in addition, her writings indicate familiarity with the Acts of the Apostles, the Epistles and the Apocalypse, and with most of the books of the Old Testament. We find her quoting passages from the Pentateuch, Kings, Proverbs, Ecclesiastes, from the Greater and the Lesser Prophets, from Tobit and Esther, but with especial frequency from the Song of Solomon, and again and again from the Psalms. In her spare leisure hours in her cell Thérèse copied out the concordant passages from the Gospel and the Old Testament. She read and compared every edition she found in the convent and was surprised and disturbed by the divergent translations. Since she did not know Latin, she had to be content with French translations and fervently wished she might be a priest in order to be able to read the Holy Scriptures in their original languages "to grasp the Divine thoughts as God wished to express them in our human language". "One must learn *the character of God* from the Scriptures", she was fond of saying. She carried a pocket edition of the Gospels about with her day and night.

[23] Mt 11:29.
[24] 2 S., 240.
[25] Petitot, 73.

Her image of God, then, was none other than that revealed in the
Holy Scriptures. The Old Testament taught her the sublimity and power
of Him, before whom the seraphim hid their faces; the New Testament
showed her the Father of Jesus Christ, and the Saviour. To Thérèse God
was always the "Divine Majesty", just as He was for Teresa of Avila. "Oh,
how good it is that God has commanded us to love Him", she said to her
sister. "Otherwise we would never have dared to." And again: "What a
joy it is, Mother, that God became a Man, so that we could love Him.
Oh, how good it was of Him to do that; otherwise, how would we have
had the courage to?"[26] "Our human nature has so strong a craving to
understand what we love; at the thought that God is pure Spirit, we
might well grow giddy. Oh, how wise it was of Him to become Man!"
When she reflected that we are entitled to call this great God Father, she
was often moved to tears. Even as a child she had experienced the closeness and the glory of God in the flash of lightnings, and her first view of
the sea at seven filled her with the same reverent and enthusiastic awe: "It
was so majestic! and the voice of the waves spoke to my soul of God's
power and grandeur." She knew that His justice was terrible towards the
impenitent sinner, and her ardour for saving souls certainly sprang in part
from insuppressible trembling before the punitive majesty of the Lord.
The terrors of divine wrath at times oppressed her heavily. When during
retreats a severe preacher impressed upon the nuns the inexorability of
Judgment, the gravity of sin, and the ease with which souls could fall,
Thérèse would be thrown into a state akin to illness; unable to eat or
sleep, she would struggle with all her might against this image of God
which her heart was unwilling to accept. A priest who knew more about
her than many others, Dom Godefroy Madelaine, reports that Thérèse
lived for a whole eighteen months in the conviction that she was damned;[27]
he considers this trial to have been a temptation of the devil. The Novice
Mistress has testified that Thérèse was once reduced to tears by the words:
"No one knows whether he is worthy of love or of hate."

We must not for a moment disregard these facts when we consider the
saint's famous childlike and sunny confidence in God's infinite mercy;
when we encounter again and again her own images of the child in its
mother's arms pressing close to its father's heart. Only within this framework do such images reveal their full depth and their genuine importance. Like an edelweiss upon a jagged peak, this blossom of her soul
lifted itself out of silent darkness towards the Infinite. She felt the presence of this terrible and invisible God at every step in her life, recognized

[26] 1 S., 15.
[27] 2 S., 528.

His hand in the fall of snow on her Clothing day, in the longed-for corn cockle in a bunch of flowers, in every moment of her existence. Day and night she repeated to Him, with closed eyes, so to speak, the words of love which He spoke in His divine mercy and mildness to fallen man, those words with which the Scriptures are filled. During the period of her blackest night of faith, that almost fatal time, the sick girl was inexpressibly moved by the sight of a white hen gathering her chicks under her wings. "I had to weep, since I thought that God had introduced this parable into the Gospel in order to make His affection believable to us. He did this to me all my life. He sheltered me wholly under His wings. A while ago I could no longer restrain myself; my heart overflowed with gratitude and love. Oh, God does well to conceal Himself from my sight, to show Himself only rarely to me and to reveal the workings of His mercy only 'as through a glass, darkly'.... I would not be able to endure so much sweetness."

The Scriptures provided a corrective for the stunted or hypertrophic malformations in the religious thinking of the day. With refreshing sanity Thérèse rejected the fabulous and fantastic conceptions of pious poetry. "The things that help me, that do me good, are not at all the nonsense we are told. The things people will accept! For example, that Little Jesus moulded birds out of mud and breathed upon them so that they came to life! The Child Jesus certainly did not work any such useless miracles! Why then would they not have been simply transported to Egypt by a miracle—that at least would have been useful, and certainly would seem an easy matter for God—they would have been there in the twinkling of an eye. But no, that was not how it was; their life was just like ours."

It is really curious that her reading in the Scriptures seems to have effected no alteration in her picture of Christ—that current and so unbiblical picture of Jesus which dominated the religious writing of the period and was given virtually definitive form in the devotional images of the post-Nazarene movement. Did this art style so rule the religious imagination of her contemporaries that no one was able to escape its stamp? Or, conversely, did this conception so ardently cultivated embody itself in Church art? A pale, gaunt figure, slim as a willow, with drooping shoulders, long locks, excessively large eyes and languid gestures—such is the portrayal of the Saviour we see on First Communion pictures, where, dressed in bright-coloured flowing garments, He is shown embracing a bewreathed child. This figure may derive from the style which was introduced into French, and thence into Catholic piety by St Margaret Mary Alacoque. During the seventeenth and even the eighteenth centuries it may have provided a necessary counterbalance to the prim, cold and intellectual elements of Jansenism and the Enlightenment. But it remained as a persistent conception of Christ in the popular imagination. This was Christ as a figure of extreme sensibility in still another sense, for it was a projection of feminine psychology into Christ. Moreover, it corresponds very closely to the "sweet Lord Jesus" of the later Pietists with their little lambs and doves. No one, confronted with such a picture, can say: "The LORD!" This Christ is solely the Friend and Bridegroom, weeping and uncomprehended, taking refuge within the small circle of the devout, where alone He can feel comfortable, begging for their consolation. And they, the devout, are the only ones in the whole wide world who are still willing to offer Him a place.

We encounter this image of Christ hundreds of times in Thérèse's writings. "Jesus is weeping", she says again and again in her letters, which so guilelessly express the innermost life of her soul. "Jesus is weeping! Oh, how that hurts Him!" (She is referring to the fact that her cousin, because of a scruple, missed going to Communion.) "Consider, darling, that Jesus dwells in the Tabernacle especially for you, for you alone; He burns with longing to enter your heart."

"Oh, Céline, Jesus asks us both to quench His thirst by giving Him our souls.... Yes, He *begs* us for souls.... Oh, let us understand His look!" [28]

"Jesus weeps—and we... we think of our sorrow, without consoling our Bridegroom.... Would it be possible for a grain of sand to console Jesus, to wipe away the tears? Who understands the tears of Jesus?"

"Céline, darling, let us make a small tabernacle in our hearts, in which Jesus can take refuge; then He will be consoled and He will forget what we cannot forget: the ingratitude of souls who leave Him alone in a lonely tabernacle.... Your heart should be a brazier at which Jesus can again warm Himself."

"Céline, you must make your heart into a little garden of delight into which Jesus can come to rest... the Spouse who cannot have anything about Him that is not virginal." [29]

"Has Jesus not established His dwelling in your heart to console Himself in it for the wickedness of sinners?" [30] "Oh, my dearest Céline, what joy Jesus has in His little harp! He has so little joy in the world; permit Him to rest in you."

Even the tremendous chapter in Isaiah on the suffering servant of God, one of the most powerful and austere passages in the entire Bible, is translated by her wholly into this curiously sentimental language.

[28] Letter 74.
[29] Letter 102.
[30] Letter 116.

All this is proof of no more than the power of religious convention. But at the same time the fact itself teaches us how inessential, in spite of everything, the language of images and concepts is, in a genuine relationship with God. These trappings we today find almost unbearable. Yet did they ever raise a barrier between Thérèse and the living Lord of her soul? Was her love, her insight, less than that of any other saint in times of greater aesthetic talent, epochs which gave us the tremendous mosaic images of Christ, or Romanesque and Gothic crucifixes?

It is all the more surprising to us to see how original and fresh her conception of the Blessed Virgin was, how it differed from the sugary and exaggerated representations of the period.

"All the sermons I have heard on Mary have left me unmoved", she said at the end of her life.[31]

How I wish I had been a priest, to be able to preach on the Blessed Virgin!... Above all I would have shown how little we really know about her life. It is not right to tell improbable stories about her, things that we simply do not know—for example, that when she was very small, three years old, she went into the Temple to consecrate herself to God with all kinds of deep emotions, whereas she probably went only because her parents told her to....

And why should we infer, from the prophetic words of aged Simeon, that the Holy Virgin thereafter had the Lord's Passion constantly in mind? "A sword *shall* pierce your soul"—one can see from that, Mother, that it was a prediction of something that would happen later.

For a sermon on the Blessed Virgin to bear fruit, it would have to show her real life, which the Gospel gives us hints about, and not an imaginary life.... Yet we can well guess that her real life, in Nazareth and later, must have been very ordinary....

The Blessed Virgin is presented to us as beyond attainment; she should be shown as imitable, practising hidden virtues; it ought to be said that she, like us, lived by faith; that ought to be proved by passages from the Gospel, such as those in which we read: "The words which He spoke to them were beyond their understanding," and again: "The father and mother of the child were wondering over all that was said of Him"[32]—do you not think this marvelling also expresses astonishment?

How gladly I sang to her:

> The straight way to Heaven thou hast made clear
> By practising always the most humble virtues.

It is not true that she had no physical pains. [This had been asserted by a priest in a letter to Thérèse.] When I contemplated her this evening, I grasped that; I understand that she suffered not only in her soul, but in her

[31] *N.V.*, 23 August.
[32] Lk 2:50, 33.

body as well. She suffered a great deal on her journeys, from cold and heat and weariness.... She fasted so often.... Oh, yes, she knows what suffering means! And good St Joseph, how I love him! He could not fast because he had to work so hard.... I see him working with the plane, and wiping his brow from time to time. Oh, how sorry I am for him! How often he experienced grief and disappointment! How often people blustered at him! How often they refused to pay him for his work. Oh, we would be astonished if we knew what a hard time they had of it. And how simple their life seems to me.... The women from the countryside came to the Holy Virgin and talked familiarly with her; sometimes they asked her to let her little Jesus go and play with their children. And little Jesus looked at the Blessed Virgin to know whether he really might go....

We know well enough that the Blessed Virgin is the Queen of Heaven and Earth. But she is more Mother than Queen, and no one should try to persuade people, as I have often heard, that because of her virtues she outshines and as it were extinguishes the glory of all the saints as the rising sun makes the stars disappear. Good God, how strange that would be: a mother extinguishing the glory of her children! I believe quite the opposite, that she increases many times the glory of the elect.

It is fine and good to speak of her virtues and prerogatives, but we must not end there. We must so speak that people will be made to *love* her. If in listening to a sermon on the Blessed Virgin we are forced from beginning to end to gasp with amazement—nothing but Ahs and Ohs—we soon have enough of it, and that leads neither to love nor to imitation. Who knows whether a good many souls may not in the end be driven so far as to feel a certain estrangement from a being so very much superior. The only prerogative of the Blessed Virgin is that she was exempted from original sin, and became the Mother of God. And even in regard to this last point, Jesus tells us: If anyone does the will of God, he is My brother, and sister, and mother.[33]

We feel here something of the honesty and strictness of thought which was the badge of honour of nineteenth-century science. But this lively feeling for the truth and nothing but the truth, which never left Thérèse—"I do not know whether I am humble, but I know this: that in all things I see the truth"[34]—by no means chilled and cracked the sincerity of her devout heart, as can so easily happen. Precisely because her image of the Blessed Virgin was free of all romantic ornamentation and exaggeration, she loved the real Virgin all the more tenderly and submissively. To her she addressed her finest verses; in her she confided like a child in its mother. So great was her delight in Our Lady, in the very fact of her existence, that she once remarked: "On the other hand we are happier than she, for she had no Blessed Virgin to love! That is sweetness more for us, and so great a one—and a great sweetness less for her!" And all

[33] Mk 3:35; *N.V.*, 23 August.
[34] *C.S.*, 266.

her love poured out once more in the childlike sentence, the last lines she wrote in her life, under a picture of Mary: "Oh, Mary, if I were the Queen of Heaven and you were Thérèse, I should like to be Thérèse in order to see you as Queen of Heaven!"

4. EXPERIENCES OF GOD

With the new name a Carmelite receives when she enters the Order there is always an epithet: Teresa of Jesus, Marie of the Eucharist, Elizabeth of the Holy Trinity, Anne of the Angels. The epithet singles out the Mystery which she is supposed to contemplate with special devotion.

Thérèse's names in religion—she had two of them—imply a consecration and an imitation. The epithet with which the world is most familiar is "of the Child Jesus"; but the two names must be taken together to define her religious significance.

The first name was promised to her at nine, as befitting this tender age, by Mother Marie de Gonzague, and was given to her at her entry into the convent. In her maturity it played a minor part. In itself, veneration of the childhood of Jesus was a precious Carmelite heritage of the seventeenth century, the classical age of French mysticism. This veneration does not, however, centre around the charm and sweetness—as might be superficially assumed—of the Child in the Crib; it is not meant as an appeal to the maternal instincts of devout girls and the mentality of small children. Rather, it concentrates upon the staggering humiliation of divine majesty in assuming the shape of extreme weakness and helplessness. Reverence for the Crib goes back to Francis of Assisi, to that first memorable occasion in the cave at Greccio when the saint prepared the bed of straw and led in the ox and donkey and the worshippers by nocturnal torchlight suddenly thought they saw the living Child in his arms. But it took the French Oratory of Cardinal Bérulle, and the French Carmel which was so strongly influenced by him, to renew this old devotional practice and lend it new meaning. "Naked, sharp and inexorable—it announces to us nothing else than humiliation to the point of death. Beneath the winsomeness and the lisping speech of the Infant is concealed the most profound mystery of the incarnate Word." Thus Bremond sums it up in his history of piety in those days.[35]

Linked with this is absorption in the mystery of disguised divinity, of divinity suddenly become impotent—that mystery which permeates the whole of Christian life, forever assuming new metamorphoses. "Even the

[35] Vol. III, 517 ff.

grace of our being the children of God, that childhood which we receive in baptism, is as it were held in the fetters of human inadequacy, in a self-abasement which commemorates *the self-abasement of the Eternal Word at the Incarnation*"—here we have a succinct exposition of the basis for the Bérulle school's worship of the childhood of Jesus.[36] Mother Margaret of the Blessed Sacrament, a seventeenth-century Carmelite (1619–1648), derived from these ideas the conception of imitation of the Child Jesus in His smallness, His silence, His helpless obedience, and developed a doctrine which in part seems to foreshadow that of Thérèse. But it is not likely that Thérèse anywhere encountered the current of this great tradition. She will have heard the name of the Reverend Mother Margaret read aloud every 26 May at table; but that was probably all. Pious souls around the turn of the century, especially in convents, remained as a rule amazingly ignorant of the time-honoured spiritual treasures of the Church. Instead of going to the sources, they read treatises and poor accounts at fifth and tenth hand. Thérèse's occasional quotation from a sermon of Tauler, of an incident from the life of the blessed Henry Suso, or of words of the Lord addressed to St Gertrude, by no means proves that she had read their writings herself. It is far more likely that she found the passages in anthologies and other such customary devotional books. At any rate, Thérèse nowhere mentions the name or the doctrines of this predecessor. And since otherwise she invariably mentions every stimulus and suggestion she consciously received with open-hearted gratitude, we may conclude with certainty that she was unaware of this kinship. It remains remarkable that this young saint, tapping directly at the very well-spring of her Order, entered upon its heritage of her own accord, revived and renewed its lost treasures out of her own original impulse. For her "little way", or, as she was also fond of calling it, her "way of spiritual childhood", as a summary of her doctrine of perfection, contains all the essential features of that "imitation of the childhood of Christ" developed in various different ways by the French school of the late seventeenth century. We shall have more to say about this later.

The early cult of the Child Jesus at first entitled its object the "little King of Glory", in order to stress the idea of humiliated majesty. Art represented the Infant wearing a crown and even equipped with the sceptre and orb of empire. But consideration of this aspect of Jesus constantly prompted consideration of the idea of the completion of the Mystery in the Passion. From, "Behold, I come to do Thy will", there is only a short span to "obedient unto death, yea, to death on the cross". Margaret

[36] Bremond, III, 514.

of Beaume herself, and her disciples outside the Order, thus early shifted constantly from the one image to the other. In the burning imagination of the Provençal seamstress Jeanne Perraud, both conceptions coalesced into an image of the Child Jesus with the instruments of the Passion. From this vision stems the endlessly repeated and varied representation of the Child no longer as an infant in the Crib, but as an earnest boy playing with the crown of thorns and the nails, or leaning pensively against a cross. This motif was disseminated in countless devotional pictures and remained popular and current long after the turn of the century, though by then its profound meaning had long since been forgotten by the pious masses.

This vision, too, played a part in Thérèse's spiritual development. This picture of Jesus as a boy had undoubtedly been familiar, to her from her own childhood. But her turning from the Mystery of the Divine Childhood to contemplation of the bitter Passion was not due to it. When she received the veil, at the age of sixteen, she herself asked Mother Marie de Gonzague to confer upon her the second name: of the Holy Face.

In *The Story of a Soul* she does not forget to record gratefully that it was Pauline who first guided her towards this devotion. Presumably Pauline had learned much in this respect from Mother Geneviève, who highly esteemed the image known as the "Veil of Veronica" and had had it placed in the chapel of the Lisieux Carmel. At the same time the roots of Thérèse's desire for this name are deeper, and multiple. The actual initial impetus, of which she does not speak in the autobiography, but which Pauline mentions,[37] was given by her father's illness. The face of the person she loved most on earth was now for ever deprived of sanity and transformed into the frightful mask of living death. Added to this was her memory of that mysterious vision in childhood, in which she had seen her father walking in the garden with covered head. With the obsessiveness of grief she pondered on the meaning of this trial which had befallen so faithful a servant of God. Combined with that was her own experience of God's turning away from her. All this was given form and significance in her mind by the "bleeding Head, so wounded". Thérèse herself says little about this. Six weeks before her death she remarked to Pauline: "The words in Isaiah: 'No stateliness here, no majesty, no beauty, as we gaze upon him, to win our hearts. Nay, here is one despised, left out of all human reckoning; bowed with misery, and no stranger to weakness; how should we recognize that face? How should we take any account of him,

---

[37] Petitot, 82–83.

a man so despised' [38]—these words were the basis of my whole worship of the Holy Face.... I, too, wanted to be without comeliness and beauty, alone to tread the grapes, unknown to all creatures." [39]

"Tomorrow I shall be the bride of Jesus 'whose face was hidden and whom no man knew'—what a union and what a future!" she wrote to Sister Marie on the eve of her Profession.

And we will remember the "pale glow from the downcast eyes in the Face of my Spouse" which alone illuminated her underground journey. From then on Thérèse always carried a picture of the Holy Face in her Breviary; during meditation there was one in front of her place in choir. During her long illness she had one pinned to the bed curtain and studied it constantly, in order to be able to bear her pain. It is deeply significant that on the Feast of the Transfiguration she used especially to venerate the Holy Face of Jesus. [40]

Again and again her poems centre around this image:

> Oh, to console You, I would be alone,
> Live forgotten, unknown by all,
> For the wholly veiled glow of Your beauty
> Has blazed mysteriously and brilliantly for me,
> And draws me there, to You, to You alone.
> Your Face is now my sole possession;
> I shall ask nothing but this treasure,
> Hiding myself, in You, from all fame,
> I will be like You, my Jesus...
> Imprint on me the divine image,
> The gentle features, so that I may be holy;
> Soon their imprint will make me so
> I will draw all hearts to You...

And again:

> Oh, consider this, that Your Divine Face
> Was unknown even to Your brethren,
> But You left us Your image, so still and bright,
> And Lord, You know, I recognized You!
> Through the tear-stained veil,
> Face of the Eternal, I saw You radiant.
> How Your veiled countenance

[38] Is 53:2–3.
[39] *N.V.*, 5 August.
[40] Ibid.

Comforts and delights my heart:
Oh, consider this!

The consecration to the Holy Face, which Thérèse composed for the novices, is a compendium of her thoughts about this Mystery.

Adorable Face of Jesus,

Since You have deigned to choose our souls especially, to give Yourself to us, we come to consecrate ourselves to You. It is as if, Jesus, we heard You saying:

"Open to Me, My sisters, My beloved brides, for My face is bedewed and My face is moist with the moisture of the night." Our souls understand the language of Your love; we want to dry Your gentle face and comfort You for the forgetfulness of men. To their eyes it is still as if You were hidden; "they see You despised and abject". O face, more beautiful than lilies and the roses of spring, from our eyes You are not hidden. The tears which veil Your divine gaze appear to us like precious diamonds, which we would garner, that we may use their infinite price to purchase the souls of our brothers.

We have heard the loving plaint of Your divine lips. We have understood that the thirst which consumes You is a thirst for love, and we wish to possess inexhaustible love in order to refresh You!

Beloved Bridegroom of our souls! If we had the love of all human hearts, it would belong only to You. Very well, then, give us this love, and then come and refresh Yourself in Your little brides. Souls, O Lord, give us souls! Above all the souls of apostles and martyrs, so that we, through them, may inflame the hosts of poor sinners with Your love.

O adorable face, we shall succeed in winning this grace from You. Forgetting our exile, by the shores of the rivers of Babylon we shall sing the sweetest melodies to Your ears. And because You are the true and only home of our souls, our songs shall not fall upon alien soil.

O beloved face of Jesus, awaiting the everlasting day when we shall at last behold Your unending Glory, our sole longing is to delight Your divine eyes by concealing our own faces so that no one upon this earth shall recognize us. Your shrouded countenance, behold, is our Heaven, O Jesus!

"O adored face of Jesus," another prayer goes, "You who are the sole beauty that delights my heart, deign to impress Your divine image upon me, so that You cannot look at the soul of Your little bride without regarding Yourself. O my Beloved, for the sake of Your love I consent never to behold the sweetness of Your glance here upon earth, never to feel the inexpressible kiss of Your mouth, but I implore You, inflame me so with Your love that it will soon consume me and I shall soon be permitted to appear before You."

It is strange that Thérèse, as soon as she came to "compose" a prayer, fell so entirely into the clumsy and bombastic prayer-book style of the period. Her own form of prayer, after all, was as simple as possible. She actually hated, we hear from many sources, the conventional devotional books and "dear little devotions of pious females" with their pretentious and empty flourishes. "It is not necessary to read from a book beautiful prayers composed for our particular need before we can be heard. If this were the case, I should certainly have to be pitied.

"The daily recitation of the Divine Office is a great joy to me... but apart from this I have not the courage to make myself search for wonderful prayers in books; there are so many of them, and it gives me a headache.... I just act like a child who can't read; I tell God, quite simply, all that I want to say, and He always understands. Prayer, for me, is simply a raising of the heart, a simple glance towards Heaven, an expression of love and gratitude in the midst of trial as well as in times of joy.... Whenever my soul is so dry that I am incapable of a single good thought, I always say an Our Father or a Hail Mary very slowly, and these prayers alone cheer me up and nourish my soul with divine food." [41]

Perhaps for that very reason she did not succeed in translating the "inexpressible sigh of the spirit" from the mute depths of the soul into anything but the rigid formulas she had learned. But however that may be, through the tiresome, sentimental and affected devotional language of these formulas there yet rings out the pure, flaming triad of her religious character: love, atonement and concealment.

[41] *S.S.*, x.

5

THE BREAKTHROUGH

1. "TELL THIS TO NONE WHO IS NOT WISE"

F OR WHAT ANSWER can there be for God, whose reality filled her life, whom she encountered in the Scriptures, in the figure of the Child in the Crib, and in the Holy Face? What answer but love, love and love alone? How oppressed Thérèse was by the dark, the terrifying mystery of malice: that man refuses God this love—the sole thing that God asks of him. The bloody, spat-upon face of Christ was the silent, fearful, never-to-be-forgotten embodiment of the response which had in fact been given to Our Lord's appeal, and which was still being given.

"He came to what was His own, and they who were His own gave Him no welcome." There was only one thing to do: to "console" Him—to use the possibly ill-chosen word of traditional piety—a word which none the less is based on Scripture and not, as some think, only upon subjective, feminine sentimentality taking liberties with the sublimity of God. At any rate, this idea is one of Thérèse's favourites, and arises from a profound, amazed shudder over the content of the tradition: "Trials of Jesus—what a mystery! So then He too was tried? He too? Yes, He was tempted, and often. 'He was alone to tread the winepress', and 'He looks to see if someone is there to *comfort Him*, and He finds none.' " [1]

To comfort Him means: to do our best to compensate for the frightful thing which can no longer be undone, not only to bewail it, but to make up for it by all possible love, devotion, loyalty and even pain, so that He will no longer be able to say that He trod the winepress all alone. It means, finally, if possible, to convert the blasphemers and the blind into lovers and believers. That is atonement: love of God and love of sinners inseparably fused into one white-hot emotion. Thérèse wanted to save souls so that God would no longer be offended and would be loved again; she wanted to love God still more so that His fire might transform her and give her power to save her brothers. Here was the innermost core of the Carmelite vocation. Whoever seriously sets out along this stream

[1] Cf. Ps 68:21.

surrenders to a vertiginous current which inexorably rushes towards a cataract: complete abandonment. Who can draw the line, saying: thus far and no farther? Whoever wishes for perfect love must at last be carried along into that greatest love which lays down life for friends. Thus Christ will be followed to the end. Physical martyrdom, a bloody death, is only one form of this fate.

Not everyone who sets foot upon this way knows where it is going to lead him. Thérèse went along it clearsighted and with calm steps. How, in such a decision, in such resolution, the true essence of Christian love is revealed! It is not an uncontrolled or intoxicated feeling, but a reality stronger than death and harder than Hell, for it is the transformation and the return of the human soul to the unfathomable, burning abyss of divinity.

> Tell this to none who is not wise,
> Since the mob is quick to criticize:
> How worthy life is of the name
> That yearns for death in the fiercest flame.

Goethe, for all his breadth of wisdom, did not know of this human potentiality; nevertheless, the above stanza sums it up as scarcely anything else could.

On 9 June 1895, in the seventh year of her life in religion, on the Feast of the Holy Trinity, this call so overtook Thérèse that she wrote out with her own hand her dedication until death. After she died her sisters found the document in the small copy of the Gospel which she had always carried over her heart.

During the Holy Mass at the high festival, Thérèse meditated upon the Mystery of God's demanding men to love Him—and men's rejections of Him. She thought of the saints who offered themselves to divine justice as voluntary victims, in order to take upon themselves the punishments reserved for those who would not hear, as Paul was prepared to be damned to save his brothers. Suddenly there flashed into her mind the perception that the same attitude and the same offer was possible with regard to divine mercy. Suppose a human soul opened itself like a vessel, no, like an abyss, and offered to receive the disdained love of God? Suppose a mortal heart offered a shelter to the unhoused love of God in this world? Would that not be one response of the kind God sought in souls? To be sure, the one who submitted to the wild lightnings of divine love, yielded fearlessly and defencelessly to them, would be destroyed by them—she realized this at once. What heart could withstand the onslaught of such an excess of love? But as others, before her, had cried out to the God of Justice, Thérèse now cried out to the God of Love: "Do not spare me!" She was fully conscious of the import of this plea, so much so that she did not venture to carry the step beyond the boundaries of obedience, since it involved a radical disposition of her own person. On her knees she obtained the consent of the Prioress—who at this time was Mother Agnes[2]—and the formula, before she would regard it as binding, had to be examined and approved by a theologian, so that no word in it would violate the teaching or tradition of the Church.

This "offering of myself as a victim of holocaust" is a unique document.

In form, and to some extent in content, it represents nothing new. Prayer books of the period are full of similar offerings, oblations and "acts of dedication": to the Blessed Virgin (there is a famous one by Grignon de Montfort), to the Sacred Heart, and so on. These oblations probably all derive from late forms of the above-mentioned "school" of the French Oratory. Common to all of them are a majestic and baroque emotional exuberance, verbosity, invocations to the whole of the Heavenly Court to bear witness, the "exaltation" of the feelings acknowledged. Common to all is the curious feature of a narrow, special, virtually legal obligation set forth in a written and signed "deed"—the word being used in the double sense of an act and of a legally valid document. For that reason, too, we may question the value of printing such formulas in handbooks for believers as "prayers for daily use". For something that was for the author a unique experience, one which perhaps reshaped his life, and which reflected a special inner destiny, can scarcely be repeated by simply anyone, can scarcely be read off to fill in someone else's devotional hour. Under such circumstances, the "deed" naturally loses its character as a binding act and is cheapened by becoming no more than a handful of exaggerated, moralistic, empty phrases.

Thérèse's oblation contains, inextricably mingled, the formulas of traditional "deeds" of this type, and new, surprising elements: the stammering of dearest desires, such as might spring from a childlike and exuberant

---

[2] There is a curious discrepancy between the sisters' accounts of this incident. Céline believes she remembers that Thérèse instantly wanted to share the happiness and grace of this oblation with her, and declares that Thérèse, "beside herself and without speaking", immediately after the Mass in which the illumination came to her, set off to see the Prioress, taking Céline in tow. "She asked for permission to suffer as a holocaust of Merciful Love *together* with me, and gave a brief explanation. Our Mother was in a hurry; she did not seem to understand fully what it was all about, but granted permission for anything Thérèse wished, so thoroughly did she trust in Sister Thérèse's prudence" (1 S., 52). Pauline, on the other hand, states emphatically that no one else knew anything about it; that only later Thérèse took two novices (Céline, and Marie of the Holy Trinity) into her confidence and told them of this oblation in order to inspire them to the same glorification of God (1 S., 22). The difference between these accounts may be due to the tendency, so apparent in the editing of the original manuscripts, to present Thérèse as in all matters unique and solitary.

religious imagination, together with the ultimate statement of the spiritual experiences of seven long years. Thus we may be justified in assuming that the text was written down in a moment of high emotion, without a thought as to its inner logic and texture, and that later it was not revised. To the reader's inner eye is presented the figure of a human being poised on a narrow, outjutting platform with arms outstretched for a leap into an unknown chasm. And before the leap, hastily, words tumbling over one another, she cries out her dearest wishes to the mysterious power to which she is about to commit herself. One wish is bolder and more improbable—indeed, let us say the words, more impossible—than the other. They are like challenges: "You see, I trust you so deeply that I expect you to do this, for my sake." And in the strength that comes from so intoxicating a confidence, the leap is made.

Thus Thérèse first asked Our Lord, whom she was permitted to receive in the Eucharist so seldom, to perform in His omnipotence a special miracle and remain from Communion to Communion "in me as in the tabernacle, never abandoning Your little Victim". Pauline has expressly testified that Thérèse conceived these words literally: she wished Our Lord to remain in her, under the sacramental species, as in the tabernacle. Thus, too, the novice who was most in Thérèse's confidence, Sister Marie of the Holy Trinity, whom Thérèse introduced to this oblation, states: "She said concerning this point: if God inspires me with this request, it is because He wishes to grant it.... For His little victim of Love God will do wonders.... On one occasion she wrote, in a poem, the lines:

> O God who holds the universe in awe,
> You live in me, a captive, day and night.

Someone suggested that the phrase should properly read 'for me', but Thérèse knew precisely what she wanted to say. 'No, no, I have expressed myself correctly', she maintained, and threw me a look as if to say: we two understand one another."

We may well wonder that the priest to whom the formula was submitted for approval did not find this idea open to objection and merely ordered the revision of the expression "my infinite desires" to "my immeasurable desires" because the word "infinite" should be applied only to the Absolute. When Thérèse's writings were examined in connection with the trial, the Holy Office took exception at least to the way this idea was expressed, as well as to the following appeal: "Take from me the freedom to be able to displease You!"—a repetition of the prayer Thérèse had made as an eleven-year-old First Communicant, that the freedom which frightened her be taken from her again.

However, the sentence which follows, "If nevertheless I fall out of weakness", reduces the literal significance of the passage and plainly indicates that in her emotion she went too far.

Furthermore, Thérèse expressed, no longer as a plea, but in tones of fullest confidence, the expectation that in Heaven she would be permitted to bear upon her transfigured body the stigmata of Our Lord, just as she shared his Passion upon earth. Such dreams of extraordinary, indeed fantastic graces and privileges are in striking contrast to Thérèse's usual sobriety and simplicity—so much so that we must spend a little more time considering the whole matter. Are we not likely to find here, beneath the painful bombast of the period, which dearly loved such fantasies, a path to true sanctity?

Among other things, by drawing so sharp a dividing line between the sacred and the profane spheres, Thérèse's period divorced sanctity from daily life. Scarcely a memory remained of the God in whom we live, move and have our being. "The World" was pictured as a place of irredeemable darkness in which moments of the Eucharistic presence of God floated like so many lost sparks. This dire picture may have driven more persons than we imagine into pantheism. Devotion to the "prisoner in the tabernacle" replaced, in considerable measure, the idea of the "presence of God". This was certainly not true of Thérèse, of course; like all saints, she had constantly a living awareness of moving before the face of God. But her almost constant dryness and inner abandonment, her constant experience with God's apparent "absence", made her long with greater intensity than others for the moments when His presence at least was beyond doubt, was tangibly there, whether or not she felt it. Thus her strange petition to be converted into a "living tabernacle" expresses nothing but her overwhelming yearning for greater certainty of His presence than the views of the period could give her. Her second petition, couched in the "image" of a desire for loss of freedom—for this, too, was an image—expressed her longing to be inseparably united to the divine will. And the third expressed, perhaps, nothing more than the confidence expressed in the Scriptures that "He will form this humbled body of ours anew, moulding it into the image of His glorified body, so effective is His power to make all things obey Him." [3]

However, it is only the second part of the oblation that contained the personal religious breakaway from the traditional to new ground.

> After the exile of this earth I hope to possess You in our eternal home. But it is not my wish to heap up merits for Heaven; I wish solely to labour for

---

[3] Phil 3:21.

Your love, solely to give joy to You, in order to comfort Your Sacred Heart and to save souls who will love You for ever.

In the evening of this brief day, I shall appear before You with empty hands, for I do not ask You, O Lord, to count my works. In Your eyes all our justice is blemished. Therefore will I robe myself in Your own justice and receive from Your love the eternal possession of Yourself. I want no other throne, no other crown than You, O my Beloved!

In Your eyes time is as nothing, a day as a thousand years. Thus You can prepare me in a single moment to appear before You.

In order to live in a single act of perfect love, I offer myself as a holocaust to Your Merciful Love and implore You to consume me entirely. Let the floods of infinite tenderness pent up within You pour out into my soul, and so let me become the martyr of Your Love, O my God!

May this martyrdom prepare me to appear before You, and break life's thread at last, and may my soul take its flight unhindered to the eternal embrace of Your Merciful Love....

O my Beloved, I would I might repeat this oblation to You countless times with every heartbeat, until "when the shadows have retired" I may avow to You my love in eternity from face to face!

Below these words was the solemn, almost legalistic signature:

> Marie-Françoise-Thérèse de l'Enfant Jésus
> et de la Sainte Face, Rel. Carm. Ind.
> Feast of the Holy Trinity, 9 June
> in the year of grace 1895.

A few days later Thérèse had the only mystical—in the narrow sense of the word—experience of her life; she experienced the divine acceptance of her oblation. She was in the choir, starting to make the Stations of the Cross. "Suddenly I felt myself pierced by a ray of fire so burning that I thought I was going to die. I do not know how to describe this ecstasy; there is no comparison which could express the intensity of that flame. It seemed to me that an invisible power was plunging me entirely into fire. Oh, what fire, what sweetness!" Thus she described the experience on her sickbed, two years later. "I burned with love and felt that one more minute, one more second, and I would be unable to bear this fire without dying. At that time I understood what the saints have said about these states, which they experienced so often. I have experienced it only once and for a single moment; then I quickly fell back into my usual aridity." [4]

The oblation is a prayer of a few pages; it takes only a few minutes to read it through. But for Thérèse it was anything but a mere prayer, something to be said in a moment of pious emotion, and then left at that. To

[4] *N.V.*, 7 July.

her it was a thing of deadly earnestness, a promise that had to be kept, a surrender that had to be repeated, day after day, and extended to the smallest incidents of daily life. With all the ruthless gravity of her nature she threw herself into this task which was to confer final form and aim upon everything her life had been hitherto. Even the two souls whom she gradually initiated into her secret seem not to have understood her fully. To them this oblation probably differed little, fundamentally, from many similar "exercises"—say, from the oblation to the Sacred Heart of Jesus which was performed every first Friday of the month by the entire community. Sister Marie of the Holy Trinity enthusiastically proposed sending the "act of oblation" out at once to all her pious relations in the world, so that they, too, might imitate it. She probably would have liked to see a "movement" spring up out of it, such as was made of the "Enthronement of the Sacred Heart in Family Life" thirty years later.

But Thérèse put a stop to this. For one thing, she feared misunderstandings—she was well aware of how easy misinterpretations were. Moreover, the matter was far too serious to her. No one could take upon himself such an oblation without being fully aware of its extent and without fully acceding to its consequences. For "to offer oneself to love as a victim does not mean accepting sweetness and consolation; it means exposing oneself to all anguish, all torment, all bitterness, for love lives only on sacrifice; and the more we would deliver ourselves up to love, the more we must surrender ourselves to suffering." [5]

And when one of the two initiates specifically asked whether the single "performance" of the oblation did not suffice for one to escape punitive justice, Thérèse replied firmly: "Oh, no, the words do not suffice. In order truly to be a victim of love, we must surrender ourselves entirely. We will be consumed by love only to the extent that we *really surrender ourselves*." To be consumed by love means that all flaws will be burned out of us during life, so that fear of what may come "after death" is no longer necessary.

"Se livrer"—this she repeated again and again, until the hour of her death: to yield, to surrender unconditionally, to abandon oneself entirely, to give one's whole being into another's keeping. But how is that done? What forms of action may be taken which are appropriate to love, worthy of love? Worthy not only of the love of the lover, whose heart may direct him to find many expressions for his emotion, but worthy of the love of the Beloved to whom the offer is made?

---

[5] S.S., Epilogue in French edition supplied by Mother Agnes.

2. EMPTY HANDS

"In Your eyes all our justice is blemished." This vital insight, one capable of transforming the whole of life, was perhaps the greatest fruit of that intercourse with God upon which the saint's "doctrine" stands as on a cornerstone. We must go back, perhaps, to the Reformation and to that neglected but inexhaustible French mysticism to find the idea thought out to its ultimate conclusions.

Thérèse had unquestionably been raised to believe in the power and importance of good works. To be sure, the Church had always taught the changeless doctrine that the merits of Jesus Christ alone underlay all human merits, and that rewards were the consequence of God's grace. But this reasoning was very remote from the consciousness of believers, especially from the devout ones; it had been almost forgotten, and only the conclusion remained, for anyone to explain as he would, or not at all. The language of piety of the period suggests little definition and little depth in this respect. The most zealous souls trusted preponderantly in their own actions—being in this very like their worldly contemporaries who believed firmly that a man's accomplishments in the world depended upon himself. The devout counted on the toil, the pain, the perseverance and the good intent behind it all—when they did not actually rely on the sheer quantity and expensiveness of their religious acts. Not for nothing did they eagerly keep account of their Masses and Communions, Rosaries and prayers, self-denial and "acts of charity", just as Thérèse had learned to do as a child. We will remember that glass of water she had denied herself in childhood, when asked whether she would not like to save a sinner, and the reassuring conclusion that she might drink after all, since the sinner was already saved by her sacrifice. At the age of fourteen she wrote to Pauline, then in the convent: "How happy I would be if at the moment of my death I could bring Jesus only a single soul which I had saved by my sacrifices!" [6] It was not uncommon for pious souls to conceive fearful sufferings for themselves, and to "offer" themselves as victims of such sufferings, in order to attain this or that end. One of Mother Geneviève's companions did this in order to obtain the definition of the doctrine of the Immaculate Conception as a dogma. The insanity, lasting more than thirty years, to which she soon afterwards succumbed, was considered by the convent community as the "cross" for the granting of this heroic request; the community believed that the definition had really been procured by her sacrifice. Thérèse must have heard this story often enough.

[6] 2 S., 294.

Twenty years after Thérèse's death Mother Isabelle of the Heart of Jesus, Sub-Prioress of Lisieux and Thérèse's most faithful disciple and interpreter (she called herself the "Herald of the Little Queen"), wrote to a young nun who wanted to offer her death to God as compensation for saving the threatened convents and monasteries of France: "What luxurious self-deception! Rather bring to the Heavenly Father the great divine offering named Jesus, whose sacrifice suffices to save all and everything, and could redeem a thousand million worlds, and more." And to a second nun: "God is powerful enough to grant us all the graces we ask of Him. We do not have to offer Him recompense or payment in return. For example, there is no need for one nun to sacrifice her own consolation to purchase consolation for another. Our Lord is kind and merciful enough to console them both. We honour Him far more by our simple trust in His generosity than by our narrow-minded calculations." And a third time she put the matter even more incisively: "For anyone to wish to build upon his works, no matter how heroic these may be, is to behave like a village idiot who meets his king and presses a penny upon him, thinking this will enrich him—and who, moreover, expects to be rewarded with lavish praise and choice benefactions. All our works are like this penny, and even less." [7]

Thérèse herself could not have expressed her "doctrine" with the force and intellectual clarity of Mother Isabelle. She who was the religiously creative person, the pioneer of the "new" way, put into practice more than she put into words, and could share her thoughts only by scattering a thousand sparks. Mother Isabelle, a highly cultivated woman, used her superior equipment to interpret and represent the bequest she was humbly administering.

Ever since Thérèse had been able to think, promises of bliss in the hereafter as the reward of our virtues had played a great part in her mind, by our standards an almost offensively great part. Zélie Martin was in the habit of managing her children by promises of heavenly rewards. Marie at the age of four was asked to give up an especially loved toy to Pauline. Her mother coaxed her by promising that this sacrifice would add "an extra pearl to your crown". Marie narrates: "I ran quickly to Mama and said, 'I've given Pauline the basket; will I go to Heaven now?' 'Yes, my daughter, you will go to Heaven.' This hope alone was sufficient to console me for the loss of my possession."

Even while her mother was still alive, Thérèse learned to ask, anxiously at first and later with assurance: "Have I been good? Will I go to

---

[7] *Life* of the Reverend Mother Isabelle, printed at Lisieux in 1914.

Heaven *because* I've been good?" During her preparation for First Communion, Marie told her again and again "of the imperishable riches which can so easily be accumulated every day, and of the misfortune it would be to kick them aside when one need only stoop to pick them up. 'Look at the people who want to be rich. How they exert themselves to earn money; and we, my Thérèse, at any moment and far less toilsomely, can earn treasures in Heaven. We can gather in diamonds with a rake. All that is necessary is to do everything we do for the love of God.' And I went away with my heart filled with joy, and with the desire also to heap up such great riches." [8]

It can scarcely be disputed that such utterances, for all their genuine faith, also represent naïve and unquestioning transference of tenacious, solid French acquisitiveness, of limitless respect for property and wealth, to the sphere of religion.

Thérèse had not the slightest misgiving in passing on this educational method when, at the age of fourteen, she took charge of children for the first time. "I did not speak of toys or sweets when I wanted these little girls to be kind to each other, but of the eternal reward the Child Jesus would give to good children." And in the zest with which the little girls took to her instruction she saw, with deep emotion, that "baptism does indeed plant the seeds of the theological virtues deep in our soul, for the hope of the joys of Heaven, even from our earliest days, is quite strong enough to encourage the practice of self-sacrifice."

It may be that our own sensitivity, and perhaps oversensitivity, to this "morality based on rewards" had made us pay too little attention to this aspect of the matter. For it cannot be denied that at least one root of that attitude springs from living faith in the Divine Word. The Scriptures speak repeatedly in many images and parables of the reward, the wreath, the crown, the treasures which we are to amass—for "where your treasure-house is, there your heart is too".[9] They do not refer to it as something we know of but should not think about too much; they urge us to think about it: "Be glad and light-hearted!" [10] And who, after all, could *believe*, really and vividly believe, in eternal bliss and vast rewards, without his life's being in some measure affected by this hope?

Perhaps, then, we may bring our critical spirit to bear only on the second root of this expectation of reward. We must ask whether this root is humble gratitude and love, consciousness of our own unworthiness and of the incomprehensible mercy of God, who deals with us according to

[8] Letter to Marie of 14 August 1889.
[9] Mt 6:21.
[10] Mt 5:12.

His graciousness and not our merits; or whether we have here unregenerate self-love which degrades this aspect of the faith to the service of its demands and wishful thinking. That the second attitude exists, follows from the first like shade from light. But restoration of the authentic Christian attitude requires not an uprooting of faith in the existence of rewards, but purification of hope for their possession.

Thérèse developed, without deviation, from a childish desire for spiritual rewards the mature attitude of spiritual hope. Certainly she was allured by the crowns, pearls and diamonds which she had been promised as a little girl. The attraction at first was no different, and no less operative, from that of the prizes, certificates and good marks she received in school—the French educational system appeals with an amazingly untroubled conscience to the ambition of pupils. But as early as the age of fifteen, when still at home, she wrote to her sisters in the convent: "And when I think that for one joyfully endured sacrifice we shall be able *to love God the more throughout all eternity!*" Very soon "Heaven" meant to her nothing but this: to see God face to face and participate in His life. Thérèse soon recognized as her only reward Him who desires to be our surpassing reward: "One single expectation makes my heart beat high: the love which I shall receive and then be able to give!" [11]

Among the nuns in the convent she frequently encountered that crude, egoistical and arithmetical hope of reward which so constantly offends against true Catholic principle. Out of a misguided view of good works and merit the nuns zealously counted sacrifices and acts of virtue, in order to present them to God as reckonings which entitled them to their legitimate recompense. They anxiously watched the fall and rise of their bank accounts in Heaven. They even seem to have estimated with keen interest the presumable stage in Heaven that their fellow nuns would attain. Thérèse reports the remark: "I did not think you would add this pearl to your crown." Such phrases were the order of the day; during Thérèse's last sickness we hear of them again and again. With saintly zeal she laboured to restore the pure meaning of the faith.

It never occurred to Thérèse to doubt the reality of the heavenly reward; that reality became the clearer the more she came to understand it as the fruit of surpassing Mercy and not the fruit of our own grasping efforts. On 17 September 1890 she wrote to Marie: "Jesus wishes to give us His Heaven out of pure grace (*gratuitement*)." However, she also never doubted that the reward would have gradations which bear a direct relation to the activities of men; incomprehensible that may be, but the

[11] 2 S., 247.

Scriptures speak of the faithful servant who added ten talents and will be set over ten cities; he who made five, over five; who gave a prophet a drink of water will receive a prophet's reward; who gave a disciple to drink, the disciple's reward. In fact: "This light and momentary affliction brings with it a reward multiplied every way, loading us with everlasting glory", says the Apostle Paul.[12] How that is done, by what secret counsels of His Mercy God "reckons" this up, was a subject that Thérèse did not worry her head about. She knew only that she loved and wanted to love, whether this love meant merit and reward or not. She knew, too, that all this love, even the purest, even the terrifyingly "selfless" love which in the eyes of men is so incomprehensible, is only a gift, is response to Him who loved us first. "That love resides, not in our showing any love for God, but in His showing love for us first, when He sent out His Son to be an atonement for our sins." [13]

How then could Thérèse possibly want to transform the fullness which He gave her into a new claim upon Him? "Her crown did not interest her at all", a fellow nun testifies with obvious amazement. "She told me that she left this matter entirely to God." [14] "If, and of course this is impossible, God Himself should not see my good works, I would not be troubled about it. I love Him so intensely that often I should like to do something to give Him joy without His knowing that it comes from me. If He knows and sees it, after all, He is as it were obliged to compensate me for it.... I should like to save Him even this effort." [15]

Let us, however, be careful not to read into such words a stoical indifference towards the promised "treasure of glory". The hopeful Christian takes all of God's promises seriously, with passionate earnestness. He stakes his whole life on them and lives joyously in the anticipation of joys. This kind of hope was the true element in which Thérèse lived. Her piety, founded in faith, tested by love, was nourished by this hope. The expectation of Heaven was the staff on which she leaned in her progress through the desert. The more she was oppressed by inner emptiness and aridity, the more fervently her whole being bent upon the blissful day when the Lord would awaken for her also and His Face would shine upon her again. But she knew at every moment that the bliss to which she looked forward as a child to Christmas, as an exile to his homeland, as a bride to her wedding, would come from overflowing grace and not as the result of her own accomplishments.

[12] 2 Cor 4:17.
[13] 1 Jn 4:10.
[14] 1 S., 50.
[15] C.S.

At fourteen Thérèse had already drawn this conclusion from Abbé Arminjon's book on the "Mysteries of the World to Come". "As I read, I experienced that joy which the world cannot give, something of what God has prepared for those who love Him. All our sacrifices seemed quite petty compared with this reward, and I wanted so much to love Jesus with my whole heart and prove it in a thousand ways while I still had the chance."[16]

"If in the hour of my death I shall see how good God is to me, how He intends to heap His affection upon me for a whole eternity—and that I can never again prove mine to Him by sacrifices—how impossible that will be to bear if on earth I had not done everything in my power to give Him joy!"[17]

Thérèse's insights do not derive from a single moment of illumination. They derive from the experience of her childhood, that being able to be good was in itself a grace; that all goodness, love, tenderness and zeal of the innocent heart were in themselves already a response to love received; that love, care, instruction and training were reflected back by the self. There followed the years of "darkness" in her childhood, of scruples and insuperable weakness which proved to her the inadequacy of even the best intentions, the most desperate efforts. Then had come the tremendous experience of her "conversion" at Christmas 1886, the gift of a stability that all her own efforts had been unable to achieve. There followed her initiation into the Mystery of the Lord's Passion, which revealed the overflowing measure of the redeeming, the loving mercy of God.

Then, when she was at last a young nun daily encountering the greatness of God in the Scriptures and the liturgy, all the claims and self-importance of human vanity definitively vanished. "Thou art my Lord, for Thou needest not my good."[18] These words from Psalm 15 are quoted only once in Thérèse's writings, but they stand invisibly above every page. Her deep, certain knowledge had its source not in philosophical considerations of the nature of man, nor in theological conceptions of the nature of God, grace or freedom. It sprang, rather, from the knowledge which indwells in love, from living intercourse with the living God. Before His Face, moreover, there also vanished, gently and imperceptibly, the apparently so stout and absolute barrier between the "sinners" out in

---

[16] *S.S.*, v.

[17] *Esprit*, 50, notes inédites.

[18] This quotation is given in the version Thérèse read and pondered. Correctly, it should read: "The Lord whom I own as my God, I confess that in Him is all my good."

the world—who are sinners because they do all possible wicked and forbidden things—and the devout souls who characterize themselves as sinners only "out of humility", when such a term is required by common decency or by the liturgy ("pray for us poor sinners!"), but who nevertheless are in all modesty conscious of being perfect or on the way to perfection, of being pleasing to God and of doing more than is commanded by the Law. Before His Face Thérèse found again the old, so often buried truth that man *is* a sinner and can never be more than a pardoned sinner, no matter what he does or does not do. Out of this new wisdom she wrote to Céline: "I tell you, when Jesus said to Magdalene, 'he loves Him more to whom more is forgiven', that can with more reason be repeated when Jesus has remitted someone his sins *in advance*. He has pardoned me everything by not letting me sin at all!" This is echoed in the famous and profound parable from the fourth chapter of *The Story of a Soul*:

> Suppose the son of a skilful doctor falls over a stone lying in his path and breaks a limb. His father hurries to help him and dresses his wound so skilfully that it heals completely. Naturally, he is quite right to love such a father and will be most grateful to him.
>
> But supposing again this doctor saw the dangerous stone, anticipated that his son would fall over it, and moved it out of the way when no one was looking; then his son would know nothing of the danger from which his father's loving care had saved him, and so would have no reason to show gratitude. He would love him less than if he had healed some serious wound. But if he did find out the truth, surely his love would be even greater? I am that child, the object of the Father's loving providence "who did not send His son to call the just, but sinners". He wants me to love Him because He has forgiven me not *much* but *everything*.

That was why Thérèse was delighted by the Gospel story of the workers in the vineyard who began at the twelfth hour and yet received the same reward as the others who had borne the burden of the day's work. Above all other saints she held dear those who had not "merited" Heaven, but had "stolen" it as she put it: the good thief and the Holy Innocents (among whom she venerated with particular love her own little brothers and sisters). One of her best poems sings the victory, won without struggle and unmerited, of the little martyrs of Bethlehem:

> O little band, transfigured and unstained,
> Beside the Lamb you march along!
> *Unmerited*, your privilege was gained,
> And you have learned the newest song.

Your victory came to you without a fight,
Yet heroes have no greater fame.
The Saviour won it for you, by His might,
O Innocents without a name.

Tucked into the copy of the Gospels that Thérèse carried on her person was a note reading: "Lord, You know that I love You!" and on the other side of the sheet of paper: "Be merciful to me; I am a sinner!"—the words of the penitent publican in the Temple.[19] She was well aware why she had burst into tears at hearing the words: "No one knows whether he is worthy of love or hate." Yet such a reaction was so strange and so unprecedented in her environment that the Novice Mistress had been astonished, and even those closest to her viewed such conduct only as a unique display of humility. They did not take seriously Thérèse's genuine conviction. Céline declares, in tones of audible amazement at such self-belittling: "Thérèse was *convinced* that without the special aid of God she would not have been able to achieve her salvation."[20]

At her sister's sickbed, Pauline said: "When I come to die, alas, I shall have nothing to give to God; I shall arrive with empty hands, and that troubles me deeply." Thérèse responded spiritedly: "It is just the reverse with me—if I had all the works of St Paul to offer, I would still feel myself to be an unprofitable servant; I would still consider that my hands were empty. But that is precisely what gives me joy, for *since I have nothing I must receive everything from God*." And again: "How I look forward to going to Heaven! But when I think of Our Lord's words: Behold, I come and bring the reward with me, to give to each according to his works, then I tell myself that He will probably be embarrassed when He comes to me, because I have none. He cannot reward me according to *my* works. So much the better, for I have confidence that He will reward me according to His."

"*Because* I have none." Others might base their hope upon laboriously acquired spiritual treasures—Thérèse's illimitable trust bubbled up solely from the springs of her jubilant poverty. What is empty can be filled. "Where there is nothing, God is", as a profound Irish proverb puts it.

Empty hands are God's delight;
All our losses are His winnings;
All our ends prove, in His sight,
To be our radiant beginnings.[21]

[19] Lk 18:13.
[20] 2 S., 410.
[21] Werner Bergengruen.

Thérèse is considered to be above all the saint of childlike trust, and she deserves the name. But her confidence did not spring from childlike ignorance of the gravity of man's fate and Christian destiny. Rather, it sprang from the abyss which devoured everything upon which men—and especially devout men—were accustomed to base their certainty before God. Thérèse trusted because God is such that one can trust Him without a pledge, because He will receive and supply, with incomprehensible love, all those who throw themselves naked into His hands, expecting everything from Him. "In our prayers we must follow the example of those stupid people who ask for things and do not know where to stop, who repeat their stammering pleas again and again, without considering propriety, and who often ask for things which no one would have thought of giving of his own accord, and which people give to them in order to be quit of them. We must say to God: 'I know well that I shall never be worthy of the things I hope for—but I hold out my hands to You like a beggar child, and I know that You will more than grant my wishes *because You are so good!*'" [22] She would not have wondered at any miracle, Pauline says; she thought God's omnipotence was always in the service of His love for us, and was therefore available to us at all times. The Lord's words to St Mechtilde touched her deeply: "I tell you that it gives Me great joy when men expect great things of Me. Great as their faith and their boldness may be, I shall give to them far beyond their merits. It is indeed not possible that men shall fail to receive all that they have hoped of My power and My mercy." [23]

Again and again Thérèse sought in the Scriptures for confirmation of her boldness. She found it in ample measure, and again and again founded her confidence upon it. "Have You not permitted me for so long to deal boldly with You, my God? As the prodigal son's father, to his eldest, to You have spoken to me: All that is Mine is yours." Up to the last she repeated: "We can never hope for too much of God, who is so mighty and merciful; we will receive from Him precisely as much as we confidently expect of Him." And sitting in the garden, sick unto death, she wrote with unsteady fingers: "Yes, I have seen it now: all my expectations will be more than fulfilled. Yes, the Lord will do wonders for me infinitely exceeding my boundless desires!"

At first these and similar words apply principally to her spiritual longings for salvation and sanctity; in temporal things, Thérèse thought, we ought to follow the example of Martha and Mary at Bethany and of Our Lady at Cana: simply confide our needs to Our Lord and leave it to Him

[22] 2 *S.*, 361.
[23] 2 *S.*, 253.

to do what He wishes about them. Such confidence rests tranquilly in God in the midst of all the tempests and darknesses of the soul. Thérèse never ceased to glory in the profound and indestructible peace in the depths of her soul, defying all pangs and anxieties, up to and into the very shadow of death. Such peace does not come from having been spared temptation, from being unassailed—for that would always be accompanied by faint, submerged fears of change. Rather, it comes from perfect consent to anything that God may send. Teresa of Avila taught her daughters to sing and pray:

> I am Thine, born for Thee;
> What dost Thou will to do with me?
> Give me wealth or poverty,
> Give me sorrow or high glee,
> Consolation or misery,
> Sweet life, sun all revealed.
> Myself I do entirely yield:
> What dost Thou will to do with me?

And so Thérèse prayed on the day of her Profession: "I offer myself to You, my Beloved, that You may do in me everything You will, unhindered by any created obstacle." [24]

During her long illness Pauline once brought the conversation around to the saints who had led an extraordinary life, like St Simon Stylites. "I prefer the saints who were afraid of nothing," Thérèse said, "like St Cecilia who accepted marriage and did not fear." This saint, whom Thérèse had first encountered in the Catacombs, always remained for her the symbol of her kind of hope, which consisted of blindly giving herself into the hands of God: Cecilia who had betrothed herself to Christ, and whom her parents had married off; yet during the forced wedding feast "her heart sang" instead of grieving and being afraid.

> O heavenly music, how your song reveals
> That Love is hope: O bride consoled,
> Sleep in God's Heart; oblivion heals
> All care, O child whom trustfulness makes bold.

There is a certain danger inherent in this insight which had to be met. Seldom can we absorb a great spiritual perception without so coming under its sway that we needlessly and fanatically play it off against all other truths. Therein lies the root of all heresies. Recognition of the

[24] *S.S.*, viii.

insignificance of human action in itself, as a factor of salvation, of the surpassing power of merciful love, contains within itself a dangerous reef. Both the German Reformation of the sixteenth and Latin quietism of the seventeenth centuries foundered on this reef. Those who passionately oppose the claim that "works" are a factor in salvation almost necessarily go to the extreme of denying the necessity and virtue of works altogether and rejecting all "religious action" as arrogance before God.

In the still and limited world of her convent Thérèse encountered this danger, too. When Sister Marie of the Holy Trinity wanted to send out Thérèse's Act of Oblation to all and sundry, she forbade it, pointing out that what she had written "might easily be misunderstood as quietism".

When Céline, reading Ecclesiastes, came across the passage: "Mercy will assign to each his place according to his works", her wits had been sufficiently sharpened by Thérèse's instruction for her to ask her young mistress: "How can that be, since St Paul says that we shall be justified through grace alone?" Thérèse replied to her "with ardour"—and with excellent theological lucidity:

> We must do everything we are obliged to do: give without reckoning, practise virtue whenever opportunity offers, constantly overcome ourselves, prove our love by all the little acts of tenderness and consideration we can muster [this is a rough approximation of her untranslatable *"par toutes les délicatesses et toutes les tendresses"*]. In a word, we must produce all the good works that lie within our strength—out of love for God. But it is in truth indispensable to place our whole trust in Him *who alone sanctifies our works and who can sanctify us without works* for He can even raise children to Abraham out of stones. Yes, it is needful, when we have done everything that we believe we have to do, to confess ourselves unprofitable servants, *at the same time hoping that God out of grace will give us everything we need*. This is the little way of childhood.

This statement is perhaps the most profound and exact presentation Thérèse ever made of "her way". It permits no further misunderstandings. She disposes of all faith in any automatic magical power inherent in human action, as a means of attaining salvation. But then, once that has been made clear, there arises courageous, ardent, transcendent faith in Him *who sanctifies our works*. He does not depend upon our sanctified works, but He knows the human heart which He created, knows how unquenchable is its longing to give itself, to dare, to serve, to create. And He who brought into being this noble urge, after the image of His own Love, who gave it glorious opportunities for fulfilment in the natural realm—He deigns, out of graciousness and mercy, to grant us a similar fulfilment in the realm of grace. He accepts what we wish to give, and, moreover, gives us the effectiveness of our gift.

The whole of the last chapter of her autobiography recounts the story of this illumination.

The love which filled Thérèse's heart to overflowing sought almost with despair for the channel of good works, in order to express itself. "*Des immenses désirs*"—tremendous longings had preoccupied her from her girlhood on. When she entered the convent and began nourishing her mind on the lives of saints, there awoke in this passionate young soul, with renewed force, her recent dreams of religious heroism:

To be Your Spouse, my Jesus; to be a Carmelite; to be, through my union with You, a mother of souls—surely this should be enough? Yet I feel the call of more vocations still; I want to be a warrior, a priest, an apostle, a doctor of the Church, a martyr—there is no heroic deed I do not wish to perform. I feel as daring as a crusader, ready to die for the Church upon the battlefield.

If only I were a priest! How lovingly I would bear You in my hands, my Jesus, when my voice had brought You down from Heaven. How lovingly I would give You to souls! Yet while wanting to be a priest, I admire St Francis of Assisi, and envy his humility, longing to imitate him in refusing this sublime dignity.

Such contradictions! How can they be reconciled? I long to bring light to souls, like the prophets and doctors; to go to the ends of the earth to preach Your name, to plant Your glorious Cross, my Beloved, on pagan shores.

One mission field alone would never be enough; all the world, even its remotest islands, must be my mission field. Nor would my mission last a few short years, but from the beginning of the world to the end of time.

But to be a martyr is what I long for most of all. Martyrdom! I dreamed of it when I was young, and the dream has grown up with me in my little cell in Carmel. I am just as foolish about this because I do not desire any one kind of torture; I would be satisfied only with them all.

I want to be scourged and crucified like You, my Spouse; flayed alive like St Bartholomew, thrown into boiling oil like St John, and ground by the teeth of wild beasts like St Ignatius of Antioch, so that I might become bread worthy of God.

Like St Agnes and St Cecilia, I want to offer my neck to the executioner's sword, and like Joan of Arc, murmur the name of Jesus at the burning stake.

My heart thrills at the thought of the undreamt-of torments which will be the lot of Christians in the time of Antichrist! I want them all to be my lot!

Open the Book of Life, my Jesus; see all the deeds recorded of the saints! All these I want to perform for You!

What can You say in the face of all this foolishness of mine for surely I am the littlest and the weakest soul on earth? Yet just because I am so weak, You have been pleased to grant my childish little desires and now You will grant the rest, other desires far greater than the Universe.[25]

This is the old dream of the saint, as the world dreams it: the superman who for God's sake ascends to divinity himself; this is the pagan, not the Christian, dream of the human demigod. But Thérèse knows very well that it is a dream. Not a single one of these desires, these wished-for grand deeds, was destined for her. And as though the Lord's will to cut her off from such sentimentalities must be emphasized to the last degree, even in the convent narrow limits were set, so that she could do nothing that would even remotely remind her of such deeds. She would have liked to tend the sick, in order to dedicate herself to the humblest of Love's services. Two of her sisters were privileged to undertake such nursing, but never she. And even if she had been vouchsafed all that her intoxicated imagination aspired to, would that not have been likewise "unjust wealth", which might just as easily lead her away from God as to Him? Were not even such exploits, like everything else, blemished in His eyes?

"These desires became a real martyrdom to me." She found the answer at last in the Scriptures, in St Paul's First Epistle to the Corinthians, "where he says we cannot all be apostles, prophets and doctors, that the Church is made up of different members, and that the eye cannot also be the hand". Sanctity, then, would not consist in each person's indiscriminate attempt to imitate every model and walk all ways at once. This answer satisfied the mind, but not the heart. Thérèse read on and found consolation in the sentences: "Prize the best gifts of heaven. Meanwhile, I can show you a way which is better than any other." [26] And there follows the great hymn of Love, the thirteenth chapter: All gifts are nothing without love; charity leads straightway to God even without gifts, and it remains when all imperfect works have passed.

Now Thérèse had found her way.

"As I thought about the Church's Mystical Body I could not see myself in any of the members mentioned by St Paul, or rather, I wanted to see myself in all of them. Charity gave me the key to my vocation. I saw that if the Church was a body made up of different members, the most essential and important one of all would not be lacking; I saw that the Church must have a *heart*, that this heart must be on fire with love. I saw that it was love alone which moved her other members, and that were this love to fail, apostles would no longer spread the Gospel, and martyrs

[25] *S.S.*, xi.
[26] I Cor 12:31.

would refuse to shed their blood. I saw that all vocations are summed up in love, and that love is all in all, embracing every time and place because it is eternal.

"In a transport of ecstatic joy I cried: 'Jesus, my love, I have at last found my vocation; *it is love*. I have found my place in the Church's heart, the place You Yourself have given me, my God. Yes, there in the heart of Mother Church *I will be love*; so shall I be all things, so shall my dreams come true.' "

For at first it *is* a dream. No human being can choose this mission, no human being can deserve it. But God does not give to us because we run and strive; He gives out of His mercy.

"I dare not fathom, Lord, all the implications of my prayer, lest I should find myself crushed beneath the weight of my audacity. I take refuge in my title, 'a little child'. Little children never realize all that their words imply, but if their father or mother were to come to the throne and inherit great riches, loving their little ones more than they love themselves, they would not hesitate to give them everything they want. They would be foolishly lavish just to please them, and go even as far as weakness. Well, I am a child of Holy Church.... My heart does not yearn for riches or for glory, not even for the glory of Heaven; that belongs by rights to my brothers, the angels and saints.... No, what I ask for is *love*. Only one thing, my Jesus, to *love You*. Outstanding deeds are forbidden me. I cannot preach the Gospel; I cannot shed my blood, but what matter? My brothers do it for me, while I, *a little child*, stay close beside the royal throne, and *love* for those who are fighting.

"Love proves itself by deeds, and how shall I prove mine? *The little child will scatter flowers* whose fragrant perfume will surround the royal throne, and in a voice that is silver-toned she will sing *the canticle of love*."

Into the midst of this rhapsody there penetrates reason's question; dreams are all very well but the mind must pay its tribute to truth:

But *what use to You*, my Jesus, will my songs and flowers be? This fragrant shower, these fragile petals, worthless in themselves, these songs of love from so small a heart will charm You all the same. Yes, I am sure of it; sure that these nothings will give You pleasure. The Church Triumphant will smile on them, and wishing to play with her little one, she will gather up the scattered roses and place them in Your divine Hands. This will invest them with infinite value, and she will scatter them upon the Church Suffering to put out the flames, and on the Church Militant, to make her victorious.[27]

[27] *S.S.*, xi.

Every word of this must be read with close attention and considered with care. Thérèse's figurative language seduces one all too easily into shallow misinterpretations, and yet conceals amazing vigour and first-rate logic and theological reasoning. These few pages represent Thérèse's creative discovery of an age-old and always new form of piety.

Every word is intended figuratively, and a good many are images of another image which in turn must be recognized and interpreted. Many of the figures Thérèse uses have more than one sense.

The prime metaphor hovering at the back of her mind is obviously a recollection of her childhood: of herself, a small girl dressed in white, taking part in the Corpus Christi procession, and being allowed to scatter a basket of flowers in the path of the Blessed Sacrament. "I used to throw them up high into the air before they fell, and when my rose petals touched the monstrance my happiness was complete." [28]

This became a symbol of everything that came later, just as childhood in all things meant for Thérèse a valid prefiguring of life. She was still a child before God and would remain so: small and dependent, able to give away only things she had herself been given. All her present activities were still like the rose petals that filled her white basket, fleeting as a breath, useless and valueless. Her affectionate language, her heart's desires, her daily needlework, her barren, sleepy prayers, her small services of love to the other sisters—all these were rose petals, no more. And rose petals, too, no more precious than the first, were her parting from her father, her life in the convent, all the hardships and dereliction of the desert, all the inexpressible loneliness and darkness, the fatal sickness which destroyed her young life, and all the torment of a death-agony lasting three unending months. All was one, all nothing but dying leaves, plaything of the winds. What was great, what small? And suppose all the great and admired works of her creative, militant brothers were to be granted to her—still, what would they be in God's eyes but scattered rose petals?

But then the miracle happens. Love stoops in answer to the foolishly bold beseeching of a child and makes the impossible possible: the Church, the holy, living Mother, picks up the rose petals. Now they are no longer a plaything and trumpery; they are the property of the "King's Spouse", now the community of the saints offers them to Our Lord. And as the pierced divine hands take them, they acquire infinite value through Him who alone can sanctify our works. Only then, when they have been dipped in the blood of divine suffering, do these poor and ephemeral things

[28] *S.S.*, ii.

merge with the redeeming sacrifice of the Heart of Jesus and pour forth again in the overflowing of His love—as ransom for the suffering brethren and strength for the fighting brethren.

> How well I know that all our honesties
> Are worthless in Your eyes, are empty signs.
> To make my sacrifices verities
> I cast them, Lord, within Your Heart's confines....
>
> In lightnings, You have handed down Your law;
> Yet will I hide, fearless, in Your Heart.
> In Your eyes even angels show a flaw;
> You, Lord, are all my virtue, all my art.
>
> To scatter flowers for You, sacrifice
> My smallest sign and my intensest dread,
> My sorrows, bliss, renunciations, joys—
> Behold, here are my roses, white and red!

Among her most charming peculiarities was her impulse to embody this conception not only in words, but in gestures. In the evening she often went with a bunch of roses to the high Cross in the convent yard, where she would scatter the rose petals over the feet of the Crucified. And even on her sick-bed, when she could no longer think and pray, she plucked apart the flowers that were brought to her and showered them around the crucifix that lay on her blanket: a touching parable of her own mute, defenceless surrender.

But if this is the case, that our poor actions are, if they are done out of love, accepted by God's love, and if they please His love because we are loved—then there is only *one* answer. Thérèse recalled the day long ago when Léonie had offered Céline and herself a basket of ribbons and bits of lace and other remnants. Céline examined the things and then nicely took a ball of silk braid, but Thérèse, the four-year-old, took firm hold of the entire basket, saying, "I choose everything", and marched off with her prize. "This trait of my childhood characterizes the whole of my life; and when I began to think seriously of perfection I knew that to become a saint one had to suffer much, always aim at perfection and forget one's self. I saw that one could be a saint in varying degrees, for we are free to respond to Our Lord's invitation by doing much or little in our love for Him; to choose, that is, between the sacrifices He asks. Then, just as before, I cried: 'I choose everything.' " [29]

[29] *S.S.* i.

Scattering roses meant two things to her: loving and suffering. "During the single day, or rather the single night of this life, there remains only one thing for us to do: to love, to love Jesus with all the power of our hearts, and to save souls for Him, so that He will be loved still more." [30] Thus Thérèse loved Him, who wishes to be loved in the least of His brethren, with that love which overcomes the weaknesses and the burdens of men by daily devotion to them, and which with gentle obstinacy plants the fruitful seedlings of kindness and mercy in the driest and stoniest soil.

But charity as the Christian ought to understand it, of the kind that Thérèse made the very essence of her life, goes far beyond these narrow confines of the immediate environment—although there is where it is hardest to exercise charity. "May your soul, *which ought to embrace the whole world*, not be squeezed into a corner of your cell", the great Teresa had warned her nuns in the first flush of the Reform. None had known as well as she how the mind and heart could shrink, how all their movements could become restricted to stubborn circling around an ego and its swollen, immoderately overstressed "spiritual life", all under the cover of piety. This morbid state could become an "occupational disease" of the contemplative. As such, it had to be always recognized and met with intelligence and clarity. The voluntarily confined inner self must open out towards the heights and depths. Only in this way could the person and her vocation remain wholesome. And love alone can shatter the rising wall.

The heart of this youngest daughter of the great St Teresa, a heart blazing with "vast desires", understood this imperative call. The passion of her desire to save souls, which had led her to the Carmel, flourished in the desert, ever growing in purity and power. The rose petals which the child strewed were intended for the whole extent of the Church Militant and the Church Suffering.

"Jesus has so incomprehensible, so uncompromising a love for us," she wrote to Céline,[31] "that He wants to do nothing without us; He wants us to share with Him in the salvation of souls. The Creator of the universe waits for the prayers and devotion of a poor little soul in order thereby to save a number of others who, like her, were redeemed at the price of His Blood."

"Oh my Céline, let us live for souls, let us be Apostles, let us above all save the souls of priests. These souls must be as transparent as crystal— alas, how many bad priests there are, how many priests who are not holy

---

[30] To Céline, 1889.
[31] 15 August 1892.

enough. Let us pray, let us suffer for them—Céline, do you understand the cry of my heart?" [32] Perhaps she was thinking of the sensational apostasy of Father Hyacinthe Loyson, a famous and brilliant preacher of her Order, who had shaken the whole of devout society in France by running off with a woman. Thérèse prayed especially for him until her death.

"She taught us", reports Sister Mary Magdalene of the Blessed Sacrament, "that God would call us to account for the priests whom we could have saved by prayer and sacrifice and did not because we were too faithless and too cowardly. 'Let us not fail in a single one of our small sacrifices for them', she used to say." [33]

At one time she cried out to a novice who was trailing along at a leisurely pace: "Does one have so much time to spare when one has children to feed?" Fired by this passion, Thérèse would also practise—and with great zeal—the most diligent sort of "accumulation of merits". But she did so not to safeguard herself against the Last Judgment, not to add to her spiritual treasures so that she might enjoy eternal felicity, but solely to "support" the children who were entrusted to her. Just as with all other possessions, both material and spiritual, love and poverty flow inseparably and as a matter of course into one another.

"Had I been rich, it would have been impossible for me to see a poor man going hungry without my giving him some of my goods at once. It is exactly the same when I acquire spiritual treasures; the moment I feel that souls are in danger of hell, I give them everything I have, and I have never yet found a moment in which I could say: from now on I will work for myself." [34] "Nothing remains in my hands. Everything I have, everything I earn, belongs to the Church and to souls. I could become eighty years old, and I should always remain equally poor." [35]

Her correspondence with her two "brothers", the young missionaries Roulland and Bellière, centred around this mysterious participation, through love, in the work of redemption.

"My sole desire is to see God loved, and I confess, if I were not allowed to labour on that task once I arrive in Heaven, I should prefer the exile to the homeland", she wrote towards the end of her life.

The great St Teresa was fond of comparing her mission to a crusade, that masculine endeavour so familiar to her as a Spaniard and a noblewoman. The "little" Thérèse preferred to see her mission mirrored in the figure of the girl heroine, the Maid of Orléans. In her many poems to

[32] 14 July 1889.
[33] 1 S., viii, 105.
[34] N.V., 12 July.
[35] Ibid.

and about St Joan, whose fate was so entirely different from hers, the historical Joan virtually evaporates into a symbol. Joan's "enemy" is the devil, not the English; the kingdom she is seeking to win is not the Crown of France, but the Kingdom of God; the salvation of France will not stop political defeat, but the tide of unbelief. In a musical playlet Thérèse put into Joan's mouth words which only thinly veil her conception of her own destiny:

> I shall pray to the Lord of hosts;
> I shall drive out the foreigners' hordes.
> I love my France, my native land,
> And I shall save her faith,
> For her I give life and heart and hand.
> For my king I will force the foe to his knees;
> Death holds no fears for me.
> I look forward to eternity.
> May God, when I pass beyond her sight,
> Console my mother in the long night.

"In the solitude of Carmel", she wrote to one missionary, "I have understood that it is my mission to win love for the King of Heaven and bring the realm of hearts under His sway." [36]

Thérèse composed a highly illuminating prayer, "inspired by a picture of St Joan of Arc".

"Lord God of Hosts, who has said to us in the Gospel, 'I have come not to bring peace, but the sword', arm me for the struggle. I burn to fight for Your honour, but I implore You, fortify my courage.... O my Beloved, I know what struggles You have destined me for.... I shall not contend upon battlefields. I am the prisoner of Your love; of my own free will I have forged the chain which fetters me to You and keeps me for ever parted from the world. My sword is Love! And with it I shall 'drive the stranger from the kingdom and proclaim You King'—within the souls of men.... Surely, Lord, You have no need of so weak a tool as I am. But Joan, Your virginal and courageous bride, has said: 'We must fight; then God gives the victory.' O my Jesus, thus will I fight for Your love until the evening of my life.... On earth You did not want to rest; I want to follow your example."

The poem to her favourite patron, the humble and cheerful missionary martyr, Théophane Vénard, also plays with the same images—in this case

[36] April 1897.

possibly stimulated more by St Teresa of Avila's "Crusader's Song" than by the example of the Maid of Orléans:

> O Christian hero, lend the splendour of your arms
> To me; to fight for sinners is my great desire,
> To suffer, spill my blood and tears.
> Oh shield me and give power to my arms.
> For them I will wage war for ever here
> And take the Kingdom of Heaven by storm.
> For Our Lord has sent fire and sword
> To earth—but He has not sent peace.

Thérèse's commentary on such verses does, to be sure, banish all suspicion that she is indulging in romantic self-glorification (and all danger of that as well). She knows quite well that in this mystical struggle "blood and tears" are the only proper weapons, and play a greater part than all heroic "action". In this was reflected the unfathomable mystery that the Son of God has redeemed sinful humanity not so much by doctrine and demonstrations of power, but ultimately by suffering pain and death. And this mystery continues to be enacted in His members.

"It seems that Jesus wishes to establish His kingdom in souls far more by sufferings and persecutions than by brilliant preaching", she wrote to one of the missionaries;[37] and again, with terrible insistence, in one of the last letters of her life: "I do not wish to be freed from sufferings here on earth, for suffering united with love is all that still seems to me desirable in this vale of tears."[38]

The resolve to suffer, as the "ransom of love", to atone by participating in Our Lord's Passion, is a fundamental element of the Carmelite vocation. To meet that requirement, generations of the Order were extremely ingenious in inventing and carrying out self-chosen mortifications. Here again the "child" Thérèse found a new and astonishingly simple way:

> So, my Beloved, shall my short life be spent in Your sight. I can prove my love only by scattering flowers, that is to say, by never letting slip a single little sacrifice, a single glance, a single word; by making profit of the very smallest actions, by doing them all for love.
> I want to suffer, and even rejoice for love, for this is my way of scattering flowers. Never a flower shall I find but its petals shall be scattered for you; and all the while I will sing, yes always sing, even when gathering my

[37] *Esprit*, 116.
[38] Ibid.

roses in the midst of thorns; and the longer and sharper the thorns may be, the sweeter shall be my song.[39]

Here, again almost wholly concealed under the flowery words, is one more of Thérèse's great discoveries for all of us. We may well call them inventions also, so newly and creatively do they spring from her heart, and so truly are they a rediscovery of something that has always been present, and that for so long was forgotten.

Such a rediscovery was needed.

Mortification of the body (including that undertaken as Christian penance) represents a highly complex and many-layered development in the framework of natural religion. Not all of its aspects need be indiscriminately approved by the Christian.

Only the half-educated think that the Christian religion "invented" physical mortification by making the body a thing of contempt. The urge to master the body's demands, and the belief that such mastery represents elevation of man and a new source of power for him, is deeply rooted. Indeed, the roots are as deep as instinct; we may speak of this urge as a spiritual instinct. And it can become just as immoderate as any other instinct. That fasting, continence and abstinence liberate, purify and strengthen the spirit, and release hitherto unknown forces, is an experience as old as religions themselves. Many forms of "magic" by which the primitive exercises power over nature or men, spring from such discipline. The major religions have repeatedly examined this phenomenon and offered varying explanations and conclusions. Revealed Christianity also accepted this part of human and religious experience and added a new meaning to the old reality. Now it was the Kingdom of Heaven which suffered violence, and which was to be won by those who employed violence against themselves. The spiritual metamorphosis which was to be wrought by Christian penance did not require any specifically prescribed forms, but it could make use of any tested exercises. Thus the body, too, acquired a symbolic language to indicate its submission to divine order, its participation in the prayers and the disciplining of the soul— "the corporealization of prayer", one writer has called fasting in the primitive Church. By this symbolic language it also expressed man's belief in the Resurrection—and the purification of the body was practised with that end in view. The tremendous ascetic movement of the fourth century, from which monasticism arose, consciously elected the sufferings of life in the desert as a substitute for martyrdom, which was no longer being imposed on Christians. From the beginning, mortification was viewed

[39] *S.S.*, xi.

as imitation of Our Lord's Passion. We have spoken of this in the chapter on Carmel.

But alongside this pure aim there inevitably followed the great temptation of all ascetics: that arrogance which is as much the classical sin of the austere as incontinence is of the lukewarm. Haughtiness appears in all its forms, from childish vanity (which peeped through the holes in the tattered cloak of the ancient Cynic and sat upon the Pharisee's ash-bestrewn head) to the finest subtleties of the drive to gain power over the souls of others. This was accompanied, at certain times, by a genuine hatred of the body and the consequent aim to humiliate and abuse this "worst enemy". There was also a curious inversion of crude materialism which sought salvation in the quantity and harshness of the mortification undertaken, rather than in the spirit animating it. And there was the deliberate intention to induce abnormal psychic states, such as visions and ecstasies, through harrowing of the body. As a rule such measures sprang less from pure longing for union with God than from the drive to win oneself a place above that of ordinary mortals.

Consequently, the struggle for preservation of the purity of penance runs through the entire history of the Church. It has always been necessary to fight for the genuine place that penance has in Christian life, and against the misunderstandings and abuses; it has always been necessary to mark out the proper boundaries for mortification. St Paul warns in the Epistle to the Colossians against the activities of the Gnostic sects who in "superstition and self-abasement and hard treatment of the body" lay claim to the sham of wisdom—and yet are in truth serving only the "gratification of the flesh".[40] St Augustine describes the two modes of mortification, physical and spiritual, and expresses a far greater preference for the latter: "To tame the spirit, to trample upon honour and prestige, is far more than to torment and scourge the flesh and wear penitential girdles. This penitential exercise is more glorious and precious, and therefore harder and costs us much more than the other."[41] St Jerome wrote with force and clarity in one of his pastoral letters: "Long and immoderate fasting greatly displeases me, especially in those who are still young in years. I have noticed that the young ass, when he tires of the journey, is fond of straying off the road." And the person who quotes these words is mild St Francis de Sales in his book *Introduction to the Devout Life*.

Scarcely a saint has matured without the bitter discipline of ruthless mortification; and yet almost every saint has moved away from immod-

[40] Cf. Col 2:23.

[41] St Augustine, *Sermo 20, de Sanctis*, quoted from Rodriguez, *Übung der christlichen Vollkommenheit*, Regensburg, 1862.

erate struggle against the flesh, has displaced the centre of gravity to inner penance. Every saint has retained a certain austerity of attitude pervading the entire personality, but this austerity has not always been expressed in particular actions. The penitential Orders place the entire life of their members under a rule of greater strictness than the average Christian in the world regards as obligatory. To be sure, the personal destiny of such Christians in the world may impose upon them hardships far greater than any demanded by monastic rules. Perhaps the austerity of monastic Orders is characterized by the principled exclusion of a number of natural pleasures and satisfactions, rather than by express prescription of the opposite of such pleasures.

The Carmel, it must be said, goes far in this direction. It grants the body no more than the necessary minimum. At first glance it seems scarcely possible that within these iron limits there would still be room for voluntary intensifications of penance. Yet the Rule provides for them. With that reverence for free initiative in matters of zeal which is so characteristic of monastic Orders, the Rule leaves open areas for action under the special inspiration of the Holy Spirit—though such actions, too, are subject to the superiors' judgment. It may be, for example, that a nun wishes to add a special fast of her own to the general fast. For example, a contemporary of our saint, who died a few years before her, Sister Miriam of Abellin, took only bread and water for half a year. Another nun may renounce the evening meal for a few months, or all drinks other than water, or may take upon herself special penances with penitential instruments. She may be actuated by a special craving for atonement or wish to accomplish a specific end. Then, there is the distinctly therapeutic character of certain penances; these may be applied when particular symptoms of well-known spiritual states appear. They are used like medicines for specific diseases, and often have a curative effect unmatched by any other means.

Inherent in this scheme are two potential temptations. The lesser one consists in this: that in epochs of spiritual deterioration the last-mentioned sober and objective application is forgotten. Mortifications cease to be cures; they are confused with games—especially when exact knowledge of the character of the penitent is ignored. There develops empty rivalry in the endurance of pain. The "ascetic" whose principal aim is record performances resembles a person who indiscriminately tries out on himself a whole host of medicines and poisons, with no regard for the labels, and who makes it a point of pride to demonstrate how many bitter and ill-tasting substances his stomach can stand, or even how many major operations he can "survive".

The second temptation is more subtle and harder to recognize because it does not spring from such crude vanity, but from the best of intentions.

It is described with great terseness and penetration in Werner Bergengruen's thoughtful novel *Der Grosstyrann und das Gericht*:

> It was your obligation to serve God according to your destiny, by your way of being, and instead you have had a great longing to serve Him with a deed. By way of being I mean a form of suffering that requires immeasurable patience, by deed a form of action that requires immeasurable heroism. The way is without end, the deed unique. The way comprehends deeds, not one deed. And so I see in the deed the temptation to escape, by means of a single thrust, the permanent necessity of the way, and to escape from it by means of an ascent and an intensification which leaves the way behind it.

In Thérèse's period, both these modes of misunderstanding had to a great extent obscured the pure concept of asceticism. "The deed" stood high above "the way" in the view of many pious souls; many perhaps dreamed of a way which would consist of a chain of "deeds" in constantly ascending order. That was how the life of saints was generally conceived. Moreover, a slavish religiosity dominated by routine could summon up little understanding for objective distinctions. The known traditional forms of penance were considered to be of equal value, generally speaking, and were recommended for imitation. The description of fearful mortifications filled a good deal of space in the lives of saints; the disappearance of such practices from ordinary Christian life and from the monasteries was greatly decried as symptomatic of the decadence of true spirituality, and of a weakening of zeal. Mortification, or, more precisely, the stress on mortification, stood at the centre of piety in the commonly accepted sense, and often it was more an end than a means.

The Lisieux Carmel was no exception in this respect. No details are available to us, except the hint in connection with the nettles Mother Marie de Gonzague used for mortification.[42] But the brief commentary on that matter suffices: "When Sister Thérèse saw with her own eyes the fruits which grew from such penances, she sought a means to attain sanctity more swiftly and surely." The old Foundress had advised moderation. "Without great prudence and great judgment, all that is nothing but vanity, and nourishes self-love", she had said. But here, as in other matters, she had been too weak to impose her will upon the convent, and above all on her successor. Like the nettles in the garden, spiritual fads flourished in spite of her humble wisdom.

We might expect Thérèse to have a false conception of penance. As a child of her time and her education, she shared, as if it were innate, the general embarrassment with the body. "My body has always been a dis-

---

[42] See Chapter iii, 3.

comfort to me—I did not feel at ease in it, and even as a child I was ashamed of it", is a sentence found among the many accounts recorded from her sickbed.[43] During her childhood illness from chorea the doctor had prescribed cold showers and compresses. But Marie soon had to discontinue them because the child, even under Marie's own ministrations, suffered too much psychologically. (In this the sisters saw nothing but admirable "heroic chastity".[44]) Céline, too, has stated that Thérèse "was ashamed of her body", and that only one thing could console her for the fact of being burdened with it: that Jesus had not disdained to assume a body like our own.[45] Another time Thérèse said: "If Our Lord and the Blessed Virgin had not gone to banquets, I should never have been able to understand this custom of inviting friends to meals. It seems to me we really ought to hide when we eat, or at least remain only among our closest relations. Invitations are all very well—but only for the purpose of talking, telling one another about travels or memories, sharing pleasures of the mind with one another." When, on the other hand, she says of herself: "I did not have the capacity for enjoyment—I always noticed that— but only a very great capacity for suffering", it seems to us that this statement represents a self-deception. Her capacity for enjoyment had been tested all too infrequently. A great physical capacity for suffering is quite generally the reverse side of an equally great capacity for enjoyment. Moreover, we have evidence on some points. Thérèse's tastes were dainty, not to say spoiled. She demanded the utmost cleanliness and neatness about her. She liked pretty, well-cared-for utensils. Having to use an ugly, chipped water jug instead of a pretty and undamaged one, or being given a sticky fork, meant "a real sacrifice" to her. Spots on clothing and furniture were painful to her. The sight of big spiders made her shiver with fear and repugnance. She loved flowers passionately, stroked with sheer delight the velvety skin of a peach, liked to compare the flavour of fruits with the scents of various flowers. On the trip to Rome she used a flask of cologne water with such pleasure that she remembered the incident even while she was being prepared for Extreme Unction, and asked herself whether at that time she had not committed a fault of excess.

To a person with such a nature the hardships of the Carmel must have been a sore trial, and must at the same time have aroused ambition—we must not forget that deeply rooted impulse in her nature towards special distinction, coupled with the youthful urge to prove herself in honourable contests. Could not both these closely related impulses find legitimate

---

[43] *N.V.*, 29 July.
[44] 1 *S.*, xiv, 8.
[45] Ibid.

outlet in the field of asceticism, here in the convent? Would it not at the same time be "exercise in perfection" to satisfy them?

No wonder, then, that the question of penance preoccupied the saint's mind. For a moment it seemed as if she would be led into the usual channels. Thérèse herself says that at the beginning of her Carmelite life she had "a strong inclination to works of penance"; as the sisters explain,[46] it was above all the reading of lives of saints which aroused such desires in her, and possibly also the example of other nuns—especially that of the Prioress, perhaps, who favoured violent and "heroic" penances for herself. The considerations that decided Thérèse against such enterprises are highly characteristic. One, as the above-quoted passage tells us, was provided by her sharp, critical, and observing mind when she compared the fruits of such efforts with the energy expended; another came from self-knowledge. She soon recognized the curious expansion of the ego which seems to be a natural concomitant of such exercises. "I would have taken far too much *pleasure* in them", Thérèse confesses frankly. "God made me realize that the sternest penance can be mingled with natural satisfaction; one must be very wary in this regard.... We must be extremely moderate in everything that has to do with instruments of penance; often nature predominates, rather than virtue." [47]

Her sole experiment in this field—wearing a small iron cross with sharp points—caused an inflammation which, as it were, opened her eyes. Probably this disability, insignificant though it was, kept her from fulfilling her ordinary daily duties. Could it be right to block the way of penance by such individual "deeds" of penance? If her strength obviously did not suffice for both way and deed, it was perfectly clear which she ought to practise and which let alone. "The devil often deceives great-hearted but unwise souls by driving them to exaggerations which injure their health and *hinder them from the fulfilment of their duty*." [48]

Thérèse had found Columbus's egg. She made the "way" itself a deed, made life a penance. The daily routine of the Carmel, as prescribed by the Rule alone, was austere enough to satisfy her thirst for sufferings and trials. Each day's evils sufficed unto themselves if the day's assignments were carried out, by the hour and minute, with honesty and thoroughness. Human nature saw to that, because human nature resents having only what is necessary every day. Why invent artificial means? Daily bread is given by God's hand—to them who understand how to receive it.

[46] *Esprit.*
[47] 1 *S.,* xii, 12; 2 *S.,* 287; *N.V.,* August 3.
[48] 2 *S.,* 290.

Thérèse soon grasped the contradictions in those nuns who thoughtlessly requested exceptions from the Rule in a hundred ways and spared themselves its austerities, only to use the strength thus gained to assign themselves extra works of penance. Such behaviour ran counter to the simplest honesty in meeting one's obligations. First of all, what was taken for granted had also to be taken seriously. "Why have we taken upon ourselves a life of austerity if afterwards we seek exemption from a whole host of things we find irksome? We must not withdraw from the slightest mortifying exercise, unless obliged to do so under obedience." [49] She viewed whatever was imposed upon her by the Prioress as coming directly from God. For that reason, too, she shunned the laxities and exceptions in the convent as if they were poison. Dom Godefroy Madelaine testifies that as a postulant Thérèse from the beginning begged the Prioress to let her practise the Rule in its full rigour. Later, too, she suffered greatly from the repeated attempts of her solicitous sisters to obtain ameliorations for her. During the harsh last winter before her collapse it became a veritable torment to her to withstand the well-meant interventions of her sisters, but she did not yield.

Ancient tradition sets one of the goals of monastic life as a "substitute for martyrdom". Consequently, it would be truly unrealistic to make such a trial easy and pleasant by small surreptitious changes and evasions. If one takes this view, everything else follows. The one inexhaustible school of mortification is work. Every ordinary task of the day must be done as precisely, as conscientiously, as composedly and faultlessly, as the strength of body and soul permits: without haste, without hesitation, without carelessness, without negligence. Anyone who has tried to do this knows well that such punctiliousness can be true penance. And in this regard Thérèse behaved like a good soldier, wringing the most out of herself. "As long as I can drag myself about, I must stick to my post", was her attitude. As long as she could walk, even though she had to muster all her strength to stagger from wall to wall, Thérèse missed none of the communal exercises; she stood when the others stood, knelt when they knelt, endured the long prayers in choir without attracting attention, in spite of headaches, nausea, fits of dizziness and that deadly weariness so characteristic of a state of advancing tuberculosis. When she came from medical treatment, during which she received painful red-hot needles upon the skin of her back, she went, without asking for a moment to rest, to her next task, even if it happened to be hanging out the laundry, when her back would suffer every time she raised her arms.

[49] I S., xiii, 44.

The other school of mortification was the practice of fraternal charity. We will recall the chapter in which Thérèse learned and practised perfect kindness towards the other nuns. Let us consider what this must have cost her. Penance and love flowed together into a single current. "How can we especially mortify ourselves when doing the laundry?" "That is easy to guess", Thérèse replied. "If you find it hard to work at the cold water, that is a sign that it is also repugnant to the others; then go to work there. If, on the other hand, the day happens to be very hot, stay by the boiling cauldron.... If we choose the most uncomfortable part of the task, we are simultaneously practising charity by letting others have the better work."

In addition to obedience and love, a third element particularly characteristic of Thérèse was added to these two, like a secret spice: to evade nothing, to meet the difficulties of daily routine, whether small or large, and to meet them not by a stoic act of will, but, as it were, with open arms. We must receive such hardships warmly, let them penetrate us, expose ourselves to them, taste them to the full without a shudder. This practice of non-resistance became for Thérèse noble tranquillity. Her neighbour in choir disturbed her, during the hour of silent prayer, by the highly irritating habit of tapping her fingernails against her teeth. This is the episode which, out of consideration for the nun in question, was recast in *The Story of a Soul* into the famous incident of the nun who rattled her rosary. Thérèse not only refrained from making any remarks, or asking for quiet; she focused all her attention upon the disturbing noise which so racked her nerves that she was bathed in perspiration. At the laundry tub the sister opposite her worked with such zeal and clumsiness that she splashed dirty water from handkerchiefs into Thérèse's face. Thérèse not only remained silent; she would not even step aside to avoid the repugnant shower.

Thérèse suffered bitterly from the damp cold of the Norman winter. Carmelite custom forbade heating in any but the common room. Anaemic as Thérèse probably was, she often could not sleep whole nights through and lay, trembling, teeth chattering, under her thin blanket. A single word would have been enough, and she would have been given better care, but she endured this for nine winters without complaint. During her last illness she revealed: "Throughout my religious life, the cold has caused me more physical pain than anything else; I suffered from cold until I nearly died of it." Only after the cold had destroyed her health did she modestly ask the Prioress whether it might not be better to heat the convent. "Too narrow observation of tradition, without considering the character of different countries and the natural dispositions of persons, is tempting God and sinning against prudence." Her advice, which could no longer help her, was followed.

In the winter Thérèse avoided, as far as possible, entering the common room or staying in it longer than necessary; indeed, she did not allow herself the slightest movement by which people involuntarily protect themselves against cold. "We should not even reveal the fact by hunching up in walking, or shivering and rubbing our hands." [50] "In the winter," Céline tells us, "I seldom saw her nestle her hands within the scapulary [which is after all for that purpose] in spite of the fact that she suffered intensely from chilblains. One day it was biting cold outside, and we were without heat; I saw that in contrast to the rest of us she kept her hands uncovered and let them rest outspread on her knees. I made a gesture, for this annoyed me, but she only smiled with her faintly mocking expression."

At one period of Thérèse's illness, a half-deaf elderly sister was in attendance in the sickroom. Thérèse, feverish and perspiring, asked her to take away a blanket. But the kindly old nun, who heard only the word "blanket", brought another; and since the patient thanked her with a warm smile, she busied herself fetching all available blankets—delighted to be doing a service for the poor girl—and heaped them on the bed. Thérèse went on smiling, and the relief nurse found her half-suffocated, running an extremely high temperature.

In the same way, in the refectory she left her mortifications to Providence and was not disappointed. We have already heard how the nuns who worked in the kitchen from the beginning gave unpleasant leftovers to the youngest sister, in the expectation that she would dispose of them. This habit lasted a full seven years, until Thérèse fell ill and the Prioress intervened. Now, when she was commanded, and therefore had to respond obediently, to report what foods disagreed with her, it came to light that she had for so long eaten the things that least agreed with her. "I never gave in to repugnance." On one occasion a significant interlude took place. Marie was placed in charge of the kitchen as procuratrix. She wanted to make up for her sister's sufferings, coddle her a little. Consequently, she often slipped Thérèse something extra at table, "but God saw to it that her taste and mine are completely opposed, and that I never had to overcome myself so much as during this period even though I seemed to others thoroughly pampered." Perhaps it was at this time that Thérèse, as a special favour, received some cider at table. However, she had to share the bottle with an old, invalid nun, and it apparently did not occur to this nun that the beverage was intended for two. She regularly drank it all herself. In order to receive none, Thérèse had only to follow the rule according to which the nuns were not supposed to ask for anything

---

[50] I S., xiii, 44.

themselves, but to leave such matters to the concern of their neighbour or the sister who waited on the others.

Later on she taught her novices nothing but little, unimpressive mortifications, of such minor quality that they would tend to shame rather than feed vanity: not to eat less than they needed, but to eat everything, in order to please the palate as little as possible; never to improve any food at table by mixing or adding condiments; to end a meal with a dry piece of bread; not to gulp down repulsive medicine, but to swallow it drop by drop. "We must well utilize the little opportunities that are offered to us if we are barred from great achievements." And these penances, small though they were, were effective.

Here again the individual items do not, taken one by one, yield a proper picture; we must regard rather the texture of the whole. For the hagiographer, as many lives of saints seem to prove, there is a certain temptation to pick out individual traits and call them "heroic", in order to elicit the sympathy and admiration of the reader. Quite rightly, such tactics soon arouse a certain emotional resistance. Really, the reader asks himself, what does this or that passing and arbitrary cross amount to, compared to the daily, inescapable tribulation of so many people who live in the world? If the devout think they must lay emphasis upon such "heroic virtues" they are answered at once—with equally false emphasis—by the scepticism of contemporaries.

"Indeed, we may say that if the medieval monk, or a saint famous for his austerities, had had to perform the same physical exertions which modern man in his occupational and athletic life carries out as a matter of course, he would frantically clasp the crucifix and call upon God, the Virgin Mary and all the saints to shield him from such horrible torments.... And today, the mountaineer who with bleeding hands forces his way up a chimney; the flyer dangling between heaven and earth; or the youthful hiker doing his thirty miles and after a sparse meal sleeping on a camp-bed—all such persons are practising that matter-of-course civilian asceticism which might make many a monkish professional ascetic capitulate."

The above comment is by Elizabeth Busse-Wilson in her sensational, and for good reasons, quickly forgotten book on St Elizabeth of Hungary.[51] She and the many persons whose prejudice she voices here have forgotten or never understood that the true difficulty of Christian asceticism lies not in single high points, in specific record achievements, but in the inexorable monotony and continuity of their penances. The hard-

[51] Munich, 1932, p. 62.

ships of "civilian asceticism", as E. Busse-Wilson calls it, cannot be denied by anyone familiar with them. But there is about them a virtually all-powerful and also indispensable charm which makes them endurable: diversion and the hope of diversion. Men can endure the greatest strains when they are conscious that these will not last, that sooner or later the trials will be relieved by their opposite, though it may be only for a short time: that hunger will give way to satiation, solitude to society, pressure to peace, weariness to rest, troublesome clothing to more comfortable garb, coercion to self-determination. This counterpoise and compensation is lacking in the convent. Furthermore, in ordinary life we are free to lessen the hardships and burdens. It is perfectly legitimate, morally, to outwit them, remedy them, eliminate them altogether. We praise the strong and skilful person who succeeds, even in the most unfavourable circumstances, in securing a maximum of advantage and relief, in reducing his exertions to the minimum. The voluntary penitent, however, may not evade the hardships that come his way. He is not supposed to fend off what is unpleasant, nor to offset it, but rather to accept and endure everything. And this he must do not as a temporary test, not as experiment, training or adventure, not as the result of destiny's bad weather, but as a form of life which will extend until his death. What ordinary person does likewise? Furthermore, in the convent this monotonous persistence in almost intangible, constantly repeated trivialities has, always and everywhere, to be invested with the weight of full religious significance, and consciously so, whereas the average man usually loses sight of it.

Thérèse took this obligation seriously and fulfilled it to the ultimate degree; it literally pervaded every moment of her day. Hence, it is all the more interesting for us to learn how little importance she attributed to individual items of religious practice, and to her own role with regard to them. We shall later return to the subject of her resolute rejection of the traditional practice of counting specific "sacrifices". As for the passion for mortification, she rejected all forms of this which kept one's mind upon the act itself and "prevented the spirit from turning to God". The famous examples of saints or devout priests did not shake her from this opinion. In regard to this she was wont to quote the words: "There are many dwelling-places in my Father's house." [52] "Certainly all mortification is praiseworthy and meritorious, if we are convinced that God asks it of us. If we are mistaken in our actions, He is nevertheless moved by our intention. But I could never bind myself to something that would keep me continually occupied.... As our Mother St Teresa says: God does not, as

---

[52] Jn 14:2.

we would like to believe, concern Himself with a heap of trivialities, and
we must not confine our souls in any respect." [53] She could be utterly
free of narrowness or pedantry in this matter because she considered active penance only the expression of love, and she knew well that love
does not always choose to express itself in the same way. "Love is the
only thing we should strive for", she instructed her sister Pauline, who
humbly questioned her. "For that reason we should always prefer the
action which we can do with greater love, whether it is 'harder' or easier
it is better to do something in itself minor than something 'valuable' if
we perform the first act more lovingly than the second." [54] All physical
mortifications weigh nothing as against charity, she used to say.

Gratitude, too, is a form of love, and one highly pleasing to God. How
can it be practised by a person who haughtily disdains everything joyful?
She would, Petitot comments,[55] have thought she were sinning against
the high virtue of moderation if she had, out of principle, denied every
innocent pleasure; she frequently found that the beauty of nature, the
charm of a flower, the fragrance of a peach, compelled her to feel loving
gratitude towards God.

It is amazing to see how she, who never sought refreshment or be-
guilement, recognized and received with childlike gladness the joys and
little consolations that fell to her from the hand of God. In the snow on
her Clothing day, in gifts of flowers for "her" Child Jesus, in the cooling
drink that a nurse brought her unasked, she saw *délicatesses de bon Dieu*,
tender proofs of God's love, which could evoke from her tears of delight
and humility.

At the beginning of her life in the convent she had followed certain rules
of penance, and at meals she had deliberately tried to spoil the taste of food
by adding salt or wormwood, or turning her mind to repulsive things while
at table. She soon moved away from such artificialities. "Eat whatever is put
before you." [56] "Later I found it simpler to offer to God in gratitude the
things I enjoyed eating." She invented little games for somehow "enno-
bling" what she continued to call the "sordid business of eating". These are
so reminiscent of the "table manners" recommended by Henry Suso in his
youth that we consider it possible that Thérèse may have taken this idea from
his biography, since she once mentions having read it.

"I imagine myself at Nazareth, in the house of the Holy Family. If, for
instance, I am served with salad, cold fish, wine, or milk with rum [in

[53] *Esprit*, 181.
[54] 2 S., 290.
[55] Page 57.
[56] 1 Cor 10:27.

the infirmary], I offer it to St Joseph, and think: Oh, how good that will be for him! To our Blessed Lady I offer hot foods and ripe fruit, and to the Infant Jesus our feast-day fare, especially broth, rice and preserves. Lastly, when I do not like the food at all, I say cheerfully: 'Today, my Little One, it is all for you.' " [57] "If I lack something, I am then thoroughly content, for then I really have something to give to the Holy Family." [58]

"I want to suffer out of love and rejoice out of love." God's Fatherhood accepts both, just as it is He who sends both rain and sunshine. Again and again this thought reappears in her poems, in "To Scatter Flowers", in "Hymn to the Innocents", and in many others:

> To scatter flowers for You, sacrifice
> My smallest sigh and my intensest dread,
> My sorrows, bliss, renunciations, joys—
> Behold, here are my flowers white and red!

> To make the souls of children white as snow
> Increase the shining band;
> Behold, Lord, my sum of joys and tears below
> I give into Your hand.

Thence, certainly, comes the curious lightness so typical of all of Thérèse's penances. She accomplished the apparently impossible feat of being, every moment, in a state of sharply focused, intense, controlled alertness, and at the same time completely unselfconscious and spontaneous in all she did. She possessed that freedom from selfconsciousness in which, as in the physical order, the subtlest forces of the soul can function unhindered, at their best. But when she prescribes this type of unselfconsciousness, are we not forcibly reminded of the Russian folk tale about the alchemist's formula: the adept will succeed in making gold only if, during his mixing and concocting, he absolutely does not think of a white bear!

4. THE VEIL

In this quandary, also, Thérèse found the only possible way. It was the way of the "veil"—that unique and characteristic attribute of her hidden face.

What shall we call it? Silence, simplicity, hiddenness, reticence? All these terms sound too ponderous, too emphatic, too deliberate, too forced. Her veil was spun so fine that no one ever saw it, and yet it protected her

[57] *C.S.*
[58] *N.V.*, 23 July.

for nine years in the narrow, exposed intimacy of a tiny convent as effectively as the fabled cap of invisibility. Her smile hid her as smoothly and as impenetrably as any visor.

Smilingly, Thérèse went through her years in the convent, graciously, guilelessly, sunnily smiling. But that smile was the most stringent instrument of her physical and spiritual penance.

At all costs she did not want to be "interesting"—not mysterious, noteworthy, enigmatic, stimulating. She did not want to attract the curious glances of the others, to seem admirable or "heroic", or provoke pity by obvious unhappiness. She wanted to be like all the others, not conspicuous, not outstanding, not much talked about. She wanted to act as if all were well, as if nothing were the matter with her, ever, as if she had no troubles. She wanted it to seem so to the other nuns, to the Prioress, to herself. Indeed, she must not merely act as if nothing were wrong; she must know that she herself was nothing special and that whatever she did, thought or felt was really not worth talking about, not worth paying attention to. The veil of ordinariness, averageness, commonplaceness, was only the outward expression of this interior knowledge; it was the guardian of all secrets between God and the soul. It was the only way in which it was permissible to suffer.

And it alone corresponded to the admonition of the Gospel: "When you fast, do not show it by gloomy looks as the hypocrites do. They make their faces unsightly so that men can see they are fasting; believe me, they have their reward already. But do thou, at thy times of fasting, anoint thy head and wash thy face, so that thy fast may not be known to men, but to thy Father, who dwells in secret; and then thy Father, who sees what is done in secret, will reward thee." [59]

There are many ways in which the fasting person can distort his face in order to impress men, almost as many ways as there are types of human beings: piteous lamentation, and proud, gloomy reticence; wild alternation of mood, and significant silence; rigid gaze, melancholy mien, curt replies, mysterious allusions, mute sighs, clenched teeth, forced good cheer. All such signs inform others as plainly as the most public announcement: "You lucky people do not know my silent struggles!" Young people especially, who fancy they despise voluble and bold complaining, are very prone to such transparently tragic histrionics which yield far more self-satisfaction than humiliating laments.

"A good little nun," the convent said of Thérèse, "very nice and friendly, very well-meaning and conscientious, but certainly nothing special. She

[59] Mt 6:16–18.

did not suffer from anything and was rather insignificant. What will our Mother be able to write about her in her obituary letter? She entered here, lived and died. Virtuous she certainly is, but that is no feat when one has so happy, uncomplicated a nature, no difficulties of character, and has not had to win virtue 'like us' by struggles and suffering."

In the Carmel such judgments carry additional weight. For these convents are marked by a militant enthusiasm for suffering; the nuns judge one another principally by the standard of spiritual struggle and victory. Their eye for scars and wounds is sharpened, and accounts of spiritual adventures, narrow escapes and perils withstood are reverently passed on from one to the other. After all, in a certain sense the aim of a Carmelite's life is suffering; she wishes to achieve a kind of mastery in suffering; and nuns are supposed to spur one another on to courage and steadfastness in suffering. What a verdict this is, then, if the community can only say, when the end of one of the band is drawing near: "She had nothing to suffer."

Even during Thérèse's last illness such comments were made, and she knew it. When the sisters and some of the novices, who already formed a kind of congregation of devotees around her, praised her merits in the convent, one voice protested: "I cannot understand why so much fuss is made about Sister Thérèse. She has done nothing remarkable; we do not see her practising virtue; and it cannot even be said that she is a really good nun."

"We do not *see* her practising virtue—*on ne la voit point pratiquer la vertu.*" This comment is beautifully significant. It is a revelation of how the nuns generally regarded virtue—as something recognizable by a certain extra effort, by audible creaking of the joints, by visible tautening of the will; by precisely what Nietzsche described as the stoic spiritual hero of his century in his wonderful chapter on the Sublime One:

> I saw a Sublime One today, a Solemn One, a penitent of the spirit: O, how my soul laughed because of his ugliness!
>
> He was draped with ugly truths, the prize of his hunting, and rich in rent garments; many thorns clung to him also—but still I saw no rose upon him.
>
> As yet he had not learned laughter, and beauty. Darkly, this hunter returned from the forest of knowledge.
>
> From the battle he returned home with wild beasts, but out of his earnestness stared one more wild beast, one yet unconquered....
>
> When he grew weary of his sublimity, only then would his beauty commence—and only then will I try him and find him delectable....
>
> Already I love in him his bull's neck, but now I would also see him have the angel's eye.
>
> Also he must unlearn his hero's will; I would have him raised up, not merely sublime; let the ether itself raise him up; let him be without will!...

Truly, his desires must not grow mute and vanish in satiety, but in beauty! Graciousness should be part of the magnanimity of the high-souled.

Arm placed above the head—that is how the hero should rest; that is how he should also overcome his resting.

But for the hero above all beauty is the hardest of all things. Beauty is never conquerable to sheer will....

But if power is gracious and descends to make itself visible, then I call such condescension beauty.

And from none other do I demand such beauty, but from you, O mighty one! Let your goodness be your last self-conquest....

You should aspire to be the pillar of virtue; it grows more beautiful and more delicate always, but inwardly harder and sturdier, the more it rises.

It is strange how aptly these stanzas delineate Thérèse of Lisieux; a more exact portrait of her could hardly be desired.

When, forty years after her death, the surviving sisters, all of advanced age, sought to summon up their memories of their convent's saint, they always recollected first the "angel's eye": her wondrously beautiful, unforgettable smile.

Thérèse was a singing soul—"*une âme chantante*"—said Dom Godefroy Madelaine, that friend of the Prioress who seems to have best recognized the young nun's personal quality. He also pronounced the considered judgment: "Never again have I encountered a soul at once so great-hearted and so humble."

The soaring bliss of her relationship with God, her one-time sunny disposition, that radiance she had possessed as a young girl before her entry, was no more. Those wings had long since been painfully clipped and were never to grow again. What she had was the result of conscious and inflexible exercise: "I do not like St Aloysius as much as the blessed Théophane Vénard, for in the life of the former it is said that he was grave and sad even during recreation, whereas Théophane was always cheerful, although he suffered a great deal."

Thérèse, too, was a source of amusement and jollity in recreation, and whenever she was not present, a sigh passed through the assembled nuns: "There will be no fun today." One nun relates that during the period of Louis Martin's illness the older sisters were always downcast and held aloof from the others a great deal, in order to discuss their sorrows with one another. Thérèse alone sat and laughed with the others as usual; but sometimes while she did so, big tears rolled down her cheeks without her seeming to notice. And Sister Marie, speaking of the same period, remarks that Thérèse seemed so strong that it occurred to no one to worry about her or console her. During her last illness, cousin Marie Guérin wrote home: "When visiting Thérèse we find her much changed, very emaciated, but displaying always the same cheerful serenity and always having something to say to make one laugh." Neither physical pain nor spiritual pangs could change this. "When I have great pain, or disagreeable things happen to me, I answer by smiling. At first I did not always succeed, but now it has become a habit which I am glad to have acquired."

"Why are you so bright this morning?" Pauline asked when visiting her at her sickbed one day. "Because of two little crosses...", she replied.

This smile was not forced, was not theatrical. It arose from the noblest kind of modesty, which shuns any baring of the inmost self, and also from an infinitely delicate courtesy reminiscent of the polished manners of the great Eastern cultures. "How do you manage to show no sign and to display such genuine serenity?" Dom Godefroy wondered when Thérèse told him what she underwent when she was visited with doubts against the faith. "I try, by God's grace, never to burden others with the trials that God thinks it well to send me", Thérèse replied.

But she also went beyond the Far Eastern ethic which views such self-control as an essential aspect of good manners. To Thérèse her smile was simply honest fulfilment of her vocation. It would be a contradiction, she taught her novices, for them to bear the burden of convent life wretchedly, with visible effort, after they had solemnly declared on the day of their Profession that they were accepting the Rule in full freedom of the will.

"The face is the mirror of the soul, and yours, like that of a contented little child, should always be calm and serene. Even when alone, be cheerful, remembering always that you are in the sight of the Angels." Or she would say, in that curious and often astonishing childlikeness of her parables: "God, who loves us, is sorry enough that He has to try us on earth—even without our constantly informing Him how hard it is for us; therefore we should not let it be noticed that we notice it. Out of *tact* we ought not to complain about heat and cold, not dry our perspiration and rub our chilled hands. Or if we do, then we must do so secretly, to make it clear that we are not reproaching God for our discomfort."

In connection with penances we have already mentioned that Thérèse adopted the rule of concealment. She suppressed all those little gestures which serve to communicate the fact that one is too hot or too cold. In the light of this we will not misunderstand Thérèse's saying that she even tried to smile when performing the prescribed scourging, "so that God would not see how it hurt me". This self-imposed rule extended to inward attitudes during prayer:

> If You would part from me,
> Treasure Divine,
> And of Your love for me
> Give me no sign,

Still I shall smile, and still
Sing as before,
Knowing that soon You will
All joy restore.

For Him I love I wish my smile to shine;
Though He to try me hides His Face from me,
For Him I wait, though night and pain be mine:
This is my Heaven, this my felicity.

This veil conceals everything: her struggles, her solitude, her election, every glimmer of heroism—everything that for young people makes the state of suffering bearable and even attractive. Nothing so tersely sums up Thérèse's fate in the convent as this often-related little incident:

During her long illness a visiting nun noticed a glass of some brilliant red drink on her table. "What is that precious beverage?" she asked. "I hope it tastes as good as it looks!" It happened to be the bitterest medicine that Thérèse had to take. "This glass is the image of my life", she later said to Pauline. "Others have thought I was continually drinking the most delicious wine, but it was full of bitterness. And yet my life has not been a bitter one, for I have learned to find my joy and sweetness in all that is bitter."

Another conversation of the same period serves to underline the point. Two months before Thérèse's death that nun whom she had so heroically befriended in spite of her natural antipathy asked her whether she had ever had any struggles, a question which, in the Carmel, was virtually insulting. " 'Oh, I certainly have', she replied to me. 'I have not had a yielding nature.... That did not show, but I have been made to feel it keenly. I can assure you that I have not spent a single day without grief and struggle—not a single one!' " [60]

We will remember that even as a child Thérèse had formed the noble habit of silence. She seemed to have a natural inclination for privacy amidst the all-embracing emotional communism of the family, if we may put it that way. Instinctively she resisted the family's urge to share every feeling and every experience. But her silence also arose from a profound religious sense of her "secrecy with God", for it is characteristic of all genuine love that it wishes to share with the other person a private area accessible to no one else. These feelings continued to govern her maturity. Thérèse quite consciously practised the useful virtue of silence, and

[60] I S., xii, 48.

the manner in which she taught it to her novices is an indication of how well she understood the temptations to flee it.

"Why do you feel your weariness so keenly and consciously?" she said to a novice who complained that no one appreciated how much work she did. "Isn't it because no one else knows about it? If someone were to say to you, 'Sister, you have done so much, do rest a bit', you would no longer feel any fatigue. I would like to see you always a brave soldier who takes seriously his brothers' wounds but treats his own as mere scratches. Blessed Margaret Mary once had two sores; she said that she really suffered only from the first because the second one could not be hidden, and so it was examined and she was pitied for it by the whole house.... That is a wholly natural feeling, but it is also making oneself common (*agir comme le vulgaire*) to wish others to know when something hurts us." "It does us so much good, gives us such strength, not to talk away our pains."

"You wound your soul", she said in all sincerity to her beloved elder sister who at every little vexation went running to Pauline for consolation. "You rob yourself of strength. We only weaken ourselves when we talk about the difficulties of battle while still on the battlefield.... If only a spark of passion is in the heart, it is better to remain silent and wait until your soul has grown entirely calm before you speak about the incident, for to converse about it often serves only to poison the heart." So she wrote to Céline.[61]

Even on her deathbed she urged Pauline, as the future Prioress: "If we wish to win illumination and God's help for the guidance and the consolation of souls, we must not talk about our personal troubles in order to relieve ourselves. Moreover, by such 'outpouring of our hearts' we do not even attain genuine alleviation; we excite, rather than soothe ourselves."[62]

"O blissful silence which gives so much peace to the soul!"

Thérèse found the great exemplar of this attitude in the Blessed Virgin. Like her, Thérèse wished to "keep all things in her heart". She revered above all the silence with which Our Lady endured Joseph's suspicions, and the way she left her justification to God.

> Mother, your silence speaks; I love its every tone
> And hear it as sweet music, sonorous harmony.
> Only a soul that builds on Heaven's help alone
> Can show its grandeur thus, and say all silently.

[61] 2 *S.*, 621.
[62] 16 September.

This silence applied not only to her own affairs; it also included tact towards others. "She never expressed her opinion unasked", one of her fellow nuns testified. And she continued, with an almost comical, but highly significant association of ideas: "That is why we now keep saying all the time in our Carmel: What do you know, that little girl! What a stir she's making! A big fuss all over the world! Who would ever have thought it possible!"

The veil meant even more than mere self-control and modest restraint. Thérèse desired not only inconspicuousness, but misunderstanding. She knew whom she was following. "O Face that was not recognized even by Your own disciples!" This was the finest flower of her devotion to the Holy Face. She overcame her pride, her desire for status—that most powerful of human impulses, which at times stabbed her young heart with fiery stings—by wearing the veil of the smile. Beneath that smile she sacrificed things profound and valid: the basic human longing for recognition, for another's understanding look into one's own heart. "Nobody understands me" is an eternally feminine and eternally youthful lament of solitude. Thérèse did not *want* to be understood. She did not want this in spite of the fact that her whole being, from childhood on, had been accustomed to the most intimate and unreserved exchange of confidences with her beloved sisters. She did not want it, even though the sisters wanted nothing more, and expected, almost demanded, that they be allowed to participate as before in her inner life. "May my face remain veiled like that of the Lord of all creatures, so that on earth no man may recognize me!" At her Profession Thérèse had worn close to her heart a letter in which she prayed: "Grant that no one may trouble about me; that I may be trampled under foot, forgotten like a tiny grain of sand."

Once more the dream of her period of decision rose up in her. "If I had not been received into the Carmel, I would have entered a Refuge and lived there unknown and despised among the poor penitents ... telling them of the Infinite Mercy of God."

Thérèse's reserve was an imitation of the reserve of Christ. It may well be objected that remarkably little of this trait is in evidence. On the contrary, *The Story of a Soul* offers effusions of amazing, and in places embarrassing, candour and detail. The same is true of the letters. The testimony at the trial proves that the three sisters were thoroughly informed, down to small details, about Thérèse's thoughts, feelings, experiences, difficulties, graces and tribulations. They themselves stress this fact again and again. We will remember Pauline's testimony that on her deathbed Thérèse said to her that she knew every wrinkle of her soul. And when Pauline was asked how she knew so precisely her sister's virtues, she replied: "From the spiritual conversations we had on days when speech was permitted, from the *constant communication* of her thoughts which I received, and which I would write down, in so far as I judged them worth recording."

During the inquiries three nuns in addition to the three sisters declared that they had enjoyed special intimacy with Thérèse. Sister Thérèse of St Augustine, who had been the object of her antipathy and self-conquest, testified: "I knew the Servant of God from 1888 to 1897; during this time we lived in a certain intimacy." The lay sister, Martha of Jesus, Thérèse's first companion in the novitiate, stated: "A special intimacy linked us until her death." And finally her novice, Marie of the Holy Trinity, declared: "Our relations were especially close and familiar.... She was always very sweet and very communicative towards me." All three report a whole series of candid utterances by Thérèse on her inner life. The same may be said of the old Novice Mistress, Marie of the Angels. And we must not forget the closeness of Thérèse's relationship with her Prioress, to whom the deepest confessions of the ninth and tenth chapters of the autobiography are addressed. In these chapters Thérèse refers often to many an intimate conversation. "I always try to be an open book to my superiors."

There were, then, at least eight nuns with whom Thérèse frankly discussed her inner life—one out of every three in the convent. Beyond that, there was her correspondence with her relatives outside, and with the two missionaries. In addition, she frequently related her own experiences and emotions to the novices in order to guide them. Her poems, largely confessions of the most intimate sort, were the common property of the Lisieux Carmel and during work were sung to melodies of familiar songs.

Where then was there any room for the reticence and concealment we have said was Thérèse's mark?

In the midst of openness. We must distinguish between a reticence consisting in refusal to speak, and the opaqueness, so difficult to recognize, so elusive, practised by our saint.

The Story of a Soul is from the first to the last page a specimen of this strange, possibly unique compound of detailed statement and strict concealment. The limits of what might be said, and was actually said, were wide—embarrassingly wide to those of our generation and to non-Latins. By French standards, and by those of the devout among themselves, for whom mutual analyses of one another's souls were normal subjects of conversation, they were not out of the ordinary.

Thérèse completely adjusted herself to these limits, never exceeding them in breadth, but only in depth. We have remarked before on the innocuous and unemphatic way she had of mentioning the most important things, whose depth and significance reveal themselves to us only after patient meditation.

It is worth noting the emphasis and unanimity with which the Martin sisters—except for Léonie—assure us that they learned nothing from *The Story of a Soul* that they had not already known. So Pauline: "There is nothing in the manuscript which we were not already familiar with from our intimate conversation." [63] "Reading her story has scarcely added anything to my knowledge of her life." [64] Marie: "I found again in it what I already knew from our life together." [65] Céline: "Reading this actually taught me nothing new; at most, she refreshed my recollection of details that I had forgotten." [66]

At one time Pauline clearly states that Thérèse did not *want* to write anything but the things the sisters already knew. "When I ordered her to write down her memories of childhood, the Servant of God replied: 'What would you want me to write that you do not already know?'" Céline, too, confirms this view (of the first part of the autobiography): "Her manuscript was in fact a family memento, intended exclusively for her sisters." [67] Thérèse's introduction strikes a similar note: "I feel really happy just to be able to tell you, Mother, of all the wonderful things He has done for me. Remember, I am writing the story of the little flower gathered by Jesus, for you alone." That this was her original aim is stressed by the heading of the original manuscript: "Story of the Springtime of a Little White Flower, Written by herself."

It would never have occurred to Thérèse to make literary use of her own spiritual destiny. Her friend Marie of the Holy Trinity at one time considered writing down the story of her vocation and conferred with her young Novice Mistress, Thérèse, saying: "My experiences are so interesting; I should like to write them down in order not to forget them, and it will certainly do me good if I read them over later." But Thérèse would not approve. "Mind you do nothing of the sort. You can't do it without permission, and I advise you not to ask. For myself I should not like to write anything about my life without an express order, and one which I had not solicited. It is more humble not to write anything about oneself. The great graces of one's life, such as one's vocation, can't be forgotten. The memory of those graces will avail you more if you confine yourself to going over them in your mind, than if you write them down." [68]

[63] 1 S., vii, 6.
[64] 1 S., i, 1.
[65] Ibid.
[66] 1 S., i, 4.
[67] 2 S., 786.
[68] 1 S., 132, No. V de Autobiographia S. D., etc.

Shortly thereafter Thérèse received from her Prioress, Pauline, the order to write her memoirs.

It may also be noted that the sisters, in their statements about the saint, make extensive use of Thérèse's own words. Often they literally quote pages from the autobiography, making only insignificant changes. In the testimony of the sisters in particular we scarcely find important additions to the material in *The Story of a Soul*. Only by assembling all available details from the history of the convent, from the obituaries of other nuns, from the memorial on Prioress Marie de Gonzague, and from virtually unnoticed incidental remarks, can we complete the saint's own confession— and see how persistently she kept her own counsel, even with those who were closest to her.

"Go forth and proclaim what glories the Lord has done to you." When this command is issued, we find in many saints the capacity for response with the utmost simplicity and naturalness: "I shall sing the mercy of the Lord for ever." From the inspiration of the Apostolic Epistles to the memoirs of the little nun of Lisieux there rings out the full chorus of those upon whom grace has been showered, who with glorious freedom proclaim the plethora they have received, knowing well that in doing so they are praising the Giver of all gifts, and not the poor vessel that accepts them. This is a chorus of pure hearts who speak of the overflowing wealth that has been confided to them without self-adulation. Not the least of the enchantments of the great mystical confessions lies in this, that they reflect such purity in the confessor.

Thérèse belongs among these. She could say with delightful honesty: "I think I am now too little to be vain." And this applies to her book as well as to her conversation. Rarely did she lift the veil of her own accord. But whenever anyone approached her with a question, whenever her reply could supply a need, clarify a confusion, refresh a weary soul, it was as though a rich vein of crystal water had been struck: transparent, abundant, in a powerful current, her reply bubbled forth. But as soon as the commandment of the moment, and of charity, had been fulfilled, the spring withdrew to its source, in perfect silence once more. Thérèse knew well that everything God produced in her was the property of the Holy Spirit. She called herself a "little bowl" of worthless clay, which the Lord nevertheless filled with food when His creatures were in need of nourishment.

That is the wonder of this candour: that she always observed the invisible limit of her silence, never badly expressed "herself", never falsified the purpose and the privilege of communication. She imparted her treasures, her "lights", as the language of the convent would put it, liberally to her sisters, to the other nuns, to the novices, to her readers. She revealed everything that would help, console, illuminate and support others. Precisely her apparently unlimited candour *when she was asked* formed the perfection of her hidden face. This candour seemed so absolute that no one believed there were things concealed beyond it. "Many pages of this book will never be read."

Thérèse's taciturnity has been questioned from another point of view. Did it not betray, the *Advocatus Diaboli* asked at the trial, a certain contempt for the judgment and opinions of others from which secret pride in knowing better, secret complacency, might be deduced? Did it not spring from a possibly unconscious sense of superiority on the part of a person who thought there was no one like herself, and who therefore preferred to do entirely without advice or instruction? Here the point is often made that Thérèse had no spiritual *directeur*, which many French Catholics regard as indispensable to true progress. The absence of such a director seems to point to concealed haughtiness.

On the other hand, it is established that Thérèse by no means thought she could do without spiritual direction. No less than six priests, with whom she discussed the problems of her soul, testified at the trial; moreover, Father Alexis, with whom she had that decisive conversation during the retreat of 1892, was not present, and several others did not live until the trial. A number of them, confessors and directors of retreats, particularly emphasize how extremely simple and modest Thérèse always was during such conversations; she sought only factual truth and clarity, forgoing all attempts to make herself important. Indeed, "she forgot herself"—something rare enough in such situations. Thérèse regarded the priests whom she applied to solely as the guardians and dispensers of God's mysteries, never as an audience of connoisseurs before whom she wished to display the beauties of her soul, and never as human beings whose personal interest, admiration or sympathy she was wooing. She wanted to learn, wanted to see rightly, and discriminate clearly, wanted to test her illuminations, premonitions and desires against the inflexible standards of the Church. She knew by experience that the ultimate and most important instruction was the one of which it has been said: "I would hear what God the Lord speaks within me." But nothing could have been farther from her thoughts than to oppose an inner voice to the instructions of His ministers who were fulfilling their office. Thérèse could honestly declare: "Jesus has, in fact, been my Spiritual Director too, though I do not mean I never opened my heart to my superiors. Far from concealing what was going on there, I have always tried to be an open book to them." It was a great sorrow to her that the priests from whom she sought guidance did not understand, or did not take seriously, her real problem. She sought for one who would, and suffered painfully because she had so little success in her search. Her own conviction of the rightness of her way did not content her—as it has scarcely ever contented any saint. She continually tried anew as soon as another retreat director or some famous priest came to the convent. The encounter with Father Alexis remained in her memory all her life as an hour of high grace because through him she had, as it were, received the blessing of the Church upon her "little way".

5. THE NOVICE MISTRESS

It appears that Thérèse initially considered the "little way" only as the course incumbent upon her personally. It constituted the series of illuminations vouchsafed to her, and their sum; it was the real story of her soul and the gist of that continual silent instruction within the innermost sanctuary of the soul of which *The Imitation of Christ* speaks so forcefully. The Scriptures were her guardian angel in the desert. She had another: her deep, keen, unshakably composed attentiveness to inner guidance which her soul, hungering and thirsting for righteousness, drew from her conscience, from prayer, and from the most commonplace incidents. "Do not harden your hearts, as they were hardened once in Meriba, at Massa in the wilderness." [69]

"I know from experience that 'the Kingdom of God is within us', that Jesus has no need of books or doctors to instruct our soul. He, the Doctor of Doctors, teaches us without the sound of words. I have never heard Him speak, and yet I know He is within my soul. Every moment He is guiding and inspiring me, and just at the moment I need them, 'lights' till then unseen are granted me. Most often it is not at prayer that they come but while I go about my daily duties." [70]

When she was entrusted with the guidance of the novices, the task imposed upon her the necessity of transmitting the light she had received to others, of directing others along her own way. Thérèse grasped the full extent of her responsibility. It necessitated her rethinking her theory and practice, casting them into a clear form and utilizing them for instruction. Thus her "doctrine" gradually came into being. It must have been developed fairly early, for Thérèse was barely twenty when she received this important assignment. With it there also awoke in her the urge to pass on the greatest of the treasures she had received, first to her beloved sisters, then to the novices in her charge, and at last to the whole world.

[69] Ps 94:8.
[70] S.S., viii.

In a conversation of 16 July[71] Thérèse admits that after her Profession her single ardent desire was to have Céline in the Carmel as soon as possible. "I desired this happiness not from natural impulse, but for her soul's sake, so that she too might travel along my little way." She probably spoke about it first with her sisters, for during the retreat of 1896 she wrote out for Marie, at this sister's express request, that outline of the little way which was inserted into *The Story of a Soul* as the famous eleventh chapter.

Pauline had become Prioress in the spring of 1893. She turned over the office of Novice Mistress to her predecessor, Mother Marie de Gonzague. There were important reasons for doing this, but Pauline was at the same time clearly aware of how little fitted the ex-Prioress was for such a task. She therefore looked for a counterpoise. "I thought I could choose no other course, in order to avert a greater evil. But to minimize as much as possible the harm she might do, I assigned Sister Thérèse to *supervise* her two companions (the lay sisters Martha and Maria Magdalena).... In reality I was counting on Sister Thérèse for the guidance of the novices."[72] That is to say, twenty-year-old Thérèse officially, though secretly, received from her Prioress the assignment to supervise her former Prioress, who was now her immediate superior in the novitiate, to observe her mistakes and if possible to correct them. A more delicate task in such a situation can scarcely be imagined. To make matters worse, the demands upon Thérèse's tact and humility were a hundredfold more complicated because this assignment did not remain between her and Pauline, but somehow became an open secret among those members of the community who disliked Mother Marie de Gonzague. The novices themselves knew quite well, as is evident from many statements, that Mother Marie de Gonzague occupied the office and dignity of Novice Mistress only "for appearance's sake", "titularly", "out of convenience", "out of consideration", "for the sake of peace", "officially", and so on. The novices understood that she "was not able to train the novices properly", and that in all essential matters they were obliged as "inconspicuously and discreetly as possible", "in order not to provoke Mother Marie de Gonzague's jealousy", "in order not to trouble the peace of the community", and "in such a manner as not to encroach on Mother Marie de Gonzague's rights"—to abide by the instructions of young Thérèse.[73]

---

[71] *N.V.*

[72] 2 S., 176.

[73] Statements by Sisters Marie, Céline, Martha, Marie of the Holy Trinity, Mary Magdalene of the Sacred Heart (2 S., 176, 186, 203, 216, etc.).

For three full years Thérèse managed this virtually impossible situation. Her own novitiate, which by custom included, in addition to the one-year postulancy, another two or three years as professed novice, was already over. Mother Agnes, however, let her continue in the novitiate, since the convent maintained a sharp separation between the community proper and the novices, and her moving on to the convent would have put an end to her usefulness.

In the spring of 1896 Marie de Gonzague was once again elected Prioress. To the general amazement and, as can be detected between the lines of the testimony, to the indignation of the community, she retained the office of Novice Mistress. The Rule provides for this in the event that the Prioress finds no suitable sister for the difficult task. As her assistant—in such a situation she is required to have one—she appointed Sister Thérèse. Since 1926 the Carmel Constitutions has stipulated that the Novice Mistress must be at least thirty-five years of age and have had at least ten years since her Profession; her assistant must be at least thirty years of age and have had five years since her Profession. In Thérèse's day there were no edicts of this sort. Yet it can scarcely have been customary to assign this office to the youngest nun in the convent, even though she already counted five years since her Profession. This difficulty was simply solved; Thérèse was left in the novitiate and dubbed "Senior Novice", without being given any other official title.

This is the explanation of the oft-repeated legend of Thérèse's humiliation in the convent (and by Mother Marie de Gonzague) in that she was made to stay among the novices for an unduly long time, was never accorded her rights as a professed nun, and all her life was deprived of a seat and vote in the Chapter, that she "humbly took her place with the novices behind the professed sisters and lay sisters". This alleged humiliation was, on the contrary, the greatest honour that could be accorded her. Everyone in the convent knew that her post presupposed "outstanding intelligence, love, piety and conscientiousness".[74] And Thérèse gratefully appreciated this distinction so unprecedented for a nun of her age. She wrote: "I can't say that Jesus makes me walk the path of outward humiliations; He is quite content to humble me in my inmost soul. I am a success as far as everyone else can see, and, if one may use such an expression with regard to the religious life, I walk the perilous path of honour; and I understand why my Superiors treat me as they do, and why God treats me in the same way. I would be of little use to you, Mother, if everyone thought I was stupid and incapable of doing anything.

---

[74] Rule and Precepts, § 229.

That is why our Divine Master has cast a veil over all my shortcomings, exterior or interior." [75]

Morbid jealousy has been called Mother Marie de Gonzague's besetting sin, and probably she well deserved this reproach. We are therefore struck by her magnanimity in assigning Thérèse the office of Novice Mistress, although not the title, which would have been inappropriate because of her youth. The embarrassing drama of convent diplomacy which was played around her for three years, and in which Thérèse was forced to take the principal role, can scarcely have escaped this clever and crafty woman. For when Mother Agnes tactfully suggested to her that Thérèse "might be useful to her in her task", Mother Marie's own followers would only too eagerly have elucidated the meaning of this "assistance". Nevertheless, at the end of these three years which had been so difficult for both parties, Mother Marie de Gonzague kept Thérèse at her side. That such cooperation was still possible between them is testimony of the Prioress's nobility of character and of the extraordinary deference, tact and modesty with which Thérèse fulfilled her delicate task. It may also be true that the Prioress's difficult temperament later got the better of her, that she had spells in which she demoted and restored Thérèse to her office "every two weeks"; that she grew jealous when Thérèse's influence seemed to her too powerful (at which times she would charge Thérèse with exceeding her authority); that Thérèse often had to carry out the humble service of an assistant in secret; and above all that the novices, with typical feminine pleasure in secrets and complications, "took refuge in a thousand deceptions" in order to enjoy Thérèse's guidance without incurring the wrath of Mother Marie de Gonzague.[76] Nevertheless, Thérèse succeeded in winning and keeping the Prioress's entire confidence. Perhaps, indeed, the whole plan for the particular form of her assistantship came from Thérèse herself. "You have said to me what Jesus said to St Peter: 'Feed my lambs'", she writes in the ninth chapter of *The Story of a Soul*. "*I begged you* to feed them yourself, and to number me among your flock. It was a reasonable request, and you did not entirely refuse it. You made me, not their Novice Mistress, but the senior novice." Thereafter Thérèse laboured hard and fruitfully together with her, for almost two full years, to train the rising generation of Lisieux. With humour and gratitude Thérèse describes their collaboration: "An artist uses many brushes, or two at least. The first and most important is used to sketch the general background, and quickly covers the whole of the canvas, while the second, the smaller one, is used to sketch in detail. I liken you, Mother, to

[75] *S.S.*, x.
[76] 2 *S.*, 210.

the more valuable brush which Jesus lovingly takes up when He has in mind some great work upon your children's souls; I am the very little brush He uses afterwards for minor details." [77] And to Céline she wrote:

> For a long time you have been asking me for news about the novitiate, especially about my work, and now I am going to satisfy you. In my dealings with the novices I am like a setter on the scent of game. The rôle gives me much anxiety because it is so very exacting. You shall decide for yourself if this be not the case. All day long, from morn till night, I am in pursuit of the game. Mother Prioress and the Novice Mistress play the part of sportsmen—but sportsmen are too big to be creeping through the cover, whereas a little dog can push its way in anywhere... and then its scent is so keen! I keep a close watch upon my little rabbits; I do not want to do them any harm, but I lick their fur glossy, and tell them when they look too much like wild rabbits. In fact, I try to make them such as the Hunter would have them, simple little creatures that go on browsing heedless of everything else.
>
> I laugh now, but seriously I am quite convinced that one of these rabbits—you know which one I mean—is worth a hundred times more than the setter; it has run through many a danger, and I own that, had I been in its place, I should have long since been lost for ever in the great forest of the world. [78]

In view of the character of the novices entrusted to her, Thérèse's task could scarcely have been more difficult. We are familiar, of course, with the tendency towards exaggeration throughout Céline's testimony whose whole aim was to glorify her sister. (This was, to be sure, unconscious, as we can see from her naïve declaration: "As far as I am concerned, I would rather she were not beatified at all than that I should represent her any different from the precise way she appears to my conscience." [79]) Probably there is exaggeration here also; Céline's intention is to show the virtues of the young Novice Mistress against the darker background of her charges. Nevertheless, this description must have some basis in reality.

"Sister Thérèse was not spoiled in the selection of her novices; they were far from the quasi-perfection of those who are sent to us today at the intercession of the Servant of God. One was tight-lipped, untamed, and fled from her instructions. Another was untalented and without a real vocation to the Carmel, and the Servant of God appeared to exhaust her energies on her without any seeming result. A third was so hard to teach that she was permitted to remain in the Carmel solely thanks to the

[77] *S.S.*, x.
[78] 19 August 1894.
[79] 2 *S.*, 799.

patience of our young Mistress—and so on. It was in such unprepared soil that she had to labour." [80]

Since we may assume that Céline was including neither herself nor her cousin Marie Guérin in this frank description, we can identify the others with relative accuracy. Among them was that young lay sister who had led a troubled, knocked-about life as a maidservant. She had experienced the squalor and ill treatment which is often the lot of the poor and had suddenly, on the advice of a priest, found herself in Carmel, where she must have had considerable difficulty adjusting herself to the religious life. She is supposed to have been the nun who could not endure Thérèse's gaze.

Another was Marie of the Holy Trinity, who came from the Paris Carmel and later became Thérèse's confidante and friend among the younger nuns. Still another was the much older lay sister Martha who, as she herself relates, asked and *received* the special favour of remaining an unlimited time in the novitiate, because of her attachment to Thérèse. Then there was Marie Guérin, who as a sickly, spoiled child had once imposed upon Thérèse her first schooling in patience and forbearance. We do not know much more about these nuns, but the numerous conversations that have been recorded betray every form and nuance of vanity and touchiness, pettiness and narrow-mindedness, obstinacy and childish immaturity. To be sure, all five, for all their other deficiencies, brought with them enough zeal and resolution to meet the tremendous demands of the Carmel, and they held on. Here was something on which to build. Thérèse's task consisted in shaping this heroic but crude material, in preventing it from growing crookedly, and in conferring upon the general well-intentioned aspiration towards perfection a clear, intelligent and durable form.

The sureness with which this twenty-year-old went to work is indeed astonishing. As Novice Mistress as in so many other things she shows no perceptible development. From the very start she knew what she wanted and how to achieve it. With her balanced nature and her already firmly established humility, the honourable assignment did not at all go to her head. She approached her pupils without any of the overenthusiasm or ebullient confidence of the young, who think nothing simpler than to educate others, convert them and bring them to one's own pitch of perfection.

As soon as I entered the sanctuary of souls, I saw at a glance that the task was quite beyond me, and placing myself in the arms of God, I did what a baby would do if it was frightened; I hid my head on my Father's shoulder,

---

[80] I S., iii, 89.

and said: "You see, O Lord, that I am too little to feed Your children. If You want me to give each one, on Your behalf, just what she needs, then fill my hand, and without leaving Your arms, without so much as turning my head, I will pass on Your riches to those who come to me for food. If they like it, then I shall know it is You, not I, to whom they are indebted; but if they grumble because they find it bitter, I will not fret. I will try to convince them that it comes from You, and take good care to offer them no choice."

The very fact that, left to myself, I could do nothing, made my task seem all the more simple; there was only one thing for me to do, unite myself more and more to God, knowing that He would give me all the rest in addition. This was no vain hope; no matter how often I have to feed the souls of my sisters, my hand is always full. I assure you that had I acted in any other way, had I relied upon my own resources, I should have had to lay down my arms at once.[81]

The following section seems to us to be, once more, couched in the form of confession, veiled instruction to the Prioress herself, to whom the chapter was dedicated. We know the frailties Mother Marie de Gonzague allowed herself especially in her guidance of the nuns; we know how she was wont to interlard conversations with discussion of her own affairs, and how much she tolerated and even fostered the attachments that usually arise from such familiarity. Thus Thérèse continues with full consciousness of her purpose:

Here, as in everything else, I must deny myself and make sacrifices. It is the same with a letter; it will be fruitless, I feel, unless I have had to overcome a certain amount of repugnance, and unless it has been written solely under obedience. Whenever I am talking to one of the novices, I take care to mortify myself by never asking questions out of curiosity. If she begins to talk about something very interesting, then changes the subject to something that does not interest me at all, I never draw her attention to the fact, for I am sure that self-seeking leads to no good.

I know that your lambs think I am very strict, and if they were to read this, they would say that it does not seem to worry me in the least to have to chase after them, and tell them when they soil their lovely fleece, or leave some of their wool caught in the wayside briars. But whatever they say, they know in their hearts that I love them, that there is no danger of my imitating the hireling "who seeth the wolf coming and leaveth the sheep and flieth", I am ready to "lay down my life for them" and I love them with such a pure love that I do not want them to know it. I have never, thanks to God's grace, tried to win their hearts to myself; I know that my task is to lead them to God and to you, Mother.

This is certainly put plainly enough. But how charming is the tact with which she promptly glosses over Mother Marie de Gonzague's faults and

[81] *S.S.*, x.

points the way to righteous peace: "I know that my task is to lead them to God and to you, Mother, His visible representative here below, to whom they owe respect and love."

In the clearest fashion, Thérèse develops the concept of true spiritual direction which is concerned solely with the subject's progress and salvation, and is not undermined by laxity or affection:

> In teaching others, as I have said, I have learnt a lot. I saw from the very beginning that everyone has to go through much the same struggle, though from another point of view there are vast differences between one soul and another; and because they are so different, I can never treat them in the same way. In some cases I have to make myself very small and not be afraid to humble myself by telling them about my own struggles and failures. It is not so hard for them, then, to make known their own faults, and it makes them happier to know that I have learnt all about it from my own experience. In other cases, the only way is to be firm, and never go back on anything; humbling oneself would be regarded as a sign of weakness. I want to do my duty, no matter what the cost, and Our Lord has given me the grace to face everything.
>
> More than once I have heard someone say: "You will have to treat me gently if you want to get anything out of me; if you treat me with severity, you will get nowhere." But I know very well that no one is any judge in his own case, and a child naturally makes a fuss under the surgeon's knife, sure that the remedy is worse than the disease; but he will be delighted at being able to run about and play when he finds, a few days later, that he has been cured. It is just the same with souls; before long, they are quite ready to admit that they would rather have a little bitterness than sugar.

The statements of her "pupils" everywhere confirm this picture. "Her guidance was very energetic", Sister Martha says. "She was extremely alert and had a very sharp eye to see our faults and reprove us. Nothing escaped her. She scolded with great gentleness, but also very firmly; she never showed herself lenient towards our faults, never deviated from something she had once said." We can sense how Thérèse's own training by Pauline served her as basis for her work with these grown-up children. "She was not afraid to displease us and so deprive herself of the popularity and the demonstrations of love which greater latitude towards our faults might have won for her."

Thérèse knew this too. "Kindness must not degenerate into weakness. When we have had good reason for finding fault, we must leave it at that, and not allow ourselves to worry over having given pain. To seek out the delinquent for the purpose of consoling her, is to do more harm than good. Left alone, she is compelled to look beyond creatures, and to turn to God; she is forced to see her faults and humble herself. Otherwise she would become accustomed to expect consolation after a merited rebuke, and would act like a spoilt child who stamps and screams, knowing well that by this means its mother will be forced to return and dry its tears." [82]

"God and Nature do not love tenderly"—these words of Goethe might well be applied to Thérèse's theory of education. It was not easy for her, for she was far more timid than we might imagine from these vigorous principles. "I would rather be corrected a thousand times than correct anyone else once", she remarked. But for all her delicacy, there seems to have been a good measure of healthy hardness hidden within her—that peculiar hereditary sign of good breeding. She knew that she brought a good many difficulties upon herself, but she took these in her stride.

"When staying with my aunt, while I was still a little girl, I was given a certain book to read. In one of the stories great praise was bestowed on a schoolmistress who by her tact escaped from every difficulty without hurting anyone's feelings. Her method of saying to one person: 'You are right', and to another: 'You are not wrong', struck me particularly, and as I read I reflected that I would not have acted in that way because we should always tell the truth. And this I always do, though I grant it is much more difficult. It would be far less trouble for us, when presented with a controversy, to say that the absent person was to blame. Less trouble— nevertheless I do just the contrary, and if I am disliked it cannot be helped. Let the novices not come to me if they do not want to hear the truth." [83]

We can easily understand that the novices at first felt no great affection for Thérèse, or that her pupils' respect was mingled with a certain measure of fear and shrinking. Those who were accustomed to her apparently effortless good nature, her obliging attitude towards every wish and demand, her alertness to any possible service she might do for her fellow nuns, might well have been surprised when she suddenly revealed so different a side to her nature. Some must certainly have interpreted this constant adaptability as servility and lack of fibre; these would have been greatly taken aback by her firmness. At the same time, the very sternness with which she insisted on her method serves us as an important measure of her docility in her relationship towards her sisters in all other respects.

The reports are as unanimous on this score as they are on her charity and obedience. Thérèse did not ask a great deal of the novices, but everything; not sometimes, but all the time; not half-heartedly, but with complete commitment of all their forces. A good many novices were inclined to think they had already performed their feat of heroism by entering the Carmel; they now wanted to rest on their laurels. Girls such as these must have thought they had good reason for resentment, for Thérèse never

[82] *C.S.*
[83] *C.S.*

relaxed her demands upon them; they had to pay a high price to satisfy her. But if her pedagogy did not meet with immediate success, Thérèse was not surprised. She realized from the start what others who plunge wholeheartedly into works of spiritual mercy often realize so late and with such difficulty: that it does not lie within our power really to help another human soul.

"At first sight it appears easy to do good to souls, to make them love God more, and mould them according to one's own ideas, but in practice one finds that one can no more do good to souls without God's help than make the sun shine in the night." [84] And again, in a letter to Céline: [85] "All the finest eloquence of the greatest saints could not bring forth a single act from a heart not possessed by Jesus. Only He can play upon His lyre."

But since she felt that the result was His affair alone, she could proceed boldly and without anxiety: "For my little birds I scatter to right and left the good grain that God puts into my hand, and then I let happen what will; I no longer trouble about it; sometimes it is as if I had sown nothing at all; but God tells me: Go on giving and giving without worrying about anything else." [86]

Given the unregenerate nature of some of her charges, the resistance sometimes assumed drastic forms. One of the novices would hide whenever she was supposed to come to Thérèse's cell for instruction, and the young Mistress had to chase her down in her hiding place. [87] Others displayed open mistrust and bluntly voiced their anger, hostility and rebellion. Since Thérèse's position was not that of one in authority, but only that of a senior novice, they thought they could allow themselves liberties they would never have dared to take with a superior. Thérèse bore all this not only with good humour, but with joy; she felt it as a counterweight to the excessive praise and admiration which rained down upon her from other quarters. She took the outbursts of the novices calmly and gratefully, as graces from God. "One day when I wanted very much to be humiliated, a young postulant happened to gratify my desire to such an extent that I could not help being reminded of the time when Semei cursed David, and I repeated the latter's words to myself: 'Yea, it is the Lord who hath bidden him to say all these things.' "

From the very start Thérèse possessed the prime qualities of a good teacher: infinite patience, lively perseverance, sober judgment which was astonished at nothing, and sincere love free of all fretful pessimism. She

[84] S.S., x.
[85] 13 August 1893.
[86] I S., iv, 316.
[87] 2 S., 278.

noted the smallest success, the smallest effort, on the part of her pupils, and gratefully rejoiced. "In the work of guiding souls," she said in conversation, "we must never simply let things take their course in order to safeguard our own peace; we must fight unwearyingly to win the battle, even if we are without hope. *What does success matter?* If we find a soul obstinate, let us not say: 'There is nothing to be done here; she does not understand anything; we must give her up; I can't cope with it!' Oh, how cowardly it is to talk that way. We must do our duty to the last." [88]

"What costs me most is having to look out for their faults, their slightest imperfections, and then fight against them to the death." But: "I have been like a sentry watching for the enemy from the highest turret of a castle. I miss nothing, and am often amazed that I see things so clearly, while I have every sympathy with the prophet Jonas, who fled before the face of the Lord rather than announce the ruin of Nineveh.... Yet I am convinced that this is as it should be."

Did Thérèse feel the great temptation of almost every professional educator: to assume a superior, critical attitude towards everybody? "Whenever I notice anyone who is not a novice doing anything wrong, I heave a sigh of relief. Thank goodness it is not my business to correct her! I hasten to make excuses for her, crediting her with her undoubted good intentions." [89]

She taught the novices the principles by which she herself lived: to practise charity, to be friendly, hard towards oneself, patient, mild and helpful towards others, to be simple and self-controlled, "to use force smilingly". "She could not tolerate it", Céline says, "when others made a to-do about childish 'sufferings'." Her method sometimes had the vigour and drastic humour we admire in Philip Neri. A sensitive and excessively temperamental novice was apt to burst into tears at the least provocation. Since neither reprimands, resolutions nor penances helped, her young Mistress ordered her to catch her tears in one of the tiny shells Thérèse used in her painting. She might cry a shellful of tears every day, no more, Thérèse said. This little joke helped.

Thérèse was very stern with those who would plume themselves upon their virtue. On a holiday when there was, by exception, dessert, one novice was accidentally passed over by the sister who waited at table. She made a remark about the "mortification" which she had accepted without complaint in the refectory. Thérèse ordered her to go to the kitchen sister at once and ask for the portion she had not received. Ashamed, the novice protested, but Thérèse remained inflexible. "Let that be your

[88] *Esprit*, 98.
[89] *S.S.*, x.

penance. You are not worthy of the little sacrifices God asks of you. He wanted you to do without your dessert; therefore He permitted you to be overlooked. He thought you would be generous enough to accept that—and you disappointed His expectation by putting your claim in a roundabout way."[90]

This same novice tells of how once, during spiritual direction, she boasted of an "act of virtue" she had performed. "It is too bad that you have spoken of this", Thérèse replied. "In consideration of all the illuminations, all the graces, Jesus has granted you, you would have been guilty indeed if you had acted differently. What is your act in comparison to all that He might rightly demand of you? Rather humble yourself by thinking of the many opportunities to practise virtue which you let slip."[91]

After a few months in the convent her beloved sister Céline felt herself to be quite heroic and asked Thérèse to compose a poem in her name, listing her sacrifices and renunciations and, as it were, holding them up to the Lord. Every stanza was to end with "*Rappelle-toi!*—Remember this!" Thereupon Thérèse wrote her longest poem, in precisely the opposite sense: the thirty-six stanzas describe the sufferings of the Lord for the sinful soul and remind the soul: "Remember this!"

But when one of the nuns honestly and without self-importance suffered from her sins and weaknesses, Thérèse respected these feelings and knew how to offer gentle, apt consolation. "Think of how we polish copper; we smear it with mud, with a material that dirties it. Afterwards, when this has been rubbed off, it gleams like gold. You see, temptations are to the soul like this mud; they serve to make the opposing virtues in us gleam."[92] "It is a great trial to have to see the dark side of everything, but that does not depend on you. Do what you can to free your heart from the cares of this world, and above all from creatures, and be certain that Jesus will do all the rest."

6. THE LITTLE WAY OF CHILDREN

But her goal was far deeper and more comprehensive than merely to reconcile the novices to difficulties or wean them from faults. Did Thérèse know that she was teaching her pupils an entirely new ideal of Christian perfection—or rather, though this she surely could not have known, one that had been forgotten for centuries? Sometimes we are inclined to think so, when we catch the faint note of irony with which she contrasts her

[90] 2 S., 710.
[91] Ibid.
[92] 2 S., 504.

"little" soul with the "great souls", those strong, heroic souls who strove to attain a flawless and insurmountable kind of perfection, who sought records in all the virtues. Strove—or perhaps put on display?

She did not have to come to the Carmel to learn this. The insight was the merciful fruit of those strange early years of darkness when she pursued the usual phantom of sanctity until her soul sickened. Then she had perceived that weakness is perfected by grace, redeemed by grace. The letters she wrote as a fifteen-year-old novice to her sister Céline are imbued with the wisdom of an experienced spiritual director: "My dearest sister, Do not let your weakness make you unhappy. When, in the morning, we feel no courage or strength for the practice of virtue, it is really a grace: it is time to lay the axe to the root of the tree, relying upon Jesus alone. If we fall, an act of love will set all right, and Jesus smiles.... You know well that Our Lord does not look so much at the greatness of our actions, nor even at their difficulty, as at the love with which we do them. What, then, have we to fear?" [93] "You are doubtless right—it costs our heart's blood to give Him what He demands. And what a blessing that it does cost it! What happiness, to bear our crosses feebly!... I, who am but a little grain of sand, will set to work without joy, without courage, without strength—and these very incapacities make the task easier for me. I want to labour only with love." [94]

This is a theme Thérèse cannot state too often: "Let us suffer, if we must, with bitterness, without courage. Jesus must have suffered in sadness; would the soul suffer at all without sadness? And we should like to suffer generously, nobly; we should like never to fall. What an illusion!" [95]

Or she replies, when Céline after the first flush of her enthusiasm complains of the cooling of her ardour: "That was only youthfulness; real courage is not this ardour of the moment, in which one desires to set out for the conquest of souls in the teeth of all dangers—dangers only lending more attractiveness to this lovely dream. Being really brave means to long for the cross in the midst of fear, while we are as it were fighting against it, like Our Lord in the Garden of Olives." [96]

At the end of her Carmelite way she would not recant this humble insight: that Jesus did not prefigure "heroism". "It is so consoling to think that Jesus, the divine hero, has felt all our weaknesses and shuddered at the sight of the bitter chalice—that very chalice he had so burningly desired", she wrote to one of her missionaries on 25 December 1895.

[93] 20 October 1888.
[94] 28 August 1889.
[95] 12 March 1889.
[96] 2 S., 395.

And a year later when she was writing for Sister Marie the marvellous letter of instruction which comprises the eleventh chapter of *The Story of a Soul*, and her elder sister had replied in tones of depression and uncertainty because she felt incapable of such lofty dedication, Thérèse wrote to her:

> My desire for martyrdom is as nothing; it is not to that I owe the boundless confidence that fills my heart. Such desires might be described as spiritual riches, which are the unjust mammon, when one is complacent about them as about something great.... These aspirations are a consolation Jesus sometimes grants to weak souls like mine—and there are many such! But when He withholds this consolation, it is a special grace. Remember these words of a holy monk: "The Martyrs suffered with joy, and the King of Martyrs in sorrow." Did not Jesus cry out: "My Father, take this cup from Me"? How can you say that my desires are the mark of my love? I realize that what pleases God in my soul is not that. What pleases Him is to see me love my littleness, my poverty: it is the blind trust which I have in His Mercy.... There is my sole treasure.[97]

"If you bear in peace the trial of being displeasing to yourself, you offer a sweet shelter to Jesus. It is true that it hurts you to find yourself thrust outside the door of your own self, so to speak, but fear not; the poorer you become, the more Jesus will love you." This, too, Thérèse was able to write at sixteen.

"You wish to see the fruits of your efforts," she wrote to Marie Guérin, "and that is just what Jesus wants to hide from you. He likes to regard by Himself the little fruits of virtue which we offer to Him. They console Him."[98]

In the same way she taught the novices: "Offer to God the sacrifice of never gathering any fruit. If He will that throughout your whole life you should feel a repugnance to suffering and humiliation—if He permit that all the flowers of your desires and of your good will should fall to the ground without any fruit appearing, do not repine. At the hour of death, in the twinkling of an eye, He will cause fair fruits to ripen on the tree of your soul."[99]

"I beg you to understand me", the wonderful letter to Marie Guérin, quoted above, continues. "Do understand me: the more wretched and the weaker we are, the more suitable we are to love Jesus, to be the victim of His love. The mere desire to be His holocaust suffices; but we

---

[97] 17 September 1896.
[98] *Esprit*, 140.
[99] C.S.

must consent to remain always poor and powerless. And you see, that is where the difficulty lies, for: 'Who will find the man truly poor in spirit? He must be sought far away', says the *Imitation of Christ*. It does not say that He is to be found among the 'great souls', but far away, that is to say, in lowness, in nothingness. Let us stay far from everything that glitters; *let us love our littleness; let us love feeling nothing*, and Jesus will come to fetch us, no matter how far away we may be, and He will reshape us in the flames of Love."

This doctrine, this basic truth of the Gospel—that nearness to God grows not out of our fullness in righteousness, but out of the receptive emptiness of our poverty—emerges even more clearly from an early letter to Marie Guérin, which already contains a precise commentary on the teaching of St Paul: "You are mistaken if you think I walk the way of sacrifice with enthusiasm. I am weak, very weak, and every day I experience this weakness afresh, to my profit. But it pleases Jesus to teach me the art of *boasting of my weakness*. That is a great grace, for in this behaviour peace of heart is to be found." [100]

"I am quite resigned, now, to seeing myself always imperfect, and I even make it my joy", she announces in the seventh chapter of *The Story of a Soul*. That is no thoughtless, empty phrase sprung from obligatory humility; Thérèse put this disposition into practice.

"It is probably true that I am not always faithful, but I do not lose courage on that account; I throw myself into Our Lord's arms, and He teaches me 'to draw profit from everything, from the good and from the evil He finds in me' [101]." "I give way to many weaknesses, but I *rejoice* in them." (In *Novissima Verba* this last phrase is given as: "I am never surprised at them.") "I cannot always raise myself above earthly trivialities—but then I withdraw into myself and tell myself: 'Oh, so I am still taking the first step—as always!' But I think this with great sweetness and without sadness. It is so pleasant [*consoling?*] to feel oneself little and weak." [102]

Let us not misconstrue these last words as meek sentimentality; their true content comes into view only when measured against the unfailing, iron self-conquest of her whole life: it is the miracle of God's omnipotence. Supported by it, weakness can take one step at a time and no more, always supported by hope, always taking the one step, until at the end of her life Thérèse could say: "I believe that since the age of three I have never refused Our Lord anything."

[100] Letter 87, July 1890.
[101] St John of the Cross.
[102] *C.S.*, 5 July 1897.

"He has exalted the lowly ... and sent the rich away empty-handed." [103] But such lowliness must be real; it must be recognized by others as well as by ourselves, otherwise it may easily lead to self-deception.

"The thought *nourishes me* that Sister X finds me without virtue", Thérèse said after an unjust reproof. "And I am happy that I seem so to myself also." [104]

A novice spoke of her desire for more strength and energy with which "to practise virtue". "And suppose God wishes to have you as feeble and powerless as a child?" Thérèse countered. "Do you think that would be less worthy in His eyes? Consent to stumble, or even to fall, at every step, to bear your cross feebly; love your weakness. Your soul will draw more profit from that than if, sustained by grace, you vigorously performed heroic deeds which would fill your soul with self-satisfaction and pride." In her inexorable hunting down of religious and ethical vanity, the saint went so far that she even preferred her "victories" to turn out to be partial and inadequate ones. For then, instead of thinking back upon them with a sense of pride, she would experience a certain humiliation at not having fought well enough. [105]

"Let us take our place humbly among the imperfect ones; let us consider ourselves little souls whom God must support from moment to moment. As soon as He sees us thoroughly convinced of our littleness, He extends His hand to us; but as long as we wish to perform great deeds on our own account, even though our pretext is zeal, He lets us alone."

A novice bemoaned her own clumsy, awkward manner and envied others—perhaps Thérèse herself—for their tact. "Whenever you feel this temptation, pray as follows: 'My God, I rejoice that I have no fine and delicate feelings, and I rejoice to find them in others.' That will be more pleasing to God than if you were always irreproachable."

Céline envied Thérèse her good memory for Scriptural passages. "Oh, now you want to possess riches again. To wish to support oneself on such things means to seek support on red-hot iron—a little scar will always remain afterwards."

Here, wholly fresh, springing up out of the depths of her own being, was resurrected the wonderfully liberating, redeeming wisdom of the great Bishop of Geneva, St Francis de Sales, who two and a half centuries earlier founded the most human and natural school of piety: "I would praise my Creator with the face which He gave me."

---

[103] Lk 1:52, 53.
[104] *Esprit*, 135, souv. inédits.
[105] *Esprit*, 135, souv. inédits; 2 S., 414.

Is not the practice of such a doctrine the death of all grand and glorious aspirations? Is this not the smuggest kind of acceptance of one's own limitations, where instead we should make the effort to overcome them by action? We already know enough of Thérèse's exercise of love and suffering not to take such an objection seriously. We know how intensely her life was given to the performance of duty, to the pursuit of good works, to the cultivation of all the virtues. In these respects she was surpassed by none. Only—and this "only" contains all—her justification and evaluation of action was new. With strict and unsparing clarity, Thérèse rejected all ascetic efforts which were directed not towards God but towards one's own "perfection" and were therefore nothing but spiritual beauty—culture. A large part of the fear of sin in devout persons is just such disguised narcissism of the soul: the tiniest sin is unbearable because it is a blotch upon the precious self, a sign of inadequate performance in self-sanctification, evidence of a remnant of earthliness. And in order that this vanity may not become ridiculous, the person must enormously exaggerate his own faults, screw himself up into the interesting hero of a tragedy of guilt—when all the while he has been guilty of only ordinary failures. Even while shuddering over the imaginary depths of his iniquity, he enjoys his own complicated personality. "The penitence that depresses us comes from vanity; penitence from God lifts our courage."

It was on this view, then, that Thérèse based her extraordinary refusal to consider her daily faults important—an attitude virtually unheard-of in devout circles. Because of her great conception of God, and her lack of illusions in her view of human beings, she assigned to these things no more significance than they deserved. How well she knew, having once been so obsessed by scruples herself, that stupefied circling around the real and imaginary wounds in the soul, that overwrought, incessant measuring, counting, calculating, touching and examining one's own "perfection", that most dangerous distraction of attention from God to the ego under the pretext of tender conscience, and even humility. All that was, she knew, confusion, darkening and even untruth. Even between human beings who love one another such conduct is forced and, ultimately, false. "I have long believed that the Lord is more tender than a mother, and I know more than one mother's heart to the very bottom. I know that a mother is always ready to forgive trivial, involuntary misbehaviour on the part of her child.... Children are always giving trouble, falling down, getting themselves dirty, breaking things—but all this does not shake their parents' love for them."

Even at fourteen Thérèse had sensed that two such incompatible facts as the ineradicable weakness of man and the unapproachable holiness of God could not be reconciled by victorious human effort alone, by trying to attain a dubious ideal of "worthiness" in the sight of God. There had to be another way. She had, after all, experienced during the difficult years of growing out of childhood how little all our own efforts can achieve, even with the best intentions. Now a solution of unprecedented boldness began to dawn upon her. "Jesus could give me the grace no longer to offend Him, or to commit only faults which cause Him no sorrow, but serve merely to humble me and strengthen my love", she wrote to Pauline in 1890.[106]

What may Thérèse have meant by that? Her most intimate experience with God led her to conclude that there are some faults for which man is not wholly responsible, springing as they do from the weakness of his nature and the limitations of his ability and freedom, faults which are unintentional. She concluded that love acts as an antidote, so to speak, to faults that it cannot entirely eliminate. Jansenism recognized no such distinction. It trained the conscience to ascribe the whole burden of every objective infraction to personal culpability, and to measure this guilt against the holiness of God. It did not pose the question of how much the person at fault loved God. This school of thought may have influenced the priests whom Thérèse was permitted to consult about her "great problem". Thus it is understandable that for years she met with no understanding and received no support for her point of view. At retreats and spiritual conferences, Thérèse had to hear again and again how easy it is to fall into mortal sin, even by a mere thought. "Throughout these days of retreat I saw her pale and upset; she could neither eat nor sleep, and would have fallen ill if the retreat had lasted any longer", Pauline reports. "It seemed to her that it must, after all, be very difficult really to offend God when we love Him."

At last, in the summer of 1892, Thérèse found in Father Alexis, a Franciscan from Caen, her long-sought, ardently wished-for supporter. It is no doubt significant that he was a popular missionary who was reputed to know more about "great sinners" and ignorant lay folk than about devout nuns and "perfect" souls. This may mean that, engaged in pastoral care as he was, he understood more about genuine human problems, about the reality of sin and atonement, than many a specialist who dabbled in techniques of perfection for advanced students of sanctity.

"I had been undergoing all sorts of interior trials at this time, which I could not explain to anyone; yet here was someone who understood me perfectly, as though inspired by God, and my soul opened out completely. He launched me full sail upon that sea of confidence and love

[106] 2 S., 255.

which had attracted me so much, but on which I had never dared to set out. *He told me that my little faults did not cause God sorrow,* and added: 'At this moment I stand in His place as far as you are concerned, and on His behalf I assure you that He is very satisfied with your soul.' "

Thérèse's happiness was complete. For four years she had groped her way along in doubt and uncertainty. "No one had ever told me before that faults did not pain God; this assurance filled me with joy, and made it possible to bear my exile patiently. My inmost thoughts had been echoed!" [107]

In the document of her *Oblation to Merciful Love* we find this thought again: "If through weakness I should chance to fall, may a glance from Your Eyes straightway cleanse my soul, and consume all my imperfections—as fire transforms all things into itself."

From this insight it was only a short step to the question of the necessity (the necessity! we are not concerned here with other considerations) of frequent confession. Then, as now, the nuns were required to make weekly confession; the more zealous made even more frequent use of the confessional. We do not know whether Thérèse did more than pose this question in her thoughts; no word of hers on the subject has come down to us. Perhaps she felt that the institution was too firmly established and too much taken for granted. Nevertheless, her conception of the matter points to a direction from which sooner or later conclusions must be drawn. It is clear enough from many of her opinions that she did not hold with timid shrinking from the Holy Eucharist on account of small faults; she was convinced that the miracle of forgiveness of sins to faithful and loving souls was constantly taking place. "If we accept with meekness the humiliation of our failure, divine grace returns instantly." [108] "The most important plenary indulgence is that which everyone can obtain without the ordinary forms: the indulgence of charity which covers a multitude of sins." [109]

Out of the very awareness that man is hopelessly bound by his natural limitations, that no man can leap over his own shadow, arose the tremendous "nevertheless" of her confidence in God's sanctifying powers. For this self as it is, this poor, limited, often utterly unbearable self is the very object God uses to reveal His omnipotence.

"We can never expect too much of God, who is at once merciful and almighty", she said—although by this famous utterance she did not mean that every prayer for the accomplishment of little desires would be heard.

[107] *S.S.*, viii.
[108] *N.V.*, 2 September.
[109] *Esprit*, 85.

"To surrender to love means to depend upon the omnipotence of God."
God will bear us on eagle's wings; God will take us home to Himself.
Thérèse was particularly fond of this image.

> My only Friend, why not reserve such boundless aspirations to great souls,
> souls like eagles, who can wing their way to the stars? I am no eagle, only
> a little fledgling which has not yet lost its down, yet the eagle's heart is
> mine, and the eagle's eyes, and despite my utter littleness I dare to gaze
> upon the Sun of Love, burning to take my flight to Him. I long to fly and
> imitate the eagles, but all I can do is flutter my small wings. I am not
> strong enough to fly.
>
> What will become of me? Must I die of sorrow at finding myself so
> helpless.... You, my Saviour, You are the Eagle whom I love; and it is
> You, the Eternal Word, who draw me on; You who flew down to this land
> of exile, to suffer and die, that You might bear all souls away and plunge
> them deep into the bosom of the Blessed Trinity, the eternal home of
> Love.... O Jesus, I know that for You the saints have done foolish things
> as well as wonderful ones, for they were eagles. I, however, am too little to
> do great things, and my foolishness lies in hoping that Your love accepts
> me as a victim; it lies in counting on the angels and saints to help me, my
> beloved Eagle, to fly to You on Your own wings.
>
> For as long as You wish, I will stay with my eyes fixed on You, longing
> to be fascinated by Your divine gaze, longing to be the prey of Your love.
> Some day, this is my hope, You will swoop upon me and carry me off to
> the furnace of love, and plunge me into its glowing abyss.[110]

The same attitude is expressed in the well-known passage from the ninth
chapter of *The Story of a Soul*, addressed to Mother Marie de Gonzague
in June 1897.

> You know that I have always wanted to be a saint; but compared with real
> saints I know perfectly well that I am no more like them than a grain of
> sand trodden beneath the feet of passers-by is like a mountain with its
> summit lost in the clouds.
>
> Instead of allowing this to discourage me, I say to myself: "God would
> never inspire me with desires which cannot be realized, so in spite of my
> littleness, I can hope to be a saint. I could never grow up. I must put up
> with myself as I am, full of imperfections, but I will find a little way to
> Heaven, very short and direct, *an entirely new way.*"
>
> We live in the age of inventions now, and the wealthy no longer have to
> take the trouble to climb the stairs; they take a *lift* [an elevator]. That is
> what I must find, a *lift* to take me straight up to Jesus, because I am too
> little to climb the steep stairway of perfection.
>
> So I searched the Scriptures for some hint of my desired lift until I came
> upon these words from the lips of Eternal Wisdom: "Whosoever is a little
> one, let him come to Me."... Your arms, My Jesus, are the lift which will
> take me up to Heaven.

[110] S.S., xi.

This often-cited comparison sounds one of the saint's favourite motifs: the image of the little child. At this point we must once more listen attentively and distinguish carefully; otherwise we shall be sorely troubled. Are we to wish Christians to model their characters exclusively upon the example of a little child? Does not this deny the earnestness, the dignity, the maturity, which are after all part and parcel of our picture of Christian living? Is there not an element of immaturity, light-headedness, coyness, creeping into Thérèse's doctrine at this point? We even find her saying: "Even poor people give a child everything it needs; but when it grows up the father no longer wants to support it, and says to it: 'You can stand on your own feet now; go out and work.' You see, that is just what I never wanted to hear; that is why I never wanted to grow up, since I felt myself incapable of earning my own livelihood, *of earning eternal life by my own efforts.*"

The final clause is the telling one; that makes us realize that here is no infantile "escape to childhood", no flight into an artificially maintained helplessness, no shirking of the difficulties of adult life. Thérèse speaks in figures, or rather, uses one figure in place of another, and her metaphors should not be taken literally. A small child is in fact incapable of earning its living; a grown man, an adult Christian, is equally incapable of earning eternal life by his own efforts. The metaphor of the child refers only to the spiritual, not to the physical, reality. Thérèse was thoroughly aware of this distinction. She remarks elsewhere quite matter-of-factly: "The Innocents in Heaven are not children; they only have the inexpressible charm of childhood. We imagine them as children only because we need images in order to understand invisible things." And her poem on the little martyrs of Bethlehem then makes exuberant, intensive use of metaphor. Underlying all her examples of "spiritual childhood" is Jesus' word: "Unless you become as little children..." just as her doctrine is everywhere based upon the Scriptures.

"Sometimes, when I read books in which perfection is put before us with the goal obstructed by a thousand obstacles, my poor little head is quickly tired. I close the learned treatise, which wearies my brain and dries up my heart, and I turn to the Sacred Scriptures. Then all becomes clear and light—a single word opens out infinite vistas, perfection appears easy, and I see that it is enough to acknowledge our nothingness, and like children surrender ourselves in the arms of God. Leaving to great and lofty minds the beautiful books which I cannot understand, still less put into practice, I rejoice in my littleness, because only little children and those who are like them shall be admitted to the Heavenly Banquet." [111]

---

[111] Letter 203, to Père Roulland, 9 May 1897.

"To remain little means to recognize one's nothingness, to expect everything from God, not to worry too much about one's faults; in a word, not to wish to lay up treasures in Heaven, and to keep an untroubled heart."

"To be little also means not to ascribe to oneself the virtues one practises, not to think oneself competent, but to recognize that God places this treasure in the hand of His little child for it to use when it has need. Finally, it means not to lose courage on account of one's faults, for children often fall, but they are too small to hurt themselves seriously."

As we see, being a child was for Thérèse only another phrase for that time-honoured goal of spiritual aspiration which other teachers have called spiritual poverty or tranquillity. But in her time the purity and simplicity of this concept had been so overladen by an accumulation of debris that even those closest and most faithful to her repeatedly misunderstood her. Just six weeks before her death the most intimate of her sisters noted: "I said to her: 'How much you must have had to struggle to arrive at the degree of perfection in which we now see you!' She replied in an indescribable tone: 'Oh... that is not it at all!' And somewhat later she said: 'Sanctity does not consist in these or those exercises and achievements; it consists in a disposition of the heart which allows us to remain small and humble in the arms of God, knowing our weakness and trusting to the point of rashness in His fatherly goodness.'"

"Oh! when I think of all I have to acquire!" a novice sighed.

"Or rather to lose!" Thérèse replied. "It is Jesus who takes upon Himself to fill your soul to the degree that you rid it of imperfections. I see clearly that you are mistaking the road, and that you will never arrive at the end of your journey this way. You want to climb the mountain, whereas God wishes you to descend it. He is awaiting you in the fruitful valley of humility." [112]

Again and again she took issue with the false ideal of flawless perfection, which can only be achieved at the cost of self-deception. "It is sufficient to humble ourselves, to endure our own faults with meekness. That is true sanctity. If there were not often something offensive to God in our faults, we would have to commit them deliberately in order to remain humble." [113]

---

[112] C.S.

[113] I S., xvii, II. A contemporary of our saint, the ecstatic lay sister at the Carmel of Pau and later in the Holy Land, the young Arab girl Miriam of Abellin, said similar things in her states of ecstasy. "In hell every virtue may be found, excepting humility;... in Heaven every sin, excepting pride."—"There are saints who became holy through pride, for they painfully fought it all their lives.... Everything comes from pride.... But it is a

Is it not piercingly clear from such words that a certain type of ambition for "self-sanctification" is nothing but the ultimate disguise of the old temptation in Paradise: to be like God? All the saints have been aware of this. Why do we see, in reading the lives of saints, primarily the things that increase our vanity instead of leading us to the truth about ourselves and God? "I entrust to Jesus my failings; I tell Him all about them; and I think, so bold is my trust, that in this way I acquire more power over His heart and draw to myself in still greater abundance the love of Him who came to call the sinners, not the righteous." [114]

For He alone is our sanctification. The work of His grace in us, the growth of divine life in the soul, the mysterious reshaping and growth to maturity in Christ, takes place silently and invisibly, like the slow germination of a seed, continuing day and night but removed from the prying eye and the irreverent clutch of curiosity. "Power is none but comes to you from the Lord, nor any Royalty but from One who is above all. He it is that will call you to account for your doings, with a scrutiny that reads your inmost thoughts", says the Book of Wisdom (6:4).

"The little ones will be judged with the greatest leniency", Thérèse paraphrases and explains this Biblical passage. "It is easy to please Jesus, to delight His heart; it is necessary only to love Him, without paying too much attention to our own faults.... A glance at Jesus and recognition of our own wretchedness makes all well again." [115]

"I know that certain spiritual directors advise us to count acts of virtue, in order to progress in perfection." How diligently Thérèse had practised this traditional method as a child. "But my Spiritual Director, who is Jesus, teaches me not to count my acts; He teaches me to do everything out of love."

Even the incessant struggle against our own bad tendencies should not be fought "in order to weave our crown, to acquire merit and win virtues", nor even "so that we may become saints", but solely "to give joy to Jesus".

Here again was the veil, now shielding what belonged to God, not only from the curiosity or admiration of others, but from her own view. "I know that many saints have passed their lives in the practice of amazing penance for the sake of expiating their sins. But what of that? 'In My

---

great grace when we have a defect to combat; that is a great grace."—"God forgives every slip to a soul which has humility. In Heaven the most beautiful trees are those that have sinned most; they have used their paltrinesses like a heap of fertilizer surrounding the foot of the trunk" (B. Stolz, O.S.B., *Miriam von Abellin*, Bigge-Ruhr, 1929, Josephsdruckerei).

[114] *Esprit*, 144, notes inédites.

[115] *Esprit*, 185; unpublished letter to Céline.

Father's house there are many mansions.'[116] . . . I try to be in no way concerned about myself and leave to Jesus what He deigns to accomplish in my soul."[117]

When we suffer too much "from ourselves", we ought simply to look the other way. "When we see our misery we do not like to look at ourselves, but only upon our Beloved. . . . God does not force us to stay in our own company. He often sees to it that this company is so unpleasant to us that we leave it. And I see no other way for us to get away from ourselves than to visit Jesus and the Blessed Virgin, by hastening to works of love."[118]

No petty book-keeping with regard to our own prayers and good works for others is required; we need not try to determine of our own accord who will receive the benefit of this or that prayer and sacrifice.

"How do you arrange your spiritual life now?" the nuns asked her when she lay ill. "My spiritual life as a patient? Why, that is very simple: I suffer, that is all. I cannot force myself to say: 'O my God, this is for the Church, this is for France', and so on. God knows quite well what He ought to do with my merits; I have given them all to Him for His pleasure. And then, it would tire me out spiritually if I were to say continually: 'Give this to Peter, give this to Paul.' I only do that hastily if a sister expressly asks me to, and then I think no more about it."

The Little Way, too, must remain true to itself; it too can be falsified and twisted. Thérèse seems to have foreseen this possibility, to have anticipated the ruses by which it could be recast into a "great" and "greatest" way, and thus be made thoroughly suspect in the eyes of many persons. For it is easy to distort this doctrine in such a way as to indicate that the Little Way is "really" the great way, little souls "really" the holiest, little works "really" world-shaking ones. "For the rest, Eternity will bring all to light, while we here go about like the children of kings in the guise of servants." That is spiritual equivocation.

No, Thérèse meant what she said. Let us recall her words about scattering flowers, which have been so often misrepresented. Everything remains what it is, large or small. The fledgling is by no means an eagle in disguise, not even an ugly duckling which will some day be revealed as a swan. Little souls are by no means supermen, geniuses going incognito through a dulled world and basking in the fact of their glory which is known only to themselves and a few initiates. The insatiable human desire to reduce those above to one's own level is fraught with danger; it

---

[116] Jn 14:2.
[117] Letter 203, to Père Roulland, 9 May 1897.
[118] Letter to Marie Guérin, 1894.

can no more be done than to assume that we are already on the level of those above us. One cannot arrive at this counterfeit equality without self-deception and hypocrisy. If it were indeed possible, it would mean annihilation of the glory of creation, which depends upon variety and hierarchies.

"I saw that if every little flower wished to be a rose, nature would lose her spring adornments, and the fields would be no longer enamelled with their varied flowers." So Thérèse begins the story of her soul.

"The great saints have laboured for the glory of God, but I who am only a very little soul work solely to give Him joy. I want to be a little flower in the hand of God, a useless rose whose appearance and fragrance nevertheless refresh Him, provide Him with a small, superfluous pleasure. And I should be happy to endure the worst torments if they served to make Him smile, even just once." [119]

Heaven will *not* provide the kind of overcompensation that servile humility expects. "When a gardener makes a bouquet, he always finds little gaps between the splendid flowers; to fill out these gaps and prettily round off the whole bouquet, he sticks moss in between. You see, that is what I will be in Heaven: a little sprig of moss among the glorious flowers God has there."

This very littleness was the sturdy base of the serene assurance with which Thérèse proclaimed the overflowing grace of Him who performed great wonders for her. "I am now too little to still be vain; I am certainly too little to coin fine phrases in order to give rise to the impression that I am very humble. Rather I prefer to confess very simply that He who is Mighty has wrought for me His wonders, and the greatest of all is that He has shown me my littleness, my inability to do any good by myself."

And yet, out of this confession of littleness there suddenly breaks forth what had for so long been prepared within her soul: the consciousness of her messsage.

"If only, my Jesus, I could tell all little souls about Your ineffable condescension. I feel that if, supposing the impossible, You could find a soul more weak than mine, You would delight in lavishing upon it far more graces still, so long as it abandoned itself with boundless confidence to Your infinite mercy!"

But as yet a clear awareness of her mission was still lacking: "But why this desire to tell others the secrets of Your love? Can You not, Yourself, reveal to others what You have revealed to me? I know You can, and I beg You to do so; I implore You, cast Your eyes upon a multitude of little

---

[119] *Esprit*, 9, souv. inédits; *N.V.*, 16 July.

souls; select from this world, I beg of You, a legion of little victims worthy of Your love!"

It was only on her sickbed that Thérèse perceived that she was destined to help lead little souls upon her way by more than such pleas alone. But from the above passage—the last sentences in the eleventh chapter of *The Story of a Soul*—it is already evident that Thérèse understood as a task what she had hitherto thought of only as a personal grace.

Who are the multitude? The term "little souls" must still be analysed, for it is ambiguous and elusive, above all because Thérèse sometimes used it in deliberate contradistinction to the desire for greatness, and sometimes used it in a more sweeping sense. Each time the difference in her usage of the term somewhat alters the content and the extent of its meaning.

At one time "little souls" are the great majority of believers, "all those who are not led by extraordinary ways". Then, more narrowly, it refers to all those who do not by nature incline to extraordinary feats, who are—we hazard the dreaded phrase—average men of good will. Finally, and in this last construction the scale suddenly tips the other way and the pan holds only a minority who are anything but average, those who have recognized their nothingness before God, who joyfully consent to it and in spite of it, indeed because of it, expect great graces from God. These, then, are souls who are capable of and called to the absolute devotion of sacrificial victims.

Perhaps Thérèse would bridge the apparently serious discrepancy between the first and the third meaning by saying that the first group contains all those who ought to and could walk the Little Way, the third those who really pursue it to the end. In the same way; a saint is not a being of a different order from the "ordinary" Christian, but is rather the term of growth to which he tends.

The prototype of the little souls is Mary, the Blessed Virgin. In her, to be sure, we are infinitely far from all ordinariness, and the term "littleness" in her case seems to express only the veil of sacred reticence which like the magic cap of fable makes her invisible to the eyes of the uninitiated. On the other hand, however, we know how earnestly Thérèse meant everything she perceived and said about Mary's humility. She understood how intensely the Magnificat is truly the prayer of little souls:

> O Virgin full of grace, you lived in Nazareth,
> I know content in lowly poverty;
> O Queen of the elect, your life was not enriched
> By raptures, miracles, and ecstasies.

Hence countless little souls upon this earth of ours
Lift up their eyes to you in confident appeal,
For it has pleased you, O Mother unsurpassed,
To be their guide upon the common road to Light.

Thus Thérèse was really speaking of the Blessed Virgin, and yet at the same time speaking of "everyone", of all the baptized upon whom God lavishes His gifts because He is God, almighty and merciful, not because one person or another is "religiously endowed" or otherwise worthy of being chosen.

"I have understood that Our Lord's love can be revealed just as well in the simplest soul as in the sublimest, if it does not offer resistance to His grace."

Thus Thérèse's message is truly a message to Christendom, and not to any restricted group of religious communities. It is directed towards the ardent heart which is consumed by passionate yearnings for greatness, by *désirs immenses*, which becomes stilled in the presence of God, and through renunciation is awakened and rewarded with unimaginable abundance. Equally, it was directed towards the anxious, inhibited, naturally limited people who possess neither *élan* nor ardour, but whose trust in God is firm as a rock, who believe that He will perform the work of their transformation in Christ, by day or night, whether he wake or sleep, so long as he follows Thérèse's simple advice: "When I can feel nothing, when I am altogether arid, I seek tiny occasions, real trivialities, to give joy to my Jesus: a smile, for example, or a friendly word, when I would rather be silent and look bored."

Her message is for the penitent. Whatever his experience of sin may have been, aberrant and grotesque, or wretched and banal, he may, through her, obtain true insight into his own "value" and an understanding of God's mercy, and henceforth continue on his way awed and grateful, ashamed and hopeful. Her message is for the innocent child who has not yet been touched by the breath of evil, and who on the "little way" daily receives back again and learns to cherish as an unmerited, blessed gift, its own goodness.

Her message is for monks and nuns, to shake them from the complacency of routine observance, from the conceit of works and merit, and to recall them to the true Gospel attitude of the unprofitable servant, to lead them back to the austere, purifying school of incorruptible love.

Her message gives joy to the Christian in the world, who has neither the time, the strength nor the desire for complex cultivation of the soul, and who nevertheless receives through her assurance that the poor in spirit who gladly affirm their poverty, without making a virtue of necessity, will be showered with goods.

We have pointed out more than once that our saint's doctrine is in itself neither new nor original. Its relation to the main stream of French, and thus Occidental, Catholic spirituality is that of a solitary late product of the classical mystic doctrine of the Oratory and of the seventeenth-century French Carmel. The very expression "the little way" can be found in the writings of the Carmelite Margaret of the Blessed Sacrament of Beaume. The biography of her exemplar, Catherine of Jesus (who died in 1627), written by her Prioress, begins with a dedication to the Queen of France by Cardinal Bérulle, founder of the French Oratory: "The Greatest of the Great has created small and great.... I speak to Your Majesty of littleness, *in honour of the little soul* whose life is dedicated to you." Margaret of Beaume deliberately calls herself the "little person", not only because of her arrested growth, which had left her no bigger than a child; she calls herself the bride of the Child in the Crib, and pronouncedly derives her mode of devoutness from littleness.[120]

The great Cardinal Bérulle, and his possibly still greater disciple Condren, preached the "spirit of childlikeness"—which was to be not so much the "spirit of the Child Jesus" as the spirit of "one of the little ones whom Jesus let come unto Him". It consisted in the "spirit of self-annihilation", detachment from all earthly things, mortification of self-will and all the inclinations to pride which are flattered by "accomplishments". Those who surrender themselves to such childhood must cease to be guided by their self-will and let the spirit of Jesus Christ fill and impel them. They must cease to be "self-belonging". Yet this attitude is not so much a tense, militant one, whose object is violence towards the self; it is not a stifling of the self, not negation, but the gentle, relaxed, peaceful abandonment of the child in its mother's arms. It is innocence rather than conscious forgetfulness of self; it banishes all the toil and fret of spiritual ambiguities, in order not to turn back to itself and seek itself in vanity, rancour or sorrow over what one has done or said, over praise or blame received, over evils seen or heard.

"The childhood of Our Lord teaches us the annihilation of our ego, obedience to God, silence, innocence without self-assertion, but with the tranquil yielding of a child to grace. The soul no longer asserts itself to attain anything, but on the contrary annihilates itself and lets itself be led, in littleness and simplicity, with pure and trusting gaze. This loss of the self's will is still another peculiarity of Christian childlikeness; symbol of it is the natural behaviour of children who trouble about nothing, abandoning themselves entirely to the care which their parents devote to them."

[120] Bremond, III, 358 ff.

Thus did the Cardinal's disciples expound the spirit of childlikeness; we might add many further examples from those assembled by Bremond in his third volume. The similarity to the doctrine of Thérèse of Lisieux is perfectly obvious.

Bérulle had as his confessor St Francis de Sales, whose convents preserved most faithfully the spirit of enlightened docility and serene simplicity which was rapidly to evaporate from the eighteenth century on. It need not surprise us, then, that the Visitation nuns were among the first to accept the new saint with gladness, although possibly also with some feeling that all the excitement over her was somewhat superfluous, and that to them at least she had nothing essentially new to say. During the preliminary investigation Léonie, a nun of the Order of the Visitation, remarked: "In all our convents Sister Thérèse is greatly revered; that is not surprising, since the spirit of her piety is *entirely ours* and that of our founder, St Francis de Sales." [121]

If we remember that the two oldest Martin girls, who so decisively shaped Thérèse's fundamental religious attitudes, were pupils at a convent of the Visitation, and that to the end of her life Thérèse regarded Pauline as her spiritual guide and "ideal in all things", we may well ask how strong a part this tradition played in her development, not directly, but by inspiring a general attitude towards life. On the other hand, we observe from their testimony in general that the two elder sisters, with a fine humility, always felt themselves to be the disciples of their younger sister. Never, in any of the published material, is there the slightest indication that they recognized ideas they had earlier transmitted.

Thérèse, too, nowhere reveals any consciousness of her indebtedness to older sources. Had she had the slightest pretext, she would certainly have appealed, with eager gratitude and conscientious devotion, to the authority of her own beloved sisters. But she unquestionably felt herself to be the advocate of something new, and she thanked her sisters rather for the confidence with which they accepted and supported her untried venture.

"Who taught you your little way of love?" Marie of the Holy Trinity asked her. "She replied to me: 'Jesus alone instructed me; not a single book, not a single theologian, has taught it to me; and yet I know from the bottom of my heart that my way is truth. I have received encouragement from no one but Mother Agnes and Jesus. When the opportunity came to open my heart, I was so little understood that I said with St John of the Cross: "Send me no more messengers who cannot tell me what I

---

[121] I S., xx, 82.

wish to know." ' " [122] It is noteworthy that no mention of Father Alexis is made here. Since Marie of the Holy Trinity did not enter the convent until 1894, the conversation with Father Alexis which Thérèse records in *The Story of a Soul* had already taken place.

Another statement by this same confidante of Thérèse is also significant. "One day she asked me whether after her death I would give up her little way of confidence and love. 'Certainly not', I replied. 'I believe in it so firmly that it seems to me if the Pope himself were to tell me I was mistaken I could not believe him.' 'Oh,' she broke in forcefully, 'one must always believe the Pope. But do not be afraid that he will tell you to change your way. I would not give him time. If when I get to Heaven, I find out that I have misled you, I would obtain permission from God to return instantly to warn you. Until then, believe in my way and follow it faithfully.' " [123]

As we can see, a small group of initiates was forming in the Carmel of Lisieux. They felt themselves to be pioneers of the Little Way and sought to win friends and relatives in the world over to it. We have already seen that Thérèse had at one time to put a check upon this movement. The members of the little band were firmly convinced that they had found in Thérèse "a treasure of immeasurable value". Nevertheless, we are justified in asking whether her faithful disciples themselves were fully conscious of what elements in the doctrine were truly innovations. The new elements are so deeply embedded and heavily disguised in the garb of traditional formulas that at first they appear to be essentially a restatement of things already more or less known and favoured in run-of-the-mill piety. We must raise the question of whether this circumstance did not contribute largely to the amazing response to *The Story of a Soul*. Thérèse's contemporaries fancied that they recognized in the book their favourite thoughts and sentiments, not at all a revolutionary upheaval or a breakthrough to something new.

If, for example, we read in the account of the ecclesiastical trial the reply of a priest who was a friend of Thérèse to a question on the value and essence of the Little Way, we are likely to think in involuntary amazement: Much ado about nothing.

"1. Remain little and practise humility.

"2. Frequently perform *easy* mortifications and little sacrifices—what Thérèse calls scattering flowers.

"3. Trust in God and practise holy surrender."

---

[122] 2 S., Animadversiones 22.
[123] Ibid.

Céline describes it in similar fashion: "The basis of her instruction was that we should not be grieved even by the sight of weakness and, because charity covers a multitude of sins, we should practise love. Her Little Way consisted in praising her weakness and her incapacity to do any good by herself." To judge by the general tenor of her testimony, Céline regarded such words in exactly the same light as if another saint said he was surprised that the world still existed in spite of his sins. "In addition, we were to look at the bright side of things, and also curb our impatience in working upon our inner selves." [124]

Perhaps we should consider a much-quoted statement by the saint herself as one of the reasons for the inadequate interpretation of her own doctrine. During her illness Pauline asked her once more to explain the Little Way which she wanted to teach to souls. Thérèse, who may then have been weary and exhausted, replied: "It is the way of spiritual childhood, the way of trust and complete self-surrender. I want to teach others the means I have always found so completely successful, to let them know that the only thing to do on earth is to offer Our Lord the flowers of little sacrifices and win Him by our proofs of love. It is the way I have won Him and why I shall find such a welcome." [125] For her sister, who according to Thérèse's own words knew every recess of her heart, such locutions were understandable; but for the uninitiated this sentence, torn out of the context of an intimate conversation and presented as a programme, fosters misinterpretations.

It is strange, and a conclusive proof of how sharply the living tradition of the *École Française* had been cut off, buried and forgotten even in Catholic France, that to our knowledge no biographer and no contemporary of the saint—not even Petitot in his admirably deep study—has referred to this obvious kinship between Thérèse and her predecessors. Partly, to be sure, this may be due to the unconscious but obvious desire of her admirers to underline the uniqueness and originality of their saint.

"One day," Thérèse relates,

Sister Marie of the Eucharist wanted to light candles for a procession. She had no matches, and seeing a little lamp burning in front of the relics, she approached, but there was only a tiny glimmer left on the charred wick. Nevertheless, she succeeded in lighting her candle, and with it all the candles of the community. Who dares to glory in his own works? I thought. From one faint spark such as this it would be possible to set the whole earth on fire. And yet, the humble little lamp would remain the first cause of this conflagration.

[124] 2 S., 610.
[125] *N.V.*, 17 July.

It is exactly the same in the community of the saints. A spark can generate great lights in the Church, doctors and martyrs. Without our knowing it, we often owe the graces and lights we have received to some hidden soul, because God wills that the saints dispense graces to one another through prayer, so that they will love one another in Heaven with a great love. How often I have thought that perhaps I owe all the graces I have received to some little soul who has prayed God to give them to me, and whom I shall not meet until I reach Heaven.[126]

Perhaps this charming parable provides the deepest "explanation" of the true meaning of the Little Way.

[126] *N.V.*, 15 July.

6

PERFECTION

All is grace.
— THÉRÈSE OF THE CHILD JESUS

IN THE NORMAL COURSE of events, Thérèse's way would have long continued in quiet and hiddenness. She might have remained Novice Mistress, perhaps become Prioress, of a gradually growing community which, however, would never extend beyond the bounds of the Lisieux Carmel. The event which made Thérèse herself and her disciples, conscious of her mission, and which produced the first and most important instrument by which she affected the world—her autobiography—was the fatal disease that attacked her when she was barely twenty-three.

From childhood Thérèse had felt with certainty that she would never live to grow old. "I have never asked God that I might die young—that to me would be a cowardly prayer; but from my childhood He has deigned to inspire me with a strong conviction that my life would be a short one", she wrote in one of the last letters of her life. Humanly speaking, there was no reason for this assumption. She had been a delicate child, and the debilitating effect of her anxiously sheltered upbringing had probably furthered this delicacy. She had always been susceptible to colds, especially in the throat, and during her adolescence had suffered a good deal from headaches and states of exhaustion. But these afflictions seemed, to a very considerable extent, to be a reflection of her psychic difficulties during the period of "darkness". And the truly miraculous conversion of Christmas 1886, far more thoroughgoing and fraught with consequences than that first inexplicable cure in May 1883, produced—together with the sudden loosening of psychic tensions—a new burgeoning of her physical energies. Since the attack of chorea at the age of twelve she had had no serious illnesses. In spite of the difficulties of making the transition, which we have already described, Thérèse withstood the severities of Carmelite life surprisingly well. It is surely evidence of how she felt physically when she wrote to Céline in 1894, shortly before that sister's entry: "I have an iron constitution." However, she added the strangely premonitory qualification: "But the Lord can break iron as though it were clay."

A year later she had the most consoling dream of her life, in which Blessed Anne of Jesus promised her that the Heavenly Father would soon call her home.

In the convent Thérèse frequently suffered from throat infections, as she had during her childhood. The year she wrote of her iron constitution granular growths appeared in her throat; the doctor treated these with corrosive silver nitrate. These growths were already a symptom of tuberculosis, but it is evident that neither Thérèse nor the other nuns had any idea of the danger, perhaps not even the doctor.[1] When Céline entered the convent, Thérèse was already under the doctor's care. Otherwise, there were no changes in her daily routine. Pauline, who was then still Prioress, for all her maternal tenderness saw no reason to make any exceptions—not even, as she later mentions herself,[2] to dispense Thérèse from the dusty or damp tasks of cleaning and laundry. Thérèse herself, of course, never thought of asking for such relief. At that time Thérèse was employed at the gate and at painting, in addition to the regular housework at which all the nuns took turns. After the re-election of Mother Marie de Gonzague she was again assigned to the sacristy; this was, as we know, her favourite office, and in addition it required no special exertion. Two months later, on the night before Good Friday, the first serious symptom appeared, a slight coughing of blood—not, as is often erroneously stated, a haemorrhage. From Thérèse's own, very exact description it is evident that she suddenly felt her mouth full of blood and spat this blood into her handkerchief. That was all, and she slept soundly through the night. Next morning she felt so well that when she went, as in duty bound, to report the incident to the Prioress, she could with good conscience ask and obtain permission "to finish Lent as I had begun. I did not feel the least tiredness or pain. Good Friday found me taking my full share of all our austerities, and they had never seemed so dear to me!"

Harsh criticism has been levelled against the Prioress because she did not immediately send Thérèse to the infirmary, but instead let her participate in the undiminished austerities of Lent. But Pauline herself informs us of the manner of Thérèse's report. "The following morning she told the Prioress; this has happened to me, but I beg you, do not attribute any importance to it; it is nothing; I have no pain and implore you to let me continue the Lenten exercises like all the others."[3] According to the

---

[1] 1 S., xix, 2; 2 S., 824. Her Aunt Dosithea, in the Order of the Visitation, had died of tuberculosis at the age of forty-nine; she had suffered from it for twenty-two years, her entire life in the convent.

[2] 1 S., xii, 1.

[3] 2 S., 566.

Manuscrits Autobiographiques Thérèse also reported to the sister who was at that time infirmarian, her close friend Marie of the Holy Trinity, requesting her, however, not to alarm the other sisters about the matter. It was the nurse's duty to recommend to the Prioress whatever health measures seemed necessary. It would seem that she, too, did not consider the case urgent.

According to her own testimony Thérèse felt better and stronger during this Lent, even though the Rule, following the ancient discipline of the early Church and of the East, permitted only one meal daily; and even though the sparse fare of that meal was made sparser by the prohibition of eggs and dairy foods—while the nuns were expected to work eighteen hours a day in the biting cold of early spring.

Thérèse herself saw only one thing in the night's incident: the sign of the Lord's arrival, His first call, "like a gentle, distant whisper". In her first physical alarm, when she felt the hot blood welling up, she thought she was going to die, "and my heart felt as if it were bursting for joy". We can imagine, then, how she knelt smilingly at Mother Marie de Gonzague's feet, with shining eyes and glowing cheeks, and radiantly asked permission to continue the Lenten practices. How could the Prioress, who was used to having her nuns come to her wailing and fussing over every smallest affliction, have sensed that Thérèse's trouble was indeed serious? Moreover, it was but two days to Easter, and she knew very well what active participation and fervent prayer on these most solemn days of the whole year meant to a devout heart. So she let Thérèse have her way. By evening, the girl's strength was exhausted. Like all the others in the convent, she had eaten nothing but bread and water, and in between the long hours of reciting the liturgy in the choir she had washed windows in the icy cloisters. One of the novices found her there, deathly pale and in a half faint; she offered to take over the work, but Thérèse sent her away. During the night she once more coughed blood.

In both cases, however, there was no more than a single discharge, "a handkerchief full", and Thérèse did not otherwise feel ill. To be sure, it takes extraordinary equanimity to sleep soundly after such an occurrence; in fact, she had conquered her curiosity to such an extent that she faithfully followed the Rule in not again lighting her lamp to find out what had happened. Not until the following morning did she examine her handkerchief! The days after Easter, with their lifting of austerities, seemed to bring about an improvement in her condition. Thérèse was taken to the doctor once more, and he prescribed various medicines for the throat.[4]

---

[4] 2 S., 824.

The sickness seemed to have passed. In the summer of that year a dry little cough developed. The doctor examined Thérèse again and "found nothing serious"; he prescribed strengthening nourishment, and Thérèse was given a dispensation to eat meat. On 12 July she was able to write to Léonie: "I am not coughing at all any more." And on 16 July she wrote to the Guérins, who were much concerned: "You insist, dear Aunt, that I tell you about my health as if you were my mother. I shall do so, but you will not believe me if I tell you that I am feeling fine, so I will let the doctor, to whom I was taken in the visiting room yesterday, say it for me. After he had honoured me with a single look, he declared that I was 'looking well'." [5] In November her transfer to Saigon was seriously considered. But the winter brought a deterioration in her condition. Her organism could no longer endure the bitter cold of the unheated building. Attacks of fever occurred and began to follow one another with increasing frequency. Nevertheless, Thérèse did not report herself ill or even ask for another blanket. Perhaps, since the fevers would always die down after a few hours, she did not think her condition yet grave enough to entitle her to any alleviation of the austerities.

After the Lent of 1897, the prescriptions of which she once again carried out to the letter, the disease broke through all her self-control and strength of will. Thérèse began running fevers and coughing constantly. Now the house-doctor attempted "energetic measures": mustard plasters, iodine paintings, massages and cauterizations. From the therapy it is evident that Thérèse was already considered "consumptive". But as is so often the case with the tubercular, her appearance was deceptive. She was still able to go about her day's work, although at what cost! She still rose at the same hour as all the others—from Easter until the feast of the Holy Cross at half past four o'clock, from the feast of the Holy Cross to Easter at half past five o'clock—performed eight hours' duty in the choir, helped to hang out washing in the open air. No one, not even the doctor, seems to have thought of the danger of contagion; Thérèse continued to take part in the community life, ate at the same table with the other nuns, used the same dishes and tableware, helped with the laundry. Gradually she lost appetite, could no longer digest her food, became emaciated. Early in May she was relieved of all work; however, she asked permission to be allowed to continue to help with the mending. In June she usually sat in the convent garden in her father's wheelchair, working on the second part of her autobiography. On 6 July she suffered a hemorrhage, followed by several others. Dr de Cornière diagnosed a severe inflamma-

[5] Laveille, 487.

tion of the lungs and forbade—at this late date!—all movement. Thérèse was moved to the infirmary; the doctor prescribed ice, mustard plasters and cupping. From then on, her physical disintegration proceeded inexorably. From 8 July to 1 August she spat blood two or three times a day, suffered from deep depression, fearful attacks of asphyxia, tormenting asthma and exhausting bouts of sweating. She was given inhalations of ether, which helped little. The disease spread throughout her entire body. She could scarcely drink, although she suffered acute thirst, became alarmingly emaciated, developed bedsores; when, to ease her during her incessant fits of coughing, she was lifted up, she felt as if she were sitting on fiery needles.

On 30 July she received the Last Sacraments. On 16 August violent, persistent vomiting began; the following day the doctor found that both lungs were so severely riddled that she could not be expected to live for more than a few days. But the slow dissolution was to last another six weeks.

On 22 August she began to suffer terrible intestinal pain; the tubercular intestines were actually beginning to die. "I have never seen this disease take such a form", the doctor declared. "What the patient is going through is frightful." Thirst tormented the dying girl like fire, but the coolest drink increased the pain, "as if fire were being poured on fire". During the last days the discharge was purulent and cheesy, with a frightful odour of decay. Thérèse lost the capacity to move her limbs and could only breathe in little cries. On 19 August she had received Holy Communion for the last time; thereafter her constant vomiting prevented her from receiving this consolation. On the evening of 30 September she died.

Disease and physical pain are so essential and profound a mystery of human existence, that scarcely any saints have been spared them. Since Christ our Lord became like us in all things excepting sin, He took it upon Himself to endure the violent maceration of His body, but by means of His Passion and Crucifixion. In the torment of the flesh there is an unfathomable humiliation of the spirit; such violence is done to it by the weight of pain that it is brought to the point of impotence and utter helplessness. It is idle to ask which is harder to bear, suffering of the body or that of the soul. We know that human beings can endure more physical pain, the more backward they are—and the more highly developed: the savage, and the person of supreme spiritual cultivation. The one endures out of a fund of crude strength, out of lack of sensitivity and, even more, lack of the power to reflect upon his sufferings and so intensify them; the other endures out of the mind's mastery over the body, no matter how slight his physical resistance may naturally be. But since in the more highly cultivated human being suffering has a more profound effect upon the soul, and since physical pain brings in its train a unique sense of isolation from all other human beings, brings depression and many anxieties, it may well be said that great physical pain constitutes the most complete form of human suffering.

Christians have frequently been contemned for their respectful view of illness; the Christian (or, the unbeliever would say, Christianity) appears to see a value in something from which human beings naturally turn away repelled. Perhaps only the Christian, with his knowledge of man's supernatural destiny, of Adam's original state before the Fall and of the resurrection of the body, truly knows what a humiliation illness and bodily suffering mean. Perhaps he alone knows how far illness is from being a mere consequence of chemical, physical, physiological factors, and how much it is mystical punishment and an effect of the Fall. But he knows also that Our Lord became the Man of Sorrows, and that we have been saved not only by His spirit, His love, and His tidings, but also by His wounds and His stripes. That our redemption has taken place through suffering of the flesh and spilling of blood may mean that it could take place in no other way. Perhaps there are sins which can be atoned for only by torment of the body—sins which begin in the soul but are expressed through the body: incontinence, violent temper, cruelty, certain forms of arrogance. And the Christian knows, too, that where a human being united with God suffers in soul and body, the mystery of Christ's Atonement is continued. "Always we, alive as we are, are being given up to death for Jesus' sake", writes St Paul, who understood these matters as did no other, "so that the living power of Jesus may be manifested in this mortal nature of ours."[6] Thus the believer sees in each person who suffers like Christ a chosen spirit, one who has been marked out, and approaches him with profound reverence.

Thérèse, too, obeyed the law which bids us imitate Christ in all particulars; it was necessary for her to be conformed to the Man of Sorrows, and this grace was granted. As if this were a necessary sequel, the disease which broke down the defences of her youth, broke through the veil of her obscurity. While the seal of death became manifest upon her flesh, the life of Jesus shone out from within her.

The first signs of the fatal disease unleashed a storm of pure jubilation in her unfrightened heart. The account of that Good Friday night, though written more than a year later, captured something of the unearthly joy

[6] 2 Cor 4:11.

she had experienced. There is no trace of fear in it, no natural trembling of the menaced body, nothing but boundless joy at the approaching home-coming. It seems almost incredible but unquestionably this feeling was her sole response to the discovery. "My heart nearly broke with joy.... Dearest Mother, I was filled with hope, convinced that my Beloved, on the anniversary of His death, had let me hear His first call—a far-off lovely murmur, heralding His approach. I assisted at Prime and at Chapter with much fervour, then hurried to kneel before you and tell you of my happiness.... The hope of soon entering Heaven transported me with joy."

This is not a grim turning of the back on life, not a weary drooping of the will to live, but an almost ecstatic yearning for the new, the eternal life, for which she had always longed and now felt tangibly close. For a few days she was carried along on the crest of this wave of emotion, which utterly put from her consciousness her physical discomfort. "My faith was so strong and vivid that the thought of Heaven made me su-premely happy. It seemed impossible that anyone could be so wicked as to have no faith. They could not possibly be sincere in denying the ex-istence of another world." [7]

But strangely enough, the discharge of blood was soon followed by another sign which kept pace with the disease and was to persist until the hour of her death. All at once this glowing, victorious faith faded away, and Thérèse learned from her own experience that "there really are souls who by their abuse of grace have lost the precious treasures of faith and hope." During that Easter of 1896 her great trial of faith began and lasted literally until her last breath. In the ninth chapter, addressed to the Pri-oress, Thérèse speaks calmly, candidly and in detail about it, but as always she does not tell all. The sparse additional testimonies of the others who knew her well are in part contradictory. All agree that Thérèse suffered from extremely violent and what she felt to be well-nigh irresistible "temp-tations against the Faith". But were these really *doubts* of her religion? It does not appear that specific, coherent, unanswerable questions about this or that tenet of the Faith arose, questions which might have threatened the whole structure. Rather, one single point collapsed abruptly: the cer-tainty of personal immortality. Did everything else remain—the belief in God, in Christ, in the Church, in the sacraments, in the Blessed Virgin, in the saints? Were these other beliefs only partly veiled by shifting mists of emotion, at times overcast, at times showing clear again? Or did the one stone that suddenly collapsed bring down all the rest with it, without

[7] S.S., ix.

the need of any direct assault upon these other tenets? Or are we here being deceived by the veil drawn so closely around the hidden face? Had everything actually become submerged in the utter darkness, and only blind, unreflecting loyalty forced her to go on speaking and writing as if all were still alive? Let us listen to her own account:

He allowed my soul to be enveloped in utter darkness. Ever since I was very little, the thought of Heaven had always been a joy to me; now it brought torment and conflict. This trial did not last merely a few days or weeks; it went on for months; and I am still waiting to be delivered from it. [At the time she wrote this it had been going on for fifteen months.] It is impossible to explain what I feel—I only wish I could. I am in a dark tunnel, and you would have to go through it yourself to understand how dark it is; but a comparison may give you some idea.

Suppose I had been born in a land which was always deep in fog; I should never have seen the beauties of nature, never a ray of sunlight. But from my childhood I should have heard about them, should have known I was in exile, and that there was another land I was bound to seek. The inhabitants of the land of fog have not made up this story; it is absolutely true, for the King of the Land of Sunshine came to spend thirty-three years here; but the darkness did not understand that He was the light of the world. . . .

Since childhood, as I have said, I had been certain that one day I would leave my dark world far behind. I do not think that this was only from what I had heard. The very desires and intuitions of my inmost heart assured me that another and more lovely land awaited me, an abiding city; just as the genius of Christopher Columbus gave him a presentiment of a new world. Then suddenly the fog about me seems to enter my very soul, and fill it to such an extent that I cannot even find there the lovely picture I had formed of my homeland; everything has disappeared.

When, weary of being enveloped by nothing but darkness, I try to comfort and encourage myself with the thought of the eternal life to come, it only makes matters worse. The very darkness seems to echo the voices of those who do not believe, and mocks at me: "You dream of light and of a fragrant land; you dream that the Creator of this loveliness will be your own for all eternity; you dream of escaping one day from these mists in which you languish! Dream on, welcome death; it will not bring you what you hope; it will bring an even darker night, the night of nothingness!"

This picture of my trial is no more than a rough sketch compared with the reality, but I dare not say more for fear it might be blasphemy! Perhaps I have said too much already? God forgive me! . . .

I expect you will think I am rather exaggerating the night of my soul; to judge by the poems I have written this year, I must appear to be overwhelmed with consolation, a child for whom the veil of faith is almost torn apart; yet it is no longer a veil—it is a wall reaching almost to Heaven, shutting out the stars.

When I sing of Heaven's happiness, of what it is to possess God for ever, I feel no joy; I simply sing *of what I want to believe.* Now and then, I must admit, a gleam of light shines through the dark night, to bring a moment's respite, but afterwards its memory, instead of consoling me, only makes my night darker than ever.

So Thérèse wrote, with childlike candour confiding the state of her soul to her beloved godmother. Towards her sisters, even to Pauline, she ventured to speak of this dark night only in occasional hints, for fear of leading them into confusion and perhaps even infecting them with her doubts. And probably also she kept silent still more in order to preserve her "veil". One day in the infirmary—her trial had by then been going on for more than fifteen months—Pauline spoke of Heaven and of the physical presence of Jesus and Mary there. In reply Thérèse gave only a long, heavy sigh. Pauline questioned her, and "she confided to me *more than usual* about her sufferings". "Oh, if you knew what horrible thoughts constantly oppress me", she said. "The reasoning of the worst materialists forces itself upon my mind. Oh, little Mother, must one think such things when one loves God so dearly!" [8] She added that she never "debated with" these dark thoughts. "I must necessarily endure them", she said. "But while they are imposed upon me, I make acts of faith incessantly."

This confession seems to us immensely important. It is apparent that Thérèse's distress was not only emotional in origin, as we might gather from her account to the Prioress; that it sprang not only from the feeling that her certainty about Heaven had collapsed, from her feeling that she was approaching absolute annihilation, from her being unable any longer to feel that joyous anticipation of eternal bliss which she had once so taken for granted. These feelings she had, but in addition she was also the prey of *raisonnements*, ideas, arguments of the materialists. She was suffering from genuine intellectual temptation; her possession of the truth was threatened by active hostility, not only by passive shadowings. "I no longer believe in the eternal life—everything has vanished", she said to that Sister Thérèse of St Augustine with whom she was linked in the strange friendship she had wrung from herself. And it is of the highest significance, if the witness remembers correctly, that she did not just say, "It seems to me *as if* I can no longer believe in the eternal life", but: "*I no longer believe*...". In another place, however, we read of Pauline's asking: "And what about the Blessed Virgin; is she too veiled?" "No," Thérèse replied with animation, "Our Lady is *never, never veiled for me*. And when I can no longer see God, she takes care of everything for me with Him. I send her especially to tell Him to try me without hesitation." [9]

[8] Petitot, 266.
[9] 2 S., 244.

No wonder that Dom Godefroy declares, as we have mentioned, that Thérèse thought herself damned for a full eighteen months. For it must be remembered that to the piety of those days every puzzled, questioning, uncertain thought about the content of the Faith was instantly equated with full-scale, sinful "doubt". Into what abysses of inner torment tempted, struggling human beings were thrust by such judgments. For as a rule anxious spiritual guides used to forbid as dangerous and impertinent all frank, clear examination of the troubling questions, the sounding of which could have eliminated so much perplexity. Newman's famous dictum that ten thousand difficulties about the Faith do not amount to a single doubt was truly not spoken without reason.

Was Thérèse in similar case? We know that by nature she had a clear, curious and critical intellect, that she was capable of and ready to ask questions, to observe, to discriminate and to judge. We can guess (for example, from her remarks on contemporary veneration of the Blessed Virgin) that she had often encountered and recognized gross distortions of the traditional content of the Faith. Had any trouble of this sort, which she guessed without being able to analyse and refute intellectually, oppressed her during those last months when, knowing that her end was near, she could no longer postpone questions, but had to decide them promptly? We can hardly assume that there now rose to her troubled mind talk against the Faith which she had heard at some earlier time— her childhood and youth had been too anxiously guarded. Hence the "arguments of the worst materialists" must have been generated by her own reason. Possibly a simple conversation with some understanding priest, a fearless discussion, attainment of a higher point of view, development of greater exactness in her ideas, might have dispelled a good many spectres. "Whenever I find myself faced with the prospect of an attack by my enemy I am most courageous; I turn my back on him, without so much as looking at him!" This was altogether in the spirit of current morality; thoughts against the Faith, as against purity, must not be dealt with; they must only be fled from and ignored. One of the priests to whom she turned in her distress found her condition "extremely dangerous". Prior Godefroy diagnosed diabolic temptation. Perhaps it was he who advised Thérèse to write down the Credo and always carry it with her. She wrote it with her blood.

This much seems established: that this prolonged and terrible perplexity was never treated with attempts to clarify and analyse. It may be that the besetting ideas, never thought through to the end, never viewed with the perspective that words give, never alleviated by answers, but only violently repressed by acts of will, gradually became obsessions. It may also be that the physical disease destroyed the beautiful spiritual equilibrium she had enjoyed since that Christmas grace of 1886, and that the old, dangerous, dark underground of her spiritual nature once more burst forth victoriously. This may have been an outbreak similar to, but more terrible than, the compulsive scruples of her childhood, a new wave of morbid obsessions swamping her now defenceless mind. It may be, then, that Thérèse knew with instinctive rightness that these things could not be attacked with the intellectual weapons of reason and argument, that they simply had to be endured and as far as possible not taken seriously. Nevertheless, in dark hours she certainly suffered from the nameless fear that such sufferings might after all represent unconscious guilt, that having such thoughts at all might be a sign of her rejection by God. In hours of insight, however, she understood that this terrible and, as she so often repeated, "incomprehensible" state was not a fault but a task, that she was required to participate in the sins of the world outside the convent walls, where violent attacks raged against the existence of the soul, against immortality and the "hereafter". She grasped that she was atoning not only by praying at a safe distance for those poor Godless souls, but by being right in the midst of them, sharing all their torments and their blindness, being one of them, and having to appeal to God's mercy. She was participating in the unfathomable Passion of Our Lord when His Father abandoned Him. And wholeheartedly, Thérèse committed herself to this suffering.

"But the darkness did not understand that He was the light of the world. But Your child, O Lord, has understood. She asks pardon for her brothers who do not believe. She is quite content to eat the bread of sorrow as long as You will. For love of You, she will sit at the table of sinners laden with bitter food, and will not rise until You give the sign. Yet in their name and in her own, may she not say: 'O God, be merciful to us sinners! Send us away justified. May all in whom the light of faith shines dimly see at last. If the table they have defiled must be purified by one who loves You, I am willing to sit there alone eating nothing but the bread of tears until You choose to take me into Your Kingdom of Light. I ask only one grace—may I never offend You!'" [10]

We must keep all this in mind when we read the last chapters of *The Story of a Soul*, the poems, the letters and the conversations of the saint from the hardest year and a half of her life. It can scarcely be believed that these joyful, blissfully jubilant, quietly peaceful, transparently childlike confessions, observations and prayers could have sprung from such a state of soul. The root of them all was the same, the same root from which Thérèse

[10] *S.S.*, x.

in childhood had derived strength during all serious crises: her loyalty towards her conscience at all costs, and her obedience, which was the garb of this loyalty. Ruthlessly Thérèse transcended her own state of mind and her own feelings. She knew what was true and real whether or not she felt, understood or experienced it. The Sun *was* in the sky, even if she were blinded. She had seen the radiant light; she knew she had seen it; and even if she no longer knew—it had vanished to such remote spaces— she still knew that she had known it once, and that would have to satisfy her. And so she wrote and prayed as if nothing had happened, as if her whole inner world had not been buried by an earthquake. She paid homage to Truth. She no longer felt and understood faith, but she continued to live it. Once again, and yet as if it had never happened before, she had stepped over the firm edge of certainty and was crossing the nocturnal abyss just as if it were solid ground beneath her feet. "God forgive me; but He knows that I try to practise my faith even though it brings me no joy. I have made more acts of faith in the last year than during all the rest of my life."

"I no longer believe in eternal life; it seems to me that there is nothing after this mortal life; everything has disappeared, and only love remains."

"I was strangely surprised to hear of this temptation against faith," says the sister to whom Thérèse spoke the above words,[11] "for her soul seemed peaceful and serene as ever; one would have thought that she was flooded by consolation, so easily and naturally did she practise virtue." Only when Céline, in rare interludes of spiritual converse, went on too rapturously or else complained about petty troubles, could Thérèse's self-control give way. Once she fled. To Sister Thérèse of St Augustine she exclaimed during the conversation quoted above: "Oh, if you knew, if you knew! If for five minutes you had to go through the trial I am undergoing! If you only knew!" How this sigh betrays her terrible craving for communication, for a single human being who would see through the mask of her smiling calm, who would at least share the knowledge and help her bear the cruel solitude of this assault. But her veil remained opaque, even at this stage.

It is as though this depression had a profound connection with the disease-wrought disintegration of her body, as though the dying body forced its instinctive fears into her mind in the form of this beclouding of her childlike faith. Autumn came, and then the winter. Every afternoon at three o'clock the tide of fever surged high. But she would not let it show. Not for nothing was Thérèse the daughter of a mother who for

[11] I S., xii, 45.

sixteen years had hidden from her own husband the fatal tumour in her breast. Not for nothing had she lived under the same roof with Mother Geneviève, who for thirty years had endured an internal growth, without complaint, until she was found lying unconscious on the floor. Thérèse was determined to die in harness. She reported on how she felt to the Prioress, but always so tersely, with so cheerful an expression, so upright a stance, so calm a voice, so untroubled a smile, that Mother Marie de Gonzague did not realize how seriously ill she was. And not only Mother Gonzague, who did not have a very keen eye for the weaknesses and pains of others. Even the eternally watchful sisters with their almost prying solicitude, and the affectionate novices who observed their Mistress so closely, noticed nothing until it was too late. Thérèse still sat upright on the hard benches, though her back was sore from cauteries and drawing plasters. She still sprang lightly and smilingly to her feet at the slightest gesture from someone else, in order to fetch, to arrange, to lend a helping hand. She still walked through the open cloisters in swirling snow and lashing rain, without even lowering her head, hunching her shoulders, drawing her cloak more closely about her, or sheltering her frozen hands in the sleeves. Anyone who saw her must have thought her insensitive to heat and cold. She continued to prevent herself from wiping the perspiration from her burning forehead, so that no one would notice how feverish she was. She still put in the long, endlessly long hours in the choir, without leaning against anything, without fainting, even when everything turned black before her eyes and she could not catch her breath. She still laughed and joked in the recreation hour, was lively, interested in everything, quick-witted and sympathetic to the others.

It occurred to no one to ascribe the flush of her cheeks or the glow in her eyes to illness. She still ate whatever was placed before her—less and less, to be sure, but who would notice that? Her cell was so far from others that her nocturnal fits of coughing went unheard. She still allowed the others to heap small commissions upon her; she drew and painted and wrote verse and letters as long as lights were allowed. Everything seemed just the same as always. Only when she was alone did her strength give out. It took her half an hour to climb the small staircase that led to her cell; she could do it only by sitting down to rest on every step. Once in the cell, undressing took her a full hour, so painful had the few necessary movements become for her. Then followed the long night when she lay sleepless from cold and shuddering with fever, coughing blood—and her mind obsessed with those uncanny, blasphemous thoughts against the Faith.

It is really incomprehensible that throughout this whole long winter no one recognized Thérèse's true state. The only explanation is that her smile, the naturalness, strength and lightness which she unwaveringly simulated, without once failing, hoodwinked the entire convent, including the doctor. It is established that she was constantly under the doctor's supervision, and he tried all possible cures and treatments upon her. Her apparently undiminished ability to perform her tasks, and her radiant good humour, concealed the ravages of the disease; it did not yet seem urgent that she be given special care and made to rest. Until the last she remained faithful to her principle of asking for no remissions of the Rule, neither requesting permission to sleep longer nor dispensation from attendance at table, choir or work. And of her own accord Mother Marie de Gonzague did not make such offers; she was far too accustomed to the nuns interceding for themselves on the smallest pretext. Moreover, the Martin sisters had always been coming to her with requests and hints concerning the youngest of them; she had had seven years of this sort of thing. Had not the sisters fretted and worried and respectfully made suggestions and reproaches ever since Thérèse entered the Carmel as a child of fifteen? And had they ever been right in their apprehensions? Had Thérèse even once been really ill in all those years? Had she not, in fact, burdened though she was by nursing, withstood the influenza epidemic which had carried away many of far stronger constitution? Had not the sisters always wanted to wrap their delicate child in cotton wool and spare her all austerities? But she, the Prioress, had not let herself be beguiled; she had remained hard and permitted this chosen spirit to go the strict way that her great heart demanded. And look what fine fruit this decision had borne! Had Thérèse not become mature, strong and robust in body and soul? To be sure, all the sisters' whisperings had not been silenced; on the contrary. But this gossip was no more important now than it had been in the past.

Thérèse's way was not made any easier by her awareness of this pulling and tugging all around her. "You did not understand me then", she said gently to her sisters when it was already too late, when she had already been lying in the infirmary for six weeks, and her sisters reminded her, with tender reproach, how often they had vainly begged her to sleep late or to ask for dispensation from night choir. "I seemed stubborn, but it was because I felt that everyone was always trying to influence our Mother. I would gladly have told her the whole truth, so that she could decide for herself, of her own accord.... I assure you, if she herself had asked me not to go to Mass, Communion or the Offices, I would have obeyed with great docility." [12] But the order did not come. Let us not forget that *The Story of a Soul* contains not a single word about these sufferings.

---

[12] I *S.*, xix, 166, 12 August.

Thérèse later regretted it as a weakness that she had spoken at all, that she confessed to Marie of the Holy Trinity her torments at night, so that when Marie was assigned to the infirmary she hastened to inform the authorities about it—with such force that at last Thérèse was given proper treatment. "Oh, I had prayed God so intensely to let me take part in all the community's exercises until my death. He did not wish to grant me this. And yet it seems to me that I could go right on with everything—it would not make me die a minute sooner. And I sometimes imagine *that if I had not said anything, no one would think me sick.*" [13]

Now that the true extent of Thérèse's illness had come to light, Mother Marie de Gonzague did what she could to provide all possible relief for this beloved daughter—little as her robust nature was ordinarily capable of sympathetic understanding of the sick. Thérèse thanks her, in the tenth chapter, in touching words: "All through my illness you have showered attentions on me and this has taught me a great deal about charity. No remedy seems too expensive to you; if one fails, then you untiringly try another. You take such care of me at recreation; there must be no draughts. All this makes me realize that I should be just as compassionate concerning the spiritual infirmities of my Sisters as you are concerning my physical ones."

Mother Marie de Gonzague appointed Céline assistant in the infirmary in place of Marie of the Holy Trinity [14] and entrusted her with the care of her sister. Céline was given a cell adjoining Thérèse, and permission to spend the entire day with her except when she had to be in choir for Divine Office. The other sisters were allowed to relieve her at intervals. Pauline's diary on her conversations with Thérèse begins on 6 April; from this it is evident that long before Thérèse's obvious collapse she must have received permission to be with her sister frequently and engage in unlimited conversation with her. [15] Laveille even speaks of daily visits by the sisters. Marie Guérin, now Sister Marie of the Eucharist, was given permission to write to her parents daily about Thérèse's health. [16] It is hard to understand how, in the face of such consideration and generosity on the part of the Prioress—in spite of the existing tensions—the legend of her animosity towards Thérèse and her sisters can still persist.

In one matter there were difficulties with Mother Marie de Gonzague. In September the doctor proposed morphine injections to alleviate Thérèse's inhuman pain. Mother Marie de Gonzague refused to give her consent.

[13] *N.V.*, 18 May.
[14] 2 *S.*, 838.
[15] Laveille, 397.
[16] 2 *S.*, 995.

She had inflexible, old-fashioned views on the grave moral effects of this anodyne and believed it was not proper to stupefy a Carmelite nun with such things. Probably she had carried away from gossip in the parlour half-understood, weird rumours about drug addicts and narcotics.[17] How little her attitude was directed against Thérèse in particular is evident from the biography of Mother Geneviève. Seven years earlier, while her beloved ex-Prioress was suffering so severely, Mother Marie de Gonzague had insisted on the same view, and there is no doubt that she would have clung to it with equal obstinacy in her own case.

Thérèse submitted to this decision like a child. She probably did not know that her sisters, according to their own admission, utilized "all possible tricks" in order to give her morphine syrup secretly, in spite of the ban.[18] Perhaps one reason for the stories about Mother Marie de Gonzague's hostility was the clash she had with the family during the very last days of Thérèse's life. The house physician, Dr de Cornière, was taking a month's vacation, and the sisters wished Dr Neele, their cousin Jeanne's husband, to assume the care of Thérèse. Mother Marie de Gonzague permitted him to come only three times; presumably she was unwilling to strengthen the family council in the infirmary by another member who, moreover, possessed the authority of a medical man. The victim of this conflict was Thérèse, for the intestinal gangrene had made its onset and was causing her fearful torments.[19]

The period from May to 30 September was one prolonged process of dying. Every few days Thérèse was given up, expected to die in a few hours, and again and again the moment of dissolution was incomprehensibly postponed. And this whole process of dying took place with uncanny clarity, as if under a microscope, and in the full glare of a probing lamp; as we read we feel as if we were standing by, watch in hand. That is what gives this period and the whole process its unique stamp. What in other human lives takes place quietly and almost without witnesses is here revealed with the nakedness and publicity of a clinical demonstration. We watch a saint die, inch by inch, and the death is preserved for us, with every sigh and every convulsion, as if in a motion picture. We witness a series of close-ups. It is a cruel spectacle, and often we feel repelled, as if such secret and delicate experiences ought not to be exposed. Or we would feel repelled if this revelation, like everything in Thérèse's life, did not have its own peculiar value, were not a witness to

[17] 2 S., 826.
[18] 2 S., 395.
[19] 1 S., xix, 218; 2 S., 825.

something. It is as if a piece of the inner, hidden tissue of Christian life had been cut out and moved under a bright light, so that we might examine it thread by thread for genuineness and purity. For while Thérèse so wearisomely died, the three sisters who tended her stood around, already absolutely convinced that this dying girl was a saint; they were resolved not to lose a single word or gesture of hers, for their own benefit and ours. They were determined to hold fast and transmit to posterity her least word. It was with this in mind that they noted her smallest gesture and her most elevated remarks. It was to corroborate this conviction that they daily asked the sick girl innumerable questions that penetrated to the deepest and most secret depths of her soul and her faith. And this is the standard the dying Thérèse must meet—not only in the eyes of her devoted sisters, who already venerated her, but in the eyes of all of us who look upon this deathbed as it stands so strangely in the limelight.

May we say that these last months were the most difficult and most dangerous in Thérèse's truly burdened life? Not at first glance, certainly. Unless we look beneath the surface it may seem that all at once the cross was removed from her shoulders. To be sure, she was gravely ill and had to suffer a great deal physically. But, after all, it was now recognized that she was sick, and she was being tended accordingly, given all the privileges illness confers. She was incomparably better off than she had been during the past winter. Through the Prioress's loving kindness she had almost been restored to the downy nest of Les Buissonnets, to the constant, exclusive, undisturbed company and care of her tender, sympathetic sisters. The barriers she had endured for so many years, which the Carmel had imposed upon her family-bound heart, were now almost entirely lifted. So, above all, the nuns who disliked the Martin clique saw it. When the sisters' paeans reached the recreation room, there were malevolent whisperings among these others; they asked what such "sanctity" was worth when the girl lived in the convent as if she were in the bosom of her family, pampered and showered with admiration.

Thérèse's relationship to the Prioress, too, had suddenly become simple, easy and joyful. Certainly the Prioress's conduct seems to show that in spite of the occasional friction which her temperament made inevitable she was really not ill-disposed towards Thérèse's beloved sisters, since she granted them everything that could possibly ease their grieved hearts. And had not her customary severity towards Thérèse changed to sincere gentleness? "For some months now, the Divine Master has completely changed His way of dealing with His little flower.... He allows her to unfold in the warmth of the bright sun. He only smiles upon her now, and this favour also comes through you, Reverend Mother."

Indeed, it seems as if even Thérèse's greatest penance might be laid aside now: her silence, her cap of invisibility. In surprising abundance, apparently without restraint, self-revelations pour from her. For during these last months there ripened in the sick girl the consciousness of her worldwide mission. Now she saw it in complete, fearless clarity. She had a bequest to make; it would be her sisters' task to receive it, administer it and transmit it. Time was pressing and her strength was daily wasting away. She had to speak as long as the respite lasted; perhaps it was so unbelievably postponed only for that reason. She had to give of herself, without timidity and unsparingly. Those few weeks of literally "galloping" dissolution were the only span of time given to her for the delivery of her message; she must complete her task before death came. Thus the silence which seemed part of her nature suddenly burst into speech, in spite of shortness of breath, exhaustion, stupefying pain, dizziness and vomiting. And her sisters, who like herself were conscious of the inexorably vanishing reprieve, drew insatiably upon her with their innumerable questions.

If there had been only a shadow of pretension, of coy modesty, secret self-complacency, only a breath of pose and theatricality in Thérèse's nature—these weeks would have revealed it. For now any such emotion could have had its heyday. Now she needed to exercise no caution or restraint, since she was no longer confronted by wariness or criticism, but only by blind, affectionate trust. Yet what danger there really was, when the hungry questions were lifting the last veil, were pushing to the verge of the possible and endurable, and even beyond. And let us not forget that her utter physical disintegration also threatened her natural self-control and her acquired mental discipline. We tremble almost as we watch the spectacle; it is as though a person sick and half-stunned were attempting to walk a tightrope, and we wonder how long will it be before the inevitable false step is taken.

The objective temptation of this last situation in her life cannot be exaggerated. The temptation presented itself all the more secretively and obscurely because it was constantly being offered her by those who loved her most innocently and sincerely, by those before whom she need feel no shyness, no guardedness, no inhibitions. What came to light at this point was the ultimate, deepest, most naked reality of her soul.

We must ask ourselves again and again how it was possible for Thérèse to survive these months unscathed, these months which she spent surrounded by the heady vapours of incense, by open veneration as of a saint. We must be no less astonished at the incomprehensible but beyond doubt perfectly genuine *naïveté* of the sisters. They were so thoroughly convinced of Thérèse's invulnerability that they did not conceive of the possibility that such veneration might be imposing a terrible burden upon her. Pauline had long been in the habit of writing down the thoughts and experiences Thérèse imparted to her, and to this zeal we owe many of Thérèse's most precious sayings. Now she did so openly in Thérèse's presence. She whipped out the *carnet*, the notebook, at every conversation, no matter how short, like a faithful stenographer with her pad. Céline, too, tells us that she kept a notebook. "It was hard on Thérèse," Pauline says naïvely, "and inhibited the outpourings of her heart, but she let me do it simply in order not to sadden me." [20]

The questions and suppositions that Thérèse allowed to shower down on her sometimes border on the comic, and it is amusing to see that she sometimes recognized them as such. With what imperturbable grace, wit and intelligence she managed to ward off many of them. But we are still more moved by the wonderful patience and the earnest, undeviating sense of responsibility which underlay her good humour. The reader, too, involuntarily thinks of the comparison that Thérèse more than once used: "I feel like the Maid of Orleans before her judges: I hope that I am answering with equal sincerity." For this was indeed an interrogation, in a far stricter sense than she thought. And like the one she referred to, it was also an interrogation before the eyes of all Christendom, of which she was as unaware as Joan before her judges.

How gently she endeavoured to free the thoughts of those she loved best from the attachment to her, which, though spiritual, was too natural, and to lead them to a deeper, purer understanding. We think sometimes of the clumsy questions the disciples of Jesus asked about the coming of the Kingdom and their rank in Heaven.

"In Heaven you will be placed among the Seraphim", said one of the sisters.

Thérèse answered, "If so, I shall not imitate them. At the sight of God they cover themselves with their wings. I shall take good care not to hide myself with mine." [21]

"To console me at your death I have asked God to send me a beautiful dream."

"That is a thing I would never do; to ask for ordinary graces is not suitable to my little way."

"You have loved God so much", said the sister, "that He will work a miracle for you, and we shall find your body incorrupt."

"Oh, no, do not be surprised if I do not appear to you after my death and if you see nothing extraordinary as the sign of my blessedness;

[20] I S., xix, 28.
[21] C.S.

remember that it is in the spirit of my little way not to wish anything to be seen of it."

"You are greatly graced; you have the privilege of not fearing death."

"Why should I be more immune to that than anyone else?" replied Thérèse. "I do not say like St Peter: 'Never will I deny Thee.'"

"The angels will come to bear your soul to Heaven."

"I do not believe that you will see them, but of course that will not hinder their being here. I should like to have a 'beautiful' death in order to give you pleasure—but do not be sad if at the moment of my death you observe no sign of joy at all in me.... Did not Our Lord Himself die a Victim of Love, and see how great was His Agony!"

"What will you die of?"—this question seems designed to evoke an answer such as "of love, of an arrow of divine love", or something of the sort. The descriptions of her agony, and the pictures painted by the sisters of the saint on her deathbed, are entirely in this spirit.

"Well, I shall die *of death*. Did not God tell Adam of what he would die when He said to him, 'Thou shalt die of death'? That is very simple!"

"Have you an inner illumination that you will soon die?" asked the sister.

"Oh, little Mother, to speak of me and illuminations! If you knew my poverty. I know nothing that you do not know also; I guess things only from what I can see and feel." [22]

"On 10th August we said to her that souls which like her had attained to the perfection of love could regard without danger their own supernatural beauty."

"What kind of beauty? I see nothing of 'my beauty'. I see only graces that I have received from God", Thérèse answered.

And then, as if she had already said too much in saying this, she added "with deep emotion: 'Oh, my sisters, how much gratitude I owe to you. If you had not brought me up so well, what a wretched thing you would have before you now—instead of what you see in me today!'" [23] They told her that the Mother Prioress and other nuns were talking in recreation about her beauty and graciousness. "Oh, what does that matter to me. That means less than nothing to me; it bores me. When one is so close to death, one cannot rejoice in such things."

"Indeed you are a saint!"

"No, I am not a saint. I have never wrought the works of a saint. I am but a very little soul whom God has loaded with His favours. The truth of what I say will be made known to you in Heaven." [24]

[22] 2 S., 415.
[23] 2 S., 311.
[24] 1 S., xix, 157, 19 August.

"I told her that I would later see to it that her virtues were properly appreciated", said another.

"One must only see to it that God is properly appreciated; there is nothing to stress about my nothingness", replied Thérèse.[25]

But with the same sureness Thérèse avoided the opposite reef, though in her situation it would have been so easy to founder on it: taking refuge in false humility in the effort to fend off such assaults. Where she wanted to confess the gifts of God, the purest humility shone radiantly in the perfect simplicity of her thanksgiving. For she believed that she *was* indeed sanctified by God's unfathomable condescension, who had done this great thing for her because of His handmaid's very lowliness. Only thus may we understand the alarming words which were twice copied down during those last days:

"You are a great saint!"

"No, I do not consider myself a great saint—*I think I am a very little saint*; I believe it pleased God to place in me things which would do good for me and others."[26] And when an ear of wheat was brought to her bed, she pulled out the heaviest. "Mother, that ear of wheat is the image of my soul. God has loaded it with graces for me and for many others. And it is my dearest wish ever to bend beneath the weight of God's gifts." Then, fearing that this thought might savour of pride, she added: "Oh, how I should like to be humiliated and abused, so that it will be seen whether I am truly humble of heart.... But still, in the past, when I was humiliated, I was very happy about it.... Yes, I believe I am humble. God shows me the truth; I feel so clearly that everything comes from Him." Another time she said to her sisters, in the midst of the silence of a night vigil: "You do know that you are caring for a little saint..." And then, as if to erase this sentence which seemed to have welled up out of deep reflections, she went on: "But you are saints too!" Probably this was intended to mean: I am no better than you; God can do the same in you that He has done in me—has certainly already done it.

Petitot sees in this understanding of herself the stamp of natural genius and compares these words with the verdicts of great artists or thinkers on their own super-eminence and the future fame of their still unappreciated works. We cannot agree with this. We find in Thérèse no signs of natural (as opposed to supernatural) genius. Rather, these words seem to express the concept of sanctity of her period, which we have already discussed. Yet they reveal also a pinnacle of religious self-detachment. At such moments

[25] 2 S., 911.
[26] 1 S., xix, 153.

the saint was capable of regarding herself as impartially as any other of God's creatures and praising God's wonders in herself as she would do for anyone else. "By God's grace, I am what I am, and the grace He has shown me has not been without fruit." [27]

How careful she was even at such times to weigh carefully what she said—that is, to specify plainly what was God's share and what her own. "Oh, it is incredible, how all of my hopes have been realized. Once when I was reading St John of the Cross I begged God to fulfil in me what He describes, that is, to sanctify me in a few years as much as if I would have reached old age, in order to consume me swiftly with His love—and He has granted my request!"

"When I think of all the graces God has shown me, I cannot keep back tears of *perfect contrition*." [28]

"What do you think of all the graces that have been heaped upon you?" she was asked.

"I think 'the Spirit of God breatheth where He will.'"

"How patient you are!"

"I have never had patience for a single moment. It is not *my* patience. It is always misinterpreted!" And again when the doctor praised her heroic endurance: "How can he say that I am patient! I sigh and whimper and cry out continually: O my God, my God, I cannot go on, have mercy, have mercy on me!" [29]

Not for a moment did she attempt to adjust herself to the saint's part she was expected to play, to the pattern all expected. Pauline suggested that she say something edifying to the doctor when he visited her. "Oh, that is not for me. Let the doctor think what he wishes. I want only simplicity—anything else is horrible to me. Believe me, if I did as you wish, it would be very wrong of me." Another time she was asked to toss rose petals to the nuns when they came as a group to bid her good-bye. Thérèse refused—she would not do that even for her little Mother's sake. Scattering roses was her personal expression of tenderness for Our Lord and His saints, not a charming gesture for human beings.

Thérèse sat one day in the garden, regarding the blue sky. Her sister, edified by her expression, said: "With what love you are looking at Heaven!"

"Oh, do you imagine I am thinking about the real Heaven? Not at all, I am simply admiring the material firmament; the other is more and more closed to me."

[27] I Cor 15:10.
[28] I S., xix, 185.
[29] N.V., 20 September.

She was profoundly grateful when her pain-racked nerves would give way and a tiny fault would shame her in the eyes of the others.

A clumsy, well-meaning nun brought her a child's toy to divert her. For the moment taken aback by the silliness, Thérèse rather coolly refused the proffered toy: "Whatever should I do with that?" Immediately afterwards she wept and begged the sister's pardon: "Oh, forgive me, forgive me, I was so rude." And when the sister did not at once forgive her for the "ingratitude", she felt sincerely and painfully guilty. "How happy I am," she said shortly afterwards, "to find myself, even so close to death, so imperfect and so needing God's grace!"[30]

Another time a sister offered her a cup of broth. At the very sight and smell of it, Thérèse was seized by an insuperable nausea and refused it with the usual formula of thanks. Incensed by what she thought was finickiness, the nun carried off the soup and vented her feelings by remarking loudly that Sister Thérèse was not only no saint, but not even a good nun. "What a benefaction that is," Thérèse said, "to hear on one's deathbed that one has not even been a proper nun!" And we willingly believe her, remembering her words about the spicy salad which was so necessary to counteract the sweets of excessive praise.

Some time before Thérèse's collapse, Pauline was standing by one day when someone asked the sick girl, who was burning with fever, to do some altogether superfluous painting. Thérèse betrayed her vexation for just a moment by flushing violently and remaining silent. "In the evening she wrote a note to me: This evening I showed you for once my 'virtue' and my 'treasures of patience'. I who am so good at preaching to others! I am glad you witnessed my failure. You did not reprove me—and yet I deserved it. But on all occasions your kindness says more to me than stern words; you are for me the image of divine mercy. Oh, how much good it does me that I have been bad! I much prefer it that I failed, than if, supported by grace, I had been a model of meekness. It does me infinite good to see how Jesus is always invariably gentle, invariably loving towards me!"[31]

"Read aloud to me from the life of a saint", she asked after some trying little incident. "My soul is hungry."

"Would you like to hear something about St Francis? You will like it; it is full of flowers and birds."

"No, not for that reason," Thérèse replied gravely, "but because I need examples of humility."

[30] 2 *S.*, 322.
[31] 1 *S.*, xviii, 8.

Until the last she knew, for all that she had called herself a little saint, how much her confidence stood in need of fear and trembling; until the last she remained faithful to her Little Way.

"I can base my confidence upon nothing, not upon a single one of my works. Thus, for example, I very much wished to be able to say: 'I have said all the offices for the dead which were my obligation.' [The Prioress had just granted her dispensation from these.] But my poverty is a true grace to me. I reflected that in my whole life I have been unable to pay a single one of my debts to God—and that precisely this, if I would have it so, might be true wealth and a source of strength to me. And so I have prayed: 'O my God, do You make up for all the debts I still owe towards the souls in Purgatory, but do it as God, so that it will be infinitely better than if I myself had fulfilled my obligations.' And I felt great consolation as I thought of the words in the canticle of St John of the Cross: 'Do Thou pay all debts.'[32] I had always referred these words to Love. I feel that is a grace which cannot be explained,... we experience such great peace in being absolutely poor, in being able to count upon nothing but God."[33]

"My Mother," she said to the Prioress, "if I were to be unfaithful now, if I were now to commit the slightest act of unfaithfulness, I would have to pay for it with frightful torments; I could no longer accept death. Therefore I never cease to ask God: My God, I beseech You to preserve me from the misery of being unfaithful to You!" What did she mean by unfaithfulness, the Prioress inquired. "If, for example, I should entertain voluntarily a proud thought, such as: I have acquired such and such a virtue; I am convinced that I can practise it. For that would mean depending on my own strength, and when one has come to that point, one risks plunging into the abyss. If I were to say: O my God, You know I love You too greatly to linger over a single thought against the Faith—my temptations would become so violent that I should most certainly succumb. But if I remain humble, *I have the right, without offending God, to commit little follies until the day I die.*"[34] "When I reflect on those words of Our Lord: 'I come quickly, and My reward is with Me, to render to every man according to his works', I think that He will find my case a puzzle: I have no works. Well, He will reward me according to His own works."

On 9 July the convent chaplain visited her and said encouragingly: "What is all this about your entering Heaven soon! Why, your crown is far from finished. You have only just begun to fashion it!"

---

[32] *The Living Flame of Love*, Stanza 2.
[33] *N.V.*, 6 August, supplemented from 2 *S.*, 907.
[34] 7 August.

"Certainly, Father, that is true. No, I have not yet woven my wreath, but God has finished it for me."

With moving simplicity, Thérèse accepted the painful weaknesses her failing body imposed upon her. Her slow starvation—for a long time she was able to take only liquid nourishment—engendered vivid fantasies of greed, as is often the case. Her imagination was suddenly filled with images of all kinds of delicious foods for which she felt a morbid craving. She and her sisters could understand this in no other terms than as another example of diabolic temptation; this time the devil wanted to lead her to gluttony and immoderation. Thérèse suffered intensely from these fantasies; she felt that all her "spirituality" was being humiliated. "All my life eating was for me only an occasion for self-conquest—and look what has become of me now. It seems to me that I shall die of hunger. Oh, how horrible that is, to die of hunger! I am suffocating in material things. O my God, come and fetch me soon!" [35] "My sisters, pray for the unfortunates who are on their death-bed. If you knew what goes on in one, how little it takes to make one lose patience! How merciful and forbearing you must be with them, no matter who they are!"

"I have never had so bad a night. Oh, how good God must be, that I can endure all this suffering. Never did I think I could suffer so much—and I think I have not yet reached the end. But He will not abandon me."

"Perhaps I shall lose my reason", she said on 19 August. "Oh, if you knew what I am going through. Tonight, when I could endure it no longer, I asked the Blessed Virgin to take my head in her hands, so that I could endure this pain!" "Oh, how I pity myself", she moaned softly. "Nevertheless, I would not suffer less."

"I am glad I have never asked God for suffering", she said to the Prioress, who visited her and gave her her blessing. "That way He is obliged to give me the courage to endure it."

"It seems to me you are made for suffering", the Prioress replied. "Your soul is tempered for it."

"Oh, for spiritual suffering, yes; I can take a great deal of that.... But as for physical pain, I am like a little child, a very little child; I cannot think at all, I only suffer, minute after minute. My mother, how much God must help one when one suffers so!" [36]

"Little Mother," she cried out to Pauline, at the end of her strength, "pray for me! If you knew how I am suffering. Pray that I shall never lose

[35] 2 S., 569.
[36] 25 August.

patience. Oh, how I need God's help. I who wished so intensely all possible forms of martyrdom—ah, one must be in it to know what it means!" [37]

More than once she confessed that the pain was driving her to the verge of suicide. "Three days before her death I saw her in such a state that my heart broke", Sister Marie of the Holy Trinity declared. "I approached her bed; she made an effort to smile at me, and said in a voice choked by suffocation: 'Oh, if I had no faith I could never endure so much pain. I wonder that many more among those who deny God do not take their own lives.' " [38]

To Pauline Thérèse had said earlier: "Be very careful, when you have to care for such patients again, never to leave poisonous medicines standing by their bedside. I assure you, it takes only a moment to lose one's control when one has such pain." And we must remember that at this time she was plunged in the deadly darkness of her spiritual night!

Even the devil had to serve her ends. When a mocking voice filled her nights, demanding: "Are you certain God loves you? Has He Himself told you so? The opinion of a few creatures will not justify you in His sight!" she employed this temptation to anchor herself still more firmly in humility, and to offset what might have been a natural inclination to listen too fondly to the "opinion of creatures". More and more profoundly she entered into a recognition of her insignificance, while those around her were already venerating her as a saint.

"I should never ask God for greater pain, for then it would be my own pain; I would have to bear it alone—and I have never been able to do anything by myself."

"In childhood the great events of my life seemed from afar like mountains I could never reach. When I saw other little girls going to First Communion, I said to myself: How shall I ever reach my First Communion? Later: How shall I ever get to the point of entering Carmel? And still later: reach my Clothing, make my Profession? And now I say the same of dying."

Continually, the darkness of her temptation accompanied the ghastly pain of her decaying body, the terrible suffocation. Only for short periods at a time did the "hissing of hideous serpents" cease in her soul. The impenetrability of this torment held her, in spite of her overflowing urge to communicate and feel the sympathy of others, in a solitude none could enter. "I have waited for Jesus all night. I have rejected many temptations. Ah, I have made many acts of faith. I too can say: 'I look to the right of me, and find none to take my part...' in the hour of my death",

[37] 2 S., 828.
[38] 1 S., xix, 319.

she added placatingly, even in her torment not wishing to offend her sister, for the psalm continues: "All hope of escape is cut off from me, none is concerned for my safety." [39]

Towards the end of August a new, inexplicable anxiety and uneasiness began. Thérèse felt that she was subject to a diabolic threat; she begged more intensely than ever for prayers. A blessed candle was kept burning all night long. She asked the nurse to sprinkle her bed with holy water. "The devil is about me. I do not see him but I feel him near me. He torments me and holds me with a grip of iron to deprive me of all consolation, trying by increasing my sufferings to make me despair. Oh, how necessary it is to pray for the dying. If you only knew! How needful is that prayer we use at Compline: 'Free us from the phantoms of the night!' . . . I believe the devil has asked God for permission to try me by such extreme suffering, in order that I may lose both patience and faith."

But precisely in this uncertainty, in this ultimate exposure to powerlessness, Thérèse knew herself to be carried by the invisible and, alas, impalpable hands of God. In them she rested, still a child, until the last a trustful child. "God has always helped me, leading me by the hand since my childhood, and I rely upon Him now. Though I should endure the extremity of suffering, I know He will be there with me."

Out of such depths, infinitely far from all lofty heroic poses, she exercised that *amor fati* which is the essence of true heroism. "I have prayed that you would not have to suffer so, and now you are suffering so terribly!" Céline lamented. And Thérèse responded: "I have prayed to God not to listen to any prayers which would set obstacles in the way of the fulfilment of His will with regard to me." [40]

And once again, this time put very childishly: "Yesterday I prayed to the Blessed Virgin that I would not have to cough, so that Sister Geneviève [Céline] could sleep—but I added: and if you do not grant my prayer, I will love you still more." When the sisters expressed their pity that even all the saints were apparently abandoning her, she said "with a kind of pride": "I believe they want to see how far I can carry my trust."

Out of this knowledge that she was being supported sprang the gentle, childlike bravery of her endurance, which was at once obedience, submission, love and simplicity. Here, too, was the source of her unwearying, vital affection for others, her tender charity, her invariable smile, her unfailing consolation for the other sisters, who were less able to withstand the sight of her anguish than the sufferer herself. Here, too, was the source of that unfathomably profound, scarcely translatable phrase of hers:

[39] Ps 141:5.
[40] 10 August.

"We who go the way of love—it seems to me we must not think of the pain that may await us in the future, because that would mean a lack of confidence. And it would be like trying to interfere with Creation—*c'est comme se mêler de créer.*" [41]

"My heart is full of the will of God; whatever is poured upon it does not penetrate to the inside; it is a mere nothing that glides off like a drop of water that cannot mix with oil." And with inexpressible gentleness flowered the peace which was the miracle of this illness, the peace the world cannot give. "You are sad, little Mother; what is the matter?"

"Because you must suffer so frightfully."

"Certainly—but at the same time, what peace—what peace!"

"Do you see over there in the garden, beside the chestnut trees, the black hole where it is impossible to make anything out? I am in such a hole, soul and body. Oh, yes, what darkness! But I am at peace." [42]

"What do you say to God?" asked the nurse who found her one night sleepless and praying.

"I say nothing—I just love Him."

Hundreds of times the silly question was asked her whether she "would rather" die or get well, would rather die sooner or later, would rather die easily or hard, would rather go on suffering or not. Did no one see the cruelty of such an inquisition? With invariable gentleness Thérèse repeated in a hundred ways: "As God wills."

"And if you could choose?"

"I would not choose." "God gives me no premonition that death is close, but only of far greater sufferings. But I am not afraid; I want only to think of the present moment." "I always suffer only for a moment; if we think of the past and future, we despair."

"God gives me courage exactly in proportion to my pain. I always feel that at the moment I could endure no more, but I am not afraid—if the torment increases, He will also increase my courage."

Again and again, from various sides and with various intentions, she was asked the unanswerable and trying question of when she would die. Would she die on a great feast day or at the moment after Holy Communion? She ignored all this. "I have never wished to die on a feast day; my death will be feast day enough for me."

"I am like a small child at the railway station, waiting for its parents to place it on the train. But alas, they do not come, and the train is leaving. Still, there are other trains; I shall not miss them all."

---

[41] 23 July.
[42] *N.V.*, 28 August.

"On the ninth [of June] I clearly saw in the distance the lighthouse which points my way to the port of Heaven, but now I no longer see it; it is as if I were blindfolded. Whatever is said to me about the closeness of my death no longer reaches me. God undoubtedly wishes me not to be so concerned with that now as I was before I fell ill. Then the thought was necessary and highly useful to me; I felt that. But now it is just the reverse. He wishes me to surrender myself like a little child which does not worry at all about what is going to be done with it."

"I need not prepare for that journey", she wrote to Léonie. "...Jesus Himself must pay all the expenses, as well as the price of my admission to Heaven." And when she was asked, almost anxiously, what right she had to be so unconcerned, since even saints had trembled at the thought of damnation, she answered with loving confidence: "Little children are not damned."

Not even concern for a "good death", as current piety then interpreted that phrase, troubled her any longer. "If some morning you find me dead, you must not be unhappy about that, for then God [*Papa le Bon Dieu*] has simply come for me. Undoubtedly it is a great grace to receive the Sacraments, but if God does not permit it, that is well, too.... All is grace."

Until the last her smile of patient—no, rather of radiant—serenity was so natural, so without any sign of being forced, that among some of the nuns the rumour spread—even at this point!—that Thérèse really was not so sick as her sisters pretended. Her request for the Last Sacraments was greeted by some with actual scorn; what an "embarrassment" it would be for her if she received them now and afterwards got up again. Even the convent chaplain, whose task it is to decide such a matter, was deceived by her peaceful gaiety to such an extent that at first he refused to administer Extreme Unction, considering it needless. "You do not at all give the impression of someone sick", Pauline afterwards said to her with gentle reproach. "And you also have no idea how to behave in order to obtain what you want!" "No, this is a trade I really do not understand", Thérèse replied gravely.[43]

The nun who had taken offence when Thérèse refused the broth—even she had the excuse that behind that peaceful smile it was impossible to guess the fatality of Thérèse's illness. Others, again, abused her patience by engaging in tiring conversations, which Thérèse charitably endured by summoning up all her strength. The Prioress, fearing precisely such importunity, had forbidden the novices to visit her; otherwise they

---

[43] 2 *S.*, 291.

would have stormed their young Mistress's door. But time and again one would slip through the barriers. A lay sister who had charge of tending Thérèse during the convent Mass later admitted candidly: "Convinced that I was in the presence of a saint, I spent the entire hour questioning her and obtaining benefit from her edifying replies—without realizing that I was subjecting my heroic patient to an excessive strain. An extremely painful fit of choking was the consequence."

It was during this visit that Thérèse asked mercy for the flies which were tormenting her, and which the sister wanted to kill. "We should spare our enemies, and I have no others."

Even malice did not remain away from the sickbed. One nun thought it incumbent upon her to inform Thérèse directly: "If only you knew how little you are loved and esteemed in the house!"[44]

At the beginning of the last phase of the disease, there seems to have been a good deal of talk about the fact that Thérèse was no longer "doing" anything and was "an unnecessary burden" on the community. There may also have been envy over the special position the Prioress granted to this patient, envy that she could be constantly tended by her own sisters and cousin, envy over the expensive medicines and the gifts of fine fruit that were sent to her by her relatives in the world. "Sister Thérèse is utterly useless. Look how slowly she walks; she certainly does not hurry. When will she ever begin to work properly?"[45] "That is my least concern", Thérèse said when the gossip was, equally needlessly, repeated to her.

Even in July Pauline said anxiously to her: "If you go on living long, no one will understand what your illness is all about." "What does that matter!" Thérèse replied cheerfully. "I shall be glad if all despise me—I have always wanted that; now, at least, I shall have it at the end of my life."

Yet sometimes she was nevertheless oppressed by the lack of understanding. "My soul feels utterly exiled—Heaven is closed to me and on the earth there is no longer anything but tribulation.... I am well aware that others do not believe I am seriously ill, but that comes from God."

Worse still is that really weird story of the unnamed nun who came every evening and posted herself silently at the foot of the bed to contemplate the sick girl for a while, *laughing*. (The original version expressly says "laughing", while the *Novissima Verba* softens this to "smiling very intensely", which scarcely means anything.[46]) Was this malice, tri-

[44] I S., xvii, 38.
[45] I S., xvii, 65.
[46] 2 S., 923; *N.V.*, 25 August.

umph, hatred? Thérèse bravely smiled back; afterwards she was utterly spent. In response to Pauline's question she replied: "Yes, it is very painful to be regarded laughingly while one is suffering—but I think Our Lord on the Cross in the midst of his torment must have been looked at in exactly that way. It says in the Gospel that they looked at Him and shook their heads. This thought helps me to offer this sacrifice to Him gladly."

On the day she received the Last Sacraments, the sisters scarcely gave her time to compose herself after Communion—so many of them wanted to see and to talk with her. "How I was disturbed in my thanksgiving! But I thought that when Our Lord wanted to retreat into the desert, the multitude followed Him, and He did not send them away. I wanted to imitate Him by receiving the sisters gladly."

She continued to share in spirit in the life of the community. One hot day she said: "Today at one o'clock I thought to myself: now the sisters will be very weary in the laundry. I therefore asked God to refresh all of you, so that the work would go forward in joy and love. And since I was feeling so bad at the moment, I was glad that I was able to suffer like the rest of you."

Thérèse was firmly convinced that she was beyond the help of medicines, and so she found it hard to use all the expensive remedies procured for her. She spurred herself into taking them by remembering "that St Gertrude was gladdened by the thought that it would redound to the good of our benefactors, since Our Lord Himself has said: 'Whatever you do to the least of My little ones, you do unto Me.' ... I have made a covenant with God that the poor missionaries who have neither time nor means to take care of themselves may profit by the medicines that are given to me."

In spite of all distress of soul and body, her lively humour remained indestructible, and the clear, austere sobriety of her mind unaffected. "Now look at our pallet!" she cried out merrily as the mattress upon which the dead were laid on the bier was placed in the adjoining room, in preparation. "It will be nicely at hand to receive my cadaver."

"Death will come to fetch you."

"No, not death, but God! Death is not, as pictures tell us, a phantom, a horrid spectre. The Catechism says that it is the separation of soul and body—no more!"

"The most beautiful angels all robed in white will bear your soul to Heaven", another sister said, by way of comfort.

"Fancies like these do not help me. My soul can only feed upon truth. That is why I have never desired visions. On earth we cannot see Heaven or the angels as they are; therefore I would rather wait until after my death."

Eloquent descriptions of the joys of Heaven, which were read aloud to her or summoned up in conversation, left her cold. "It is not that which attracts me."

"What then?" (How much this question betrays.)

"To love, to be beloved, and to return to earth to teach love for our Love!"

This is the thought which now incessantly occupied her mind. Or rather there were two: the promise of the "shower of roses", the graces and benefactions she would send, and the consciousness of the "mission" now beginning for her, to teach others the Little Way. The two strands cannot always be disentwined; Thérèse's mission included both: temporal aid in earthly needs, and instruction of souls in how to follow her Way.

Thérèse spoke so precisely, in such detail, of the work she would do after her death, of the nature of the shower of roses, that many persons tend to see her as gifted with prophetic vision. We would doubt this; it seems to us to be belied by Thérèse's admitted spiritual darkness during those very weeks and months. How could she simultaneously remain completely blind as to her own immortality and every possibility of a life hereafter, and nevertheless envisage with such clarity her own existence in Heaven and capacity to influence the course of affairs upon earth? These two states of mind seem scarcely compatible. It is not impossible that in her consciousness the sense of approaching annihilation should have alternated with visions of coming glory as swiftly and arbitrarily as dreams in a delirium. But we are inclined to see Thérèse's numerous conversations and promises of future deeds as a reaction against her temptations, as exercises in hope. Deaf, blind and insensible to the other world though she was, her faith and confidence in God's faithfulness were sufficient for her to dare to promise: "So it will be—because God is God! because everything I paint for you in my boldest exaggerations is mere gossamer to what He has reserved for those who love Him." This was a pure, overwhelming, wonderfully defiant act of faith.

"After my death I will let fall a shower of roses.... God would not inspire me with this desire to do good on earth after my death if He did not intend to realize it. Otherwise He would rather inspire me with the desire to rest in Him—don't you think?"

"I feel that my mission is soon to begin, to make others love God as I do, to teach others my 'little way'. I will spend my Heaven in doing good upon earth.... I will not be able to rest until the end of the world, when the Angel has said: 'Time is no more!' Then I shall rest and be able to rejoice, for the number of the elect will be complete."

Thus the twelfth chapter of the *Histoire* collects a number of her statements. More and more intensely, Thérèse saw herself in the likeness of the beloved heroine of her childhood, the Maid of Orléans.

"The saints also encourage me in my prison; they say to me: 'As long as you are in chains you cannot fulfil your mission; later after your death, will come the time of your conquests.' "

With what exactitude Thérèse pictured these conquests to herself, as a person before his vacation might carefully go over in his mind the pleasures of the holiday, imagining them and enjoying them in advance. This seems surprising when we consider how resolutely she had just rejected all fantasies of Heaven. Now she herself let her fancy play in a way she had never allowed herself earlier; perhaps this mood corresponded to the period before her entry, when she had dreamed of martyrs' torments and crusaders' exploits. It may also be that those childish, tasteless pictures of Heaven drawn by the others may have been partly what occasioned her temptations against the Faith, and that she fled from them into the sober, stern acceptance of our ignorance. The pictures she painted for herself were a kind of antidote to these others— although we must confess that sometimes her own language did not differ from them too greatly. Once she pointed to a passage in a missionary magazine describing the appearance of a white-garbed saint at the bedside of a sick child. "That is how I shall be", she said. A month before her death Céline remarked: "To think that the sisters in the mission Carmel in Indochina still think you will be coming...." "I will come to them soon", Thérèse replied quite matter-of-factly. "If you only knew how swiftly I shall make my rounds, once I am in Heaven. I will help little children to baptism, I will aid priests, missionaries, the whole Church."

Sister Marie tells a tale that sounds utterly Franciscan. Thérèse was sitting in the garden, watching her set traps for the greedy birds. She begged for the lives of the little thieves. "I must destroy them", Marie apologized. "Otherwise we will have no cherries or strawberries next year." "Please let the birds be", Thérèse said. "You will see, when I am in Heaven I will send you fruit enough!" Marie yielded, in order not to grieve the sick girl, and thought no more about the matter. But next summer at harvest time two large baskets of fruit actually arrived from another convent, and this gift was thenceforth repeated every year.

"When you set out for Africa, I will follow you, no longer only in thought and prayer", she wrote to Father Bellière. "I shall always be with you, and with a believing heart you will feel the presence of the little sister whom Jesus placed by your side, not for a mere two years, but until the last day of your life." [47]

[47] 3 February 1897.

"Will you look down upon us from Heaven?" the sisters begged her. "No, I will come down", Thérèse assured them.

Far more remarkable is the manner in which, during the last fourteen days of her life, she concerned herself about her own relics, if we may put it that way. She expressly and of her own accord asked her sisters, in whose presence she was utterly unembarrassed and felt secure against giving offence, to gather carefully the rose petals which she was accustomed to scatter over her crucifix. "Don't lose a single one of them, my sisters; they will later serve you to give joy to many souls."

From the very beginning of her confinement to her bed, Sister Marie had been collecting her loose hairs, convinced that these would soon be considered relics. (Marie of the Holy Trinity did the same, although Thérèse may not have known this.[48]) This need not surprise us, nor that the sisters dabbed up on linen cloths the tears wrung from her by pain and weakness and greeted an eyelash found on such a handkerchief as precious booty. But what is strange is that Thérèse with full consciousness not only tolerated such practices, but supported them; that she even ordered them to preserve her clipped nails—a matter that the *Advocatus Diaboli* specially mentioned.[49] All that is disquieting and might almost overthrow our image of her at the very end, if we were not to assume that even this, so altogether unprecedented in the history of the saints, may well have been a unique expression of boundless hope—permissible in self-defence against the unbearable onslaught of temptation which whispered to her that her soul and body were doomed to total annihilation. Or was there behind it some inner command of which we know nothing? Plucked from the context of superabundant, irrefutable testimony of unshakable humility and simplicity, such incidents would be extremely offensive. But the overwhelming unanimity of those other voices must silence our qualms.

In point of fact innumerable miracles have been performed by means of all these things. We do not know and will never know—for here the veil drops impenetrably over the hidden face—what degree of inner certainty was given to Thérèse in the midst of her darkness. What is it that radiates through such words as these: "In Heaven God will do all I desire, because on earth I have always done His will"? Or: "Yes, now I know it: all my hopes will be fulfilled in abundance. Yes, Our Lord will do wonders for me infinitely exceeding my vast desires!"

She was also concerned about the influence her autobiography was to have.

[48] 1 S., xx, 144.
[49] 1 S., 17.

Pauline had at first taken no great account of the notebook which her sister obediently handed to her for her feast day in 1896. She knew what was in it, after all. When Thérèse's condition grew so much worse in May, Pauline read the notebook again, and suddenly it acquired great importance in her eyes. She recognized in it her sister's spiritual legacy. Now she became burningly concerned with the problem of how this treasure was to be garnered and distributed. By the exercise of some diplomacy, she prevailed upon Mother Marie de Gonzague to order Thérèse to continue it. In June, sitting in the garden in her wheelchair, Thérèse wrote the ninth and tenth chapters. The work was a great strain; at the end she could scribble down only a sentence at a time and wrote in pencil because dipping pen in ink was too trying. At this time she herself seems not to have thought about any wider distribution, for she began the section: "I will simply do as I am told. I do not seek to know what use this manuscript could be, and have no hesitation in saying, Mother, that I should not be in the least disturbed if you burnt it before my eyes without even reading it."

It had probably been said to her, Petitot avers, that her notes might later be employed for the obituary letter.[50] From the conversations at her sickbed, however, it seems to us evident enough that Pauline and Thérèse soon agreed that the work required publication in the broadest sense. They frequently said that the autobiography should be sent out to "many souls" and "all sorts of souls" in order to show them the Little Way. Yet Thérèse remained quite tranquil in the midst of all these ambitions. "Suppose our Mother throws the whole thing into the fire?" Pauline fretted. "Oh, that would not trouble me in the least; I would still not doubt my mission. I would simply think that God intended to fulfil my desires in another fashion."[51] Again and again she said: "Souls must be told..." The famous passage in chapter 10 of *The Story of a Soul* beginning: "If I had committed all the crimes it is possible to commit..." was inserted by Pauline at Thérèse's express request after a conversation on 11 July. "Souls will understand that at once; this example [of the death in love of the converted sinner in the desert] will encourage them." Could Thérèse really have been thinking only of souls in Carmel? Pauline told her again and again what profit readers would reap from what she had written. "But how well they will see that everything comes from God! Whatever glory I win from it will only be a present made me from His prodigality, nothing I have any right to of my own accord. Yes, *all* will be convinced of that." "*Tout le monde*"—to be sure this phrase in French often means

[50] Petitot, 152.
[51] Petitot, 150.

only "very many" or "a number of people". But even taken in that sense, more are signified than the Carmelite nuns. Sometimes it is quite clear that Thérèse was using the phrase in its literal sense: "Mother, these pages will do so much good; people will learn to know God better from them. Oh, I am sure of it, *everybody* will love me for them." [52]

At the beginning of August the sisters discussed publication frankly at least once. Reading between the lines we can see that they were aware of the hardihood of such an undertaking and what a departure it would be from Carmelite tradition. "Mother, after my death you must not talk with anyone about my manuscript, until it is *published* with the consent of our Mother. If you do differently, the devil will set more than one trap for you in order to prevent and ruin the work of God—a very important work. . . .

"As for my mission, it will be the same as with Joan of Arc: the will of God will be fulfilled in spite of human jealousy."

We ask ourselves—may the saint forgive us the question!—whether here too the long abandoned child's dream of *gloire*, of the glory of earthly immortality, did not rise up for the very last time and become a shimmering, elusive vision before her dying eyes. It is a question without an answer.

We know only this, and perhaps it casts a ray of light upon the riddle, that in her last days Thérèse experienced a kind of judgment upon her past life and upon the testimony she had written. It is as though all the devout words she had said a hundred times over were being weighed in a new, inexorable balance, all her youthful enthusiasms and dreams of love, all her wise doctrines and exacting demands upon others. "Oh, my mother, what does it mean to have written beautiful words about suffering? Nothing, nothing! One must experience it to know what such effusions are worth!" she cried out one day in extreme anguish. But six days before her death she looked at Pauline as though remembering these words, which had made a painful impression upon her sister, and said: "Now I feel it clearly: what I have said and written is true—*all of it*. It is true that I asked to suffer greatly for God—and it is true that I still desire to do so."

This affirmation sounds altogether new, a "yes" arising shining and unimpaired out of the unfathomable depths of tribulation.

"Yes, my God, yes, yes," she murmured again and again under her breath in the midst of her torment, "I will suffer it all gladly—all."

"What would you do if you could begin your religious life over again?"

"I think I should do as I have already done."

Thérèse had felt little fear of death during the months of this long-drawn-out agony. She looked forward to the "great crossing" as she once called it, with a kind of timid, but solemn confidence. It is as though the peacefulness of her understanding of God's designs cast a cloak over her own emotions, just as her inner darkness cloaked her joyful anticipation of bliss. All the agitated and troubled questionings and speculations around her, the predictions now of imminent death, now of surprising recovery, scarcely touched her. But it is not hard to sense how she deliberately kept aloof from such speculations. "If my heart were not already full, and room were left for passing feelings of joy and sadness, then bitterness would flood in, but such transitory feelings scarcely ruffle the surface, of my soul; a peace that nothing can mar reigns in its depths. Ah—and yet these are great trials."

With a strange joy she observed the visible disintegration of her own body, regarded her waxen, skeletal hands. "I am already becoming a skeleton... I am in process of dissolution—Oh, what joy that gives me!" This was no morbid pleasure in horror, but a deep sense that the true revelation of her nature was impending. "What we shall be hereafter, has not been made known as yet." [53] The same feeling probably prompted her remark at the sight of her own photograph: "Ah, yes, that is the envelope—when will we see the letter? Oh, how I wish to see the letter."

Sometimes it would seem as if the peaceful, unshakable joy that animated her in the midst of her darkness was directed more towards her parting from the earth, which she felt so intensely as a prison, than towards the bliss of the hereafter, which in this "night" had passed beyond her ken. "Were it not for this trial, which is impossible to understand, I think I should die of joy at the prospect of soon leaving this earth."

"I am like a child who is constantly promised a piece of cake; it is shown to him from afar, and when he runs up to take it, the hand is drawn back."

The prospect of possible recovery was the sole thing that really alarmed her. What a depth of experience of suffering is betrayed by this fear of continuing life.

"I have surrendered myself entirely, whether it be to life or to death. I would *even* be glad to get well again in order to go to Indochina, if that is God's will."

When she was at last taken to the infirmary on 8 July, the exclamation slipped from her: "I have only one fear—that my condition might change again for the better!"

---

[53] 1 Jn 3:2.

"How strange it would seem to you if you should after all get well again!" the sisters said to her as late as 18 August.

"If that were God's will, I would be very happy to make this sacrifice for Him. But I assure you, it would be no small thing—to have gone so far and have to go back again."

Three weeks before her death:

"If you were told that now, this very moment, you must die suddenly—would you be frightened?"

"Not at all. With what joy I would leave this earth!"

"Then I suppose it would be a grave disappointment to you to get well again?"

"No, not that either. If I should recover, everyone would certainly look at me in astonishment—and I would say that I was quite content to be well again in order to go on serving God on earth, since that is His will. I have suffered as if I were going to die—*eh bien*, I should simply begin all over again."

But in the midst of this affirmation there came, strangely, a little lost sigh: "And yet—how little I have lived!"

Thérèse was weary, truly weary unto death. "Yes, I am like a traveller, exhausted and harried, who collapses when he reaches his destination. But I fall into the arms of God." Her frayed soul was no longer capable of strong emotion, of reviving. "If you only knew how the thought of soon entering Heaven leaves me unmoved. Certainly I am very happy at the prospect, but I cannot say that I feel vivid joy or ecstatic rapture— Oh, no." Whereupon her sister's anxious question immediately came:

"Still, you would rather die than live?"

"Oh, my little Mother, I can only repeat to you: No, I do not desire the one or the other. I only will what God wills; it is what He does that I love."

At the last she had come to the point of wishing her end might come more swiftly for the sake of the others, "because I tire my nurse so, and because I feel how it hurts my sisters to see me so ill.... Ah, I would like to take my leave."

Quite late and only occasionally, flickering fears for her own fate passed like flashes of lightning through her composed spirit, fears of dying!... "I am afraid because I have feared dying. But I have no fear about 'after death', and I do not regret life—Oh, no! I only say to myself with a kind of anxiety: what is this mysterious separation of soul and body? This is the first time this feeling has come to me, but I soon give myself up to God's care." [54]

---

[54] 11 September.

"Ought I really to fear the devil? I do not think so, because I have always done everything under obedience."

"When will the Last Judgment come? Oh, how glad I would be if I had already gone through it. And afterwards—what will be afterwards?"

But at noon on 29 September she said to the Prioress: "Mother, is this the agony? How shall I ever be able to die? I shall never manage it."

In the evening of that painful day, during which her suffocation grew steadily worse, Céline begged her for a parting word. "I have already said everything.... It is finished. Only love counts."

"This is pure agony, without a ray of consolation", Thérèse said to Pauline in the morning of her last day. But a false final surge of strength deceived her again. "No, I am not going to die. Perhaps it will go on for months. I no longer believe in myself dying; I can only believe in my suffering."

Then the fear returned, this time nakedly: "If this is only the agony, what will death itself be like?"

"And it will be worse tomorrow—so much the better."

"Dear Mother, the chalice is full to overflowing! But God will not forsake me.... He has never forsaken me."

"Yes, my God, everything You will, but have mercy on me! My God, my God! You who are so good! Oh, yes, You are good! I know it."

Towards three o'clock she stretched out her arms in the form of a cross. Mother Marie de Gonzague placed a picture of Our Lady of Mount Carmel on her knees. Thérèse threw a glance at it. "Oh, Mother, commend me quickly, quickly to the Blessed Virgin. Prepare me to die well!"

"Your preparation is complete," the Prioress replied, "for you have always understood and practised humility."

Thérèse considered for a moment; then, with simple greatness, she made her witness: "Yes, I feel it; my soul has ever sought the truth. I have understood humility of heart." And as if adding a last word in confirmation of her legacy: "All I have written about my thirst for suffering—Oh, it is really true."

Her forehead was purple, streaming sweat, and inside her mind there swiftly passed the images of her short, sorrow-filled life. All was well as it had been—she submitted to all that had been given her and took nothing back. A glow of noble pride transfigured given her, contorted though it was by suffocation.

"I do not regret surrendering myself to Love." [55]

---

[55] "With *pride!*" these are the words used in the eyewitness's account (2 *S.*, 933). It is a pity that this original boldness and grandeur was weakened, for the sake of conformity to standardized notions, in the *Novissima Verba* to the feeble formula, "with firm confidence".

Again and again she whispered this sentence under her breath.

Then the fear of death surged up once more: "I cannot breathe... I cannot die... I will gladly go on suffering."

At five o'clock the funeral bell called the Carmelites to gather around the deathbed. Communal prayer guides the one who is called to the threshold which she alone must cross.

For two hours Thérèse choked and fought, but there seemed to be no change in her condition. At seven o'clock the Prioress dismissed the wearied nuns and remained alone with the Martin sisters.

"Mother, isn't this death yet? Am I not going to die?"

"Yes, my child, it is the agony, but perhaps God wills that it be prolonged for a few hours."

The dying girl attempted to smile. "Ah, very well then... very well! I do not wish to suffer less!"

Then, looking at her crucifix: "Oh, I love Him! My God, I love You!"

After these words her head fell back. For the second time the bell rang out its hasty summons, and the nuns of the community poured back into the room. "Open all the doors!" the Prioress said, and it seemed to Pauline as though at that moment this same command rang through Heaven. The sisters knelt around the bed. Thérèse's face became bright and clear; the horrid colour of suffocation vanished; her eyes opened once more, turned upwards, radiant and filled with amazed bliss. This look lasted about as long as a Credo. Then she closed her eyes, gave a little sigh, and died. It was almost half past seven in the evening.

7

THE RIDDLE OF GLORY

Go and tell John what your own ears and eyes have witnessed; how the blind see, and the lame walk, how the lepers are made clean, and the deaf hear, how the dead are raised to life, and the poor have the gospel preached to them.
—MATTHEW 11:4–5

I. HERALDS AT WORK

MY POOR LITTLE ANGEL," Pauline had written to Thérèse in June of the year she died, "the saints in Heaven can receive fame and glory until the end of the world, and they favour those who so honour them. *Eh bien*, I shall be your little herald; I shall proclaim your feats of arms; I shall endeavour to bring others to the love and service of God through all the illuminations which He has vouchsafed to you, and which shall never pass." [1]

Now Thérèse had completed her life's journey. And the sisters prepared to keep this promise, which henceforth became their burning mission in life, the true fulfilment of their lives. All three attained remarkably advanced ages. Mother Agnes died at ninety-one, Marie at eighty, and Sister Geneviève, born in 1869, is still living [1956; she died in 1959 at eighty-nine]. We may perhaps see it is a disposition of Providence that these three women were enabled to devote almost half a century to the work of glorifying their sister. From a purely historical point of view, the probability is slim that Thérèse's legacy would have been so well cared for in other hands.

There is fair evidence that even while Thérèse still lived her sisters were already counting on her formal canonization. "What you have written here may well some day reach as far as the Holy Father", one of them said "in an intimate group" in the sickroom. Thérèse replied only with a little joke, we read in the *Manuscrits Authentiques*. Canonization presupposes miracles, strictly checked, unquestionably authenticated miracles. Such miracles, moreover, would have to come in response to prayers—

[1] N.A.T., I, p. 48, footnote 3.

since in her lifetime Thérèse had worked none—which presupposes appeals to her, presupposes her being known and trusted. Hence Thérèse had to be introduced to the greatest possible number of believers, who must be moved to admiration of and veneration for her. With fervour and also with remarkable strategy, the three sisters directed their efforts to this goal. We must admire the complete confidence with which they devoted themselves to their belief in the importance and mission of their barely deceased youngest sister, all the more so since at the outset their faith was based exclusively upon her own words.

In the beginning Thérèse did not make their task easy. Some incidents took place in the convent immediately after her death. The perfume of violets and roses was noticed mysteriously here and there in the house and interpreted as a manifestation of the departed nun. A lay sister penitently pressed her brow against the feet of the dead girl lying on the bier, begged her pardon for having once offended her, and was immediately cured of her chronic headaches. But such things are related in many convents of recently departed devout nuns. To be sure, letters gratefully reporting help and the granting of requests, and ascribing graces to the intercession of Thérèse, soon increased in number, especially after the publication of the autobiography. But the first sensational and literally *usable* miracle did not take place until 1906, almost *nine* years after Thérèse's death. This was the sudden, complete healing of a seminarist dying of tuberculosis, Abbé Anne, who lay apparently in the last moment of the death-agony.

Shortly after Thérèse's death there appeared at the Carmel of Lisieux a number of postulants who had been converted by her book and awakened to their vocation. Two of them, distinguished by high social connections and considerable gifts, became Prioresses in succession and regarded the attainment of Thérèse's beatification as their mission in life. They too died young and are today venerated quietly in the Carmel as forming a "triple constellation" with the great saint.

But the beginning had to be made by the sisters entirely alone.

They started at once with the inscription on Thérèse's grave; after overcoming the Prioress's initial resistance they had placed on the simple cross the words: "I will spend my Heaven in doing good upon earth." Among the uniform graves of the nuns this inevitably attracted attention and probably gave rise to the first inquiries and the first appeals to Thérèse.

Christian people have always harboured a strong, never satiated yearning for encounters with saints, for the physical witness of the reality of that other world. The faintest tidings have ever been sufficient to fan that smouldering craving to a blaze, and to set in motion an eager, intensified listening, watching and waiting. This readiness was certainly well nourished by conversation and letters after the death of Thérèse.

Meanwhile, the Prioress and Mother Agnes prepared for the printing of Thérèse's autobiographical writings. Knowing what we know now, it is no longer possible to maintain the thesis that the handsome volume was actually intended only to take the place of the usual obituary letter, and that to everyone's wonder it raced out into the world like a sudden forest fire. Apart from the notes on the sisters' bedside conversations with Thérèse, we now also have the detailed correspondence which the Prioress conducted with her spiritual counsellors on the advisability of publication. We know what preparations and corrections were made in the manuscript. Moreover, for the first edition two thousand copies were printed—to the alarm of many of the nuns, who wondered what they were going to do with such a burden of unsaleable books. Presumably a fairly wide circle had already been prepared for the publication of the volume.

The Bishop, who was required to issue the Imprimatur, at first showed no great eagerness; a cautious attitude towards female imaginativeness was needful, he thought. The sisters recalled Thérèse's words that the devil would place obstacles in the path of the project; probably this opposition, short-lived though it was, only increased their zeal. By 7 March, barely half a year after Thérèse's death, the Bishop yielded, and in October the book appeared. The Carmel, in keeping with contemporary taste and the principal tendency of the book itself, proposed as a title: "A Canticle of Love, or the Passing of an Angel." Dom Godefroy Madelaine cautiously toned this down to "The Story of a Soul".

Here, too, we must be amazed at the unconscious sureness with which these nuns, who after all were entirely ignorant of all advertising methods, found precisely the right way to impress their beloved Thérèse upon the attention and imagination of the rest of the world. Pictures of Thérèse, which they began producing *en masse*, were done in the smooth, agreeable manner of the century's utilitarian art, corresponding precisely to the mass taste of the period and merging its devotional ideal with the person of the charming young girl. The manuscript was treated in the same way. "Passing of an Angel"—this title perfectly renders the tone of the stylization. Every lovable unevenness in character or behaviour was eliminated, even where it would have made the figure of Thérèse more vigorous or more interesting. A great many insertions and additions, very skilfully selected and placed, stressed the excellences of her environment, brought out the virtues of her parental household, underpainted, overpainted, emphasized and underplayed. It would take a detailed special study to analyse the incredibly intelligent technique by which the sisters achieved their end. The truth was never tampered with—that must be said again, expressly and emphatically. Nevertheless, a fabulous array of tiny accents, dabs of colour, lighting effects, remodelled and retouched the total picture so that it conformed perfectly to the current ideal. Even without these embellishments Thérèse fitted that ideal pretty well; as it was, the desired portrait and the reality were not only joined as closely as possible; they were completely fused. Thérèse became an angel in human form.

We have spoken in our first chapter of the tremendous success of the autobiography, which succeeded even beyond the sisters' vaulting expectations.

Devout souls continually requested mementoes of Thérèse, and the sisters went into mass production of pictures to which were pasted tiny bits of cloth or wood from objects Sister Thérèse had used. Clothes and linen, blankets and bed curtains were cut to bits and used in this way. Even the slats of the bed and the boards from the floor of her cell were chopped up. And Céline, who was in charge of this stock, was amazed how swiftly it melted away. During the twelve months from July 1909 to 1910, a staggering 183,348 little pictures and 36,612 relics were sent out on request—all this before the canonization proceedings had begun. From 1897 to 1925 the output reached the incredible figure of 30,500,000 pictures and 17,500,000 relics.[2]

The proceedings of the trial also mention the objections which arose inside the convent to all this activity. "I could understand it if so much fuss were made about the memory of Mother Geneviève [the founder of the convent] or Sister Adelaide. But Sister Thérèse, of all people? Why is she not left in her concealment among the Innocents? What has she ever done to claim any more attention?" one nun said. And: "No question about it, all this has been instigated by her sisters. But let us wait and see; the truth will be made known."

The truth has come to light, but not in the way that Sister Aimée meant.

Abbé Domin remarked at the trial: "Perhaps somewhat too much zeal was applied to the distribution of books, pictures and other objects pertaining to Sister Thérèse. But I do not think these efforts were intended to manufacture a reputation of sanctity out of nothing. Her sisters in the Carmel certainly were not indifferent to the success of their efforts—but I am certain that they acted with the greatest purity of intention."[3]

There is, then, no need to conceal the fact that human agency played a considerable part in the origination and propagation of the devotion to Thérèse. During the trial the *Promotor Fidei* (who is popularly called the Devil's Advocate) likewise pointed out that certain matters which in such

[2] Laveille, 445, note.
[3] 2 S., 972.

cases are usually called the result of Divine Providence must in this case be ascribed to human diligence. Thus, for example, Portuguese bishops granted indulgences to readers of the book, which certainly powerfully increased its prestige among the devout, and aided its distribution. The Reverend T. Taylor, one of the first British devotees of the saint, requested the Archbishop of Westminster to attach the same award to the English edition. However, he received the reply: "Possibly too much haste has been displayed in proceeding with this cause; we have heard that the role which the relations have played in the affair might compromise the success of the cause in Rome. Consequently, His Grace takes the view that it would be more prudent to bide our time." [4]

Even those who gladly and believingly accept the shower of roses must distinguish clearly between the supernatural phenomena of signs and portents, and the highly natural results obtained by modern communication media, through the magic of publicity and advertising. A vast propaganda apparatus naturally stimulated interest and trust throughout the world. If today the name of the "Little Flower" is appealed to on all the continents, modern technology—which pious circles are so fond of condemning as a possible invention of the devil—has contributed greatly to that outcome.

At times, too, we must feel that some French missionaries brought to the fore the veneration of *"la petite sœur de France"*, as they significantly called her, not for spiritual reasons alone. Sometimes it was a bit too much of a good thing when they proclaimed "God and Thérèse" to the natives in their charge, as though veneration of this saint were the second highest duty of a Christian. The result was that the king of one black tribe in Africa appointed Thérèse "regent" of his country. Here and there, in fact, veneration of the Blessed Virgin took second place to that of the little Carmelite. Moreover, the "popular demand" for her canonization, as we may see by the content of numerous petitions collected in the first volume of the *Summarium*, had some thoroughly earthly motives in the background.

But taken all in all, this zeal and what came of it, must be viewed in the light of the words of Gamaliel: "If this is man's design or man's undertaking, it will be overthrown; if it is God's, you will have no power to overthrow it." [5] Indeed, what if there had been no divine confirmation of these efforts? Then their colossal extent and the very publicity would have only underlined the failure—let us frankly say, the ridiculousness—of all merely human propaganda in such a cause. Thus we must rather be amazed by the boldness and firmness of the sisters' conviction, that they could risk such a fiasco.

---

[4] I S., Proc., fol. 186.
[5] Acts 5:38–39.

Similar cases are, after all, well known in the Church. There has never been a lack of efforts to awaken or promote veneration of some person who died in the odour of sanctity—though perhaps never have such means been employed on such a scale. We are all familiar with those prayer leaflets which urge readers to appeal to this or that Servant of God, and to communicate to the promoters the success of these prayers. In 1916 a young Visitation nun died in Como, Italy, who was in many respects a younger sister of Thérèse. Possibly with the example of Lisieux before their eyes, and with the expectation of similar results, a group who venerated her published a small selection of her writings. In fact, the far more dramatic claim was made that these writings were the result of mystical dictation by the Sacred Heart of Jesus to His "little secretary", set to paper by order of the nun's confessor. In 1923 the epilogue to a brief biography boasted that the little book was already distributed through eighteen countries of Europe and overseas, and in five languages. "Not a day passes but that reports of graces received, unexpected aid, rescue and protection of all sorts come into the convent at Como.... This simple nun, who lived in deepest concealment throughout her entire span of life ... finds her greatest joy, now that she is in possession of God, in consoling everyone who seeks refuge in her.... The graces are beyond count."

But how little has since been heard about Sister Benigna Consolata Ferreri.

Behind all the vigorous human efforts we find, in the "shower of roses", in the miracles that actually took place, the *divine* testimony. God "played a part" in these things. He Himself sanctioned the bold words of a dying girl, justified them and abundantly confirmed them before the eyes of the world.

The tremendous sale of the book, and the numberless conversions connected with it, must be esteemed a part of this divine testimony. For both are by no means to be taken for granted. For a few decades it was fashionable to hail *The Story of a Soul* as a "pearl of world literature". It was asserted that Virgil and Dante might sooner be lost than this precious book, that no unbeliever could resist the magic of a work over which "millions of believers have shed tears", or that it "inevitably captures by storm for God even the most reluctant doubter". But as early as 1921 a Roman decretal bluntly stated that the salutary results produced by reading the book are altogether disproportionate to the "narrow and purely human limits of its origins".

"We may unhesitatingly say", observes Father Petitot, "that no one would be able, without special preparation and preliminary studies, to recognize the worth of *The Story of a Soul* at first reading."

Father Pichon, too, the devout old Jesuit who was confessor to almost the entire Martin family, and who was also the only priestly spiritual director Thérèse ever had, said in the trial: "As for the causes of the absolutely extraordinary spread of her reputation for sanctity, I can only say that it seems to me *entirely inexplicable* unless we assume an equally extraordinary intervention by Divine Providence. Certainly the booksellers have spared no efforts to push the book, but in this they have rather followed an existing movement than created one themselves. The attraction this biography exerts upon people's minds cannot be explained by any amount of advertising." [6] It must be remembered that Father Pichon would be the last person to wish to detract from Thérèse's fame.

The rector of a theological seminary commented that the strong demand might also—though this would certainly not be the sole reason—be connected with the "eminent sentimentality" of *The Story of a Soul*. After all, best-sellers sometimes owe their success to their weaknesses as well as their good qualities.

Our present knowledge of the extent and nature of the editorial revisions supports such judgments, which only a few years ago would have been resented as blasphemies. In saying this we must stress once more that had the unrevised manuscripts been published at that time, they would most assuredly have had a far smaller chance of a good reception and popularity. (Only now, when Thérèse's fame shines in full radiance, have the manuscripts appeared.) But in any case, no natural explanation of the impression aroused by the book suffices.

There is, moreover, another vital circumstance to consider. Such texts as *The Story of a Soul* may seem startlingly unique to the unbeliever or the outsider, may open up to him an unknown world. But to the good Catholic of the turn of the [twentieth] century this book was just another, though slightly different specimen among dozens of devotional books of a similar type. Why did this particular one attract attention, since it stood out neither by form nor apparent content?

2. THE HAGIOGRAPHER'S TEMPTATION

At this point the hagiographer's great temptation begins.

His particular field—the literary portrayal of a saint—has undergone radical changes since about the turn of the [twentieth] century. Not the saint as a devotional figure, as exemplar, guide or rescuer now forms his chief concern, but the saint as a human being. Hagiography in the early

---

[6] 1 S., xxi, 95.

liturgical sense was concerned with reporting the *magnalia Dei*, the great deeds of God, as they were performed in and by a mortal soul. Now hagiography has become biography of a canonized individual; history and psychology hold the floor, and the attempt is made to set forth and explain the sanctity of a saint as if it were the accomplishment of any other famous person: from heredity, environment, education, encounters, crises, aids, hindrances and inevitable catastrophes, and from sociological and historical conditions.

The merits of the new methods are great indeed. In the course of generations the saints had been reduced to little more than remote and abstract models of virtue, or romantic figures of fable. The new mode of portrayal brought them back to earth in a most profound sense. Not the least of its services was that it countered the scornful and vicious attacks of almost two hundred years of blatant rationalism which had pictured the Christian saints as fanatics, idiots and psychopaths, or as asocial, morbid nuisances. With all due scholarship the new biographical approach uncovered a handsome gallery of greatly gifted figures in all the branches of human endeavour.

Such a revision of older views reassured and strengthened Catholics who in other respects also were labouring under an oppressive sense of inferiority. But gradually this new emphasis, originally only a supplementary one, outweighed everything else. Imperceptibly a new attitude crept in and soon became a cliché: saint and hero, saint and genius, were held to be interchangeable concepts. Sanctity was seen as the flowering of a splendid, rich, well-born human spirit, its highest pinnacle. Canonization was the recognition and proclamation of a hero and genius in the religious plane. This thesis can indeed be convincingly borne out by many figures in the calendar of saints. There are very many rulers and thinkers, founders and conquerors, organizers, pioneering teachers and social reformers among them, as well as sufferers, martyrs and miracle workers, persons gifted with inexplicable powers far exceeding those of average humanity.

But in Thérèse's case the limitations of this theory are made clear. The premises are simply lacking. We may well say without exaggeration: whatever elements of sublimity, mystic powers and extraordinariness are today read into the life and personality of the saint of Lisieux are retrospective projections of the startling, dazzling fact of her posthumous glory. So great is the gulf between this glory and her appearance on earth that some persons, unable to reconcile themselves to this, would pretend that no such gulf exists and impose what appears to be a simple casual link between the two.

Thérèse has been so glorified, it is argued, *because* her achievement and her character merited precisely this kind of response. Her glorification reveals the enormous power and uniqueness of this achievement and character. Some admirers prove psychologically, some in an almost mercantile manner, that her glorification necessarily is exactly proportionate to her human qualities, her merits here on earth. There is the temptation to say that it is due not to abundance of grace, altogether unmerited, not the Spirit of God breathing where it will, but rather the payment of a debt—as if God were acknowledging what He owes to this wonderful creature of His, and making manifest His settlement of the account by elevating her to such dizzying ascent.

We may willingly discount a great deal in such speeches and writings as due to oratorical rhetoric, the excitement of a great festival, the exultation of a battle won at last, the Latin temperament, and occasional surges of ecclesiastical nationalism. But no matter how much we forgive, a residue remains which we cannot accept. First of all, there is an implicit axiom never directly spoken, but indirectly urged a thousand times over: that merit and glory correspond to one another in a manner demonstrable to human reason: that it is possible to determine by statistical figures how close a human being stands to God. And this is theologically insupportable.

Secondly, in order to prove this untenable thesis Thérèse's activities and accomplishments or her personal qualities must be enormously exaggerated. Yet what fantastic merits must an individual possess if the "hurricane of glory" is no more than fitting for her? The question reveals the absurdity.

In the preceding chapters we have attempted to describe Thérèse' brief life and her swift growth to maturity and perfection as conscientiously as possible. In all reverence, but in all seriousness also, we venture to say bluntly: Nowhere have we encountered anything extraordinary. We have observed a little, constricted, wearisomely monotonous life. Thérèse was no precocious genius, no frustrated Cleopatra, no Carmelite Simone Weil, no repressed Titan, but a very sweet provincial girl with all the qualities resulting from her origins and environment. She was considerably gifted, but somewhat inadequately educated, and she had certain inborn weaknesses. Her attitude to the world was narrow, her taste poor. Thérèse was a typical "little soul". *And as such she became the great saint whose light shines over the world.*

Her express "doctrine" is not hers alone, nor is it her principal message to us. Her nature, as it really was, is an indispensable part of that message. Without it, the doctrine leads to falsifications and misinterpretations. In a far more profound sense than she herself could know—and, let us say it, than the sisters in the exclusiveness of their particular view could guess—the story of her soul is simultaneously the representation of her Way. Thérèse was, as St Bridget of Sweden said of herself, a messenger with a letter from a mighty Lord. The letter contains for us, in the language of her time, the age-old message that the good tidings are for the poor. How fitting it is that it is brought to us by one of those poor upon whom were heaped such immeasurable gifts.

Are we in any way belittling Thérèse, are we being unjust to her, when we deny her the resounding epithets of genius, child prodigy, complex soul? On the contrary. She has no need of easy superlatives; upon her such trappings sit ill. They have been clapped on her only by the uncertainty of persons who were discomfited by the uncomprehended littleness of Little Thérèse.

Even the closest inspection cannot extend the catalogue of her deeds. Certainly she would have been capable of considerable accomplishments—she is to some extent the equal, to some extent the superior of a good many contemporary foundresses of religious congregations. But Providence did not permit her to produce any tangible work during her lifetime. Her words about empty hands remain, not as a self-deprecating pretty phrase, but as a literal report. Nor is the situation any different in regard to her virtues. Thérèse did no more than was required by her Rule and her status as a Carmelite. *How* she did it is her sole claim to fame—but one which she shared with many nuns in her own house. Her way of life is distinguished outwardly from that of Mother Geneviève or her own sisters only by its brevity. It may be that she did not exceed in "virtue" many of her fellow nuns in the Order, those now dead and those still living. But for the passionate and unremitting labours of her three sisters, no one would have heard any more or less about her than about thousands of other anonymous devout nuns.

A similar statement may be made about her suffering. Certainly Thérèse fulfilled to the limit the subjective measure of her capacity for suffering, and more no one can do. But objectively it was in no way extraordinary. Every human being is a mystery, and a saint all the more so. For in the saint his hidden springs become public, and his public aspect an unfathomable riddle. Nevertheless, it is permissible to study and evaluate the known, established facts. Thus it is possible to judge on the basis of reliable documents whether a person lived in the midst of an amicable or a hostile environment, whether he experienced love and recognition, or harshness and contempt. We may say, for example, that St Francis Xavier suffered and died more forsaken than Thérèse, who lay in her cell at Lisieux, surrounded by those she loved most in the world. Or that John of the Cross, Henry Suso or Margaret Mary Alacoque endured more malice and cruel persecution by the fellow members of their Orders than did our saint.

The same is true also of the degree of her inner trials to the extent that these are outwardly verifiable. Objectively, these nowhere exceed the bounds that are normal and ordinary in any highly developed form of Christian and conventual piety. The eighteen months of her spiritual darkness stand against almost as many years of blackest night of the soul in the life of Henry Suso, the great Dominican mystic; against forty years of complete inner desolation on the part of a St Jane Frances de Chantal. In collected letters of great spiritual guides like St Alphonsus Liguori or Father de Caussade we may read of similar inner agonies, often lasting a lifetime, reported by a great many well-known and also anonymous friends of God. And not everyone who was so tested knew at the same time that he was surrounded by a superabundance of faithful, consoling love, as did Thérèse; very few of them could aver, as could she, that such darkness was pierced by blissful, reinvigorating shafts of heavenly light.

In reading Thérèse's letters and autobiography we must never forget that she lived in the late nineteenth century. The age was marked by a naïve and wholly unconscious delight in pomposity. Let us think of the Gothic railway stations and schools, the Renaissance façades on post offices and stock exchanges. Does it therefore follow that we would find Gothic souls in girls' boarding schools, Borgias and Michelangelos at the ticket-windows?

The spiritual language of those decades corresponded fairly well to the architecture. What other age dealt so lavishly in that grave word "martyrdom"? Every banal, commonplace worry was dignified by the word. Anyone who was raised in a convent school can supply a dozen illustrative stories. How naïvely Thérèse, too, treated such a word is indicated, for example, by a letter to Céline. The older girl had dreamed that she was actually a martyr who had died by the sword. Her younger sister replied: "My Céline's dream is very pretty (*très joli!*)—and perhaps some day it will be fulfilled. But while we wait for that, let us begin our martyrdom already. . . . Before we die by the sword, we shall die by pinpricks."

Today the use of such overblown metaphor (which often verges on the comical, as when, for instance, lily and grain of sand are to plunge together into the arena) alienates us. Wherever Thérèse does not fall victim to it she is plain-spoken enough and repeatedly makes the point that her life, far from being extraordinary in any way, contains nothing which is not within reach of all little souls, that her writings hold something for everyone, "except those who are called to extraordinary things", and that, far from being a martyr, she has always been protected and treated with tender care.

This mode of speech was neither pose nor deception, but simply a habit. We have no need, out of false piety towards our subject, to take it literally and then artificially build upon it a superstructure of startling conclusions.

It is necessary to keep three circumstances in mind. First there is the well-known fact that persons in voluntary or involuntary seclusion, whether in prison, boarding school, convent or sickroom, very soon suffer a peculiar distortion of their sense of proportion. Since they lack all material for comparison, and since human beings nevertheless must give their emotional life play, the degree of their reactions becomes almost independent of the initial stimulus. We know how prisoners can experience the most powerful psychic upheavals over a bird on the windowsill, even over a mouse or a spider; we know what a bud on a flower stalk can mean to a sick person. Similarly, in convents tiny incidents, affronts, preferences, nuances of human relationships, which in the outside world would scarcely be noticed, take on the most formidable importance.

Secondly, we must never overlook Thérèse's *youth*. She herself, as well as her sisters, always made a point of her unusual maturity, and Thérèse was thoroughly convinced that in spite of her few years she had attained the grace of perfection. For all that she gladly played with the name and image of being a little child; when Sister Marie once asked her—perhaps teasingly, "So then you are a baby?" she replied very gravely: "Of course a baby—but one that thinks very deeply. A baby who is also an aged matron!" Nevertheless, and this is one of the most winning traits of her nature, she could never entirely deny her girlhood. Indeed, why should she have done so? Delight in things "poetic", in sublime and romantic words, fills her letters in particular, but it breaks out again and again in her autobiographical notebooks. Her correspondence with Céline sometimes reminds us of that ironical passage in one of Arnold Bennett's novels in which two sisters are described: "Their ages were fifteen and sixteen; this is a period in which any girl of sincere mind must admit that she has no more to learn, since after all she has learned everything in the past six months." Thérèse employs almost the same words in addressing Pauline: "At the beginning of my spiritual life, when I was between thirteen and fourteen, I used to wonder what else there was for me to learn. It did not seem possible that I could ever understand perfection any better than I did already." Although she shows her progress towards inner maturity by straightway withdrawing that assertion, she retained a good deal of this attitude. It is touching to read what she wrote to Céline on the latter's twenty-second birthday: "You know, we two together are now forty years old! Considering that, it isn't surprising that we already have such vast experience in so many things, is it?"

We may well agree with the judgment of a Carmelite Prioress that age and experience presumably would have changed many of Thérèse's views.

Let us not forget the sober, humble comment of the ageing Cardinal Newman: "The greater part of our devotion in youth, our faith, hope, cheerfulness, perseverance is natural—or, if not natural; it is from a εὐφυία which does not resist grace and requires very little grace to illuminate. The same grace goes much further in youth as encountering less opposition—that is, in the virtues which I have mentioned.... Old men are in soul as stiff, as lean, as bloodless as their bodies, except so far as grace penetrates and softens them. And it requires a flooding of grace to do this. I more and more wonder at *old* saints. St Aloysius or St Francis Xavier or St Carlo are nothing to St Philip."[7]

Thirdly, the sisters in their editorial work were so anxiously concerned for the flawlessness of their heroine that they eliminated from the manuscript tiny details for which scarcely any reader would have blamed Thérèse: for example that at eleven she still could not comb her own hair and was in the habit of crying piteously every day when her big sister did her hair for her. They suppressed also the fact that Father Pichon, when he assured the fifteen-year-old Thérèse that she had never committed a mortal sin, had added the routine pedagogical remark: "But if God were to forsake you, you would be a little devil instead of a little angel!" Or that even in the convent Thérèse would say the Rosary reluctantly when alone, and only at the cost of self-conquest. It is strange that, given this microscopic eye for "imperfections", one trait completely escaped the sisters which is certain to take the ordinary reader aback. Probably the sisters never even noticed it, since it was after all the product of their own training. We are referring to the staggering self-assurance of the girl, and her extreme egocentricity.

We will remember that as a child Thérèse did not think herself pretty because at home no one spoke of her looks. Her attitude towards her inner physiognomy seems to have been quite different. The sisters had taught the child to record her little sacrifices and acts of virtue in a notebook, and even on her sickbed we see how the constant questioning almost forced Thérèse to have too high an opinion of herself. The few published fragments of letters from relatives to Thérèse are effusively complimentary.

"You said to me [in a letter] that *everything about me pleased you*, that I was God's special favourite, that He did not make me climb the rough ladder of perfection like others, but had placed me in a lift [an elevator] in order to have me with Him sooner", she wrote to Mother Agnes.

How undisguisedly her letters and other writings reveal Thérèse's tender and naïve delight in herself! The little white flower, the fledgling, the

---

[7] *Life of John Henry Cardinal Newman*, by Wilfrid Ward, 1:574–75.

little jewel, the tiny lamb, the radiant lily, the little bride—who else ever spoke of self in such a variety of pet names? To be sure, all this was rendered harmless enough by the fact that it expressed her gratitude to God and was evoked by the most sincere desire to give the questioning sisters and the Prioress exactly what they expected, exactly what would satisfy them. It was all innocent, the innocence of a beloved woman mirroring her beauty in the rapt eyes of her lover. A Franciscan friar, who was also an expert graphologist, was shown Thérèse's handwriting without being told whose it was. His comment was that the writer would naturally have been suited to a career as a model or mannequin! Startling as this verdict is, its basis may lie in Thérèse's intense desire for self-expression. In the narrowness of her life Thérèse found only one form of outlet for that impulse: to offer to her beloved sisters her spiritual beauties. Continually every passing nuance of emotion, every imperceptible change of mood, was caught as by a camera upon the sensitized paper of an overalert consciousness. We see this again and again in the *Novissima Verba*. And how microscopically Thérèse analyses the feelings of her childhood and puberty in the section of her autobiography which she wrote for Pauline. She could not have learned to do this only while she was writing these pages. Her letters, too, betray the same burning interest in her own spiritual life, and her constant preoccupation with it.

Never would Thérèse, as did the German mystic Margarete Ebner, have been able to say about her youth in the convent: "How I lived then I cannot say, because at that time I did not pay attention to myself. I know only this much: God had me always faithfully in His paternal care." Or: "When I hear from lovers of God that God does great things with them, I have no desire for anyone to know of the things that God has wrought in me."

Alas, *great* saint though she is, how intensely Thérèse was by nature, in spite of all the detachment she practised and achieved, "overladen with self"—as another holy mystic, he too a person of excessive sensitivity, defined his own great problem. How deeply this thorn was sunk in her flesh.

In spite of the resolute silence of *The Story of a Soul*, in spite of the silent smile which was the grimmest instrument of her penance, opposing as it did the most violent impulse of her nature—every page of her writings, every poem and every letter, reveals the passionate, unappeasable intensity of her self-scrutiny, self-palpation and self-analysis. How long and how closely she must have studied her face in the interior mirror in order to achieve a depiction of herself so successful down to the subtlest nuances. Even the protagonists of her successful dramatic sketches, which sent her fellow nuns into raptures—her Maid of Orléans and her

Stanislaus—are scarcely veiled self-portraits. What delighted Thérèse about her fraternal patron, the "little martyr" and missionary Théophane Venard, was again the similarity to herself. Was she ever able spontaneously to love anyone whose personality differed in quality from her own—except Mother Marie de Gonzague?

To say all this is not to reproach her, certainly not to accuse her of sin, and perhaps not even of a "flaw". We are dealing here with one of those ambivalent qualities which become positive or negative according to the manner with which their possessor deals with them. In the destinies of saints precisely such qualities are of prime importance. Young Francis of Assisi's bent towards eccentricities, Ignatius's intelligence, Philip Neri's leaning towards practical jokes—what would these three saints have been without these elements in their characters? Certainly not what they are. Such tendencies, which in other amalgam might have been highly dangerous, serve to complete their earthly as well as their transfigured selves. Without her egocentricity Thérèse might well have lacked that enormous fascination which so overcame her sisters and, through the medium of pictures and her book—composites though these were in some respects—affected the multitudes so powerfully. It would seem that a person has to be at ease with himself in order to exert such attraction over others.

These three circumstances probably explain, *in part*, why Thérèse cherished the conviction that her insights and illuminations were unique and unprecedented. Provinciality is all too apparent in her childlike astonishment at the "secrets which Jesus has revealed to His little bride", and in the wild enthusiasm with which her sisters hailed these secrets. Certainly many of her ideas were unusual and bold within the Jansenistic narrowness of the Lisieux Carmel. Yet it remains a psychological riddle why her elder sisters apparently never recognized the origins of these ideas. Again and again they insist—and this has come to be a standard view of Thérèse—upon the inspired originality of their saint's "doctrine".

"The Lord alone was her guide"—these words have even found their way into the Office for her Feast. We have already touched upon this matter in our discussion of her "veil". "Jesus alone was my guide. I thought that God used no intermediary for me, but preferred to act directly." Was not Thérèse perhaps a little mistaken here? Few young people recognize that the domestic climate, the atmosphere of their families—especially if complete harmony prevails—influence them far more strongly than occasional conversations with strangers. When what they have absorbed through all the pores of their being for the first time emerges into their rational consciousness, they think they are hitting on their own ideas or have received a sudden inspiration. This is not to say that Thérèse, like most religious people, did not know herself to be guided by the constant gentle hints, warnings and appeals of the inner voice, of the "truth that speaks without sound or words". But can the same be said of her religious *opinions*? Her mother and father, her sisters—were not these prime influences and inspirations? Had not Thérèse at Les Buissonnets unconsciously taken in with every breath a well-defined doctrine? Had that not entered deep into her flesh and blood? She reproduced what she had received in her home environment without ever realizing the origin of these ideas. "You are my light—you are my sun—you are the way that leads to Heaven—you are a harp, a song—you are the angel whom Jesus has sent to prepare my way—you are the lift which will carry me without effort into the infinite regions of love—you are my living Jesus." Such are some of the phrases from notes she addressed during her years in the convent to Mother Agnes.

In any inventory of Thérèse's intellectual property no one will ever be able to separate the items which belonged to Pauline from those which were entirely her own.

Not quite so intensive, but very deep nevertheless, was the tie with Marie, as well as that with Celine, Thérèse's "twin soul", with whom she already felt on earth "like two drops of dew flowing together".

We must study the letters of the other sisters in order to see how indistinguishable the giving and receiving was. The diligent editors of the sources have already determined that many of Thérèse's best known and most characteristic phrases and parables, such as the "grain of sand" and the "elevator", actually derive from Mother Agnes. Thérèse's language was also plainly influenced by Father Pichon, whose one printed letter could almost be confounded with hers. Thérèse herself gratefully acknowledged the mutely eloquent example of Mother Geneviève, the aged founder of the convent.

The same thing may be said of her relationship to the great tradition of the Church. The powerful influence upon her of *The Imitation of Christ* never abated, no more than did that of Abbé Arminjon. To be sure, Thérèse thought she had profited by the works of St John of the Cross only between the ages of sixteen and seventeen. She was fond of asserting that she could learn nothing from books. But the minute source analysis of the original manuscripts proves that she continued eagerly to read his works even on her deathbed. She meditated on them, quoted from them, and emphasized that her Little Way of humility and love was "no different from that of our father St John of the Cross". In support of this contention she cited his own verse:

> Descending into the depths of my own nothingness
> I was then so raised up that I attained my goal.

We have already referred to the strong Salesian influence in our discussion of the Little Way.

It is as if the sisters feared they would detract from the glory of their darling if they admitted the slightest intellectual or spiritual influence from any quarter upon the growth of her mind. This went so far that they even deleted all passages in which Céline came too close to the protagonist of their spiritual drama. Thus they expunged Thérèse's candid admission that at home her sister had exceeded her in zeal for self-invented penances; that Céline had prayed together with her for the conversion of Pranzini; that during the famous papal audience Céline, too, had dared to address Leo XIII. In spite of many other insertions in praise of their father, they did not add, in connection with the Pranzini story, that ardent sympathy for sinners was a prominent feature of the family life. Whenever the Martins heard of an obstinate case, the entire family flung itself into his "conquest" and held novenas to St Joseph for him. This we learn from Father Piat. But the story as it is given in *The Story of a Soul* is apparently intended to create the impression that Thérèse all by herself formed the idea of praying for Pranzini, and all by herself achieved his conversion—whereas this was plainly no more than her first conscious experience with such intercessory action.

No one was permitted to stand beside Thérèse. She had to remain unique in all things. Even their ardently loved mother had to linger in the shadow of the youngest, by decree of the elder sisters. How otherwise can we explain the fact that Thérèse's dying agonies were never compared with those of Madame Zélie—when her conduct was literally the very image of her mother's? Zélie Martin, too, during two frightful years of the last stage of cancer of the breast had endured pain with terrifying heroism, had uncomplainingly carried out all her duties—the heavy, complex duties of housewife, wife, mother and businesswoman. She had rejected all special care, would have no night nurse, slept in a room far from the others, so that her cries of pain would not be heard. Half-dead, she would have herself supported by the arms so that she might be taken to early Mass and High Mass and still did not think she was dispensed from Sunday Mass, although she almost collapsed in the street. Finally she was confined to her room—where one day her daughters surprised her, deathly pale and gasping for breath, still forcing herself to kneel to say the Rosary. All the pleadings of her husband and her daughters could not persuade her to be less strict towards herself. At the last she could no longer even lie in bed; so great was her pain that she had to get up and stagger about every quarter of an hour. A whisper, a footstep in stockinged feet, caused her dreadful agonies. Through all of this she never thought she was enduring anything special. At the end she lay for three days with swollen arms and legs, wholly incapable of moving or communicating. But she smiled and showered loving looks upon all about her.

Saintlike suffering and death is also reported of the *sainte fille*, the aunt who was a Visitation nun. Like Thérèse, she died of tuberculosis. On her deathbed she declared that out of her entire life—of forty-seven years—she could recall no single voluntary, deliberate sin. "I do not at all concern myself with thoughts of the last torments, nor of the death-agony, for I am so convinced that God will give me all the necessary grace to bear it that I do not worry about all that", she said. And: "I am afraid of nothing. Our Lord sustains me. *I have the grace of the moment, and I shall receive it to the end.*" Do not these words, spoken in 1876, sound utterly "Theresian"?

So, too, when we read the few fragments which Father Piat quotes from letters of the four sisters written during the period of their father's sufferings, we would readily wager that no one who is not a specialist in Theresiana would be able to distinguish the lines written by the saint from those of her sisters. They all spoke a single language of the heart and employed a single style.

Why should we not hearken to that Prioress of the Irish Carmel at Blackwell who laughingly commented that by the standard of *The Story of a Soul* her entire convent could be canonized? Or to the Austrian Carmelite who stated that in her house little Thérèse's obedience would not stand forth because it was the general attitude and taken for granted? Or the hospital director who wrote us stating that he could name dozens of his Protestant nursing sisters—"I believe this is not saying too much—in whose lives and at whose deathbeds I have with my own eyes observed the same conduct."

Anyone, too, who is somewhat familiar with the many pending canonization proceedings of persons who lived during that period; anyone who has read a few dozen of the now mostly forgotten lives of devout souls of the past hundred years; and anyone who has had the good fortune to encounter saintly persons of that generation, or to live with them—will observe the striking family likeness stamped upon all of them. Almost to the point of monotony the same features are repeated: pure, childlike love of God, boundless confidence, burning zeal for souls, patience, kindness, simplicity, faithfulness in small things, forgetfulness of self, and, above all, the veil of unconscious or deliberate, deeply desired obscurity.

Thérèse, we will remember, once spoke of herself as a sprig of moss in the bouquet among showy flowers. This winsome image captures, over and beyond what she intended, with astonishing precision her place in the Church. For never does a single moss plant occur by itself in nature;

never could it fulfil its function alone. "Moss" immediately evokes a picture of an agglomeration, a carpet; it is in the nature of this kind of plant to appear in colonies.

In the landscape of the Church there is also "moss"—that modest ground cover of quiet, little Christians who are, as individuals, inconspicuous and unimportant, but who, as a vast united body which remains constant through the centuries, form the protective carpet around the roots of life, conserving for these the nutritive moisture. Without them there would be no towering giants of the forest. From this point of view, Thérèse is a special example of this widespread, scarcely mentioned but always indispensable spirituality whose individual advocates would be ashamed of so high-sounding an epithet as spirituality. Unadmired, taking their conduct for granted, they live their lives, almost completely hidden by their unconscious protective coloration, or regarded only as the insignificant foils which serve to set off their apparent opposites: the splendid, the extraordinary, the great and noble specimens. In essence this phenomenon remains the same; its forms are extremely varied, often wholly alien to one another, yet surprisingly brought together by that underlying element. Thus the middle-class idyll of Les Buissonnets, all plush and mahogany, is linked with the fantastically heroic experiment of Charles de Foucauld in the Sahara; so, too, the present-day work of his growing band of *Petits Frères et Sœurs de Jésus* in urban slums, in the hovels of Indian pariahs, in the trailer camps of vagabonds and in the most modern factories is traceable to innumerable individuals in cliché-ridden, strait-laced convents; the controversial pioneering adventure of the worker-priests with the colourless, commonplace life of competent and incompetent mothers of families and working girls. In the worn-out survivals of dying social forms as well as in the dramatic, far-flung preliminary projects for future Christian ways of life there is growing, silently and indestructibly, that moss which is the floor of sanctity.

Therefore Thérèse is neither old-fashioned nor timely; she belongs to no front or faction. In her, rather, the age and youth of the Church meet one another, the permanence and the rebirth of the Church, in a timeless present.

And with this, her frail young figure is suddenly revealed as an eschatological sign: in the shadow of that mysterious promise of Elijah in the closing verses of the Old Testament which says that this last messenger before the great and terrible day of the Lord will "reconcile heart of father to son, heart of son to father".[8]

---

[8] Mal 4:6.

The riddle of this destiny cannot be "explained". Only in the Beatific Vision will we be able to see more, and contemplation of the various entrance ways to the Eternal City, of the paths by which we have come to God, will constitute a large part of our bliss. So the hidden face of the saint of Lisieux remains for ever obscured, and perhaps more thickly veiled by the shimmering weave of its incomprehensible glorification than by all the earthly veils, some of which we have been privileged to lift.

Yet our last observations lead us close to a conclusion of the highest importance. Perhaps they provide us with a new interpretation of this mystery—one interpretation which is, it must be admitted, as open to question and as controvertible as any other.

The characteristic mark of the form of Christian existence we have just described is its invisibility. Thérèse was called forth from her obscurity among the Innocents, as the stern nun put it, in order to make this form of life visible to all the world. She is the flower, the crystal, the quintessence of a type of devotion which is far broader and older than her own sphere of life. She was altogether an inheritor, not of the hollow, pompous, sentimental façade which overlay the true face of the Church in the late nineteenth century, but of that substance which rested deep beneath like buried treasure, nameless but unimpaired. Under all outer forms, under scars and decay, the roots of Christian existence lived on, unrecognized, anonymous and silent, but wholesome and pregnant with life, just as in autumn and winter the coming spring lives and waits within the inert soil and the rootstocks of seemingly dead vegetation.

It is strange how life so often anticipates theory, and how reflection only slowly catches up with it. While in religious literature and from pulpits the "grand style" of sanctity was still being lauded and preached, its future form was already secretly in being beneath the threshold of consciousness. Those lovers of God did not recognize themselves, nor were they recognized, precisely because of the yawning gulf between themselves and the idealized concept of the supersaint. They were unconscious of what they stood for, or else they shied away from speaking of it as though that would be exposing nakedness, or else as though it would be the greatest brashness to trouble anyone with such notions.

Thérèse's vocation was a constellation of fortunate elements. Everything came together, as in the coagulation of a crystal, to make possible the "phenomenon" that was Thérèse. There was the remarkable spiritual climate, created by her family, in which everything could be talked out without embarrassment. There was her own overstimulated awareness of herself, which enabled her to bring into consciousness things that in others remain on the margin of knowledge. There was the gift of language, which enabled her to express her discoveries; the insatiable curiosity of her sisters to learn of them; and Thérèse's wonderfully happy experience of being a favourite child—that experience which gave her the security to believe that she was regarded by God with the same, or rather with infinitely deeper affection, than by her family.

The uniqueness of Thérèse's message did not lie in what she confided to her loved ones, but in the fact that she dared to express it at all, and that she was able to do so. Only because of this have we heard of it. Only because of this has the form of life which has always flourished so silently acquired a face and a voice. Only because of this have countless persons realized that this existence of theirs is a "way", even a way to sanctity, a way to perfection; that there is an inherent value in all the things which seemed to themselves not worthy of attention.

In this respect, it seems to us, Thérèse far exceeded the narrow boundaries of any kind of personal fame. She is the sole saint who has become a symbol to modern times. Perhaps this is one deep cause of the fantastic response to her person and her message. In her the archetype of the little saint became visible once more. And that type is truly the "heart of the Church", the marrow of the Church—that, and not the *petites saintes* of adolescent piety. In the quiet life of Thérèse there was revived the ancient, original, Gospel concept of sanctity, of the baptized Christian whose whole life reflects Christ in all its elements, who is saintly not because he does or says special things which set him off from others, but because he is a tiny member of Christ present in the world and because he endeavours to walk worthily in the path of his vocation. That is the sanctity of which Newman, another of Thérèse's contemporaries, speaks when he says that Christians in the world must be like the soul in the body, animating, effective and invisible.

Many of us certainly must learn by great effort to turn our eyes from the search for heroes and geniuses and direct them upon something so tiny that it must be studied under a microscope, as it were, until a form emerges from the muddle of dashes and dots. But when we do, we will learn to perceive the unique beauty of this poverty, as strict, clear and poignant as the beauty of bare branches against a barren sky, as the transparency of a sun-bathed landscape before spring has fully begun. We will sense that every cell and fibre of such life is more than its own mere nature, that it is soaked and filled to the brim and transfigured into the light and the power to which it has surrendered itself.

During the trial a famous exorcist made the remarkable statement that he had often heard from the mouths of possessed persons of the power of the "little virgin" over demons—*parce qu'elle était une âme détruite*. Because she was an immolated, a consumed soul—that seems to mean that she had really completely surrendered her narrow, fettered ego, had left it behind her in that depth of self-renunciation to which the Gospel refers when it speaks of those who lose their souls. When we regard the photograph taken of her in the garden during her illness, the still, seated figure with hands folded weakly in her lap and her remote, patient gaze, we catch something of this ultimate liberation.

Certainly Thérèse was *also* a person of the highest piety, in the contemporary sense of this word. Who can or would wish to deny that? But are the subjective pinnacles of her experiences, enthusiasms, formulations, really so important? Do details such as her early vocation, her oblation, her favourite forms of prayer—which were so much determined by her character—really matter?

In another life such features would seem the peaks of religious experience. In Thérèse they are interesting, but inessential. For they are precisely the features which no one can voluntarily "imitate" or make his own, whereas she felt that she stood for those things which are capable of being passed on and imitated, which are accessible to everyone of good will. Thus she herself distinguished between the elements of primary and secondary importance in her spiritual life.

Moreover, all the more superficial features also belong to the character of the era, as innumerable forgotten diaries and letters can prove, innumerable spiritual directors testify. They are after all not much more than the pretty glistening crest of foam upon the deep swell; it can pass, but the force of the wave remains. What do all the transports of youthful infatuation weigh against the enduring love of marriage?

These poems, prayers, letters and written ecstasies are blossoms, not fruits, charming "games" of her age and temperament, her nation and period. For us they are valuable because without them we would have learned nothing of the other element, because without these trimmings which so enchanted people, the storm of petitions, which called down the shower of roses, would scarcely have begun, and the "Little Way" would not have received the approbation of the highest ecclesiastical authority.

In Thérèse herself during every hour of her life, the sustaining foundation of the Church was made manifest. The details of this fabric were too small individually to be singled out by the eye; but together they formed the ground out of which everything else grew.

Thérèse thought and talked like a nun of her period. She had amazingly little understanding of "the world", of the natural, ordinary life outside the convent walls. But she *lived* the sanctity and transparency of ordinary human life. Her essential experiences of God, and her conclusions from them, were not founded upon or inspired by the special insights of the mystics, nor upon the tradition of the Carmelite Order. They derived from the homely traditions of a good family, from the simple everyday, catechism-nourished devotion of father and mother. Thus she became—like Francis de Sales, her great spiritual ancestor—a teacher of that lay spirituality which is so much discussed nowadays; just as, conversely, all monastic piety has always been nourished by the primordial example of marital and parental love. Only God knows the number of souls who share in the honour and the reward of this one saint. In her glorification there is revealed, as through a rent in the curtain, both as consolation and promise, and comprehensible to the earthly heart, a gleam of that which awaits the lowliest in our Father's House.

St Pius X is said to have prophetically called Thérèse, whose full rise to fame he did not live to witness, the greatest saint of the century. May we be permitted to understand him in that way. He, the saintly Pope who restored to the ordinary Christian the forgotten heritage which for centuries had been the privilege only of the clergy or of the most devout—free access to the Eucharist; he who again recognized that the participation of the laity was the lifeblood of the liturgy and thus broke down the artificial dividing wall between clergy and people—an act of enormous significance—he may well have understood that this little Carmelite stands for innumerable souls, for the legions of those who preceded her along her way as well as the legions of those to whom she revealed it for the first time. Therefore she stands precisely on the crossroads between the "old" and the "new" piety. She is a remarkable example of the invincible powers of renewal in the Mystical Body of Christ, of the activity of the Holy Spirit, whose creative power is ever at work. And she is all that precisely because she lived so apart from and so innocent of all the discussions and disputes over reform and rebirth.

It is a source of deepest happiness to see in the Church this process of self-purification for once not manifesting itself in the form of protest against abuses, or conflict and strife with the world, but welling up from the clear spring of a child's soul.

In Thérèse there gathered and became purified the deep, intimate, essential unchanging elements of the Faith and of Love. As the perfected butterfly breaks out of the chrysalis, so she emerges transformed from the shrivelling shell of her period and appears before us as the pure embodiment of Christian reality. To be sure, she represents also a perfection of the period's religious ideal; but in fulfilling the law of her own being, she overcomes it. She who knew only obedience, only listening, unquestionably accepted the highly questionable elements in her contemporaries' piety. But the burning purity of her touch melted away all the old slag. What she grasped and what she embodied is once again the beginning, the core, the original meaning. We see in her girlish face the hidden face of the Church, the Face of the Hidden Church, which in the chaos of time flowers, eternally young and beautiful, to greet the returning Lord.

NOTES

I. TO "ORIGIN AND HERITAGE" (see pp. 29–48)

Also characteristic of the family, unfortunately, was its utter intolerance and lack of understanding of any form of religious expression which departed from the accepted norm. This appears in literally tragic form in the fate of Léonie, the third oldest of the surviving children. She remained always the problem child of the family, and we might almost say its stepchild. Like Marie, she died at the age of eighty, in June 1941, as a nun of the Visitation at Caen. The obituary letter on her which was published as a special issue of the *Annales de Ste Thérèse*, reveals in deeply moving fashion her beautiful, unappreciated and sorrowful life.

Léonie's was the hard lot of being, among her physically and spiritually more fortunate sisters, the ugly, sickly, stupid and disobedient child—or, at least, so she was considered. She differed so much from the others that the family was helpless with regard to her, did not know what to do with her. All efforts to force her into the domestic pattern of virtue and piety, by the exercise of more or less gentle pressure, failed completely. There remained, therefore, nothing to do but to isolate her, to send her off by herself to various boarding schools, and leave her to her own resources. Clumsy pedagogy drove her further and further into obstinacy and defiance, even though she possessed a tender and sensitive heart. At one time, when she was already fourteen years old, she was utterly terrorized by a maid, and a long time passed before her mother discovered this. Slow and awkward she managed her lessons with the greatest difficulty, and there remained great gaps in her education. The "reading of prayers" which was required every day at a certain hour gave her no joy, and she objected strenuously to it. This seemed to her pious mother to put her salvation into serious peril. Nor was she consoled when Léonie instead eagerly asked for stories from the life of Jesus and wept as she listened to the account of His Passion; such signs of religious sensibility were irregular and therefore undesirable. That Léonie was incapable of combating her faults by voluntary "sacrifices" and refused to count her self-conquests by placing little discs of cork into a drawer, worried her mother as if she were resisting divine grace. The poor little thing, regarded and treated by all as a dreadful black sheep, became more and more intractable. Zélie Martin actually asked herself the painful question, as a letter to her sister in the convent indicates, whether Léonie's recovery from many severe children's diseases, for which she had once prayed so fervently, had really been a blessing. "Let her live if she is to become a saint", the mother had prayed at the child's sickbed. Madame Zélie

411

died just about the time that Leonie had at last found her way to her mother's heart. The father and the older sisters were again at a loss; immediately after the move to Lisieux had been completed they sent the adolescent girl off as a boarder, who was allowed out only on rare days, to the convent school run by the Benedictine nuns in Lisieux—the same school Céline and later Thérèse attended as day pupils. Thus Léonie was excluded from the intimate family life at Les Buissonnets, while the other members of the family turned towards one another with even greater tenderness, as compensation for the severe loss of one sister.

After her return home, Léonie remained as forsaken as ever, and even the still unknown saint among her sisters contributed towards the fate which it was hers to bear. Léonie lived like a stranger amid this closely linked, extremely intimate family. She alone was not informed when Thérèse's vocation was being discussed. Her repeated entries and departures from two convents before she found her proper home are scarcely ever mentioned in the saint's memoirs, nor does Thérèse say a word about Léonie's care of their father, nor her loneliness after Céline had entered the Carmel and she remained behind with her aunt and uncle.

Léonie Martin must have suffered frightfully from emotional isolation and inferiority feelings. Nevertheless, it seems to us that the mother's prayer at the sick child's bedside was granted. In reading of her quiet life, so entirely overshadowed by the fame of her canonized sister, we cannot escape the surprising impression that Léonie was spiritually the most unique and original of the sisters—not excepting our saint herself. When the Martin sisters were sending farewell letters with "commissions for Heaven" to their mortally ill Aunt Dosithea, Léonie asked her to win for her the vocation to be a *true* nun. This apparently struck the others as impertinence—at any rate Marie was for commanding her to strike out the word "true", arguing that it was stupid and meaningless. No one understood the child's defence that she did not want to be just a nun, but a genuine, holy nun. For the family, a nun was in herself a holy and supernatural being; they thought the qualification foolish and brazen. In their period of extreme pious extravagance, Céline and Thérèse with common accord made fun of the older girl's quiet devotional exercises, although they did so with no malice whatsoever. They ignored completely her example of heroic charity towards a sick poor woman. And yet Léonie remained attached to her sisters all her life with an unembittered, unenvying, faithful love and touchingly humble admiration.

Léonie lived what Thérèse lived and taught, the Little Way of perfect humility and simplicity. She did so wholly unconsciously and without ever suspecting that she was acting in any extraordinary manner. Not she, but the youngest sister, was chosen to bring to Christianity this new message of life with God. For along with purity of heart, Thérèse also received the gift of strength of mind, which is essential to the apostle. The older girl never belonged to the small band of disciples who carried the message out into the world. Perhaps the others did not think her worthy of it, or capable of grasping it. Yet it seems to us that in her actions she followed the Little Way with a force fully the equal of her sister's and did so for half a century longer.

2. TO "THE MENACE" (pp. 66–85)

We possess various detailed descriptions of the disease: the account by Thérèse herself in *The Story of a Soul*, and the accounts by Marie, Léonie and Céline, and by the maid Marceline Husé in the documents of the trial (1 *S.*, i, 37, 38, 92, 115; xviii, 9; also supplementary material in 2 *S.*). Then there is the account by Laveille in his biography (pp. 111–23).

All the biographers we have encountered regard the disease as unquestionably one of the three or four really "mystical" events in the saint's life, which was for the most part so devoid of wonders. It is called a perplexing, inexplicable, alien, mysterious disease. Laveille (p. 117) expresses directly the views of the Martin family and of the Lisieux Carmel: "Then the old enemy at once seized upon this state of weakness, and God temporarily allowed him power over her body which he violently tormented and would have destroyed if he had been able." As we have seen, Thérèse herself also states that her illness was produced by the envy of the devil; but we must remember that her opinion was formed when she was eleven and a half years old and simply took over her sisters' views. All the witnesses emphasize with a certain satisfaction that medical science was helpless; hence the cure could only have come about by a miracle.

The diagnosis of the physician, Dr Notta, was completely forgotten in the twenty years that intervened between the illness and the ecclesiastical investigation. Dr Notta was by then no longer living, and so far as we know no book on the saint, even one so careful and thorough as Laveille's, even mentions his diagnosis.

Jeanne Néele, *née* Guérin, who was the wife of a doctor, remembered the medical diagnosis and has reported it as follows: "The doctor treating the case called this disease St Vitus's Dance. Nevertheless, it seems to me that he was somewhat hesitant about this diagnosis and suggested that something else might be present—but what?" Dr Notta treated the illness as a nervous disease.

It is, of course, difficult even for a physician, and certainly for a layman, to obtain a reliable diagnosis of a disease after the passage of fifty years, especially when he can base his opinion only on descriptions by laymen, and many of these supplied twenty and more years after the event. Most of the witnesses were young girls at the time; moreover, they had long since formed a fixed explanation of it all which was repeated for decades and probably influenced considerably their recollection of the facts. We have, however, submitted these facts, as far as they were available, to several physicians, and their medical opinions agree that the clinical picture conforms almost precisely to that of *chorea minor*, popularly known as St Vitus's Dance. The deviations from that clinical picture also form a consistent pattern.

Chorea is a nervous disease that occurs principally in childhood, most often between the ages of eleven and thirteen, more commonly in girls than in boys, and usually in the spring. It lasts on the average from eight to twelve weeks and is curable in most cases. "Chorea children" usually have a delicate, anaemic, nervous constitution. According to older medical views, frights and shocks are the principal causes of the disease. The modern view holds that genuine chorea is not a neurosis, but an infectious disease with a definite agent in which organic susceptibility plays a large part, and that it is related to rheumatism of the joints. The fact that a psychic shock often marks the onset of the disease is explained as the result of a weakened state: the child, already infected, is more violently shaken by unpleasant experiences—so that in this case cause and effect are reversed.

A distinct preliminary stage is characteristic of chorea. Patients display neurasthenic symptoms; they become fidgety, clumsy, cross and sulky, complain of weakness, headaches and loss of appetite. Then the involuntary muscular movements gradually begin: grimaces, trembling, shaking; in severe cases this condition mounts to muscular anarchy. The body is tossed back and forth; the limbs, head and trunk are hurled savagely against wall and bedstead, so that the child must be guarded carefully to prevent severe injury. Often the children do not remain still for a minute, although they are utterly exhausted from the continuous muscular effort. In intervals occur states of rigid stupor, such as Thérèse evidently had. In rare, but severe cases, acute mental disturbances, like states of delirium, are observed; the patient experiences intense anxieties and may even attempt suicide; in some circumstances there are also fears accompanied by vivid hallucinations, while the consciousness remains unclouded. During the disease the child's emotional attitude is usually one of anguished anxiety, more rarely of irritability and abnormal elation.

Any unprejudiced observer will be struck by the astonishing agreement between the clinical picture of this disease and the illness of little Thérèse. Symptom upon symptom appears to be identical.

In addition to this genuine, infectious St Vitus's Dance there is another disease, similar to chorea, which is based upon imitation. If, for example, a genuine case of chorea appears in a class, similar symptoms will often appear in some of the affected child's schoolmates. These will be psychogenic rather than organic, and this illness usually runs its course in much milder form than genuine chorea.

From certain descriptions by Céline and Jeanne Guérin it would seem that during her attacks Thérèse actually turned somersaults—a movement which a child suffering from chorea cannot perform. Another striking feature which is difficult to reconcile with the clinical picture of genuine chorea is Thérèse's own statement that "whenever the pain eased a little I thoroughly enjoyed myself weaving crowns of daisies and forget-me-nots for the statue of Our Lady". This recollection is so precise, even to naming the flowers, that we can scarcely dismiss it as an instance of faulty memory. But how can a child who had so lost all muscular control, in the last and most intense stage of the disease, perform work that requires such a fine touch, when even a healthy child may lack the skill to handle the delicate stems of such flowers, and the thin threads that are used to tie them?

We must also consider the observation of Marceline Husé that the first, temporary recovery on Pauline's Clothing day came after a harmless initial stage lasting a week, and that only afterwards did the severe convulsions, hallucinations, and so forth, begin. This statement stands alone, contradicted by the evidence of several other witnesses who maintain that the striking improvement came right in the middle of the severest symptoms. In the trial (1 S., ii, 115) Marceline contradicted herself, agreeing with the other witnesses that Thérèse had suffered intense anxieties and hallucinations from the very start, that is, from the conversation with her uncle which precipitated the disease, and that these recurred several times a day. Léonie, too, recalls this. The first description accords with the picture of genuine chorea; the second would stand as an argument against this diagnosis, and as a link in the second syndrome; other links are the somersaults, pantomimes of self-destruction, Thérèse's falling out of bed without hurting herself, her observing her own attacks while fully conscious, and the apparent comas during which, as she expressly states, she heard everything; and finally, the strange intervals between violent attacks in which she regained complete coordination, so that she could weave wreaths.

All these latter symptoms are the well-known ones of the psychogenic disease. In consonance with them is a hitherto unnoticed account of Léonie's on the strange lingering effects after the miraculous cure. "The doctor... recommended to us, after her cure, to protect the patient from all violent agitation." (Children suffering from chorea frequently incline to relapses, during which milder repetition of the symptoms of the disease occurs.) "In the month following her recovery I happened to oppose her twice—in both cases I was entirely in the wrong. At that she fell down and remained for a brief span, for several minutes, stretched out in a state of rigidity of body and limbs. This then stopped of its own accord. However, neither delirious states nor violent movements reappeared. These two incidents remained the only recurrences. Later, no trace of the illness ever appeared again" (2 S., 131). This symptom is not characteristic of chorea relapses.

Apparently these incidents remained unknown to the other sisters. In answer to the question repeatedly asked by the ecclesiastical court, they emphatically stated that no symptoms at all ever reappeared. It is possible that Léonie and Thérèse agreed not to mention these attacks to the others—Léonie out of anxiety, because she was at fault, and Thérèse out of kindness for this problem sister, in order to spare her scolding from the others. It may also be that the two girls who shared this somewhat troublesome secret did drop a hint to the elder sisters about it, putting the matter vaguely in order neither to worry them nor to deceive them. Possibly there is an allusion to this in Marie's statement: "Except for one or two falls, which happened without visible cause while Thérèse was walking in the garden *within the week following her recovery*, there was never again any similar incident in her entire life." If, on the other hand, we assume that these were separate occasions, we would have at least four different symptoms of relapse before the disease finally disappeared.

Evidently Dr Notta did briefly consider the possibility that his little patient was suffering from a hysterical illness, for Marie quotes him as saying: "Call it what you will—*to me* this is not hysteria!" (2 S., 80). Céline also quotes him as remarking to Uncle Guérin: "In a fourteen- or fifteen-year-old such phenomena might be easily explained, but never in a child of eleven" (1 S., xviii, 9). We need not discuss the question of what recognition medicine in those days accorded to childhood hysteria; until fairly recently this abnormality was ascribed only to adults. Moreover, Dr Notta was no psychiatrist; he was primarily a surgeon and general practitioner. And given the almost Chinese privacy of the French family in general and the Martin family in particular, it is more than questionable whether the doctor was ever given the slightest explanation of the fact that his little patient had suffered a deep and prolonged psychic shock. He would hardly have looked for a real hysterical attack within the bosom of so good, affectionate a family. Thus he had little choice but to diagnose the illness as the familiar childhood disease of St Vitus's Dance and to treat it accordingly. But Jeanne Néele-Guérin, whose statements stand out by their remarkable objectivity and lucidity, emphasizes that he was never quite satisfied with his diagnosis of chorea—although his dissatisfaction did not have the meaning which the biased family attributed to it.

It need not surprise us that the Martin family insisted so stubbornly, and so single-mindedly, on the theory of unnatural, diabolical causation, so much so that they completely ignored the medical opinion which they had heard for a full ten weeks. "Nervous diseases" meant, to the late nineteenth-century middle class (and all traces of this feeling have not yet vanished) something dishonourable, which cast a blot upon the entire family, and which were best not spoken of. The derangement their father later suffered as the result of his cerebral stroke was also seen in this light; significantly, the Martin daughters always stressed that it was a humiliation and were offended by all references to it on the part of other nuns.

Moreover, the entire concept of such diseases was far more nebulous and uncanny to these pious girls than the idea of devils, possession and miraculous cures. They had heard of nervous diseases only in rare, passing gossip and whispers, whereas diabolic possession was a regular element in devotional literature; detailed descriptions and highly imaginative illustrations of it filled their reading matter. If their darling little Thérèse, the quietest and best of children, suddenly began kicking and raging in her nightgown, screaming and making horrid faces, this could not possibly have any natural causes. The devil must be behind it! Dr Notta's remark that science was impotent in this case—which it actually is in the most advanced cases of chorea—was promptly interpreted to mean that this was no matter for human arts at all. And the failure of the medical treatment seemed to them to confirm such an assumption.

After the miraculous cure, and during the following years, the more the sisters' conviction grew that Thérèse was one of the elect, destined for extraordinary things—and especially after her death, with her reputation for sanctity so rapidly mounting—hindsight produced its customary illusion. Looking back upon the disease, the sisters supplied that feature so important in hagiography: early persecution by devils. Moreover, the miraculous character of the cure also provided an inference as to the mystical nature of the whole disease. The more extraordinary the peril, the more indispensable was supernatural intervention. Only an act by the Blessed Virgin could break the power of the demons.

Furthermore, most of the witnesses seem to have been unconsciously eager to fend off any possible suspicion on the part of the public that the little girl may have suffered from some mental disturbance. The sisters were intent upon preserving the saint's personality and hence her doctrine from all misunderstandings which might throw doubt upon the credibility of her message. Out of this impulse, it seems to us, the entire group of witnesses stressed Thérèse's complete mental clarity throughout her illness. "I did not hear her say a single nonsensical word," Marie avers, "*and not for a moment was she in delirium*"—this in spite of the fact that we owe to Marie the most vivid and precise description of Thérèse's fear—hallucinations. Thérèse herself says quite without embarrassment: "I do not know how to describe that strange illness. I said things I did not think, and did things as if I were forced to do them in spite of myself; *I seemed to be delirious all the time*, but I am sure I never lost my reason for a moment." Obviously, Marie had this account in mind, rather than her own recollections, when she testified. Léonie, objective as ever, says: "My sister has written that during this disease she did not lose consciousness of what was going on around her. I learned about this detail only from her own account; without this express statement we would have had to assume, judging by appearances, that her delirium was almost complete and lasted almost continually."

Marceline, with the observing eye of the servant, unbemused by any theories, seems to have seen the reality most keenly of all; her statement (1 S., 115) surprisingly confirms Thérèse's own evidence: "It seemed to me as if she retained consciousness even during the attacks—and after the attack she remembered what had happened." This, at least, distinguishes the illness clearly from epilepsy (as does, incidentally, the fact that Thérèse never injured herself when she threw herself out of bed).

The insistence that there were no aftereffects of the illness also seems partly prompted by concern lest the miraculous quality of the cure be in any way obscured. But the extent to which the sisters permitted this zeal to colour their memories certainly went too far at times, for we find one of them saying: "Never did the slightest trace of the evil reappear, not even anything similar; afterwards Thérèse was neither impressionable nor nervous." Thérèse herself, Céline and the others have on the contrary indicated clearly enough that during the period following the cure Thérèse was excessively sensitive and constantly on the verge of tears. We have discussed at length this condition, against which Thérèse contended for years.

The slight relapses we have mentioned were probably also concealed from the closest and most sympathetic relatives, for Cousin Guérin testifies: "Never again did any of the symptoms of this illness appear, and my father used to say that if it had been a nervous disease left to its natural course, some traces would have been evident in Thérèse's temperament later on." That statement makes fairly evident the reciprocal relationship, in this case, between the family's observations and their convictions.

SELECTED BIBLIOGRAPHY

I. SOURCES

1. Documents of the beatification and canonization proceedings, as contained in the Summaries of 1914 and 1920. The full titles of these two volumes of documents are:

   (a) *Bajocensis et Lexoviensis Beatificationis et Canonizationis Servae Dei Sor. Theresiae a Puero Jesu Monialis Professae Ord. Carmelitarum Excalc. in Monasterio Lexoviensi Positio super virtutibus, etc.* Cited: 2 S.

   (b) *Positio super introductione Causae Bajocensis sue Lexoviensis Beatificationis et Canonizationis Servae Dei Sor. Theresiae a Puero Jesu Monialis Professae Ord. Carmelitarum Excalc. in Monasterio Lexoviensi.* Romae 1914. Cited: 1 S.

2. *Handbuch der Unbeschuhten Karmeliterinnen bei ihren gottesdienstlichen Verrichtungen.* Vienna, 1915.

3. *La Révérende Mère Geneviève de Sainte Thérèse, Fondatrice du Carmel de Lisieux, 1805–91.* Carmel de Lisieux, 1912.

4. *Les Annales de Sainte Thérèse de Lisieux.* Edited by the Office central de Lisieux. Seventeen annual issues: 1925–1942.

5. *Lettres de Sainte Thérèse de l'Enfant Jésus.* Carmel de Lisieux, 1946.

6. *Manuscrits Autobiographiques de Sainte Thérèse de l'Enfant Jésus en 4 Tomes.* Edited by Fr François de Sainte-Marie. (Facsimile, Les Manuscrits, Introduction par P. François de Sainte-Marie, C.D., Notes et Tables, Table des Citations.) Carmel de Lisieux, 1956. Cited: *M.A.*

7. *Novissima Verba.* Office central de Lisieux, 1926. (The saint's conversations from 1 May to 30 September 1897, as taken down by her sister Mother Agnes of Jesus.) Cited: *N.V.*

8. *Pluie de Roses. Extraits des tomes I à VII.* Office central de Lisieux, n.d.

9. *Pluie de Roses.* Tome VII: 1923, 1924–1925. Office central de Lisieux.

10. *Regel und Satzungen der Unbeschuhten Nonnen des Ordens der Allerseligsten Jungfrau vom Berge Karmel.* Würzburg, 1928.

11. *Sainte Thérèse de l'Enfant Jesus,* vie par Monseigneur Laveille. Office central de Lisieux, 1925. Cited: Laveille.

12. *Sœur Thérèse de l'Enfant Jésus et de la Sainte Face, morte en odeur de Sainteté au Carmel de Lisieux le 30 Septembre 1897 à l'age de 24 ans.* Lisieux, 1911. This volume contains:

(a) *Conseils et Souvenirs.* Cited: *C.S.*

(b) *Histoire d'une Âme, écrite par elle-même.* Cited: *S.S.* (*The Story of a Soul*, English translation by Michael Day, Cong. Orat., London and Westminster, Md., 1957).

(c) *Lettres* (Fragments) (Fifty fragments of letters, grouped by addressees). Cited by dates.

(d) *Poésies* (Forty-five poems).

13. Various obituary letters issued by the Lisieux Carmel, n.d.

II. PORTRAYALS

1. Alençon, P. Ubald d', O.Cap. *Sainte Thérèse comme je l'ai connue.* In: *Estudins Franciscans*, Revista Mensuel, dirigida pels PP. Caputxins. Barcelona, 1926.

2. Balthasar, Hans Urs von. *Thérèse von Lisieux, Geschichte einer Sendung.* Olten, 1950. An English edition is contained in *Two Sisters in the Spirit.* San Francisco: Ignatius Press, 1992.

3. Bernoville, Gaëtan. *Sainte Thérèse de l'Enfant Jésus.* Paris, 1926.

4. Combes, André. *Introduction à la Spiritualite de Ste Thérèse.* Paris, 1948.

5. Combes, André. *Le Problème de l'Histoire d'une Âme et des Œuvres Complètes* de Ste Thérèse de Lisieux. Paris, 1950.

6. Combes, André, and others. *La Petite Ste Thérèse de M. van der Meersch devant la critique et devant les textes.* Paris, 1950.

7. *Copie de la Circulaire envoyée aux monastères du Carmel après la mort de Mère Isabelle du Sacré-Cœur, Religieuse Carmélite de Lisieux, 1822 à 1914.*

8. *Die heilige Theresia vom Jesuskinde und vom heiligsten Antlitz, 1873 bis 1897. Ihr Leben, beschrieben von einer Karmelitin des Klosters der heiligen Maria Magdalena von Pazzi in Florenz.* German edition translated by Dr Josef Tress. Berlin, 1927. Cited: *Flor.*

9. *Die Schwestern der kleinen heiligen Theresia.* Edited by Albert Dolan and Joseph Stang. Innsbruck, 1932.

10. Dubosq, Mgr. René. *Sur la vraie physiognomie de Sainte Thérèse.* Office central de Lisieux, 1927.

11. Ghéon, Henri. *The Secret of the Little Flower.* English translation by Donald Attwater. London and New York, 1934.

12. Kirch, Konrad, and Adolf Rodewyk. "Theresia vom Kinde Jesu", in *Helden des Christentuins.* Vol. 2. Paderborn, n.d.

13. *L'Esprit de la Bienheureuse Thérèse de l'Enfant Jésus. D'après ses écrits et les témoins oculaires de sa vie.* Office central de la Bienheureuse Thérèse, Lisieux (n.d.; before 1913). Cited: *Esprit.*

14. Meersch, Maxence van der. *La Petite Sainte Thérèse.* Paris, 1947.

15. Moré, Marcel. "La Table des Pécheurs", in *Dieu Vivant.* No. 24. N.p., n.d.

16. Nigg, Walter. *Grosse Heilige.* Zürich, 1946.

17. Petitot, R. P. Henri, O.P. *Sainte Thérèse de Lisieux. Une renaissance spirituelle.* Paris, 1925. Cited: Petitot.

18. Piat, R. P. Stéphane Joseph, O.F.M. *Histoire d'une Famille.* Office central de Lisieux, 1946. Cited: Piat.

19. Sinthem, P. Peter, S.J. *Werden einer Heiligenseele.* Innsbruck, 1928.

20. Stern, Karl. "St. Thérèse of Lisieux", in *Saints for Now.* Edited by Clare Boothe Luce. San Francisco: Ignatius Press, 1993.

ABBREVIATIONS

C.S.	*Conseils et Souvenirs* (see I, 12, a above)
Esprit	*L'Esprit de la Bienheureuse Thérèse* (see II, 13)
Flor.	*Die heilige Theresia vom Jesuskinde* (see II, 8)
Laveille	Mgr Laveille, *Sainte Thérèse de l'Enfant Jesus* (see I, 11)
M.A.	*Manuscrits Autobiographiques* (see I, 6)
N.V.	*Novissima Verba* (see I, 7)
Petitot	H. Petitot, *Sainte Thérèse de Lisieux* (see II, 17)
Piat	S. J. Piat, *Histoire d'une Famille* (see II, 18)
1 *S.*	*Summarium 1* (see I, 1, b)
2 *S.*	*Summarium 2* (see I, 1, a)
S.S.	*The Story of a Soul* (see I, 12, b)

INDEX

Adelaide, Sister, 390
Agnes of Jesus, Mother. *See* Martin, Pauline
Aimée, Sister, 390
Alexis, Father, 237–38, 314–15, 332, 344
"alms of smiling", 115–16, 243, 304–7, 325, 373, 375
Aloysius, St, 250, 306
Alphonsus Liguori, St, 397
Annales de Sainte Thérèse de Lisieux, 10n3, 11, 40, 197n43
Anne, Abbé, 388
Anne of Jesus, Mother, 237, 348
aridity, 136, 221–29, 247–49, 251, 268
    See also doubt; faith
Arminjon, Abbé, 127–30, 276, 402
arrogance. *See* pride
Ascent of Mount Carmel (John of the Cross), 251
asceticism
    abuse of, 55, 292–94, 296
    Carmelite, 134–42, 171, 196, 300–301
    history of Christian, 139–42, 188, 265, 291, 297
    psychology of, 222–26
    purpose, 195–96, 290–94, 297
    voluntary, 135–38, 296–302, 360
atonement
    Carmelite vocation, 290–96

substitutionary, 137–39, 138n126, 264–66
    See also asceticism; love; suffering
Augustine, St, 292

Béguines, 192
Bellière, Abbé, 188–89, 288, 379
Benigna Consolata Ferreri, Sister, 392
Bennett, Arnold, 398
Bergengruen, Werner, 278n21, 294
Bernoville, Gaetan, 199
Bérulle, Cardinal, 258–59, 342–43
Bible reading, 126, 251–54, 283
Birgitta, St, 396
Bloy, Léon, 128
Bremond, H., 19, 196, 258, 342–43
Brernanos, Georges, 21
Bridget of Sweden, St, 396
Brocardus Rule, 140
brothers, spiritual, 188–91, 288, 379
Busse-Wilson, Elizabeth, 300–301

Carmel at Lisieux, 12, 132–42, 194–99, 201–7, 218–21, 317
Carmelite Rule
    acceptance guidelines, 200
    focus, 140–42, 290–94